Dimensions of Social Welfare Policy

SEVENTH EDITION

Neil Gilbert

University of California, Berkeley

Paul Terrell

University of California, Berkeley

Allyn & Bacon

Boston   New York   San Francisco
Mexico City   Montreal   Toronto   London   Madrid   Munich   Paris
Hong Kong   Singapore   Tokyo   Cape Town   Sydney

Senior Acquisitions Editor: *Patricia Quinlin*
Editorial Assistant: *Carly Czech*
Senior Marketing Manager: *Wendy Albert*
Production Editor: *Maggie Brobeck*
Editorial Production Service: *TexTech International*
Manufacturing Buyer: *Debbie Rossi*
Electronic Composition: *TexTech International*
Cover Administrator: *Kristina Mose-Libon*

Photo Credits: Page 137: © Pearson Education/PH College; p. 168: Paul Terrell

Library of Congress Cataloging-in-Publication Data

Gilbert, Neil
    Dimensions of social welfare policy / Neil Gilbert, Paul Terrell. —7th ed.
      p. cm.
    Includes bibliographical references and index.
    ISBN-13: 978-0-205-62574-1
    ISBN-10: 0-205-62574-6
    1. Public welfare.   2. Social choice.   3. Public welfare—United States.
4. United States—Social policy.   I. Terrell, Paul.   II. Title.
HV41.G52 2010
362.973—dc21   2008055072

10 9 8 7 6 5 4 3 2 1   HAM   13 12 11 10 09

Allyn & Bacon
is an imprint of

PEARSON

www.pearsonhighered.com

ISBN-10:   0-205-62574-6

ISBN-13: 978-0-205-62574-1

For Evan, Jesse, Nathaniel and Nicole—the lights of my life.
N. G.

For my boys, Josh, Ben, and Sean, with love.
P. T.

Contents

3 *A Framework for Social Welfare*
Policy Analysis   56

4 *The Basis of Social Allocations   88*

Capsules

The following is a complete list of numbered capsules appearing in the Seventh Edition.

Figures

The following is a complete list of numbered figures appearing in the Seventh Edition.

Tables

The following is a complete list of numbered tables appearing in the Seventh Edition.

Preface

Those who write about social welfare policy analysis encounter many opportunities to argue their own points of view. They are also tempted to slip prescriptions into the analysis, because the subject matter deals with compelling issues of human welfare. We recognize that many readers would like a book that provides solutions to the weighty problems of social welfare, whether or not they agree with our views. If they agree, they can congratulate themselves on their wisdom; if they disagree, they can affirm their own position by dissecting our biases and our logic. In either case, a book that gives firm and sure direction generally provides more immediate gratification than one that analyzes the terrain and debates the hazards of the different roads that can be taken.

Nonetheless, we offer few explicit and firm prescriptions for social welfare policies. (In the few cases where we *do* prescribe, it is less by design than from an inability to resist temptation.) Readers are forewarned that they will not find many specific answers to questions of social policy in this book. Rather, we attempt to share the intellectual challenges that are confronted in making social welfare policy choices. "Good" and "just" answers to fundamental questions in social welfare policy are not easy to come by. When addressed seriously, these questions require a willingness to abide complexity, an ability to tolerate contradictions, and a capacity to critically appraise empirical evidence and social values. Professionals engaged in the business of making policy choices require patience and intellectual curiosity.

To speak of policy choices implies that plausible alternatives exist. In this book, our second objective is to present and illuminate these alternatives. This edition is organized around what we consider to be basic dimensions of choice in social welfare policy. We place these dimensions of choice in a theoretical framework, providing ways of thinking and analyzing social welfare policies that are applicable to a wide range of specific cases. With this framework, we explore policy alternatives, the questions they raise, and the values and theories that reveal different answers. Ultimately, the purpose of this book is to equip students with the knowledge to come to grips with the complexities of social choice and to appraise and further develop their own thoughts on social welfare policy.

In preparing this Seventh Edition, we have been gratified by the extent to which our basic concepts of social policy choice-making have remained applicable and useful since the book's original publication in 1974. We are equally impressed with the significant changes in the structure and content of U.S. social welfare programs. When we were preparing the First Edition, social welfare was at the apex of thirty-five years of growth fueled by the expansion of social protection through new entitlements and publicly-financed programs. As we complete the Seventh Edition, social welfare provisions are under tremendous pressure from the soaring costs of social security benefits and care for the elderly, the competitive demands of globalization, and a world economy in considerable crisis. Established benefits are contracting and programs are being reshaped by increased targeting, privatization, and work-oriented incentives—as entitlement to social protection gives ground to an emerging philosophy of public support for private responsibility.

New To This Edition

In response to these historic shifts, we have incorporated into this new edition an analysis of recent important developments in social welfare policy. These include the welfare reforms of 2006 (Chapter 8); strategies for cultural responsiveness in service delivery (Chapter 6); the new social accounting, which introduces alternative frameworks for comparative analyses of social welfare expenditures in the advanced industrial countries (Chapter 2); and the historic trends leading to the rise of the Enabling State (Chapter 2). We also discuss Charles Murray's proposal for an annual guaranteed income of $10,000 for each adult (Chapter 4), the new technology of electronic benefit transfers (EBTs) (Chapter 5), and new data on basic needs budgets (Chapter 3).

Acknowledgments

We would like to thank the reviewers who commented on the manuscript of this edition: Francis Origanti, Creighton University, Omaha, and Fontaine H. Fulghum, Rutgers University, New Jersey.

1

The Field of Social Welfare Policy

"I don't think they play at all fairly," Alice began, in rather a complaining tone, "and they all quarrel so dreadfully one can't hear oneself speak—and they don't seem to have any rules in particular: at least, if there are, nobody attends to them—and you've no idea how confusing it is all the things being alive: for instance, there's the arch I've got to go through next walking about at the other end of the ground—and I should have cro-queted the Queen's hedgehog just now, only it ran away when it saw mine coming!"

Lewis Carroll
Alice's Adventures in Wonderland, 1866

Students entering the field of social welfare policy quickly come to feel somewhat like Alice at the Queen's croquet party. They confront a puzzling and complex landscape, with changing features and hazy boundaries.[1] Its knowledge base is fragmented and less than immediately related to the realities of day-to-day social work. Yet the study of this terrain is central for those who work in the social services because, to a large extent, social welfare policy shapes the forms of practice that professionals use and determines the client systems they serve. To a significant degree, both the supply of and the demand for services reflect social policy choices.

The objectives of this introductory chapter are to provide a general orientation to the field of social welfare policy and to illustrate the interrelatedness of practice and policy analysis. By presenting the subject matter of social welfare in its varied aspects, we hope that students will become interested in and comfortable with the subject of policy studies, and recognize its importance and power. The purpose of this book, as the title suggests, is to develop an operational understanding of social welfare policy by identifying its essential dimensions of choice.

We will begin by exploring three major perspectives—institutional, analytical, and political—that illuminate the field of social welfare policy. The focus on *institutions* identifies the key social structures, like families, churches, and voluntary agencies, that give shape, character, and boundaries to welfare activities. The focus on *analysis* indicates different approaches to studying and understanding policy, and for relating

1

policy knowledge to social work practice. The focus on *politics* explores the interrelationships between society and government in the field of social welfare.

Institutional Perspectives on the Study of Social Welfare Policy

Social welfare policy is an elusive concept, and one could easily exhaust an introductory chapter simply describing alternative approaches to its definition. This we will not do; nor will we review the ongoing discussion over the relationships among social policy, public policy, and social welfare policy.[2] Suffice it to say that no single definition is universally, nor even broadly, accepted. However, some effort is necessary to stake out boundaries and to form a common realm of discourse. Skirting the conceptual swamp of social policy, public policy, and social welfare policy distinctions, we will focus instead on examining the functioning of those major institutions in society that structure and provide social welfare.

All human societies organize their essential functions—child-rearing; the production, consumption, and distribution of goods and services; social protection; and so forth—into certain enduring patterns of conduct. All societies, for example, maintain institutions with responsibilities and expectations for raising and training the young. One primary institution seldom exhausts the patterns a society uses to deal with its essential functions. Although the family is the primary institution for socialization, for example, it is by no means the only one. Religious and educational organizations and social service agencies also assume some socialization responsibilities, although socialization is not their *primary* activity.

There are six fundamental social institutions within which the major activities of community life occur: kinship systems, religious organizations, workplace sites, economic markets, mutual assistance arrangements, and government organizations. As indicated in Table 1.1, society's basic day-to-day activities are organized in one or more of these spheres. And each of these spheres, to one degree or another, also carries out important social welfare functions.

Kinship

The family has always served as society's major institution for social, economic, and emotional support. The family is also the key instrument of socialization, helping society to transmit knowledge, values, and patterns of behavior from one generation to the next. As an instrument of social welfare, families constitute networks of assistance based on blood and mutual attachment. Parents, for example, "invest" in their children's future by providing for their health, their physical well-being, and their education. And families, in all societies, embody sets of reciprocal obligations to care for and protect one another. More specifically, families play an important role in at least four critical welfare arenas—caring for elderly and disabled relatives, caring for grandchildren, providing economic support, and providing help in emergency situations like natural disasters.

TABLE 1.1   *Institutions, Organizations, and Functions*

Social Institutions	Key Organizational Forms	Primary Functions	Social Welfare Functions
Kinship	Families	Procreation, socialization, protection, intimacy, emotional support	Dependent care, interfamilial financial support
Religion	Churches	Spiritual development	Faith-based health, education, social services
Workplace	Businesses, factories, farms	Production of goods and services	Employee benefits
The market	Producers (firms) and consumers (households)	Exchange of goods and services for money	Commercial social welfare goods and services
Mutual assistance	Support groups, voluntary agencies, foundations	Mutual aid, charity, community support, philanthropy	Self-help, volunteering, nonprofit social services
Government	Federal, state, and local governments	Raising and distributing resources for public purposes	Antipoverty, economic security, health, education, social services

It is estimated that there are 34 million unpaid caregivers in America providing an average of 21 hours of care per week and spending approximately $2400 out of pocket yearly per relative.[3] Millions of adults provide care to elderly relatives. Family caregivers are overwhelmingly women—mothers, daughters, spouses—and many live with the person needing help. A full 80 percent of all family caregivers provide care seven days a week.[4]

Providing care for elderly parents is a particular burden for working adults, who often must balance caregiving with their job obligations. A recent study estimated that 15 percent of the workforce actively and regularly provides assistance to older family members, often substantially interfering with their careers due to stress and absenteeism. About two-thirds of these working caregivers are women.[5]

Many millions of adults raise children with disabilities—often adult children—who suffer severe mental and physical challenges. With the developmentally disabled, in particular, living far longer than in the past, parents often continue to care for their sons and their daughters into old age. And the care, more than ever before, is often technically demanding. Routine assistance—helping with eating, bathing, shopping—continues, but the explosion in home-health technology frequently requires caregivers to maintain ventilators, administer intravenous medicines, and monitor and implement complex treatment regimens. Care that once had to be handled in hospitals is now often delegated to family members.

Over two million children live without their parents, some staying informally with relatives, others placed with relatives under the jurisdiction of child welfare agencies.

The prevalence of kinship care has grown rapidly since the 1990s, with grandparents in particular serving as foster parents, often assisted by public subsidies.[6] Stepping in for drug-abusing sons and daughters who are unable to care for their own children, grandparents often take on the responsibility for full-time custody and care. Today, it is estimated that nearly 3 percent of U.S. children live in some form of kinship care.[7]

Grandparent care, while it can have its downside, has the potential to advance several important child welfare objectives. Perhaps most importantly, it helps reduce the trauma that typically occurs when children must be separated from their parents. Living with grandparents certainly reduces the stigma of being a foster child. And keeping care in the (extended) family also helps children maintain their ethnic, cultural, and family identities.[8]

The role that families play in helping single mothers' transition from welfare to work is also becoming increasingly clear as welfare reform is implemented. Mothers in poverty often rely on *their* mothers, and other kin, for childcare, transportation, and financial support, in addition to emotional support and practical advice. While the magnitude of family care that is provided isn't certain, it appears that nearly half of all single mothers receive an appreciable level of help from their parents.[9]

Families provide financial and in-kind assistance to their members in a number of ways beyond those mentioned. Such help frequently takes the form of financial assistance such as children helping aging parents with nursing or medical care expenses, or parents helping children to buy homes or deal with financial emergencies.[10]

One very significant source of interfamilial "welfare" is child support, especially income support from absent fathers.[11] Child support levels, unfortunately, are low and far from universal—only 43 percent of poor mothers, for example, received court-ordered child support in 1998. Court-ordered awards, furthermore, don't guarantee payments, so the actual proportion of poor women receiving child support is just 25 percent. Among never-married mothers, just one in four have court orders, and only 14 percent receive payments.[12] Nevertheless, custodial low-income parents as a group

CAPSULE 1.1 • *Kinship Security*

It is patterns of kinship which most often cover us in our undertakings, provide us market opportunities, and even shield us from the importunings of the state. We do not hope to receive tuition, childcare, or a kidney from a business associate, but we do from relatives. Marriage is that device which extends to us a social security network of obligated kin. . . .

Marriage provides a kind of capital. Married couples, more than single parents, have parents and grandparents as a resource. House loans, emergency aid, care payments, cash gifts, and job opportunities come disproportionately from these relatives. Over one-fourth of all new home purchases depend upon gifts from parents. Having four parents and eight grandparents attached to every marriage broadens the base of economic support, for us as for the Inuit.

David W. Murray, "Poor Suffering Bastards: An Anthropologist Looks at Illegitimacy," *Policy Review*, 68, Spring 1994, 13.

receive about $16 billion annually in child support payments, a figure that is about a fifth of the value of their public benefits.[13]

International family aid, "remittances," provide considerable assistance from immigrants in rich countries to their relatives in the less developed world. In 2006, for example, over $45 billion in "migradolares" (migrants' dollars) was sent to Latin America from immigrants from the region. In many countries, the value of these gifts exceeds the amount generated by many sectors of the local economy, such as exports and tourism. In Haiti, for example, remittances constitute 17 percent of GDP.[14]

It is estimated that three-quarters of Latino immigrants in the United States send regular support to their native countries. In money transfer offices in Hispanic neighborhoods, customers send electronic money orders regularly to assist parents and siblings back home with housing, food, small businesses, and education. And while most of these immigrants hold low-paying jobs, their payments average about $200 a month. One migrant worker, quoted in the *New York Times*, said, "We make sacrifices now so that our families can live better and so that one day we will live better back home."[15]

Finally, relatives are essential resources in response to emergencies, both natural and otherwise. As reported by the the *Washington Post*, for example, "hundreds of thousands of people displaced by Hurricane Katrina seem to be disappearing—into the embrace of their extended families."[16] As in similar relief efforts in the past, it is families that provide the first line of assistance when misfortunes occur, dwarfing all other forms of private agency or government help.

Religion

Religious institutions manifest the spiritual aspect of human society through the ceremonies and observances that form systems of worship. But churches also sponsor elaborate social welfare provisions ranging from informal support and counseling to multimillion-dollar health, education, and social service programs.

The Church of the Latter Day Saints (Mormons), for example, operates over 600 food production projects for the poor, including twenty canneries and numerous meat-packing and dairy operations supplied by church-owned welfare farms. One estimate indicates that each year about 200,000 church members receive nearly 32 million pounds of commodities from Mormon storehouses and auxiliaries.[17] The Mormons also run Deseret Industries, which provides work and shelter for the elderly and people with disabilities, places members in jobs through church-sponsored employment offices and organizes an extensive program of child welfare, foster care, and adoption services.[18] Similarly, ultra-orthodox Jews in Borough Park, Brooklyn, have created their own welfare arrangements by pooling resources to support not only religious schools but also a network of social services including group homes, family counseling, and a volunteer ambulance service, in addition to food programs for the poor.

Catholic, Jewish, Muslim, and Protestant welfare organizations, of course, have explicit social welfare objectives, implemented both through professionalized agencies such as Catholic Charities and more informally through counseling by priests, ministers, and rabbis. The range of church-related services has been broadened in recent years by "family ministries" and "family life education" programs focused on married couples and their children, premarrieds and singles, and people facing problems such as alcoholism and divorce.[19]

The potential of sectarian programs expanded considerably in 1996 with the enactment of welfare reform's "charitable choice" provision, which authorized states to contract with religious bodies for antipoverty services. "Faith-based services," in vogue ever since, are said to harness the enthusiasm and resources and moral character of churches and church members to help solve the problems of the poor.

The magnitude of these programs is growing rapidly. Religious bodies provide billions of dollars in aid to the needy annually. Nearly 500 congregations, for example, participate in the Christian Community Development Association's activities to address inner-city problems. Other congregations sponsor drug and alcohol, sexuality and job training programs, often providing people tangible as well as spiritual resources that help them address life problems.

Workplace

Workplace organizations—factories, farms, universities, corporations, social service agencies—typically promote the welfare of their employees by providing job-related goods and services, along with regular paychecks. One's job is the most important single source of financial support for most U.S. citizens—both by providing the income necessary for everyday life and through welfare arrangements attached to the job, generally known as fringe or occupational benefits. The word *fringe*, however, seriously understates the importance of these benefits, since their value often constitutes nearly a quarter of a typical worker's overall compensation.

Along with pensions, the most important fringe benefit is health insurance. Unlike most Western nations, which provide health benefits through public programs, U.S. citizens generally obtain their health benefits through their employment; in 2006, indeed, nearly two-thirds of all working adults had employment-related insurance. Health insurance, even when employees share the costs with contributions of various sorts, still costs employers about $3000 per worker per year. On a per car basis, indeed, General Motors spends more on employee health care than it does on steel.[20]

Many firms also provide benefits such as sick leave, parental leaves, college tuition for the children of employees, gyms, legal and dental services, relocation assistance, and low-cost housing. Unions occasionally provide special benefits to supplement the public system of unemployment insurance. And many human services such as on-site childcare and alcohol and drug counseling are provided as part of company-sponsored EAPs (employee assistance programs). Some companies hire social workers and psychologists for such tasks, others rely on ordained ministers and priests to tend to their employees' emotional needs.[21]

The Market

Although theoretically there are several ways in which goods and services can be produced and allocated in society—centralized state control is one system, private altruism another—the most ubiquitous and successful economic institution in modern

CAPSULE 1.2 • *The Social Service Congregation*

The black church—usually at the forefront of successful black movements in the United States—finds itself in the 1990s becoming more of a social service agency than a spiritual, soul-saving institution.

"We're called to be everywhere," said the Rev. J. Alfred Smith Sr., pastor of the 4000-member Allen Temple Baptist Church in East Oakland. "We're doing a hell of a lot more than we were 10 years ago. Things have gotten worse for the masses."

With black neighborhoods increasingly beset by unemployment, crime, violent death, drug abuse, AIDS and family separation, ministers say they need more than a Bible and a pulpit. St. Augustine's Episcopal Church of Oakland opened its doors more than 20 years ago to the Black Panthers' first breakfast program in the East Bay. The breakfast program has long been dissolved but the church now provides groceries for 70 families each month, in addition to supporting scout troops, after-school tutorial programs, drug and alcohol dependency counseling and the Caring Family Project.

"I do feel we are being pressed to do more social work," said the Rev. Charles Carter of St. Augustine's. "You can't speak to someone about God if they're hungry. You can't save minds unless you educate them. If you're going to save their souls you have to save their bodies, too. They are tied together."

Black churches—since the first one rose in Philadelphia in 1787—have been a political and social force from the abolitionist movement to the civil rights era. "It [the church] is the only institution we own lock, stock and barrel," said the Rev. Amos Brown of San Francisco's Third Baptist Church in the Western Addition.

Andrew Billingsley, a professor at the University of Maryland and author of "Climbing Jacob's Ladder: The Enduring Legacy of African American Families," wrote: "In addition to what it does for its members, the black church as an institution has always reached out to serve important functions for the black community as a whole. It is in this respect both preserver of the African American heritage and agent for reform. Indeed, no successful movement for improving conditions of life for the African-American people has been mounted without the support of the church."

With government spending on social programs shrinking, the black church has had to feed and clothe the hungry and the homeless, provide jobs, rein in young gang toughs, react to violence in the neighborhood, and share its space with government and other programs.

From "New Role Thrust on the Black Church" by Gregory Lewis, *San Francisco Examiner*, February 28, 1993.

times for satisfying people's material desires is the private marketplace. Typically identified with capitalism, the market brings together buyers, sellers, and producers in reasonably satisfying and efficient transactions, its "invisible hand" allocating society's resources according to mutual needs and desires.

A primary component of the marketplace in industrial societies is the business firm that, together with nonprofit organizations and governments, creates and distributes a nation's goods and services. Most basic human needs, of course—clothing, food, housing, transportation—are typically met through market transactions among private firms and consumers. In recent years, furthermore, there has been a dramatic increase in the involvement of private firms in areas of social welfare that once were largely the domain of nonprofits or government. According to Lester Salamon, a massive

CAPSULE 1.3 • *Butchers, Brewers, and Markets*

It is not from the benevolence of the butcher, the brewer, or the baker, that we expect our dinner, but from their regard to their own self-interest.

We address ourselves, not to their humanity but to their self-love, and never talk to them of our own necessities but of their advantages.

Adam Smith, *The Wealth of Nations*, 1776.

"marketization" has occurred as private firms have "upstaged" traditional agencies in almost every service arena.[22]

Major childcare chains, for example, many operating on the franchise principle, run more than 2000 daycare centers—about 10 percent of all centers nationwide. Even in more traditional social service areas, such as child welfare institutions, group-home care, and residential treatment, more than half of all programs are run by proprietary establishments.[23]

The biggest profit-making operations of all are in the health field, where major corporations operate 14 percent of all general and 44 percent of all specialty hospitals, own two-thirds of all nursing homes, and hold a 78 percent share of the home health industry.[24] One of the newest and fastest growing parts of the U.S. healthcare system—free-standing emergency centers—is almost entirely a commercial enterprise. Major private corporations such as Upjohn Labs have also expanded into the home-health field and drug and alcohol treatment services.

We don't want to give the impression that the profit sector is entirely the domain of major corporations. At one end of the market continuum are thousands of individual and small group entrepreneurs who directly provide health and social services. These include private practice psychiatrists, social workers, marriage and family counselors, and laypeople who operate family daycare and board and care homes. It has been estimated that as many as 25 percent of the members of the National Association of Social Workers are in private practice for at least part of their work week.[25] It is clearly the hope of many MSWs to go "solo," hang out their shingle, and "do good" providing services that clearly are in demand—most of which revolve around personal relationships, individual insecurities, and sex, alcohol, and drug problems.

Mutual Assistance

The fourth major institution of modern society—mutual assistance—is perhaps the most explicitly focused on social welfare activities. Variously characterized as charity, philanthropy, informal help, or social support, these arrangements express society's need for mutuality, its recognition of interdependence, and its desire to promote community well-being and to assist the less fortunate. Whether viewed as a function of altruism or enlightened self-interest, mutual assistance constitutes an essential part of community life.

Most mutual assistance represents society's natural response to everyday need. Whereas traditions of self-help go far back in U.S. history, they increasingly constitute a critical resource for millions of people. One notable development of recent years has

CAPSULE 1.4 • *Tocqueville On Mutual Aid*

Americans of all ages, all stations in life, and all types of disposition are forever forming associations. There are not only commercial and industrial associations in which all take part, but others of a thousand different types—religious, moral, serious, futile, very general and very limited, immensely large and very minute. Americans combine to give fêtes, found seminaries, build churches, distribute books and send missionaries to the Antipodes. Hospitals, prisons and schools take shape in that way.

If they want to proclaim a truth or propagate some feeling by the encouragement of a great example, they form an association. In every case, at the head of any new undertaking, where in France you would find the government or in England some territorial magnate, in the United States you are sure to find an association.

Alexis de Tocqueville, *Democracy in America*, 1835.

been a reawakened interest in informal helping systems, along with a reconceptualization of the ways in which professionals and lay helpers can work together.

How do friends, neighbors, and peers help? Neighbors check in on the sick and disabled, making sure all is well, sometimes helping with housework and cooking and shopping and babysitting. Friends provide loans and emergency living arrangements. Self-help groups—small, nonbureaucratic, nonprofessional—assist people facing emotional problems. College students, for example, serve as peer-to-peer counselors confronting issues such as eating disorders, relationship violence, and sexual harassment. Working face to face with others who share and understand their predicament, millions of people receive psychological support and learn realistic strategies for problem solving.

It is estimated that 7 percent of U.S. citizens belong to self-help groups.[26] Among the most common are the following:

- Parents Without Partners (single parents and their children)
- La Leche League (nursing and other new mothers)
- Candlelighters (the parents of children with cancer)
- Alcoholics Anonymous (recovering alcoholics)
- Al-Anon (family members of alcoholics)
- National Alliance for the Mentally Ill (families and friends of the seriously mentally ill)

Beyond self-help and informal support is the extensive and multifaceted system of formal voluntary associations that provide expression to the philanthropic impulse. Organized on a nonprofit basis and aimed at addressing community welfare needs, approximately 66,000 voluntary agencies today provide an array of services for disadvantaged children, families, adults, the elderly, and a variety of special-need populations. These agencies, generally small in size compared to government bodies and governed by citizen boards of directors, coexist with a vast population of other nonprofits serving educational, health, research, and cultural purposes.[27]

CAPSULE 1.5 • *The Twelve Steps*

The twelve-step program, pioneered in the late 1930s by Alcoholics Anonymous, has been embraced by self-help groups dealing with over 200 separate problems, ranging from overeating and gambling to sex and love addiction.

The twelve "spiritual steps to personal growth," the guiding intervention for all "recovery," were formulated by Bill Wilson, AA's cofounder, in 1939. They are:

1. Admitting powerlessness over alcohol—that our lives had become unmanageable.
2. Coming to believe that a Power greater than ourselves can restore us to sanity.
3. Making a decision to turn our will and our lives over to the care of God, as we understand Him.
4. Making a searching and fearless moral inventory of ourselves.
5. Admitting to God, to ourselves, and to another human being the exact nature of our wrongs.
6. Being entirely ready to have God remove our defects of character.
7. Humbly asking God to remove our shortcomings.
8. Making a list of all persons we've harmed and being willing to make amends to them all.
9. Making direct amends to such people wherever possible except when to do so would injure them or others.
10. Continuing to take personal inventory and when we are wrong to promptly admit it.
11. Seeking through prayer and meditation to improve our conscious contact with God, praying only for knowledge of His will for us and the power to carry that out.
12. Having a spiritual awakening as the result of these Steps, carrying the message to others, and practicing these principles in all our affairs.

"The Twelve Steps of Alcoholics Anonymous" Copyright © A.A. World Services, Inc. The Twelve Steps are reprinted with permission of Alcoholics Anonymous World Services, Inc. ("AAWS"). Permission to reprint the Twelve Steps does not mean that AAWS has reviewed or approved the contents of this publication, or that AAWS necessarily agrees with the views expressed herein. A.A. is a program of recovery from alcoholism only - use of the Twelve Steps in connection with programs and activities which are patterned after A.A., but which address other problems, or in any other non-A.A. context, does not imply otherwise.

Government

Governmental institutions, according to the *Encyclopedia of the Social Sciences*, deal with the "control of the use of force within a society and the maintenance of internal and external peace . . . as well as control of the mobilization of resources for the implementation of various goals and the articulation and setting up of certain goals for the collectivity."[28] Among the most important functions of the modern state, of course, are raising and allocating resources for social welfare purposes. So important, and so huge, is the role of public activity in this area that the modern state is often defined as a "welfare state." And today's polity, at least in the industrial world, *is* organized to support welfare. Broadly, the modern state is organized to ensure economic prosperity and social stability, and, more specifically, material security; minimum standards of health, education, and housing; and protection against the contingencies of modern life that interfere with people's well-being.

Evolving Institutions and the Welfare State

The nature of society's helping arrangements is critically influenced by the balance that exists among its institutional sectors. That is, the various systems of provision have distinctive characteristics and distinctive costs and benefits. The help that families provide, for example, is immediate, emphatic, caring, and unbureaucratic. However, family help can be onerous, emotionally exhausting, and costly. Families can be destroyed financially by the needs of sick and dependent relatives. Family care is also limited by ties of marriage and blood. It provides nothing for those beyond the boundaries of family altruism who are without kin of their own. And families, of course, can be the *source* of social problems, as in the case of domestic violence and child abuse.

Similarly, while workplace benefits provide critical resources for many employees, they bypass many others, often those with the greatest needs. Approximately a third of all full-time workers, for example, lack employee-based health coverage while many of those *with* coverage still must pay a substantial share of the overall cost via co-payments, co-shares, and deductibles. And two-thirds of all workers lack any sort of company provided retirement plan.[29]

Low-wage, intermittent, and "pink collar" workers, clearly, rarely have the "armload of perks" available to better paid, professional, and unionized employees. And even when benefits *are* available, they frequently don't extend to family members. Finally, of course, occupational benefits ignore individuals who are unconnected to the labor market.

Gosta Esping-Anderson calls these disparities in occupational coverage a "severe dissynchrony between individual and collective utility."[30] When a significant portion of the "privileged" labor force receives liberal benefits, he continues, the "broad solidarity behind the public social security system is likely to diminish," undermining basic programs that serve the entire community.[31]

Public services have their own pluses and minuses. Although they can be impersonal, inefficient, and bureaucratic, they can also ensure that all needy individuals are helped and that no one is allowed to fall below a certain minimum standard of living. They can redistribute societal resources and promote equality. They can reduce the stigma of private charity, making benefits a right rather than a handout.

Although social welfare functions are distributed among all the major institutions of society, the balance among them varies considerably. In the historical context, welfare functions evolved separately, institution by institution. In the simplest societies, most aspects of life revolve around the family—with religious, governance, economic, and mutual aid activities all organized through the kinship structure. As societies grow in complexity, individuals and groups begin to take on discrete social functions, and with increasing specialization there evolve independent religious, governmental, economic, and mutual aid organizations.

If each of the major social institutions of society serves at least some welfare functions, is it possible to think in terms of social welfare *itself* as an institution? This question, it turns out, is one of fundamental conceptual importance, although only in recent times has it been explicit. Prior to the twentieth century, social welfare was a subject matter of relatively modest scope. It was only when prevailing social arrangements became unable to deal with the emerging needs of industrial life that the publicly organized system of social welfare enlarged. The first major spurt of governmental welfare in the United States resulted from the recognition that the family, religious and economic institutions, and the instruments of voluntary mutual aid and local government were unable to address the enormous social distress caused by the Great Depression of the 1930s. This realization resulted in new demands being placed on government, especially national government. This change—frequently described as a shift from a *residual* model of social welfare to an *institutional* one—corresponded to the emergence of the U.S. welfare state.

The traditional (i.e., *residual*) view is that social welfare itself is not a significant societal institution, but rather a supplemental activity necessary only when the "normal" helping channels fail to perform appropriately. Viewed as a temporary response to the failures of individuals and major institutions, social welfare is seen as a set of activities that, while necessary at times, is undesirable and expendable. Residualists argue that it is inappropriate to place social welfare on an equal standing with the primary institutions shown in Table 1.1.

Speaking at the Conference of Charities and Corrections in 1914, Dr. Abraham Flexner expressed one aspect of the residual conception of social welfare in comparing social work with the recognized professions:

> A good deal of what is called social work might perhaps be accounted for on the ground that the recognized professions have developed too slowly on the social side. Suppose medicine were fully socialized; would not medical men, medical institutions, and medical organizations look after certain interests that the social worker must care for just because medical practice now falls short? The shortcomings of law create a similar need in another direction. Thus viewed, social work is, in part at least, not so much a separate profession as an endeavor to supplement certain existing professions pending their completed development.[32]

Competing with this conception is the *institutional* view of social welfare as a distinct pattern of activities serving not as a safety net to catch the victim after all else has failed but rather as an integral and "normal 'first line' function of modern industrial society."[33] Perceived as a basic social institution, social welfare carries none of the stigma of the "dole" or "charity." It is seen, instead, as a primary means by which individuals, families, and communities fulfill their social needs.

Much of our understanding of these competing models depends on how we comprehend both the causes and the magnitude of unmet needs in society. In both models, the major institutional structures of society are viewed as ineffective to some degree in meeting people's needs. The fundamental issues are these: To what extent is this an anomaly reflecting mainly the deficiencies of *some* individuals and just a *small margin* of institutional malfunctioning? To what extent is it a *normal* consequence of institutional limitations and individual failure? An answer of "very much" to the first question and "very little" to the second relegates social welfare to the status of a residual safety net. Reverse these answers and social welfare emerges as a basic and distinct social institution.

The answers to these questions, however, remain equivocal. In this regard, Wilensky and Lebeaux's 1958 assessment is still accurate:

> While the two views seem antithetical, in practice American social work has tried to combine them, and current trends in social welfare present a middle course. Those who lament the passing of the old order insist that the [institutional conception] is undermining individual character and the national social structure. Those who bewail our failure to achieve utopia today argue that the residual conception is an obstacle which must be removed before we can produce the good life for all. In our view, neither ideology exists in a vacuum; each is a reflection of broader cultural and societal conditions.[34]

While the debate continues, it is difficult to ignore the vast importance of the social welfare enterprise in modern society, *and* the primary role of government in it. Although the development of social welfare as a separate institution doesn't entirely equate welfare with government—national government in particular—there is no denying that modern societies demand a major public role, a role that is most frequently conceptualized in terms of the welfare state.

Analytic Perspectives on the Study of Social Welfare Policy

Analysts tend to approach the field of social welfare policy in several interrelated ways. The major approaches to analysis can be described in terms of the three P's: *process*, *product*, and *performance*. Each approach examines social policy questions that are primarily relevant to the professional roles of planning, administration, and research. Professionals engaged in these activities devote most of their resources and energies to questions concerning the process, product, and performance of social welfare policy. In actual agency practice, all three roles may be performed by the same worker. In such cases, the worker tends to draw equally on the knowledge and insights generated by all three modes of study. However, in most large organizations, planning, administration, and research tasks are specialized, and practitioners tend to be more interested in the insights of one analytic approach than in others. Even when the roles of planner, administrator, and researcher are highly compartmentalized, however, requirements for handling "outside" tasks seep into the job.[35]

Similarly, it is important to underscore that these three approaches are overlapping and interrelated. This is a shorthand way of saying that conceptual distinctions tend to capture the core qualities of a phenomenon, but, by their very nature, do not well portray subtle and relative characteristics. Frequently, policy analysts may employ different combinations of approaches in their investigations. In the volume *Fiscal Austerity and Aging*, for example, Carroll Estes and others trace the *process* of legislative development concerning the needs of the aged, describe the various programs that were *products* of this legislation, and evaluate their *performance*.[36]

Whatever the practice, however, it is theoretically useful to distinguish among these analytic approaches because each addresses different types of questions. Later on in of this chapter we will describe what we believe to be the policy-relevant tasks of the *direct*-service practitioner.

Studies of Process

Studies of process focus on the dynamics of policy formulation with regard to sociopolitical and technical variables. Political science and history are two of the major academic disciplines on which process studies are based. Process study is most concerned with understanding how the relationships and interactions among the political, governmental, and interest group collectivities in a society affect policy formulation.

Studies of process are employed as points around which policy assessments are organized, usually in the form of case studies of the political and technical inputs to decision making. Process studies may be long-range studies of the development of an entire social welfare system or studies of the development of specific programs. Examples of the former are James Leiby's historical analysis, *The History of Social Welfare and Social Work in the United States*,[37] and Heffernan's political/economic analysis, *Introduction to Social Welfare Policy: Power, Scarcity, and Common Human Needs*.[38] Analyses of specific programs include Martha Derthick's *Uncontrollable Spending for Social Service Grants*,[39] Linda Gordon's *Pitied But Not Entitled: Single Mothers and the History of Welfare 1890–1935*,[40] Gilbert and Specht's *Dynamics of Community Planning*,[41] and Theda Skocpol's *Boomerang: Clinton's Health Security Effort and the Turn Against Government in U.S. Politics*.[42]

One powerful analytical tradition, deserving of special note, interprets the welfare state in terms of class, culture, and oppression. Marxist perspectives continue to be well represented in the literature, with recent examples advancing feminist interpretations of social welfare activities using a vocabulary of sexism and an oppressive "family ethic." Views from the left, such as Piven and Cloward's sociopolitical analysis, *Regulating the Poor: The Functions of Public Welfare*, see welfare programs shaped by dominant classes and interests, whether described in terms of a ruling class, patriarchy, the "establishment," or a power elite.[43] The alternative perspective sees fundamental governmental decisions as the result of a broad range of citizen interest, advocacy groups, technical policy experts, elected officials, and individual voters, in addition to "power" groups in business, finance, and their associated elites. This "pluralist" approach denies the determining influence of a dominant class, gender, or race, viewing the welfare state instead as a product of myriad social, political, intellectual, and economic forces.

Studies of Product

The product of the planning process is a set of policy choices. These choices may be framed in program proposals, laws and statutes, or standing plans that eventually are transformed into programs. The analytic focus of product studies is on issues of choice: What is the form and substance of the choices that make up the policy design? What options did these choices foreclose? What values, theories, and assumptions support these choices?

Essentially, the analytic approach employed in this book is that of a product study. Although widely employed in a variety of academic disciplines, product study is the least developed form of social policy analysis. Analyses usually focus on one or another issue of choice that is germane to a specific policy, but there is no systematic framework for placing the generic issues of policy design in a broad context. Examples of these issue-specific studies are cited in the following chapters as we attempt to explicate a generic view of social welfare policy from this analytic perspective. In Chapter 3, we will address the development and utility of this approach in greater detail.

Studies of Performance

Performance studies are concerned with the description and evaluation of program outcomes. Studies of program outcome are more amenable to objective, systematic observation than studies of process and product because program boundaries are more sharply delineated. Performance can be measured through the collection of qualitative and quantitative data and through the application of a wide range of methodological tools from various academic disciplines. Research methodology as taught in the social sciences and in professional schools provides the major technological and theoretical knowledge and skill for these kinds of studies.

From this perspective, investigators ask two types of questions: First, how well is the program carried out? Second, what is its impact? With regard to the former, programs are monitored to see what they consist of, whether they are reaching their target population, how much they cost, and so on. Impact is measured as "the difference between pre-program behavior and conditions and post-program behavior and conditions that can legitimately be attributed to the intervention."[44] Some examples of performance studies are Jason DeParle's *American Dream: Three Women, Ten Kids, and a Nation's Drive to End Welfare*,[45] Segal and Aviram's *The Mentally Ill in Community-Based Care*,[46] and Berrick and Gilbert's *With the Best of Intentions: The Child Sexual Abuse Prevention Movement*.[47]

Performance studies, of course, are frequently carried out by analytic staff attached to the legislative bodies responsible for policy oversight. The U.S. Government Accountability Office (formerly the General Accounting Office), for example, monitors and assesses federal social programs on a regular basis for the Congress. Among their studies are evaluations of Head Start, public housing for the mentally disabled, and McKinney Act Homeless legislation.[48]

Intellectual debate is generally more vigorous in the arena of process studies than in work concerned with product and performance. That is not to say that there is no controversy with respect to product and performance studies. Rather, the issues at stake in the latter two arenas most frequently stem from the political, economic, and social context within which programs are developed, whereas the issues that underlie process studies are more likely to be related to intellectual and philosophical assumptions *about the social context itself*. For example, an analysis that is focused on a particular program's design might deal with such issues as whether there is utility in charging a fee for the use of a social service (as we do in Chapter 7), or whether there are advantages or disadvantages to offering benefits in cash versus in kind (as we do in Chapter 5). Analyses of performance seek to measure the effects, effectiveness, and efficiency of social welfare programs. In these studies, the purposes and objectives of the policies and programs are taken as a starting point. But in studies of process, analysts attempt to come to grips with such questions as, What large political and economic forces in society brought about these social welfare policies and programs? What are the factors that determine how communities meet changing social needs? The ways analysts deal with these questions are strongly influenced by their own cultural and philosophical values and by their *Weltansicht*, or worldview.

The concepts used in this book to analyze the products of policy can be applied to social welfare programs in all national contexts. Similarly, the analytic methods used in the study of social welfare policy products (i.e., separating the components of choice in program design and examining the values and theories associated with these choices) do not vary in any considerable way from one social context to another. However, the study of process is heavily dependent on the analyst's basic intellectual and philosophical assumptions. The analyst is often guided by overarching ideas about the nature of human society; frequently, analysts may not even be aware of how these assumptions influence their own thinking.

Political Perspectives on the Study of Social Welfare Policy

The classic debate in the politics of social welfare pits individual versus community values, two competing perspectives that offer starkly different expressions of the good society and the proper role of government within it (Table 1.2). Individualism, a philosophic orientation emphasizing the pursuit of individual (rather than collective) interests, embodies a faith in the opportunities afforded ordinary people to succeed in life by dint of their own aptitudes and ambitions. For many, the widely held belief that achievement and effort go hand in hand constitutes our basic ethos, the primary element of the "American exceptionalism" that accounts for our success as a prosperous, free nation.[49]

The community perspective, on the other hand, reflects a very different understanding of proper conduct in society, one that recognizes the importance of common action on behalf of common goals. The community impulse views social action—not individual action—as the key component of a society's well-being, and a necessary check on the divisiveness inherent in unchecked self-advancement.

The governing postulate of individualism—every person being responsible for his or her own fate—represents the traditional vision of the American Dream. The postulate is built on a broadly held premise that those who work hard and self-reliantly will be rewarded with material success. The implication, of course, is that those who fail do so because of personal inadequacy, lack of effort, or insufficient skill.

Individualism as a philosophy finds its economic expression in the principle of *laissez-faire*, the theory that society works best when people can freely advance their own material self-interest within an unimpeded private marketplace. The social welfare corollary is that the private expression of private interests results in an optimal state of welfare, with the entrepreneurial spirit producing jobs, wealth, and economic security

TABLE 1.2   *Political Perspectives on Social Welfare Policy*

	The Individualist Perspective	**The Community Perspective**
Political Ideology	Conservative	Liberal/Progressive
View of Social Problems	Problems reflect bad choices, personal dysfunction, culture of poverty	Problems reflect fundamental socioeconomic circumstances, barriers to access, lack of opportunity
View of Markets	Unregulated markets and private property ensure prosperity and welfare	Unregulated markets create dangerous economic cycles, unemployment, urban blight, poverty and inequality, and environmental degradation
Responsibility of Government	Residual perspective— government should be small—a modest and decentralized adjunct to private institutions	Institutional perspective— government should be large enough to advance social welfare on behalf of the broad community
Social Policy Agendas	Rely on market, voluntary, and religious arrangements; provide a minimum safety net focused on the poor	Rely on public leadership; provide broad program coverage to insure full opportunity, economic security, and basic social goods

for all. As columnist George Will put it, individualism and free-market capitalism have created "the most efficient anti-poverty machine the world has ever seen."[50]

Individualism, and the value it places on the private institutions of society, constitutes the fundamental element of political conservatism. When it comes to "social interventions," then, priority is given to families, churches, businesses, and private associations, not the state. The rival perspective is represented in the economic and political ideas, parties, and movements of the left. Long associated with various strands

CAPSULE 1.6 • *The Individualist Perspective*

All of us can sense a disturbing disposition on the part of many to seek solutions to their problems from sources outside themselves. Because life today is complex and interdependent, we seem always more ready to lean on government than upon ourselves. Such an approach can never retain the health and vigor of America. Rather, we must believe in and practice an approach founded on individual initiative, individual self-reliance, individual conscience, and individual voluntary effort.

Dwight David Eisenhower, 1957.

of democratic socialism, progressivism, and modern liberalism, the community orientation holds that citizens—as a matter of right—are entitled to a "fair share" in society. For the left, social problems are less the product of personal inadequacy than of socioeconomic malfunction. For much of the twentieth century, the core assumption was that the problems of modern society were rooted in the greedy self-seeking of industrial capitalism. During the Progressive Era and the New Deal, for example, the left was preoccupied with confronting concentrated economic power and the problems of monopoly.

Nowadays, the community approach is advanced less in the language of socialism and class conflict and more in the language of socioeconomic factors, opportunities, and social welfare. Although fully reconciled to the basic structures of capitalism, the left nevertheless still views individualism—in personal conduct and in markets—as a source of inequality, social problems, and domination by social and economic elites.

The politics of right and left confront each other most directly in rival views of the role of government. Not surprisingly, individualists are suspicious of government action. While Ronald Reagan, on several occasions, stated, "The best thing government can do is nothing," nevertheless, conservatives rarely reject the worth of public action completely. We need a military, public roads, basic education, and a structure of law to enforce the rules of fair play. But when it comes to social welfare, conservatives resist going beyond the minimum safety net required to protect the social order. They resist government action because public welfare is seen as undermining personal responsibility and impeding the marketplace. This was the rationale in 1935 for opposing Social Security—people wouldn't responsibly plan for their own futures if they were assured a retirement income—and it is the conservative rationale today for opposing health and social service initiatives.

The community principle, on the contrary, values government as the expression of the democratic will of the broad citizenry, the one institution in society with the authority to protect the interests of all against the agendas of the few. For Franklin Roosevelt, "liberalism" was simply "plain English for a changed concept of the duty and

CAPSULE 1.7 • *The Community Perspective*

Little good is ever said for government as a whole. The public sector of the economy is seen, not as a cause of wealth or form of income, but a burden on the economic system. We believe we are enriched by the production of automobiles, or cosmetics, but depressed and impoverished by expenditures on public education or food stamps for the always undeserving poor. [But] public services are not, in any respect, inferior to private goods and services. Clean streets are as much a part of our standard of living as clean houses. Public health measures are as likely to save lives as private hygiene. Our liberties are greatly enlarged by our public services—by good schools, good law enforcement, ample opportunities for recreation and self-development. Collective decision making is, simply, an indispensable feature of public activity.

John Kenneth Galbraith, 1986.

responsibility of government toward economic life."[51] For the left, the mission of government is to balance market forces, to modify the power of elites in favor of the whole, and to ensure economic management for growth, employment, and fair wages. Whereas conservatives advocate the residualism of the "safety net," progressives stress active public responsibility to guarantee that basic human needs are addressed. In practice, progressive social policy is based on a broad social justice ethic, advancing an allocation of resources that reduces inequalities in society, whether they take the form of income differences or excessive disparities in education, health, or housing.

Individual and Community Approaches to Planning

The individual and community perspectives can be applied to planning—the process of policy formation—as well as to the actual substance of policy. For many years during the mid-twentieth century, indeed, planning—its hows and whys and by whoms—was one of this country's most politically divisive issues. At first, the debate followed the traditional contours of left–right politics. Friedrich Hayek, for example, writing in 1944, saw the dispute between "modern planners and their opponents" not in terms of the desirability of planning per se, but in terms of the merits of alternative planning arrangements and the degree to which they allowed for the expression of *individual* interests. For Hayek, the question was whether the smaller "natural" institutions of society—individuals and groups—were to be involved in determining their own interests or whether plans would be centrally and bureaucratically determined. It was the latter course—centrally planned change—that Hayek perceived as the "road to serfdom."[52]

Since the 1960s, this dispute has lost its edge. Certainly, the collapse of the planned "command economies" of eastern Europe and the Soviet Union eroded most of the world's faith in socialist arrangements that relied on centralized long-range schemas for economic and social development. Few modern planners anywhere in the globe still advocate unitary, nationally determined economic plans. But even before the great upheavals of 1989 and 1990 changed the face of Europe, skepticism had been growing with the very idea that a single national entity could possess the information, vision, and resources to advance the public interest in any sort of fair, efficient, or comprehensive fashion. While systematic planning, in the sense of a process that relies upon a set of evidence-based procedures for thinking about and influencing the future, remains an essential element behind good public policy, the old "rational" planning model—identifying broad community goals, identifying and evaluating alternative strategies to achieve them, selecting the optimal strategy, implementing it, and evaluating results—is rarely possible in a society such as ours with sharp disharmonies of interest, powerfully organized constituencies, and political structures that magnify differences rather than commonalities.

This is not to say that planning for social justice is irrelevant. But it does suggest that effective social planning must be cautious, sensitive to diverse opinion, appreciative of the limits of broad-scale interventions, and able to organize and mobilize common interests on behalf of social change.

Why Policy Analysis Is Relevant to Social Work Practice

The study of social welfare policy, and the choices and dilemmas involved in its formulation, is of vast importance to professionals who are responsible for carrying out policy—in particular, those who devote the major portion of their energies and resources to direct services.

The social worker providing direct services to clients—whether a mental health worker, disability case manager, probation officer, or protective services worker, to identify just a few—can play an important role in the formulation and execution of social policies. Indeed, it is well recognized that the separation of policy formulation from policy execution is a delicate division, more characteristic of a porous membrane than of the solid line of bureaucratic hierarchy. Experienced practitioners often exercise considerable discretion in executing broad directives, and so shape as well as discharge organizational policies.

The importance of practitioner discretion for policy interpretation increases as organizations grow larger and more complex. Too frequently, however, the charge to the practitioner is delivered in clichés like getting "politically involved." Such demands can be demoralizing to professionals, particularly to those whose major energies are devoted to addressing the complex problems of individuals and families. At best, a general call to arms without more specific instructions about which arms to use and how to use them is only temporarily inspiring; at worst, it is likely to leave many feeling inadequate.

A second reason for the direct practitioner's sense of inadequacy in policy formulation is that this task is not as well defined as others. In mental health and child welfare, for example, the actual doing (social work) and the objects of one's work (cases) are relatively clear. Many of the methods used in direct practice allow professionals to work within a series of fairly well-defined roles that usually have a high degree of consonance. The process by which policy is formulated, however, involves a wide range of roles that often strain against one another. Direct service, finally, tends to be *individual* practice—one social worker handling one case. Policy formulation, very differently, involves the efforts of many.

The fact that the direct practitioner's major functions are remote from the final decision points in the process of policy formulation makes many students less than enthusiastic to take courses in social welfare policy. Direct practitioners are more inclined to concentrate on the development of interactional skills, on learning how to conduct themselves as professionals, and on how to engage clients, colleagues, and community leaders and groups. The study of social choices and social values may seem abstract and theoretical. But professionals who ignore social choices and social values in favor of developing practice skills are like musicians playing background music to a melody that seems to come from nowhere. Like musical themes, the directions and goals that are reflected in social welfare policy are neither accidental nor aimless; they develop because people make choices. One has to understand the range of choices, the values implied in the alternatives, the framework within which these choices are made, the various means by which these choices are implemented, and the methodological tools that can be used to assess the consequences of these choices.

Although direct service workers may be unconcerned with policy design, they are affected by it in important ways. In the long view, policy choices affect the technologies direct service workers use. Consider, for example, the ways in which changes in federal policies have affected the character and extent of the social services in the public assistance system. The 1962 amendments to the Social Security Act placed great value on the provision of supportive casework services to welfare clients, and this choice was supported with substantial financial resources. In 1967, federal policy changed, and, along with the administrative separation of income and services, individualized therapeutic interventions were significantly deemphasized in favor of concrete social services like job training and childcare and family planning. These priorities were advanced with "matching" grants whereby the federal government paid $3 for every $1 spent by the states. Federal expenditures, in addition, were open-ended, meaning unlimited. Given this enticing arrangement, states expanded their volume of social services and hired many new service workers, and costs by the early 1970s soared to more than $2 billion annually, up from practically nothing a decade earlier.

As a consequence, Congress enacted Title XX to the Social Security Act in 1974, which placed a "cap" (financial limit) on federal expenditures. In 1981, allocations for Title XX were reduced, but states were given virtually free reign in designing social services programs and targeting beneficiaries. Since then, the program's basic structure has remained virtually intact, although its ability to address social problems has been drastically reduced because funding has remained stagnant in dollar terms, which means significantly reduced in inflation-corrected terms. Federal Title XX spending, currently around $1.7 billion annually, is considerably less than half the inflation-adjusted amount of 1981.

Social workers have also been powerfully affected by policy changes outside of Title XX—policies, for example, that expanded funding for particular types of services. Funding for the homeless, people with HIV/AIDS, and teen runaways expanded the nature and scope of social work services. The Welfare Reform legislation of 1996, which converted public assistance into a block grant, giving states broad authority to use their funds for social services instead of cash grants, resulted in a very significant boost for programs like daycare, transportation, case management, and substance abuse counseling that supported single mothers transitioning to the workplace.

Similarly, federal child welfare and mental health policies have structured the nature of social work practice at the service delivery level. The "permanency planning" thrust of national child welfare legislation, for example, has powerfully influenced the decisions that local case workers make when trying to balance child safety and family preservation. Decisions concerning substitute care when children are unable to live at home—choices between foster care and adoption and kinship care options—similarly are influenced by the federal policy framework.

In the mental health field, the deinstitutionalization of several hundred thousand mentally disturbed individuals after the mid-1970s drastically reduced the need for in-hospital social services while expanding the demand for community-based services.

Mental health social workers today, in addition to providing direct counseling, are required to weave together fragmented housing, health, income support, and social service programs on behalf of their individual clients, a job requiring a realistic and thorough understanding of services legislation and service organizations. Practitioners with the conceptual tools to analyze the dimensions of policy are far more likely to be effective in endeavors like these than social workers ignorant of such techniques.

Whether or not the direct practitioner *is* conversant with social welfare policy, the public assumes that those engaged in providing services possess pertinent information about social welfare programs, their nature, and their consequences. Legislators, politicians, and community groups frequently turn to substance abuse workers, probation officers, and mental health case managers for information and advice, and what they say is treated seriously—whether ill or well-informed—because of their status as professionals. There is, then, at the very least, a professional obligation to be knowledgeable about policy matters.

Finally, many students now being trained for direct practice will, later on, become planners, managers, and researchers because these positions are frequently filled within agencies on the basis of seniority. Direct service professionals who will ultimately perform policy-related roles would be wise to link some part of their formal education to planning, organization, and analysis. From a career point of view, it is essential that the direct practitioner have at least an appreciation of the dimensions of the field of social welfare policy, if not an intimate knowledge of its specializations.

Emerging Issues: Feminist Perspectives on Social Welfare

Recent scholarship has supplied an important new perspective to the conventional models of social policy analysis, a perspective that emphasizes the role of women. Feminist perspectives bring women qua women into the study and interpretation of social welfare in valuable and diverse ways.

One body of research, for example, focuses on the vulnerabilities of women in society—in families, in the workplace, in schools—and documents and analyzes a range of social inequalities. A considerable body of scholarship has examined issues such as violence against women, women's health, and sexual harassment. The feminization of poverty—the singular economic risks facing single mothers and elderly women—is one concern of significance. Especially vulnerable to economic dependency, women are particularly reliant on welfare-state programs. Over 90 percent of all Temporary Assistance for Needy Families (TANF) households are headed by women while women compose nearly two-thirds of all Social Security recipients. Another issue is the wage gap. Women still earn less than 80 cents for every dollar earned by men in similar occupations, and while a portion of this discrepancy reflects personal choice—some women, for example, deliberately choose lower-paying jobs in order to secure the flexibility they need to handle family concerns—much of it results from long-standing prejudices regarding the proper role of women in the workplace.

A separate corpus of study has examined the role of individual women, women's social agencies, and the women's movement more generally in the evolution of the social work profession and social welfare policies and programs. Historical analyses of women's roles in the development of income support, social services, and protective legislation for women—such as wage and hour laws governing industry—have significantly expanded our body of knowledge about the reciprocal relationships among social policy, the role women play in society, and the particular circumstances of women facing significant social and economic needs. Theda Skocpol's *Protecting Soldiers and Mothers: The Political Origins of Social Policy in the United States,* for example, focuses on the political mobilization of middle-class women in the Progressive Era a century ago and its role in creating "maternalist" social policies through mothers' pensions, health programs for women and young children, and workplace regulation.[53]

A more conceptual scholarship has formulated a body of theory that attempts to explain the evolution and character of social welfare institutions, and social policy itself, as a reflection of deeply rooted, and deeply pernicious, cultural mores and conventions. The feminist left, for example, views the traditional nuclear family as the embodiment of "patriarchy"—male privilege and female servitude. Traditional gender roles give men the responsibility to provide financial support for the family, along with the authority to "head" the household and exploit and subordinate women and children. Women, restricted to the role of wife and mother and confined to the household sphere, are prevented from pursuing opportunities in the broader economic, social, and cultural world.

Feminist scholars and activists—while broadly committed to greater gender equality—differ substantially in their approach to the question of political strategy. Christina Hoff Sommers, for example, describes policy remedies to women's subordination in terms of first- and second-wave feminism.[54] First-wave, or equity, feminism reflects the traditional liberal agenda of political rights and expanded opportunity. Equity feminists, in the tradition of the suffragette movement of a century ago, focus on practical opportunities for women in all the institutional sectors of society— schools, the workplace, and the political realm. Among the key issues of concern are abortion rights, daycare, and child support.

Equity feminists also recognize the importance of choice for women. This not only means opportunities equal to those provided men, it means support for women who select traditional roles—such as stay-at-home mothers. While recognizing that women face enormous challenges, first-wave feminists are less likely to see women as victims of patriarchy than as common partners with men in an effort to broaden opportunities for all the many categories of society's disadvantaged and marginalized.

Second-wave feminists take a broader and more radical view. "Gender feminists" seek to confront the fundamental inequalities they see as inherent in society's basic institutions—families in particular. All women—little girls to old ladies—are viewed as victimized by deep and pervasive cultural and social restraints, restraints that impede their progress, limit their possibilities, and significantly contribute not only to social problems but also to psychological and emotional disorders, such as low self-esteem, clinical depression, and anorexia.

CAPSULE 1.8 • *Patriarchy and Welfare*

During the twentieth century, the expanding welfare state continued to support patriarchal dominance while mediating reproductive relations on behalf of the productive needs of capital. The emergence of the modern welfare state, marked by the enactment of the 1935 Social Security Act, signaled the institutionalization of public or social patriarchy. Instead of simply assuming patriarchal control, the state began to systematically subsidize the familial unit of production through the provision of economic arrangements. They redistribute needed resources, offer nonworking women and single mothers a means of self-support, and provide the material conditions for the pursuit of equal opportunity. Welfare state benefits that help women to survive without male economic support subsidize, if not legitimate, the female-headed household and undermine the exclusivity of the male-breadwinner, female-homemaker family structure. As a social wage, welfare state benefits increase the bargaining power of women relative to men. . . .

The ideology of women's roles is deeply encoded in social welfare policy. It is well-known that social welfare laws categorize the poor as deserving and undeserving of aid based on their compliance with the work ethic. But the rules and regulations of social welfare programs also treat women differently according to their perceived compliance with the family ethic. . . . Assessing women in terms of the family ethic became one way the welfare state could mediate the conflicting demands for women's unpaid labor in the home and her low paid labor in the market, encourage reproduction by "proper" families, and otherwise meet the needs of patriarchal capitalism.

From *Regulating the Lives of Women: Social Welfare Policy from Colonial Times to the Present*, by Mimi Abramowitz. Reprinted by permission of South End Press.

Second-wave feminists see society as inherently sexist in its dominant values, and this sexism is "reproduced" in politics, economics, and social policy. Male supremacy, the primary cause of women's subjugation, must be the primary target of change. Confronting it requires not just liberal reform, political rights, and better social programs, but an overall attack on the inequalities built into the fundamental conventions of our culture, our language, and our understanding of male–female relationships.

In the social policy realm, second-wave feminists interpret the development of welfare legislation as a reflection of women's subjugation in the family. The traditional role of women as wives, mothers, and "unpaid domestic laborers"—the traditional family model known as the "family ethic" in feminist parlance—powerfully influences the life circumstances of women. As wives and mothers, most obviously, women find their economic opportunities limited. Without savings of their own, without marketable skills that can produce a wage, they are dependent on male breadwinners. Single mothers, the divorced, and the widowed find themselves vulnerable to poverty and insecurity. But the "family ethic," more generally, also influences the character of the social programs that have developed to address these problems, since the welfare state represents the underlying values and institutions of the broader society. For Mimi Abramovitz, for example, the welfare state has supported "patriarchal dominance while mediating reproductive relations on behalf of the productive needs of capital. The

CAPSULE 1.9 • *Ms. Information*

I do not believe that women in American society are oppressed, or members of a subordinate class. It is no longer reasonable to say that as a group, women are worse off than men. The truth is that American women are among the freest in the world. Feminism in this country has become a parody of itself. We need a forward-looking movement, guided by common sense and fairness; instead, we've got political correctness, victim politics, and male bashing.

More women than men now go to college, for example. Yet for many women's studies professors and contemporary feminist leaders such good news is no news. The most vocal among them persist in complaining that the United States is a "patriarchy" that subordinates women. In fact, the more things improve for women, the angrier their rhetoric grows. Harvard psychologist Carol Gilligan asserts that young women in today's American society undergo a "psychological foot-binding." One leading feminist text refers to American society as a "rape culture."

Does it really matter that a small group of statistically challenged activists and scholars say and believe a lot of false things about women in America? The answer is that it does matter. Third World women, many of whom really are grievously subordinated, desperately need help. But most of our prominent women's organizations are preoccupied only with saving American women from the ravages of patriarchy.

The women's movement has been hijacked by a small group of chronically offended gender feminists who believe that women are from Venus and men are from Hell. Women who value harmony between the sexes and who are concerned about the plight of subjugated women throughout the world will have to find a way to get the movement back.

From "Ms. Information" by Christina Hoff Sommers, *The Wall Street Journal*, March 25, 2003. Reprinted by permission from The Wall Street Journal, © 2003 Dow Jones & Company. All rights reserved.

emergence of the modern welfare state, marked by the enactment of the 1935 Social Security Act, signaled the institutionalization of public or social patriarchy."[55]

This kind of analysis has been critiqued for its preoccupation with gender exploitation and its disdain for the values—love, domesticity, marriage, motherhood—associated with customary family arrangements. Nevertheless, presenting gender as a central organizing principle for analysis has powerfully modernized policy studies, highlighting a range of issues long ignored or excluded from serious examination. Gender may be a less "determining" status than ever before in history, but women remain vastly overrepresented among the most vulnerable sectors of society. Whatever the ultimate origins of today's gender inequities—oppression, customs, socialization, law, biology, or ignorance—they clearly need to be challenged. Along with race, class, and ethnicity, gender provides a valuable lens for understanding social policy, assessing it, and transforming it.

Notes

1. See, for example, Martin Rein, *Social Policy* (New York: Random House, 1970), 3–20; Kenneth Bouding, "The Boundaries of Social Policy," *Social Work*, 12(1) (January 1967): 3–11; Richard Titmuss, *Essays on "The Welfare State"* (London: Unwin University Books, 1963).
2. See, for example, David A. Gil, "A Systematic Approach to Social Policy Analysis," *Social Service Review*, 44(4) (December 1970): 411–26.

3. AARP Bulletin, July–August 2007, 27.
4. National Center for Health Services Research and Health Care Technology Assessment. Research Activities 87 (July 1997).
5. Maggie Jackson, "More Sons are Juggling Jobs and Care for Parents," *New York Times*, June 15, 2003.
6. "Children in Kinship Care Gaining Ground," New Federalism Series No. B-68, The Urban Institute, April 28, 2006.
7. U.S. Department of Health & Human Services, *Report on Kinship Foster Care*, June, 2000.
8. Devon Brooks, "Kinship Care and Substance-Exposed Children," *The Source*, 9(1) (Winter 1999): 1.
9. Stacey J. Oliker, "Examining Care after Welfare Ends," *Focus* (2) (Spring 1999): 38. Oliker notes that ethnographic studies of welfare tend to emphasize the importance of family networks while surveys show a more modest level of help.
10. U.S. Bureau of the Census, *Who's Helping Out? Support Networks among American Families* (Washington, D.C.: U.S. Government Printing Office, 1988).
11. "Greater Child Support Is Linked to Parents Who Visit Children," *New York Times*, April 24, 1999, A14.
12. Roberta Blank, *It Takes A Nation* (Princeton, N.J.: Princeton University Press, 1997), 44.
13. Ibid.
14. Eduardo Porter, "Flow of Immigrants' Money to Latin America Surges," *New York Times*, October 19, 2006.
15. Ginger Thompson, "Big Mexican Breadwinner: The Migrant Worker," *New York Times*, March 25, 2002, A3.
16. Blaine Harden, "Families Quietly Shelter Dispossessed Kin," *San Francisco Chronicle*, September 8, 2005.
17. "Mormons and the 'Sin' of Being Poor," *San Francisco Examiner*, December 19, 1982, A16.
18. Ibid.
19. Sheila Kamerman and Alfred Kahn, *Helping America's Families* (Temple University Press, 1982) 202.
20. Eduardo Porter, "Rising Cost of Health Benefits Cited as Factor in Slump of Jobs," *The New York Times*, August 19, 2004.
21. Barnaby Feder, "Ministers Who Work around the Flock," *New York Times*, October 3, 1996, C1. For a general discussion of EAPs, see Kathryn Troy, *Meeting Human Needs: Corporate Programs and Partnerships* (New York: Conference Board, 1986); and Paul Kurzman and Sheila Akabas (eds.), *Work and Well-Being: The Occupational Social Work Advantage* (Washington, D.C.: NASW Press, 1993).
22. Lester Salamon, *America's Nonprofit Sector, A Primer* (New York: The Foundation Center, 1999), 118.
23. C. E. Born, "Proprietary Firms and Child Welfare Services," *Child Welfare*, 62(2) (1983): 109–118.
24. Salamon, 55.
25. Harry Specht, "Social Work and the Popular Psychotherapies," *Social Service Review*, 64(3) (September 1990): 345.
26. R.C. Kessler et al., "Patterns and Correlates of Self-Help Group Membership in the U.S.," *Social Policy*, 27 (1997): 27–46.
27. Salamon, 111–12.
28. Roy Wallis, "Institutions," *Encyclopedia of the Social Sciences*, 14 (New York: MacMillan, 1968), 410.
29. Robert B. Reisch, quoted in David Sanger, "The Last Liberal (Almost) Leaves Town," *New York Times*, January 9, 1997.
30. Gosta Esping-Anderson, "Occupational Welfare in the Social Policy Nexus," in Michael Shalev (ed.), *The Privatization of Social Policy* (New York: St. Martin's Press, 1996).
31. Ibid.
32. Abraham Flexner, "Is Social Work a Profession?" Presented at the Conference of Charities and Corrections, May 17, 1915.

33. Harold Wilensky and Charles Lebeaux, *Industrial Society and Social Welfare* (New York: Russell Sage, 1958), 138.
34. Ibid., 140.
35. For example, in Robert Perlman and Arnold Gurin, *Community Organization and Social Planning* (New York: John Wiley and Sons, 1972), an entire chapter is devoted to various ways in which the administrator of a direct-service agency is engaged in community organization and social planning tasks.
36. Carroll L. Estes et al., *Fiscal Austerity and Aging* (Beverly Hills, Calif.: Sage Publications, 1983).
37. James Leiby, *The History of Social Welfare and Social Work in the United States* (New York: Columbia University Press, 1978).
38. Joseph Heffernan, *Introduction to Social Welfare Policy: Power, Scarcity, and Common Human Needs* (Itasca, Ill.: F. E. Peacock, 1979).
39. Martha Derthick, *Uncontrollable Spending for Social Service Grants* (Washington, D.C.: Brookings Institution, 1975).
40. Linda Gordon, *Pitied But Not Entitled: Single Mothers and the History of Welfare 1890–1935* (New York: Free Press, 1994).
41. Neil Gilbert and Harry Specht, *Dynamics of Community Planning* (Cambridge, Mass.: Ballinger Publishing, 1977).
42. Theda Skocpol, *Boomerang: Clinton's Health Security Effort and the Turn against Government in U.S. Politics* (New York: W.W. Norton, 1996).
43. Frances Fox Piven and Richard A. Cloward, *Regulating the Poor: The Functions of Public Welfare* (New York: Vintage Books, 1993).
44. Howard Freeman and Clarence Sherwood, *Social Research and Social Policy* (Englewood Cliffs, N.J.: Prentice Hall, 1970), 13.
45. Jason DeParle, *American Dream* (New York: Viking, 2004).
46. Steven P. Segal and Uri Aviram, *The Mentally Ill in Community-Based Care* (New York: John Wiley and Sons, 1978).
47. Jill Duerr Berrick and Neil Gilbert, *With the Best of Intentions: The Child Sexual Abuse Prevention Movement* (New York: Guilford Press, 1991).
48. See, for example, U.S. General Accounting Office, Early Childhood Programs, GAO/HEHS-94-169BR, May 1994; Public Housing: Housing Persons with Mental Disabilities, GAO/RCED-92-81, August 1992; Homelessness: McKinney Act Programs and Funding, GAO/RCED-91-126, May 1991.
49. See Byron E. Shafer (ed.), *Is America Different? A New Look at American Exceptionalism* (New York: Oxford University Press, 1991).
50. George Will, syndicated column, November 16, 1984
51. Alan Brinkley, *The End of Reform: New Deal Liberalism in Recession and War* (New York: Alfred A. Knopf, 1995), 10.
52. Friedrich A. Hayek, *The Road to Serfdom* (Chicago: University of Chicago Press, 1944), 32–42.
53. Theda Skocpol, *Protecting Soldiers and Mothers: The Political Origins of Social Policy in the United States* (Cambridge, Mass.: Belknap Press of Harvard University Press, 1992).
54. Christina Hoff Sommers, *Who Stole Feminism?* (New York: Simon and Schuster, 1994).
55. Mimi Abramowitz, *Regulating the Lives of Women: Social Welfare Policy from Colonial Times to the Present* (Boston, Mass.: South End Press, 1988), 32–33, 39–40.

2

The Modern Welfare State

The test of our progress is not whether we add more to the abundance of those who have much; it is whether we provide enough for those who have too little.

Franklin Delano Roosevelt
Second Inaugural Address, January 20, 1937

You must rank me and my colleagues as strong partisans of national compulsory insurance for all classes for all purposes from the cradle to the grave.

Winston Churchill
Radio Broadcast, March 21, 1943

Central to any consideration of the 20th century are the huge steps taken in the direction of human well-being . . . in nutrition, in shelter, in the enjoyments, which no one should minimize, of a modern standard of living. Our century began with a small number of rich and a large, meager mass. The century is ending, in the fortunate countries at least, with a very large comfortable community.

John Kenneth Galbraith
New Perspectives Quarterly, Winter 1996

The contemporary welfare state embodies the idea that government has a significant responsibility for social protection; in this sense, every modern industrial state is a welfare state. All utilize public action to ensure that neither bad luck nor economic distress nor social disadvantage fully determine the life chances of citizens. All have programs explicitly directed to combating misfortune and advancing opportunity and, as the U.S. Constitution states, providing "for the general welfare." And all spend substantially on social welfare—more than for any other single activity. In most, indeed, social welfare spending accounts for well over half of all government spending, with the majority of civil servants planning and implementing social programs.

The Evolving Welfare State

Chapter 1 described the development of social welfare in the United States in terms of an evolution from a "residual conception," where helping was principally a function of families and charities, to an "institutional conception," where the nation itself provides a broad range of social and economic protections. For Wilensky and Lebeaux, writing in 1958, the residual approach, represented by old-fashioned poor-law welfare (i.e., cash assistance for the poor), coexisted in the United States with an emerging institutional approach—something like the welfare state—represented by social insurance, public education, and other programs designed to help all individuals and families, not just impoverished ones.[1] This coexistence remains.

While the evolution from residual to institutional has characterized many societies, the road to the welfare state has followed different contours in different countries. In recent years, indeed, a significant body of scholarship has provided a portrait of its distinctive core processes and elements.[2]

Whatever their individual differences, however, all welfare states have evolved through a series of common historical sequences. These stages, presented in Table 2.1, provide a developmental overview of the welfare state from its inception through the reorientation that has characterized recent decades.

Inception

The welfare state was born over a century ago in an era of industrial change and great social and political ferment. For long periods prior to the end of the nineteenth century,

TABLE 2.1   *The Evolving Welfare State*

	Inception 1880s–1930s	Growth 1940s–1950s	Maturation 1960s–Mid-1970s	Transformation Mid-1970s On
Political Developments	Growth of democracy; universal adult suffrage, development of union movement, social democracy, modern liberalism	Broad political consensus favoring increasing social spending; labor parties powerful in Europe, Democrats in the United States	New political constituencies advance civil and social rights for minorities, women, the disabled, and others	Conservative resurgence; tax revolt; weakening of unions; new intellectual critiques of the welfare state
Economic Developments	Golden era of unrestrained capitalism; economic dislocations of industrialization	Triumph of Keynesian economics after the Great Depression; powerful post–World War II economic growth; low unemployment	Sustained prosperity and improved living standards through the mid-1970s; 1973 "oil shock" weakens Western economies	Slower economic growth; stagnating personal incomes; increased inequality; rise in European unemployment; increased demands on social security and health programs from an aging population

(continued)

TABLE 2.1 *Continued*

Key Social Policies	Poor law tradition gives way to new initiatives in social security (pensions, unemployment, health care); public spending reaches 5 percent of GDP	Growth in coverage of basic social security, health care, public aid programs, and family allowances	Broadened range of income, health care, and social service programs; public spending by mid-1970s averages 25 percent GDP in Europe, 20 percent in United States	Few new programs; some erosion of public assistance safety net; modest curtailment in social security programs; spending levels stabilize
Role of Government	Beginning of national welfare leadership; decline of private institutions and localism	Broad expansion in national social financing, regulation, "universalization" of the constituency of the welfare state	New program emphasis on social and economic rights for minorities, excluded groups, and urban poverty populations; major increase in public employment	Reagan (U.S.) and Thatcher (U.K.) seek to reduce the size and scope of the welfare state; decentralization; privatization
Key Dates and Events: England and Europe	1886: Germany adopts health insurance; 1911: England enacts National Insurance Act; 1921: Austria adopts first family allowance	1941: British Archbishop Temple coins the phrase "welfare state"; 1942: Beveridge Plan provides welfare blueprint for post–World War II English society	1966: New Ministry of Social Security created in Great Britain; provides more generous supplementary benefits; 1971: New benefits to help the chronically ill	1979: Margaret Thatcher becomes Britain's Prime Minister, privatizes public housing and reduces pension payments
Key Dates and Events: United States	1913: Progressive federal income tax initiated; 1935: Social Security enacted	1953: Federal cabinet-level Department of Health, Education, and Welfare created	1964: War on Poverty initiated by Lyndon Johnson; 1965: Medicare and Medicaid enacted	1980: Ronald Reagan elected President; 1994: Republicans gain control of U.S. Congress; 1996 AFDC repealed

of course, all nations had some public responsibility for welfare. The British Poor Law, for example, had replaced church responsibility for the relief of pauperism with government responsibility in 1603. But it was not until the invention of social insurance that traditional poor relief—and the dominance of the residual model—began to give way to modern welfare.

Conceived in Germany in the 1880s, and very rapidly spreading throughout the industrialized countries of the world, social insurance emerged in response to a common set of circumstances—the decline of rural agriculture, the transformation of farmers and peasants into factory workers, and the jeopardy faced by increasing numbers of families as economic cycles of boom and bust disrupted their livelihood. Facing the issue of how to shield families from the hazards of industrial society, government leaders—often joined by labor and business—found an answer in social insurance.

The origins of welfare states throughout the world date to the enactment of these compulsory public programs. Recognizing the growing numbers of people who faced years of grinding destitution when they could no longer work, social insurance sought to *prevent* the most common risks of the industrial order—those associated with illness, old age and death, unemployment, and accidents—rather than dealing with them after the fact. On humanitarian and religious grounds, social insurance provided a minimum cash allotment to help people manage their lives with dignity, without the uncertainties and stigmas of private charity or poor relief. On political grounds, it represented the growing strength of the working class; given a greatly broadened franchise, ordinary people were able to demand, and secure, help from government. And the value of social insurance in promoting social harmony was not lost on the political and economic elites of the era. If workers had something to look forward to when they could no longer work, something to protect their families' futures, they would be far less likely to feel alienated from the labor force, resentful of their employers, or partial to radical politics.

The "birth" of the welfare state is usually traced to Germany's initiation of health insurance in 1883. Much of Western Europe soon followed Germany's lead, introducing health, accident, old-age pension, and unemployment programs prior to World War I, with the United States belatedly enacting its national insurances during the Great Depression of the 1930s. Workers' compensation developed to meet the needs of industrial workers who were incapacitated by accidents. Health insurance responded to the risks of sickness. Pension insurance emerged to help those who grew too old or feeble to work.

The accumulation of these programs made social welfare something very different, in scope and intent, from the traditional poor-law state with its focus on destitution and relief. Social insurance represented recognition that private charity and family support—and help from friends and church members—simply weren't sufficient in the modern world. So governments took on new protective responsibilities, sponsoring, regulating, and financing insurance programs for certain risks and certain workers. The programs were compulsory; workers in particular job categories (at first, typically, manual workers and farmers), and often employers, had to participate. These workers, and their employers, had to pay at least a portion of the costs. And, most critically, social insurance provided a legal claim to benefits, making it an essential right of modern political life.

Although social insurance represents the *sine quo non* of the welfare state, its defining minimum, the emergence of modern welfare was accompanied by significant state action in other areas of social concern. State-sponsored public health and sanitation initiatives were common in the decades immediately before and after the turn of the twentieth century. Broad public education—especially at the secondary level—became commonplace by the outbreak of World War I. Workplace safety legislation and public housing were similarly widespread, and in the interwar period (1918–1939), child allowance programs were initiated throughout Europe providing cash help to ordinary families. Perhaps most significantly, the emerging welfare states all broadened their instruments of taxation—generally by imposing progressive taxes on income—to provide the wherewithal for their rapidly expanding responsibilities.

Finally, the evolving welfare state refined many of the old institutions and principles of poor relief. Called "public assistance" or "social assistance" in the modern era, these means-tested antipoverty programs, typically directed to particular groups of the needy, remained an essential safety net element in Europe and, far more so, in the United States, especially for those not connected to the labor market and therefore not covered by social insurance.

Growth

The years of the mid-century—the 1940s and 1950s—marked a period of significant expansion in the scope of social welfare activities, and the principal component of that growth, at least in terms of spending, was the elaboration of the social insurance initiatives of the earlier decades. Simply stated, once they had begun, the basic programs of income protection—for retirement, for the loss of a job, for accidents—progressively and insistently expanded in scope and coverage, shielding an increasing portion of the population and absorbing an increasing slice of the budget. With the passage of time, programs that originally had been designed to address narrow circumstances and specific groups were liberalized, amended, and broadened toward universal coverage. At the same time, benefit levels, first established at near subsistence levels, were liberalized to meet mainstream standards of reasonableness.

In Germany, for example, the original programs of social insurance had been restricted to factory laborers. Within twenty-five years, however, most workers—farm and nonfarm, commercial and industrial—were covered. In England, the system of

---

CAPSULE 2.1 • *In the Beginning*

Social insurance first took hold in the 1880s in Germany. Germany was, like the United States, industrializing very rapidly, a generation after England, but the historical context was different. The German government was dominated by a landed aristocracy, a proud ruling class, authoritarian but paternalistic, pious and public-spirited. It wanted modern industry, the basis of national wealth and imperialist power. Its leaders were displeased by the disorganization, exploitation, and misery of the English proletariat, however, and contemptuous of the English philosophy of liberalism and laissez-faire economics that seemed to justify it. Prince Otto von Bismarck, the prime minister, was sensitive to workers' grievances and in fact willing to pacify the workers through constructive measures for their welfare. In 1881 he introduced in the Reichstag a legislative program that ultimately created national health insurance (1883), accident insurance (1884), and disability and retirement insurance (1889).

James Leiby, *A History of Social Welfare and Social Work in the U.S.*, 1978, 197–98.

unemployment safeguards was broadened from its 1911 focus on seasonal employees to nearly the entire labor force.

What this process of expansion produced, especially after World War II, was the inclusion of the middle class in the fabric of the welfare state. As social security benefits were universalized, all income groups grew to rely on public income support. As health, housing, and education programs became basic citizen entitlements, the welfare state drew in skilled workers and professionals. This extension of welfare accelerated after World War II, reflecting a new consensus that broad, national social planning was part of the modern state's responsibility to advance citizen well-being.

In Western and Northern Europe, in particular, the welfare state rapidly matured. After 1945, previously *ad hoc* welfare arrangements were integrated into comprehensive welfare systems. Social services, in the European sense of the term—provisions for education, housing, healthcare—expanded. Social insurance broadened both in terms of the populations and the risks covered. And health insurance, family allowance, and full-employment policies were established. These combined developments, according to Tony Judt, created something quite new—a broad-scale, cradle-to-grave, and at least mildly redistributive welfare state. Post–World War II Europeans, in his words, "ate more and (mostly) better, lived longer and healthier lives, were better housed and clothed than ever before and, above all, were more secure."[3]

While the European concept of a benevolent "welfare state" never fit comfortably into America's political lexicon—the term in the United States has always been used principally as one of derision—the World War II period brought about an expanded social sector on this side of the Atlantic as well. Not unlike Europe, the United States, with remarkably little controversy, expanded protections. Immediately prior to World War II, for example, survivors, spouses, and dependent children of covered workers were added as beneficiary categories under America's social insurance system, Social Security. In 1956, disability insurance was added. And over the course of the post-War decade, social security protections were widened to include farmers, household workers, and the self-employed. By 1960, a full 90 percent of the labor force was covered.

In addition, the exigencies of World War II and the prohibition on salary increases for workers led to special tax code provisions in the United States that provided powerful incentives for businesses to sponsor pension and health insurance plans for their employees. At the same time, the progressive income tax broadened from a "class to a mass" tax, providing an expanded fiscal base for social efforts.

Maturation

Measured in terms of real spending, the growth of welfare states in the 1960s and early 1970s was unprecedented. By 1975, the nations of Western Europe devoted, on average, about a quarter of their gross domestic product (GDP) to public social welfare; in the United States, the figure surpassed 18 percent. This increased spending partly reflected the continued expansion of the core social insurances (in significant measure, a consequence of the aging of the population in most all industrial nations) and partly reflected new initiatives aimed at improving the circumstances of the poor, minority groups, single-women household heads, and others in society who had only a weak attachment to the labor force. As economic growth and prosperity advanced through-out the West, liberalized social attitudes created not only a new sensitivity to social injustices, but also a new readiness to support programs aimed at civil rights and eco-nomic opportunity. In Europe, for example, social policies broadened to aid the un- or underemployed through an assortment of job training, employment subsidy, and liber-alized sickness and work initiatives. At the same time, many welfare states themselves became "virtual employment-machines," promoting full-employment policies and often providing, within the public sector, a significant source of new jobs.[4]

The welfare state expanded markedly in the United States as well, despite the United States' continuing reluctance to adopt the ideology of social welfare in any explicit fashion. Rising tax revenues in the early 1960s provided U.S. policymakers the opportunity to respond relatively painlessly (in a fiscal sense) to the heightened demands for social change created by the Civil Rights movement. The programs of the Great Society—job training, food stamps, Medicare and Medicaid, mental health, and social services—powerfully advanced the U.S. welfare state, creating, in particular, policies directed toward improving the circumstances of black Americans, a group at that time still largely excluded from mainstream society. Their political exclusion was addressed by a variety of civil and voting rights enactments that, for the first time, enfranchised African Americans in the southern states. Housing and public accommo-dation laws significantly reduced long-standing patterns of segregation in schools, residences, offices, and public buildings. And, most germane to the welfare endeavor, new social legislation provided a range of services and benefits focused on the urban ghettos in which a large portion of African Americans lived.

Transformation

In 1973, the Organization of Petroleum Exporting Countries (OPEC), the oil produc-ers' cartel, more than doubled the world price of crude oil, precipitating the "oil shock" that signaled the end of the economic golden age of the post–World War II era and the beginning of the "modern" period of slow growth, uncertain social progress, and increased questioning of the usefulness and affordability of social policy. In the fifteen years prior to 1975, social expenditures in Europe and the United States grew at an aver-age of 6.5 percent per year. In the decade after, they grew at just 3.4 percent annually.[5] Since the early 1990s, public social spending has been increasing a bit in most countries, as indicated in Table 2.3 (see page 43). Throughout the rich world, however, even in the most advanced welfare states, social spending has come under increased scrutiny as slug-gish economies combined with increased demands for benefits—many of them driven by aging populations—have produced high levels of unemployment and economic insecu-rity, growing inequality in income and wealth, and increasing class resentments. These social and economic strains, described in some detail in Chapter 9, have produced differ-ent political results in different countries. But in all countries, welfare has been under critical scrutiny.

In England and America, the reaction against social welfare—especially during the 1980s—was particularly virulent. The victory of Margaret Thatcher's conservatives in Great Britain in 1979 and the election of Ronald Reagan in the United States in 1980

CAPSULE 2.2 • *The Golden Age*

In the Golden Age, all the problems which had haunted capitalism in its era of catastrophe appeared to dissolve and to disappear. The terrible and inevitable cycle of boom and slump, so murderous between the wars, became a succession of mild fluctuations thanks to—or so the Keynesian economists who now advised governments were convinced—their intelligent macroeconomic management. Mass unemployment? Where was it to be found in the developed world in the 1960s, when Europe averaged 1.5 per cent of its labor force out of work and Japan 1.3 per cent? Only in North America was it not yet eliminated. Poverty? Of course most of humanity remained poor, but in the old heartlands of industrial labor what meaning could the Internationale's "Arise, ye starvelings from your slumbers" have for workers who now expected to have their car and spend their annual paid vacation on the beaches of Spain? And, if they fell upon hard times, would not an increasingly universal and generous Welfare State provide them with protection, undreamed of before, against the hazards of ill-health, misfortune, even the dreaded old age of the poor? Their incomes rose year by year, almost automatically. Would they not go on rising forever? The range of goods and services offered by the productive system, and available to them, made former luxuries part of everyday consumption.

Eric Hobsbawm, *The Age of Extremes*, 1994, 267.

advanced explicit crusades against the welfare state. For Reagan and Thatcher and their New Right *laissez-faire*-ist allies, the decades of post–world War II welfare growth were themselves viewed as a primary cause not only of economic decline but of community and family decay as well.

In the United States, cutbacks have been noticeable in several program areas. Cash welfare payments were cut substantially after the enactment of welfare reform in 1996, federal housing benefits have been reduced, and public aid for noncitizens and drug and alcohol abusers has been slashed. Social Security in the United States (and several European nations) has been trimmed by increasing the age for full eligibility.

We label this stage "transformation" because it is clear that changes in the last few decades represent something far more significant than modest corrective accommodations. In much of the world, indeed, this past generation's welfare changes have represented a philosophical rejection of the liberal ideology of welfare entitlement. In the 1990s, for example, the welfare reaction in the United States came not only from the New Right but also from political moderates. Bill Clinton campaigned for the presidency in 1996 with a promise to "end welfare as we know it" by placing a time limit on welfare receipt. And the Progressive Policy Institute (PPI), the policy arm of middle-of-the-road Democrats, advanced measures to transform the very essence of social policy. The PPI's blueprint in the 1990s, for example, called for a "third way" between *laissez-faire* and traditional welfare statism:

> [We] must replace the welfare system with a new strategy for enabling America's poor. While the welfare state is organized around the goal of income maintenance, the enabling state should be organized around the goals of work and individual empowerment. Above

CAPSULE 2.3 • *Laying Off Nanny*

Almost everywhere [in Europe today] there is a realization that the welfare-state ideal has gotten out of control.

From Britain to Italy, a drive is on to eliminate waste and corruption and to prune bloated bureaucracies. Tax incentives are being offered to the well-off to opt out of state pension schemes. Means testing is now commonplace. Services that once were free, such as hospital beds and child care, now attract charges. The age at which state pensions are paid is being raised.

Some of the reforms seem little more than common sense. Dutch students will soon be unable to travel free on public transport or to claim unemployment benefits as soon as they graduate. Private pension funds have been legalized in Italy after a 20-year debate. Retirement at 58 will soon be a thing of the past in Germany, and "bad weather" payments for construction workers are to be scrapped. So is a Dutch program that paid jobless artists to paint.

No European country proposes to dismantle the "nanny state" entirely; the belief that it is government's duty to care for those in need is too deeply rooted, and grass-roots resistance is too fierce.

But even left-of-center politicians tacitly accept the need for change. In a gloomy speech to the European Parliament last week, socialist Jacques Delors, the European Commission president, warned that the European Community will have 30 million unemployed if Europe does not become more competitive.

all it should help poor Americans develop the capacity they need to liberate themselves from poverty and dependency. And it should do so directly, by-passing whenever possible public bureaucracies and service providers, and placing responsibility and resources directly into the hands of the people we are trying to help.[6]

These ideas resonated with the position taken by the Organization for Economic Cooperation and Development (OECD)—the influential alliance of thirty, mainly European, welfare states—calling for a shift from a "passive" to an "active" society under which "the welfare system should be refocused and made less generous in terms of eligibility and benefits" and passive income supports should be replaced by measures designed to put people to work.[7] Even in progressive Sweden, "the idea of welfare according to need has at least partly been replaced by incentive-oriented policies."[8]

The era of transformation does not signal a significant decline in welfare activity. Reforms for the most part have tightened eligibility in some areas, reduced benefits in others, and shifted some activities to the private sector. But the fundamental core of the welfare state—universal retirement and disability programs, healthcare guarantees, unemployment insurance—continues to expand while "residual" means-tested programs for the poor have largely been maintained. The few major attacks on welfare state fundamentals—such as President George Bush's attempt in 2003 to privatize Social Security—have been soundly rejected. Pretty much everywhere big government is as big as ever.

Theories of Welfare Growth

Assuring significant economic protections to the mass of citizens was one of the key achievements of the economically advanced nations in the twentieth century. The progress in approximately 100 years from the tentative, haphazard, and partial "welfare" of family, church, and volunteer-based charity to the systematic universal welfare of the modern state, of course, didn't emerge in a historic vacuum. State welfare was not simply an idea that suddenly won over the hearts and minds of the leaders of the West. The welfare state, although it was established on an intellectual foundation of considerable cogency and appeal, won out over alternative views of public responsibility because of two indispensable phenomena: democracy and prosperity. Without universal suffrage, the dominant political *modus operandi* never would have become hospitable to the idea that the primary purpose of government was to serve the needs of people. Without material prosperity, the costly social insurances, health, housing, and social service programs of the modern era would simply not have been affordable.

In its political dimension, the welfare state developed hand in hand with electoral democracy. The expansion of voting rights to workers and to women—a process largely complete in Europe and the United States by 1918—increased demands for social protection and economic fair play. The universal adult franchise created a new electoral politics powerfully influenced by socialist ideology, working-class interest groups, and policy agendas promoting the responsibility of the state for collective well-being. According to "power resources" theorists, the expansion of social welfare paralleled the growing power of unions and parties on the left.[9]

In much of Europe, and to a degree in the United States, this broadened electoral participation shifted politics leftward. Social legislation that prior to World War I had seemed radical became the norm (first in Europe, then in the United States), with the atmosphere of progressivism most tangibly expressed in social services, workplace regulation (particularly the eight-hour workday), and social security. New labor-oriented parties strengthened in all the European countries, and the older liberal parties abandoned their traditional *laissez-faire* orientation. By the time the Great Depression of the 1930s arrived, the response, most everywhere, was to expand the welfare state, with governments seeking to rescue their economies and assist their citizens through regulation, planning, and economic assistance.

For the standard-bearers of the welfare state—social democrats (in Europe) and New Deal/Great Society liberals (in the United States)—the major business of government became personal dignity and material well-being. Voters demanded welfare, whether or not they called it that, and modern political regimes aggressively advanced its instruments—income transfers, social services, minimum standards, and fair shares for all. From this perspective, the contemporary welfare state represents the hard-won political victory of ordinary working people over traditional economic and social elites.

One of the best-known explanations of the political dimension of the welfare state is that of T. H. Marshall, who interpreted the growth of welfare in terms of the historic evolution of the meaning of citizenship.[10] As industrial society developed, according to Marshall, the bonds tying people to their communities changed. In traditional preindustrial societies, human relationships were based on ascribed statuses; the individual's place in society was determined at birth and usually did not change. The social mobility and rapid change of modern societies, however, required a different form of social solidarity, and citizenship provided a "direct sense of community membership based on loyalty of free men endowed with rights and protected by common law." Civil, political, and social rights, according to Marshall, constituted the elements of citizenship, and these rights were perceived as developing through an evolutionary process. Civil rights (e.g., the right to trial by jury) develop first, political rights (the right to vote) next. These, in turn, lay the groundwork for social rights (the right to education and welfare).

Interestingly, Marshall did not believe that citizenship rights necessarily eliminated inequality; in fact, he argued that these rights often developed to ensure the stability of their social systems. The classic illustration is Bismarck's concession of social rights to German workers in the 1870s and 1880s. Bismarckian social legislation was quite explicitly intended to reduce the force of socialist demands for full civil and political rights.

Largely independent of politics is the economic dimension—the emergence and development of the welfare state as a corollary of modern industrialization. There is no question but that the phenomenal expansion of economic productivity that came with the Industrial Revolution created the means and the expectations for a welfare-oriented society. It was industrialization, of course, that created the need for a new welfare system. Although politically oriented theories view the welfare state as a response to increasing demands from emerging political forces, economically-oriented theories see welfare resulting from the essential character of modern industrial economies and their needs for labor, efficiency, and markets. One influential body of theory interprets welfare expansion in terms of "technological determinism," a theory that sees government action responding to the imperatives of economic modernization.[11] Industry's "need" for a highly educated, well-trained, reliable workforce, for example, is seen as leading to health, welfare, and educational legislation to ensure the development and protection of that workforce. This view posits that modern societies, whatever the exact nature of their political ideology, are converging in their essential features, increasingly mixing individual freedom and state controls.

A final explanation of the welfare state interprets the emergence of social programs as a facet of capitalist self-protection. Far from viewing the welfare state as a working-class victory, Marxists see social welfare as a strategic antidote to the instabilities of capitalism, a procedure for moderating class conflict and protecting the interests of commanding elites. In this sense, the welfare state is a "handmaiden" to capitalism, a way to regulate and control the conditions under which work is organized and wealth is distributed, a mechanism to pacify the working class and keep it subservient. *Regulating the Poor*, by Richard Cloward and Frances Piven, provides one powerful analysis of the U.S. system of social welfare from this perspective; James O'Connor's *The Fiscal Crisis of the State* is another.[12] Marxism, of course, like technological determinism, is "grand" theory, useful for analyzing entire systems, but less helpful for looking at parts. And because Marxism is primarily focused on economics and class interest, it tends to ignore the independent influence of values, ideologies, and political institutions in the development of social welfare programs.

Is America Exceptional?

Although all welfare states share a variety of common attributes, they are markedly distinct in many of their essential aspects. They differ in size, in their relative emphasis on program fields, in their structure and financing, and in their underlying philosophical orientations. Some of the most dramatic of these differences separate the welfare states on both sides of the Atlantic, with the United States generally characterized as substantially less welfare oriented. The thesis of American exceptionalism, introduced in the previous chapter, has been widely advanced as a way of explaining the significant differences between the United States and Europe.

Although both U.S. and European welfare states have sponsored large and complex systems of social insurance since World War II, the two traditions diverge sharply in their underlying ideology and their protective breadth. European welfare states have been importantly motivated by a social ethos valuing equality and social solidarity, whereas the United States has cautiously developed its programs, emphasizing means-testing and private (philanthropic, as well as corporate) welfare provision.

These different orientations color the spirit, the scope, and the magnitude of social welfare in their respective societies. Europe, with powerful labor organizations and social-democratic political parties, early on adopted a range of collectivist welfare policies, policies not only guaranteeing income security to employees unable to continue in the labor market, but also to ordinary, employed working-age families. And while these policies have been transformed in recent years (see Chapter 9), Europe remains at the high end of the social spending scale. The United States, more individualistic in its political culture, developed its social programs relatively late in the century, and never adopted many of the state sponsored programs popular in other countries. Child allowances, national healthcare, broad labor market protections, and public housing and housing subsidies—all common features in Europe—have been either unknown or of modest significance in the United States. Furthermore, in the United States, national welfare authority has remained rudimentary, with great areas of responsibility left in the hands of state and local officials, officials often tending toward highly restrictive orientations, and the business sector. In the United States, for example, most workers gain access to healthcare via employer-sponsored health insurance rather than a state-run program.

Welfare Goals

One of the great triumphs of the twentieth century has been the accommodation of capitalism and social justice—the development of productive stable market economies supported and advanced by the mass of ordinary citizens enjoying middle-class standards of living.

The world of developed market economies—the world of contemporary welfare states—posits the obligation of government to act when society's private institutions do not properly function. Organized public welfare is at the very core of Western societies, improving the daily lives of major segments of the population and adding to the

CAPSULE 2.4 • *American Exceptionalism*

Although above average in educational expenditures, the United States, unlike Canada and most European welfare states, lacks national health insurance and family allowances, and both public assistance and unemployment insurance in America remain ungenerous by international standards and uneven in their coverage across the states and across population groups at risk. Only in the area of old-age, disability, and medical coverage for retired workers who have been stably employed does the United States compare well to other industrial democracies, and benefits in these areas are channeled not only through the public sector but also (with encouragement from tax breaks) through privately negotiated fringe benefit schemes.

Thus, the United States has one of the "least developed" welfare states yet is experiencing a period of unusually intense political attacks against that incomplete and ungenerous welfare state—attacks not only directed against rising levels of social spending, but also questioning the fundamental legitimacy of existing and potential public efforts to cope with evident, growing problems of poverty and social insecurity.

From Theda Skocpol, "America's Incomplete Welfare State: The Limits of New Deal Reforms and the Origins of the Present Crisis" in *Stagnation and Renewal in Social Policy* ed. by Gosta Esping-Andersen, Martin Rein, and Lee Rainwater (Armonk, NY: M.E. Sharpe, 1987). Copyright © 1987 by M.E. Sharpe, Inc. Reproduced with permission.

stability and humaneness of the economic order. Welfare states across the globe have not only substantially increased the level of economic protection, they have provided access to critical health and education services. Welfare safety nets generally ensure basic levels of well-being to the poor; economic supports reduce the hardship of recession; and social insurance, for the first time in history, has largely severed the traditional linkage between old age and poverty. Although the nature of these achievements varies from country to country, all welfare states have succeeded in institutionalizing extensive structures of provision that have remarkably improved the well-being of society's most at-risk groups.

But what, exactly, is the welfare state? How is it to be defined? Although many definitions have been offered, perhaps the most substantive, in a programmatic sense, is that of Asa Briggs, who saw the essence of the welfare state in those governmental activities that were intended to "modify the play of market forces" to improve the well-being of citizens not able to manage on their own.[13]

Briggs specified three particular goals for the welfare state (see Table 2.2) and three corresponding forms of policy. The first goal is helping people maintain their economic security when various "social contingencies," such as unemployment, divorce, or old age, make normal self-support impossible. One thing welfare state policy does well, and with considerable efficiency, is to buffer people from large drops in their standard of living when their income is interrupted. The largest welfare state programs—indeed, the first pillar of all welfare states—are the social insurance policies that prevent economic insecurity by offsetting lost income.

TABLE 2.2   *The Three Pillars of the Welfare State*

Goals	Policies	Beneficiaries
Economic security: protect citizens from common life risks by replacing lost income	Social security: social insurance against illness, unemployment, disability, retirement, death of a spouse	The working population, retirees, and their families and dependents
Material sufficiency: provide a basic floor of social protection	Public assistance: cash relief and social services	The poor and disadvantaged
Basic services: ensure access to critical goods and services	Education, health care, housing, nutrition	All citizens

The basis of eligibility for these policies, it must be noted, is not chiefly poverty. These policies are not limited to those who are made poor by events beyond their control. The basis for governmental intervention, rather, is the loss of income from employment. Unemployed workers, for example, may not be impoverished, but they are generally entitled to unemployment insurance benefits; retiring workers may have reasonable earnings, yet they are entitled to retirement benefits. Social insurance programs like Social Security protect against the range of conditions that results in a loss of job income. Because they are universal—because they cover everyone, regardless of income—these social security programs are the costliest element in the budgets of all welfare states.

Briggs's second goal, "guaranteeing individuals and families a minimum income irrespective of the market value of their property," makes sure that people achieve at least a minimum level of material sufficiency. This is the antipoverty goal of the welfare state, and it is expressed in public assistance programs aimed at the poor. Some of these policies provide services, typically aimed at building skills and independence and helping the disadvantaged move into mainstream society, and some provide cash.

Poverty relief, of course, has always been implicit in poor law and public assistance legislation. In the United States, indeed, it was a principal domestic priority by President Lyndon Johnson in 1964 when he declared "unconditional war on poverty in America." Antipoverty policies, in contrast to Social Security, are targeted on those who fall below a recognized minimum income. They are not meant to assist the broad spectrum of the population, but rather aid special groups with special needs. One of the most common ways of determining eligibility for these programs is by a means test, an administrative procedure that limits benefits to those whose incomes and assets fall below a certain, usually very modest, level. Because these programs are focused on the relatively small proportion of citizens who are poor, they are considerably smaller in magnitude than universal social insurance policies.

The third welfare state goal identified by Briggs, "ensuring that all citizens without distinction of status or class are offered the best standards available in relation to a certain agreed range of social services," means helping people secure those fundamental goods and services that society considers essential. The leading example of such a basic service, of course, is public education. Free public schooling at elementary and secondary levels is provided as a basic right of citizenship in all welfare states; parents are compelled to send children of specific ages to school. Higher education is typically not free, but governments often subsidize tuition and otherwise help students and their families meet college costs. Such help may or may not bear any relationship to financial need in the narrow sense, but it is given in recognition of the difficulties most families have in planning for—or borrowing for—the costs of college, and also in the faith that society as a whole benefits from encouraging more people to seek higher education. In addition to education, contemporary welfare states generally promote nutrition programs, daycare, and housing. In most welfare states (but not the United States), free, comprehensive, universal healthcare is a right of citizenship. In the United States, this has never been a goal of public policy although a considerable amount is spent on health, especially for the elderly and the poor.

Although these three objectives serve to define a core public policy agenda in all advanced industrial economies, it is not entirely accurate to say that the institutional model has won the day. Despite its significance in contemporary life, the welfare state remains an ambiguous, vulnerable enterprise, retaining important elements of residualism. Eligibility requirements, for example, often reflect the concept of public intervention as a last resort, available only when personal resources have been exhausted. Although it is an essential political and economic institution in Western Europe, the United States, Canada, New Zealand, Australia, and Japan, the welfare state is nevertheless subject, as we have seen, to sustained political criticism.

A final word is important on the issue of redistribution, which is traditionally a basic concern of the social democratic, progressive left. Briggs's model says little about the role of the welfare state in achieving redistribution in society, in promoting policies that seek some significant measure of socioeconomic equality. Little has been said about redistribution simply because, although not uncommon, it is hardly an essential feature of welfare states. Although a prominent theme among the early socialist theorists of "womb to tomb" social welfare—the British Fabians in particular—and still a guiding principle among the nations of Europe with powerful social democratic movements, particularly the countries of Scandinavia, it is not, nor has it been, universally characteristic. The organization of social welfare in the United States, Japan, Austria, New Zealand, France, and most welfare states, indeed, has largely followed the model pioneered by Germany, systems largely built on social insurance, with eligibility for benefits related to prior employment and benefit levels related to prior salary or wages. Although egalitarian, redistributive principles have made some headway in all welfare countries (most, for example, have universal child allowances and universal access to healthcare), the ideal of comprehensive, generous benefits for all, based on citizenship (à la Marshall) rather than a connection to work, is hardly dominant.

Welfare Scope

The enormous scope of the welfare state in all the rich nations of the world attests to its fundamental role in contemporary society. Perhaps the most conventional way of indicating this scope is by examining government social spending, the public outlays devoted to addressing basic human needs, as a portion of a nation's overall economy. Although this approach understates the size of the welfare institution because it omits *non*governmental expenditures, it nonetheless yields an impressive picture. (An alternative way of calculating welfare spending is described at the end of this chapter.)

The OECD statistics in Table 2.3 show that government social spending relative to GDP has remained remarkably steady in the major welfare states since 1990. While there is significant variation *among* nations, with public spending ranging from 15.9 percent of GDP in Ireland to 31.3 percent in Sweden, the overall trend is mildly upward. Far from being dismantled, welfare states continue to invest substantially in essential programs to fight poverty, combat insecurity, and guarentee essential services.

The United States, as Tables 2.3 and 2.4 indicate, follows the general pattern. While remaining on the lower end of the expenditure scale, public social spending has increased in real terms from 13.3 percent in 1980, to 14.6 percent in 2000, to 16.2 percent in 2003. As indicated in Table 2.4, the major element in the American social welfare budget is Social Security, a program that between 1950 and 2007 enlarged from $800 *million* to $586 *billion* annually, from less than 0.2 percent of GDP to 4.3 percent. Most of this growth occurred prior to 1980—Social Security's GDP figure has been

TABLE 2.3   *Public Social Welfare Spending (Excluding Education), Selected Counties, as Percent of GDP in 1980, 1990, 2000, 2003*

	1980	1990	2000	2003
Australia	10.9	14.1	17.9	17.9
Austria	22.6	23.7	25.3	26.1
Canada	14.1	18.4	16.7	17.3
Denmark	25.2	25.5	25.8	27.6
France	20.8	25.3	27.6	28.7
Germany	23.0	22.5	26.6	27.6
Ireland	16.8	15.5	13.6	15.9
Italy	18.0	19.9	23.2	24.2
Japan	10.3	11.2	16.1	17.7
Mexico	NA	3.6	5.8	6.8
Norway	16.9	22.6	22.2	25.1
Spain	15.5	20.0	18.1	17.3
Sweden	28.6	30.5	28.8	31.3
United Kingdom	16.6	17.2	19.1	20.1
United States	13.3	13.4	14.6	16.2
EU Average, 15 Countries	19.9	21.9	22.5	23.9

Source: OECD Factbook, 2007.

relatively stable since, although it will be increasing in the future as the baby boom generation retires.

Medicare and Medicaid, health programs that didn't exist until the mid-1960s, also continue their relentless expansion and now compose over 5 percent of GDP. Public assistance—Supplemental Security Income (SSI), Temporary Assistance for Needy Families (TANF), and Food Stamps—the antipoverty programs commonly identified as "welfare"—continue as far smaller programs, comprising in the aggregate less than 1 percent of GDP but holding their own as a portion of the economy. And several *new* programs in education (No Child Left Behind), prescription drugs (Medicare Part D), work support (daycare, the Earned Income Tax Credit), and child health (State Child Health Insurance Program) have substantially expanded the social budget.[14]

While indicating the strength of the American welfare state, in terms of its size, Table 2.4 gives only an indirect indication of who benefits from social spending. In the United States, clearly the greatest portion of welfare growth reflects spending on the elderly, spending not only in the form of pension payments under Social Security and similar social insurance programs, but also in the form of medical (Medicare and Medicaid) and public assistance (SSI) programs focused on older people. Of all the factors

TABLE 2.4 *U.S. Public Social Welfare Spending, Selected Programs, 1950–2007 (in $ Billions and % GDP)*

		1950	1960	1970	1980	1990	2000	2007
Social Security	$(B)	0.8	11.6	30.3	118.5	248.6	409.4	586.2
(OASDI)	%GDP	0.2%	2.2%	2.9%	4.2%	4.3%	4.2%	4.3%
Medicare	$(B)	—	—	6.2	32.1	98.1	197.1	375.4
	%GDP			0.6%	1.1%	1.7%	2.0%	2.7%
Medicaid	$(B)	—	—	2.7	27.4	78.1	207.5	324.9
	%GDP			0.3%	1.0%	1.3%	2.1%	2.6%
SSI	$(B)	—	—	—	6.4	16.1	30.7	37.2
	%GDP				0.2%	0.3%	0.3%	0.3%
AFDC/TANF	$(B)	0.5	1.0	4.9	12.4	19.0	24.8	25.4
	%GDP	0.2%	0.2%	0.4%	0.4%	0.3%	0.3%	0.2%
Food Stamps	$(B)	—	—	0.6	9.1	15.9	18.3	34.9
	%GDP			0.1%	0.3%	0.3%	0.2%	0.3%
EITC	$(B)	—	—	—	1.2	4.4	26.1	38.3
	%GDP				<0.1%	<0.1%	0.3%	0.3%
Veterans' Benefits	$(B)	6.6	5.4	8.7	21.2	29.1	47.1	72.8
and Services	%GDP	2.3%	1.0%	0.8%	0.4%	0.4%	0.5%	0.5%
Unemployment	$(B)	2.4	3.0	3.4	18.1	18.9	23.0	35.1
Compensation	%GDP	0.8%	0.6%	0.4%	0.6%	0.3%	0.2%	0.3%

Source: Budget of the United States Government, Fiscal Year 2009, *Historical Tables*; U.S. Census Bureau, *The Statistical Abstract of the United States*, 2008. All figures in current dollars. Statistics for Medicaid and TANF are for 2005.

accounting for the transformation of modern public budgets, none matches the increased size, and effective demands, of the elderly. At the U.S. federal level, indeed, almost all spending growth since 1960 can be explained by expanded benefits for the retired.[15]

The figures in Table 2.4 also indicate the very considerable degree to which the U.S. welfare state has become an instrument of middle-class well-being. Social Security, most notably, comprises a network of medical and income entitlements aimed at providing economic security over the life cycle for ordinary families, a network that absorbs more than half of all dollars spent on social welfare. Though the public at large often views the welfare state as "welfare"—public assistance and food stamps and the rest of the safety net—these programs, in the aggregate, are exceedingly modest in size.

Another way of expressing this middle-class tilt is to note the very modest size of *redistributive* spending. In the United States, social policy—very much in the Bismarckian tradition of work-based social insurance—is closely linked to employment. Social Security is the largest single program, and benefits under Social Security are strongly tied to previous earnings. Relatively affluent workers, in other words, become relatively affluent retirees. Programs that focus on the poor (public assistance) are small, and programs that aim to distribute basic services to all, regardless of income level (like national healthcare), are generally absent.

CAPSULE 2.5 • *"The Revolution No One Noticed"*

While Americans were preoccupied with the turmoil of the 1960s—the civil rights movement and the war in Vietnam—a revolution no one noticed was taking place. For many years, the argument for increased attention to social welfare in America had followed clear lines: The United States was spending the largest portion of its budget for defense; programs for people who were poor, sick, aged, or minorities were underfinanced. Social welfare proponents contended that in order to be more responsive to the needs of its citizens, the nation should "change its priorities" and spend more for social programs to reduce poverty and less on wars like that in Vietnam. The argument ended with a call for a change in national priorities.

In a single decade America's national priorities were reversed. In 1965, national defense expenditures accounted for 43 percent of the federal government's budget; social welfare expenditures (social insurance, health, and public assistance) accounted for 24 percent. While the mass media focused on the war in Vietnam and Watergate, a revolution in national policy from "guns to butter" was occurring. By 1975, defense accounted for only 26 percent of the federal budget and social welfare expenditures had grown to 42 percent of the budget. Twenty years later, in 1995, social welfare expenditures account for about 55 percent of the federal budget. Health programs alone (primarily Medicaid and Medicare) comprise about 18 percent of the total budget. Only 18 percent of the 1995 budget is devoted to national defense. Social welfare is clearly the major function and major expenditure of the federal government.

Diana DiNitto, *Social Welfare, Politics and Public Policy* (Allyn & Bacon, 2000), 37.

Social, Occupational, and Fiscal Welfare

The realms of welfare state policy may be seen from another perspective, one that goes beyond direct spending and beyond a focus on the public sector. This approach, first designated by Richard Titmuss, sees not one but three complementary systems of welfare: social, occupational, and fiscal.[16]

The *social* component discerned by Titmuss corresponds to the "direct expenditure" approach utilized by OECD and U.S. government agencies to organize the spending data in Tables 2.3 and 2.4. As has been noted, they equate social welfare with the provision of a range of publicly sponsored goods and services—income support, health, social services, and the like. The *occupational* system, on the other hand, comprises the system of welfare associated with employment, chiefly the workplace benefit arrangements identified in the previous chapter. *Fiscal* welfare, finally, involves the income side of the budget coin. Specifically, it identifies those features of the tax system, such as deductions, exemptions, and credits, that advance explicit social objectives.

According to Titmuss, all three welfare systems share a fundamental social character and goal. That is, each constitutes a primary area of collective intervention aimed at meeting individual and societal needs. Although many question the appropriateness of defining the welfare system in such extensive terms, today there is broad recognition among scholars and analysts, as well as among policymakers themselves, not only of the important role played by each of these separate arrangements in affecting citizens' well-being but also the varying ways in which each of the systems affect one another. There is also considerable evidence that over the past several decades the scope of fiscal and occupational welfare has grown at least as rapidly as traditional social expenditures.

The Titmuss model illuminates the broad range of organized welfare and the artificiality of narrowly equating welfare with government outlays. For Titmuss, analyses of welfare that limit themselves to public outlays present distorted, and overly sanguine, views of the true character of the welfare state. One of the most obvious distortions can be seen in how the beneficiaries of organized welfare activities are identified. Because workplace welfare generally mirrors employment status, its benefits are distributed in much the same ways as wages and salaries. That is, health, pension, and other perquisites of employment are first and foremost a function of job status. One must be employed, or related to someone who is employed, to receive them. And because their value generally increases with income, managerial and professional workers are eligible for broader and more lucrative benefits than blue-collar or intermittently employed workers.

Although occupational welfare is restricted in scope, and inversely related to need, it is nevertheless extremely important to a broad segment of the population. In the United States, where these benefits are particularly salient, job benefits make up close to half of an average worker's compensation. In 2000, for example, 103 million workers and family members were covered by private, chiefly workplace, pension plans that provided $342 billion in benefits.[17] Private firms also offer medical insurance for current workers and, often, their dependents, and also retirees. Many provide life insurance to employees' dependents. A smaller number of firms offer programs such as adoption services, health promotion, legal assistance, child and elder dependent care, and drug and alcohol counseling and treatment.

For Titmuss, occupational welfare constitutes a form of "collective intervention" because its scope and character reflect public policy. In other words, despite their nominal "private" character, job benefits are significantly influenced by government. Public policy in the form of special tax arrangements—notably the deductibility of employee benefit costs as a regular business expense—has been a powerful inducement for private employers to sponsor health and welfare programs. From the employees' point of view, fringe benefits are also especially advantageous, because benefits such as health insurance are not taxed, whereas an equivalent cash payment—provided as salary—would be. Other employer-provided fringe benefits, such as pension contributions, are tax deferred until retirement, at which time they are subject to several tax advantages. Thus, although these benefits have a cash value that is the equivalent of wages in the employment contract, this cash value is substantially tax exempt. To the extent that these benefits escape taxation, they constitute government subsidies ("welfare," it might be argued), in the same manner as other social provisions.

The chief idea of Titmuss's third classification—fiscal welfare—is that the tax system itself serves as an important instrument of social policy, above and beyond its role as a source of revenue. Acting through a number of special tax measures, fiscal welfare advances welfare objectives in much the same fashion as direct spending. Federally financed public housing and housing allowances for the poor, clearly within the realm of direct social welfare, are akin to benefits derived from such fiscal measures as the income tax deduction for interest payments on home mortgages. Similarly, deductions and credits for charitable contributions, occupation-based health and pension plans, and childcare are substantially equivalent to direct subsidies. As Titmuss stated, the "tax saving that accrues to the individual is, in effect, a transfer payment. In their primary objectives and their effects on individual purchasing power, there are no differences. Both are manifestations of social policies in favor of identified groups in the population."[18]

In an effort to quantify the value of such fiscal measures and increase public awareness of their importance, Stanley Surrey, a one-time U.S. Treasury Department official, invented the concept of the "tax expenditure." According to Surrey, these are "deviations" from the normal tax code that serve to affect the private economy in ways that normally are achieved by spending. Surrey estimated the value of these deviations, which were not counted in ordinary budget tabulations, to be about one-quarter of the regular federal budget.[19] As a result of Surrey's work, Congress in 1974 ordered an annual accounting of tax expenditures to accompany the regular federal budget.

The large number of people that benefit from tax expenditures, and the view that these provisions amount to a form of public subsidy, has led some analysts to claim that "everyone is on welfare."[20] For others, however, there are important differences between a system of fiscal measures such as tax expenditures and traditional social welfare. Irving Kristol, for example, challenges the view that these benefits are similar to direct social welfare provisions. To think of tax deductions as subsidies, he states, "implicitly asserts that all income covered by the general provisions of the tax law belongs of right to the government, and what government decides, by exemption or qualification, not to collect in taxes constitutes a subsidy."[21] In other words, allowing citizens to keep money they earned that is spent or invested in ways that benefit the individual or society is not the moral or functional equivalent of taking money from those who can afford to pay taxes and distributing it as cash benefits to those in need.

Tax expenditures—loopholes, to their detractors—are, of course, different in many ways from direct spending. For one thing, like occupational welfare, they disproportionately benefit the better-off the most. Often described as upside-down subsidies, they generally provide the greatest dollar value to those in the highest tax brackets. The deductibility of charitable contributions, for example, clearly helps voluntary hospitals, universities, and social services agencies, but it just as clearly reduces the tax liability of the rich far more than of ordinary taxpayers. Because the poor usually pay no federal income taxes at all, of course, they get no immediate benefit.

Whereas tax expenditures can be portrayed as returning funds to the private sector, lessening public intrusion, and forgoing public income to promote private action—all conservative preferences—Titmuss is clearly correct in his contention that tax policies constitute critical elements in social policy. Although the overall distribution of these indirect outlays does not help the neediest, taxation remains a key instrument for implementing public aims. Fiscal welfare and occupational welfare are analogous to regular spending, and all three systems must be assessed if one is to understand, or to affect, the nature of contemporary social welfare. Occupational, fiscal, and social welfare can each be assessed as a distinct phenomenon, but their interactions have a major bearing on the nature of the overall welfare system.

The occupational system, for example, frequently supplements public provisions, as with retirement pensions. In areas such as health insurance, it often provides support where government action is absent. Of course, meeting social needs through the occupational system can discourage the development of public policy to meet needs. Broadly available job-related health insurance, for example, has undoubedly lessened presures for government-provided universal healthcare. For Titmuss and others on the traditional left, occupational welfare—welfare principally for the middle classes and well-to-do—often undermines support for the mainline welfare state. Public provision is already a dubious public objective; an expanded occupational system, it is recognized, reduces the constituency for government efforts on behalf of the disadvantaged.

The provision of social welfare transfers through indirect tax expenditures, such as deductions for mortgage interest and exclusions on employee benefits, has grown dramatically in recent decades. Since 1970, for example, the number of tax expenditure items in the federal code increased by almost one-third, providing over $500 billion in tax breaks in 2008.[22] In the area of income maintenance alone, the value of benefits funded through indirect outlays grew at a far faster rate than benefits financed through direct expenditures.

Regulatory Welfare

There is, as mentioned, a significant limitation in utilizing a conception of social welfare that is restricted to concrete benefits—be they occupational or public; income, goods, or services; or funded through outlays or through tax arrangements. All such benefits ignore the importance of other, less tangible, sorts of interventions. At all levels of government, public activities that enhance community well-being involve more than simply the allocation, directly or indirectly, of income or services.

Social welfare objectives, most immediately, are also advanced by the regulatory powers of government. Regulatory powers, of course, have long been used to pursue health and safety goals in employment, daycare, and housing and the licensing and certifying of residential facilities and hospitals. Today's social regulation, far broader in scope, advances a variety of explicit social objectives, many of which couldn't otherwise be pursued because of budgetary restrictions.

One such area of regulation imposes obligations on the private sector to help needy groups such as children and the handicapped, therefore reducing the need for direct public programs. Thus, for example, many state and local governments have enacted childcare ordinances affecting developers of commercial properties. In San Francisco, a typical instance, major developers must either provide on-site care for employees' children or else pay $1 per square foot into a special fund to support centers throughout the city.[23] At the state level, Massachusetts has extended access to healthcare throughout the commonwealth by requiring private businesses to provide medical insurance to all their employees. Other states require private insurance plans to cover a variety of populations and procedures. For example, employers may be obligated to extend insurance coverage to family dependents, such as newborns, as well as to disabled workers, those needing alcohol treatment, and those requiring home healthcare. California and other states prohibit insurance companies from denying coverage for the services of social workers, dentists, podiatrists, speech and hearing therapists, and professional counselors and psychologists. In recent years, several states and municipalities have required large employers (Walmart is often the specific target) to spend a portion of their personnel costs on health care.

Such mandated benefits—benefits by regulation—permit government to address social and health problems without having to spend money or raise taxes. Regulation, of course, is not without costs. The private sector pays in one fashion or another, either through higher insurance rates or higher consumer prices. Some regulations may even result in firms withdrawing benefits. It has been argued, for example, that state-mandated programs have caused many small employers to drop employee health coverage altogether. In a similar vein, many contend that stringent rent control ordinances lead to a decreasing number of available rental units.

Social regulation also affects the realm of private life and families. In the 1980s, for example, a broad political consensus emerged in support of federal regulations to ensure fair child-support payments from absent parents. To increase payment levels and to enforce compliance with court-ordered child-support rulings, federal law strengthened the influence of government over family behavior. The 1984 Child Support Enforcement Amendments required states to establish procedures for withholding support payments from the wages of delinquent (i.e., nonpaying) parents. Later enactments required paternity determinations at birth and compelled states to establish and utilize uniform standards for child-support payments. Perhaps most important, the 1988 Family Support Act required states to withhold wages in cases in which court child-support orders were violated. Despite the rather elaborate structure of

CAPSULE 2.6 • *Regulating a Living Wage*

Gov. Martin O'Maliey of Maryland signed the nation's first statewide living wage bill yesterday, giving fresh momentum to a movement that seeks to raise wages through legislation.

Under the law, employers with state contracts will generally have to pay workers a minimum amount—$11.30 an hour in the Baltimore-Washington corridor and $8.50 an hour in the rural counties, where wages and prices are usually lower.

"This law lifts tens of thousands of families out of poverty and into the middle class,"

said Tom Hucker, a first-term Democratic delegate to the Maryland House. "Today Maryland shows the rest of the country a good way to honor work and fight poverty."

Nationwide, 145 cities and counties have enacted living-wage bills, which generally require businesses that receive government contracts—and sometimes those that receive subsidies—to pay an amount above the federal or state minimum wage. The highest living wage in the nation is $14.75 an hour in Fairfax, California.

by Steven Greenhouse

From "'Living wage' laws gain momentum across U.S.", by Daniel B. Wood, *The Christian Science Monitor*, March 15, 2002. © 2002 The Christian Science Monitor. All rights reserved. Reproduced with permission of Christian Science Monitor (www.csmonitor.com).

regulatory inducements and penalties, however, absent parents continue to shirk their obligations—at present only 30 percent of moms who are owed support actually receive it.[24]

One of the most interesting developments in public social regulation is represented by the "Living Wage" movement. Since 1994, when Baltimore enacted the country's first ordinance requiring private organizations contracting with the city to pay a "living wage," nearly 150 municipalities, and one state, generally prompted by local grassroots alliances of labor, religious, and civic organizations, have similarly obligated businesses receiving public money to pay their workers decently. These laws often stipulate a wage level equivalent notably higher than the poverty line.

Such regulatory interventions can advance welfare state goals. Although someone winds up paying for each measure—be it employers, employees, or separated parents—such approaches substantially broaden the range of ways in which government can address problems. Regulatory substitutes for spending programs, especially attractive in an era of fiscal constraint and tax and spending limits, are likely to expand in importance in the years ahead.

Emerging Issues: The New Social Accounting

Social welfare is pluralistic and multifaceted, involving major institutional sectors, governmental levels, and societal realms organizing help to people through a complex enterprise of formal and informal, profit-making and altruistic, and private and public endeavors. It is only recently, however, that efforts have been made to quantify the total welfare contributions of all these sectors of society. While government social welfare spending (as shown in Tables 2.3 and 2.4) is still widely employed by policy analysts, researchers, and journalists as the conventional measure of the generosity of welfare states, the limitations and distortions of this approach to social accounting are increasingly being recognized.

The most fundamental limitation is the equation of welfare and government spending. Quantifying a nation's welfare effort as total public social welfare spending as a percent of GDP—while a convenient and commonly employed measure of the "welfare effort," the generosity, of welfare states—is not the only measure that can be used. Over the last decade, indeed, it has become increasingly evident that this standard of social accounting provides a deeply flawed, deeply distorted view of a country's actual efforts to provide social welfare.

As we have explained, in addition to the checks written directly by government, a comprehensive measure of a nation's "welfare generosity" should include other sources of spending that promote individual and family welfare. Consider, for example, the hypothetical case of Edith and Alva, citizens of Americana and Nordica, respectively. At the end of the year, they both owe their governments $9000 in income taxes. Alva pays her taxes and then receives a childcare grant in the form of a $1000 check from the government. Edith's government gives her a $1000 childcare tax credit, which reduces the taxes she pays by this amount. Which country is more generous in providing social benefits? Which is making the greater "welfare effort?"

By the conventional measure of direct expenditures, Noridica is $1000 higher on the generosity scale than Americana, which gives the equivalent childcare subsidy through a special tax deduction. But tax expenditures like these are not the only measures that need to be weighed into a comprehensive calculation of welfare effort. Taxes also count. What if Alva's $1000 government subsidy was included as part of her annual income and taxed at a rate of 30 percent, while Edith's subsidy was tax free? On the scale of direct expenditures, Nordica still rates $1000 higher on generosity and welfare effort, although at the end of the day, Edith ends up with more money in her pocket to pay for childcare. In addition to income taxes, there are considerations of sales and value-added taxes, which also reduce the amount of cash subsidies that beneficiaries actually consume on goods and services. In this way, many governments "claw back" significant portions of the social benefits they offer by taxing them.

Beyond spending and taxing, as already noted, governments can also create and manage social expenditures through their powers of regulation. Thus, for example, if Edith received neither a cash grant nor a tax credit for childcare, but her employer was legislatively mandated to provide employees $1500 worth of childcare services annually, she would receive subsidized childcare valued at more than twice the amount of Alva's childcare grant after direct taxes. Yet Nordica would *still* appear to offer a more generous childcare benefit, since the value of mandatory private benefits do not show up on the conventional ledger of direct public expenditures. Mandatory private social benefits, in fact, *have* been enacted in many countries such as Belgium, Denmark, the Netherlands, Germany, Sweden, Norway, the United Kingdom, and the United States. These off-the-ledger arrangements for social protection usually include employer payments for absence from work due to sickness and maternity leave as well as required pension contributions to employer-based or individual pension plans.

Finally, a full accounting of social expenditures should include social transfers from private sources. Thus, voluntary private social benefits form another component in the comprehensive measure of welfare effort. From an individual recipient's point of view, it does not much matter whether, for example, in Edith's case, her employer is required by law to provide childcare or whether this benefit is granted voluntarily. Voluntary provisions, of course, are frequently allocated by private nonprofit organizations (whose philanthropy is stimulated by government tax concessions, as we will discuss in Chapter 7).

By the mid-1990s, as data on the various sources of social spending became available, researchers at the Organization for Economic Cooperation and Development developed a comprehensive new ledger for social accounting.[25] As illustrated in Table 2.5, this ledger allows us to compare how countries measure up both on the conventional scale (public social spending as a percent of GDP) *and* on the new measure, "net total social expenditure," which incorporates the cumulative value of benefits distributed through direct public expenditures, tax expenditures, publicly mandated private expenditures, and voluntary private expenditures.

This comparison shows how introducing a new method of social accounting significantly changes the national ranking on social expenditures. Measured by total public spending as a percent of GDP, Denmark stands second in welfare effort, Germany is fourth, and the United States, at twentieth, comes in close to the bottom of the list. But ranked on the most comprehensive measure of social spending—net social spending—Germany jumps to number one, the United States moves up to sixth place, and Denmark moves down to seventh. Calculating by the new social accounting, European countries and the United States allocate roughly equivalent proportions of their resources to social welfare transfers, but in different ways.

Ranking countries on their social expenditure in relation to the percent of their GDP is only one type of measurement for comparing how states seek to provide for social welfare. It comes from a perspective that ignores population size and wealth, which makes the meaning of comparative state efforts difficult to interpret. Consider, for example, country X, which has the same size population but three times the GDP of county Y. If country X spends twice as much on social welfare as country Y, each of its citizens is on average receiving twice the amount of social benefits as in country Y— yet country X will be ranked lower in social expenditures as a percent of GDP. What does this mean? Is country X making less of a social welfare effort than country Y? Is it less active in promoting social expenditure than country Y? That interpretation can be made only if one assumes that state action in the realm of social welfare should be proportionately equivalent regardless of population size and wealth. It is unlikely that citizens in country X seeking to maximize their social benefits will flock to country Y because it has a higher social welfare expenditure ranking.

This suggests yet another way of comparing social expenditure—in terms of per capita spending. For an accurate comparison, the per capita spending is controlled for purchasing power of different currencies. When social expenditure is calculated on the scale of per capita spending, as seen in Table 2.6, some of the countries' ranks are quite different from where they stand based on expenditures as a percent of GDP.

TABLE 2.5 *Two Ways of Measuring Social Expenditures in Twenty-Three OECD Countries, 2001*

Country	The Conventional Accounting—Public Social Spending as % of GDP	Rank Order	The New Social Accounting—Net Social Spending as % of GDP	Rank Order
Sweden	29.8	1	26.0	3
Denmark	29.2	2	22.5	7
France	28.5	3	27.0	2
Germany	27.4	4	27.6	1
Austria	26.0	5	21.8	10
Finland	24.8	6	20.0	15
Belgium	24.7	7	23.2	5
Italy	24.4	8	21.9	9
Norway	23.9	9	20.9	12
United Kingdom	21.8	10	23.3	4
Netherlands	21.4	11	22.1	8
Czech Republic	20.1	12	18.5	16
Iceland	19.8	13	18.4	17
Spain	19.6	14	17.0	18
New Zealand	18.5	15	15.9	20
Australia	18.0	16	21.1	11
Slovak Republic	17.9	17	16.7	19
Canada	17.8	18	20.3	13
Japan	16.9	19	20.2	14
United States	14.7	20	23.1	6
Ireland	13.8	21	12.5	21
Korea	6.1	22	10.0	22
Mexico	5.1	23	6.2	23

Source: Data on social expenditure as percent of GDP are from Willem Adema and Maxime Ladaique, *Net Social Expenditure, 2005 edition*, OECD Social, Employment and Migration Working Papers # 29 (Paris: OECD) annex 3.

While Sweden remains ranked third in both net social expenditure and per capita spending, the United States climbs from sixth to first when the metric shifts to per capita spending.

TABLE 2.6 *Rank of Twenty-Three OECD Countries on Net Social Expenditure Per Capita, Adjusted for Purchasing Power Parity (PPP)*

Country	Net Social Spending Per Capita in PPP Order
Norway	2
Denmark	8
Sweden	3
Austria	10
France	4
Belgium	7
Germany	5
Finland	13
Netherlands	9
United Kingdom	6
Italy	15
United States	1
Canada	11
Australia	12
Ireland	16
Spain	17
Japan	14
New Zealand	18
Czech Republic	19
Slovak Republic	20
Korea	21
Mexico	22
Iceland	N.A.

Source: Neil Gilbert, "Comparative Analysis of Stateness and State Action: What Can We Learn From Alternative Measures?" Paper presented at the Conference on the Occasion of the German EU Presidency, jointly organized by the Social Science Research Center, Berlin and the European Foundation for the Improvement of Living and Working Conditions, Dublin, May 7–8, 2007, Berlin, Germany.

Notes

1. Harold Wilensky and Charles Lebeaux, *Industrial Society and Social Welfare* (New York: Russell Sage, 1958), 138.
2. See, for example, J. Ambler (ed.), *The French Welfare State* (New York: New York University Press, 1991); R. Cos, *The Development of the Dutch Welfare State* (Pittsburgh: Pittsburgh University Press, 1993); Christopher Pierson, *Beyond the Welfare State* (University Park, Pa.: The Pennsylvania State University Press, 1991).
3. Tony Judt, *Post War—A History of Europe Since 1945*, 74–76.
4. Gosta Esping-Anderson, *The Three Worlds of Welfare Capitalism* (Princeton, N.J.: Princeton University Press, 1990), 149.
5. Organization for Economic Cooperation and Development, *The Future of Social Protection* (Luxembourg: OECD, 1988), 11.
6. Will Marshall and Martin Schram (eds.), *Mandate for Change* (New York: Berkeley, 1993), 228.
7. Organization for Economic Cooperation and Development, *Economic Surveys: Netherlands* (Paris: OECD, 1991), 89; and OECD, "Editorial: The Path to Full Employment: Structural Adjustments for an Active Society," *Employment Outlook* (July 1989).
8. S. Marklund, "The Decomposition of Social Policy in Sweden," *Scandinavian Journal of Social Welfare*, 1(1) (1992): 10.
9. See Paul Pierson, "The New Politics of the Welfare State," *World Politics*, 48(2) (January 1996): 150–53.
10. T. H. Marshall, *Sociology at the Crossroads and Other Essays* (London: Heinemann, 1963).
11. See Reinhard J. Skinner, "Technological Determinism," *Comparative Studies in Society and History*, 18(1) (January 1976): 2–27; and J. K. Galbraith, *The New Industrial State* (London: Hamish Hamilton, 1967).
12. Frances Fox Piven and Richard A. Cloward, *Regulating the Poor: The Functions of Public Welfare* (New York: Pantheon Books, 1971); James O'Connor, *The Fiscal Crisis of the State* (New York: St. Martin's Press, 1973).
13. Asa Briggs, "The Welfare State in Historical Perspective," *European Journal of Sociology 2* (1961): 221–58.
14. Richard Wolf, "How federal spending has climbed since 2001," *USA Today*, April 3, 2006).
15. Rudolph Penner, "Federal Government Growth: Leviathan or Protector of the Elderly," *National Tax Journal*, 44(2) (December 1991).
16. Richard Titmuss, *Essays on the "Welfare State,"* 2nd ed. (London: Unwin University Books, 1958), 34–55.
17. *Statistical Abstract of the United States, 2007*, table 542.
18. Titmuss, *Essays on the "Welfare State,"* 44.
19. Stanley Surrey, *Pathways to Tax Reform* (Cambridge, Mass.: Harvard University Press, 1973).
20. See, for example, Mimi Abramowitz, "Everyone Is on Welfare: The Role of Redistribution in Social Policy Revisited," *Social Work*, 8(6) (November/December, 1983): 440–45.
21. Irving Kristol, *Two Cheers for Capitalism* (New York: Mentor, 1978), 194.
22. U.S. Budget for Fiscal Year 2009, Historical Tables, *Analytic Perspectives*, Table 19–3.
23. *San Francisco Chronicle*, October 8, 1985, 10.
24. Sherry Glied, et al., "Consider it Done? The Likely Efficacy of Mandates for Health Insurance," *Health Affairs*, November/December 2007.
25. Willem Adema, Marcel Einerhand, Bengt Eklind, Jorgen Lotz, and Mark Pearson, *Net Public Social Expenditure: Labour Market and Social Policy Occasional Papers No. 19* (Paris: OECD, 1996).

3

A Framework for Social Welfare Policy Analysis

Even when armed with this much greater scientific knowledge, contemporary societies will, of course, face difficult choices between simultaneously held but competing values or objectives. . . . The precise balance between adequacy and equity in the determination of social insurance benefits, between equal access to minimum security and retention of the principle of local autonomy, between the interests of different social classes in allocating the costs of social security measures, or between the claims of family obligation and responsibilities to the wider community illustrate the nature of these ultimate and difficult value choices. Yet while there is no guarantee that democracies will act rationally in formulating their social policies, it is also abundantly clear that they cannot even be expected to do so unless they are made aware of the full implications of the choices available to them.

Eveline M. Burns
Social Security and Public Policy, 1956

Traditionally, courses in social welfare policy have emphasized the study of process and performance. In courses organized around process, students have learned about social, political, and technical processes in policy formulation, and in courses organized around performance they have learned about the details of social welfare programs in operation. A major advantage of the study of performance is its focus on factual and substantive material: it describes and evaluates programs. Here, too, lies its major shortcoming: the substance of social welfare programs is continually changing. Moreover, these programs are so numerous that one or two courses can cover only a segment of the field. Under the Title XX Amendments to the Social Security Act alone, for example, states offer more than twenty different categories of service (see Table 3.1).

As indicated in Chapter 1, a third approach to the study of this field is to focus on the set of fundamental social policy choices that have to be addressed in planning the welfare state. From this perspective the analytic task is to distinguish among and to dissect the essential components of policy design rather than to examine the sociopolitical processes through which policy is developed or to evaluate policy outcomes.

The basic components of policy design to which this task is addressed may be seen as dimensions of choice. In this chapter, we present a framework for analyzing basic choices in the design of social welfare policy.

With this analytic approach, we will use program descriptions as examples to formulate and substantiate general concepts of policy design. Because we are mainly interested in illustrating the concepts that are useful in the analysis of social welfare policy, rather than in understanding the details of specific programs, there will be a certain eclecticism in the selection of these examples; we include large and small programs, pieces of programs, existing programs, and proposed programs, some of which may never leave the drawing boards and others that have not yet arrived on the public agenda.

As Eveline Burns has suggested, the major advantage of this approach is that it equips students with a convenient set of concepts that can usefully explain and illuminate a wide range of policies.[1] The broad application of our analytic framework is conveyed through the use of historical examples, such as the War on Poverty/Community Action and Model Cities Programs of the 1960s, and the Older Americans Act and the Seattle and Denver Income Maintenance Experiments of the 1970s, along with the recent developments in welfare reform under the Personal Responsibility and Work Opportunity Reconciliation Act of 1996, as amended in 2006.

An analytic framework is an intellectual tool that helps to order reality by culling and distilling the essential elements of complex phenomena. Before elaborating the analytic framework around which this book is organized, let us say a few words about the general character of social welfare policy—our conceptual foundation on which the framework is constructed.

Benefit Allocations in the Social Market and the Mixed Economy of Welfare

In trying to construct an analytic framework that will help us understand the vast array of social welfare measures ranging from the Social Security Act of 1935 to the Personal Responsibility and Work Opportunity Reconciliation Act of 1996, we must grapple with the question: What are the common elements in social welfare policies? There is no single answer to this question with which everyone engaged in policy analysis will agree. Obviously, the apparent commonalities in the design of social welfare policy vary according to the level of abstraction on which the analysis is conducted. In this respect, an analytic framework is somewhat like a microscope; it provides a conceptual lens through which the phenomena under investigation may be studied. Like a microscope, most analytic frameworks do not have a wide depth of focus. Rather, they tend to lock on some level of abstraction that magnifies and draws our attention to a distinct set of concepts. The analytic framework we use in this book places social welfare policy in the context of *a benefit-allocation mechanism functioning outside the economic marketplace*. As Marshall has observed,

> In contrast to the economic process, it is a fundamental principle of the Welfare State that the market value of an individual cannot be the measure of his right to welfare.

The central function of welfare, in fact, is to supersede the market by taking goods and services out of it, or in some way to control and modify its operations so as to produce a result which it would not have produced itself.[2]

To say that social welfare allocations are made outside the economic marketplace offers a rather nebulous picture of the conceptual domain within which social welfare policy operates. To clarify this domain we must draw a distinction between social and economic markets. This distinction rests on the principles and motives that guide the allocation of provisions. The social market of the welfare state allocates goods and services primarily in response to financial need, dependency, altruistic sentiments, social obligations, charitable motives, and the wish for communal security. In contrast, benefits in a capitalist society are distributed through the economic market, ideally on the basis of individual initiative, ability, productivity, and a desire for profit.[3] As illustrated in Figure 3.1, the social market contains both a public and a private sector. The public sector encompasses federal, state, and local governments and accounts for the largest portion of goods and services distributed in the welfare state. Provisions allocated through the private sector of the social market include the informal efforts of family and friends, the services provided by voluntary agencies and, occasionally, by profit-oriented agencies. The last overlap with the activities of the economic market, which to some extent blurs the boundary between the private social welfare sector and the economic market.

The allocation of provisions in the social market involves both the financing and the delivery of benefits, and these roles are not always performed by the same unit. A public agency, for example, can hire its own staff to provide daycare services for low-income mothers, or, through purchase-of-service arrangements, it may pay to have the service provided by a voluntary agency, a profit-making enterprise, or by members of the client's family. In this manner the roles of public, voluntary, profit-oriented, and informal units are variously combined. The resulting variety in the modes of benefit allocations constitutes what is commonly referred to as the mixed economy of welfare.

Although profit-oriented agencies and organizations still constitute only a small segment of the social market, their numbers have been growing since the mid-1960s.

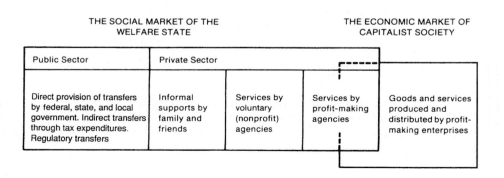

THE SOCIAL MARKET OF THE WELFARE STATE   THE ECONOMIC MARKET OF CAPITALIST SOCIETY

Public Sector	Private Sector			
Direct provision of transfers by federal, state, and local government. Indirect transfers through tax expenditures. Regulatory transfers	Informal supports by family and friends	Services by voluntary (nonprofit) agencies	Services by profit-making agencies	Goods and services produced and distributed by profit-making enterprises

FIGURE 3.1   *Social and Economic Markets of Welfare.*

In the 1980s and 1990s, proposals for the expansion of profit-oriented enterprises in the social market gained serious consideration. Even a voice from the left such as Robert Reich advanced a scheme for government and business partnerships aimed at integrating social welfare and economic development. Under this arrangement, Reich says, "We can expect that a significant part of the present welfare system will be replaced by government grants to businesses that agree to hire the chronically unemployed."[4] Public funds for social services such as daycare, healthcare, and disability benefits would be allocated to businesses, eliminating the need for government administration. Joined in this way to business institutions, social welfare provisions serve an important purpose by contributing to the formation of human capital. Herein lies what is certainly the strongest attraction of such alliances—they confer on welfare activities the legitimacy and value of a productive force promoting growth in the market economy. Inserting profit-oriented agencies into the welfare state imbues the social market with the spirit of capitalism and inclines the *modus operandi* of social welfare allocations toward that of the market economy.

At present, proprietary agencies and institutions are prominently represented in many health and social service areas, including home support services such as attendant care, transportation, meals-on-wheels, childcare, and job training.[5] One conspicuous area of growth has been in nursing home care. Whereas about one-half of nursing home costs are paid with public (mainly Medicaid) funds, close to 82 percent of all nursing homes are operated on a for-profit basis.[6] As noted, this service area is typically referred to as the nursing home "industry"; the childcare "industry" looms on the horizon.

For many, of course, mixing welfare services with the market economy runs counter to the communal and charitable ethos that typifies the humanistic character of social welfare. The merger of welfare programs and private enterprise assumes a harmony among social and economic purposes that is far from self-evident. Reward for merit and productivity is hardly consonant with support for benefits based on need and dependency. A system that encourages risk taking for financial gain is unlikely to invest serious effort in the pursuit of equality and security. The fundamental issue is how a capitalist society deals with conflicting objectives such as meeting need versus rewarding merit, promoting freedom versus providing security, and providing equality of opportunity versus ensuring equality of outcome.

The functioning of the social and economic markets in industrialized capitalist societies is based on a complex relationship between individual ambitions and collective responsibilities, a relationship that is filled with tensions and contradictions. Marshall suggests that these tensions help maintain a constructive balance between charitable and profit-making impulses (or need and merit) and so contribute to a healthy society.[7] It is difficult to imagine that such a balance might be improved by an influx of profit-oriented agencies to commercialize the social market.

Some analysts argue that because social welfare policies entail benefit allocations outside the market, they provide for unilateral exchange or "social transfers" (from society to the individual) rather than reciprocal or "market exchange" (from buyer to seller).[8] Although we will analyze social policies as unilateral designs for allocating benefits that are usually free or well subsidized, it should be recognized that those on

CAPSULE 3.1 • *Rights, Responsibilities, and the Communitarian Perspective*

American men, women, and children are members of many communities—families; neighborhoods; innumerable social, religious, ethnic, work place, and professional associations; and the body politic itself. Neither human existence nor individual liberty can be sustained for long outside the interdependent and overlapping communities to which all of us belong. Nor can any community long survive unless its members dedicate some of their attention, energy, and resources to shared projects. The exclusive pursuit of private interest erodes the network of social environments on which we all depend, and is destructive to our shared experiment in democratic self-government. For these reasons, we hold that the rights of individuals cannot long be preserved without a communitarian perspective.

A communitarian perspective recognizes both individual human dignity and the social dimension of human existence.

A communitarian perspective recognizes that the preservation of individual liberty depends on the active maintenance of the institutions of civil society where citizens learn respect for others as well as self-respect; where

we acquire a lively sense of our personal and civic responsibilities, along with an appreciation of our own rights and the rights of others; where we develop the skills of self-government as well as the habit of governing ourselves, and learn to serve others—not just self.

A communitarian perspective recognizes that communities and polities, too, have obligations—including the duty to be responsive to their members and to foster participation and deliberation in social and political life.

A communitarian perspective does not dictate particular policies; rather it mandates attention to what is often ignored in contemporary policy debates: the social side of human nature; the responsibilities that must be borne by citizens, individually and collectively, in a regime of rights; the fragile ecology of families and their supporting communities; the ripple effects and long-term consequences of present decisions. The political views of the signers of this statement differ widely. We are united, however, in our conviction that a communitarian perspective must be brought to bear on the great moral, legal, and social issues of our time.

"Preamble" from *Communitarian Platform*. Used by permission of the Institute for Communitarian Policy Studies.

the receiving end often incur stringent obligations. As Zald points out, "Although many welfare recipients may not pay money for the service that they receive, they may pay much more: gratitude, political acquiescence, and the like. Thus the lack of reciprocity depends on specification of coin."[9]

Indeed, since the 1990s, a new emphasis has emerged focusing on the responsibilities associated with citizen claims to social benefits. In public discourse on social policy, a central question has been, If social benefits constitute the *rights* of citizenship, what *responsibilities* accompany these rights?[10] Lawrence Mead's analysis of the social obligations of citizenship opened the debate about how to weigh citizens' rights to public aid against the obligations to perform as dependable members of the community.[11] According to Mead, the entitlement to benefits should be conditioned on the performance of appropriate behaviors, such as working in available jobs, contributing to the support of their families, learning enough in school to be employable, and respecting the law.

Elements of an Analytic Framework: Dimensions of Choice

Although entitlements to welfare are increasingly being joined to individual responsibilities, benefits remain social transfers allocated outside the economic marketplace. Within the benefit-allocation framework, social welfare policies can be interpreted as choices among principles determining *what* benefits are offered, to *whom* they are offered, how they are *delivered*, and how they are *financed*. The elements of this framework, of course, are not physical structures of the sort a microscope might reveal. Rather, they are social constructs that are used in the intellectual processes of making choices. The major dimensions of choice in this framework may be expressed in the form of four questions:

1. What are the *bases* of social allocations?
2. What are the *types* of social provisions to be allocated?
3. What are the strategies for the *delivery* of these provisions?
4. What are the ways to *finance* these provisions?

A few words are in order about the genesis of this approach. Eveline Burns utilized this general framework in her seminal study, *Social Security and Public Policy*, focusing on four types of decisions that informed program design in the realm of social security: (1) those related to the nature and amount of benefits; (2) those concerned with eligibility and the types of risks to be covered; (3) those regarding the means of finance; and (4) those relevant to the structure and character of administration. Our analytic approach in this book seeks to extend the pathways of policy analysis charted by Burns and others.[12] These dimensions of choice cut across the entire field of social welfare policy rather than simply delineating choices specific to a single program sector.

We treat the bases of social allocations, types of social provisions, strategies of delivery, and modes of finance as "dimensions" of choice because each will be examined along three axes: (1) the range of alternatives within each dimension, (2) the social values that support them, and (3) the theories or assumptions that underlie them. This framework is illustrated in Figure 3.2.

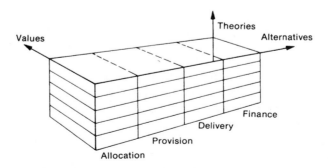

FIGURE 3.2   *Dimensions of Choice.*

Choices Regarding Allocations and Provisions

The first two dimensions of choice are expressed in the question, *Who* gets *what*? The *bases* of social allocations addresses the "who" of social welfare policy.

Social welfare policies always include some designation of beneficiaries, those whose welfare is to be enhanced through policy implementation. Although these policies are supposed to serve the abstract interests of society-as-a-whole—the elusive "public interest"—direct and immediate benefits are usually distributed differentially among segments of the population. Social welfare policies, of course, cannot help everybody equally. Choices are required, and they are continually made as trade-offs among what policy planners think is desirable, what circumstances necessitate, and what the public will countenance.

Numerous criteria are used to determine who is eligible for social provisions. These criteria include marital status, employment status, residence, family size, health, age, education, military service, ethnicity, gender, religion, and income. Our concern in examining the bases of social allocations, however, is not to catalog the many possibilities that may be employed to define eligibility. Rather, the issues of choice we address focus on a set of general principles that inform the design of eligibility criteria. *The bases of social allocations refer to the choices among the various principles upon which social provisions are made accessible to particular people and groups in society.*

The bases of social allocations are the guidelines for the operational definition of eligibility criteria. What benefits people become eligible to receive involves policy choices about the *nature* of the social provision. In policy analysis the traditional choice has been whether benefits are offered in *cash* (money) or *in-kind* (goods or services). There are, however, other types of benefits that are commonly distributed through social policy, such as vouchers, power, and opportunities that permit different degrees of consumer sovereignty than the in-cash/in-kind dichotomy. In Chapter 5, we analyze the range of alternatives in this dimension of choice. Our objective is to distinguish the various forms of social provision and their implications for consumers of social welfare benefits. Thus *questions about the nature of social provisions refer to the kinds of benefits that are delivered.*

Choices Regarding Delivery and Finance

The third dimension of choice addresses alternative strategies for delivering social provisions. Here the choices are not about "who" and "what," but rather about "how." That is, after decisions about the "who" and "what" of policy are resolved, arrangements must be made for getting the provisions selected to the eligible consumers. The ways delivery systems are designed to achieve this objective are of crucial significance to the first two dimensions of choice because it is through the delivery mechanism that policy guidelines regarding eligibility and the nature of provision are operationally expressed. Broadly speaking, benefit delivery strategies refer to the alternative organizational arrangements among providers and consumers of social welfare benefits in the context of local community systems (i.e., neighborhood, city, and county), the level at which the overwhelming majority of providers and consumers come together.

Consider, for example, a proposal for new job counseling services. Should they be centrally located in a downtown facility or dispersed in small neighborhood units? Should counselors be trained professionals or local residents? Should the services be offered if they duplicate similar services that already exist? Should they be incorporated under a unified administrative umbrella that includes related education and transportation services? Should the services be provided by a government agency, a nonprofit organization, or a profit-making organization? These choices all influence who gets served and the type of benefits they receive, policies about the nature of provisions and bases of allocations notwithstanding.

In examining the design of delivery systems, one usually discusses strategies to enhance the flow of services from providers to consumers, a point to which much of the literature in this area is addressed. Since the federal social service reductions of the 1980s, however, increasing attention has been given to strategies for rationing services and for contracting publicly funded activities to private agencies. When we examine this dimension of choice in Chapter 6, we will analyze strategies for facilitating service delivery, as well as considerations of public versus private auspices.

If social welfare policies are viewed as benefit-allocation mechanisms functioning outside the marketplace, choices must also be made concerning the sources and types of financing. It is important to recognize the distinction between funding benefits and delivering them. To clarify where funding ends and delivery begins, it is helpful to think in terms of a simple flow chart. Funding choices involve questions concerning the *source* of funds and the fashion in which funds *flow* from the point of origin to the point of provision. Delivery choices involve the *organizational* arrangements that move social provisions, either in cash or other forms, from providers to consumers.

Some of the major financing alternatives concern whether money is derived from public, private, or mixed sources; the level of government involved; and the types of taxes levied. Financing also involves the administrative conditions that govern funding arrangements, such as grant-in-aid formulas, and the "strings" attached to aid. This dimension of choice will be examined in Chapters 7 and 8.

Although the dimensions of allocation, provision, delivery, and finance will be analyzed separately in the following chapters, each with its own range of alternatives, it should be emphasized that most decisions are interdependent in the design of social welfare policies. For instance, a decentralized delivery system results when the social provision is in the form of power, as in policies for greater parental control of local education that aim to transfer decision-making authority from professional bureaucracies to service consumers. Similarly, the bases of social allocations and methods of finance are closely interwoven when eligibility for benefits involves some form of payments, as in subsidized user charges and contributory social insurance.

These four dimensions of choice encompass fundamental issues in the design of social welfare policies. The process through which these issues are resolved raises a different set of choices, choices that concern the design of decision-making arrangements and the extent to which they emphasize the roles of political leadership, citizen participation, and professional expertise, issues that will be discussed in Chapter 6.

An Example: The Transformation of Social Services

At this point, we will tie the dimensions of choice to a concrete case so the reader can see how the framework is applied. The selected case involves the evolution of social services since the early 1960s.[13] The focus is on social service provisions originally established under several titles of the Social Security Act: Titles I (Old Age Assistance), IV-A (Aid to Families With Dependent Children), X (Aid to the Blind), and XIV (Aid to the Permanently and Totally Disabled). Incorporated into Title XX of the Social Security Act in 1974, these provisions were refashioned into their current form in 1981 as the Social Services Block Grant. There are, of course, other sources from which social services emanate, such as the Adoption Assistance and Child Welfare Act of 1980; the Older Americans Act, first legislated in 1965; and the Anti-Drug Abuse Act of 1988. The reason that the Social Services Block Grant has been selected as the focal point of analysis is that it provides a considerable source of funds and it delegates the fundamental choices determining their use to state and local governments.

Any discussion of developments in the social services over the last forty years must consider the evolution of federal spending in this area. The 1962 Social Security Act amendments were the first to give specific emphasis to the role of the social services in public assistance. Between 1962 and 1972, federal grants to states for social services grew from approximately $194 million to $1.7 billion annually, a rather significant, and largely unanticipated, increase. When state estimates for 1973 indicated a potential increase to $4.7 billion, Congress, which until then had largely ignored the program, took action, enacting a $2.5 billion ceiling on federal expenditures.[14] This ceiling on social service funding rose for a while but was reduced to $2.4 billion in 1981 when social services funding was reconsidered and redesigned as the Social Services Block Grant, also known as Title XX of the Social Security Act. Since then, federal spending has gradually eroded to its current level of $1.7 billion a year.

Although it is important to appreciate the growth of federal Title XX funding as a force in the general development of social services, the focus of this case study is on the substantive program changes that have accompanied the changing levels of federal support. In this analysis, the overall rise in federal expenditures can be seen as a quantitative backdrop to a significant qualitative transformation.

Numerous changes in the nature of the social services have occurred since they first gained solid financial support in 1962. There has been a consistent broadening of eligibility standards and an enlargement of the population receiving services. In 1962, eligibility was limited to public assistance recipients, former recipients, and others who, in light of their precarious life circumstances, were potential candidates for public assistance. The government defined "potential recipients" as those who might reasonably be expected to require financial aid within one year of their application for services. Whereas these standards offered the *possibility* of extending services beyond the immediate public assistance population, it was not realized in practice. At that early stage, both program funds and trained social service workers were in relatively short supply. Because political support for the 1962 amendments was predicated on the idea that intensive social work services would reduce the size of public assistance rolls, the recipient population clearly held first priority on service allocations. Despite those immediate limitations, the possibility of extending service eligibility was established in principle.

This principle was applied in the Social Security Act amendments of 1967. Under these amendments, individuals became eligible for social services if it was determined that they might become welfare recipients within the next five years. Even more significant was the introduction of the concept of "group eligibility," whereby residents of low-income neighborhoods and other groups (such as those in institutional settings) could become eligible for service.

By 1972, people who were not receiving welfare were well represented among the social service clientele, and their number was growing. One reason for this was that the 1967 amendments had provided a loophole through which states could squeeze many locally funded services into the federal program, where they became eligible for 75 percent cost reimbursement.

The Title XX Amendments of 1974 ushered in a new set of eligibility criteria that further extended entitlements. Under the enactment, the federal government designated three categories of people who were eligible for services: (1) *income maintenance recipients*, (2) *income eligibles*, and (3) *universal eligibles*. Income maintenance recipients were those receiving public assistance, including Supplementary Security Income and Medicaid; these recipients are poor according to already-existing means-tested standards. Title XX regulations required each state to target at least 50 percent of its federal funds for people in this category. Income-eligible recipients included those who earned up to 115 percent of their state's median income. States could offer services free of charge to those whose income did not exceed 80 percent of the state median. For those earning between 80 and 115 percent of the median, services could be offered on a subsidized basis for reasonable income-related fees. The universal category referred to services that were available free of charge to all without regard to income: information and referral services, protective services for children and adults, and family planning. In 1978, a fourth category, *group eligibility*, was added. This category allowed states to designate groups of people with similar characteristics—for example, the elderly and the institutionalized mentally ill—as service eligible if it could be shown that 75 percent of the group's members had incomes less than 90 percent of the state's median income.

When Ronald Reagan's 1981 Omnibus Budget Reconciliation Act superseded Title XX with the Social Services Block Grant, federal eligibility requirements were eliminated altogether, leaving states free to exercise whatever standards of eligibility they desired. Despite the discretion afforded them, however, most states continue to employ much the same eligibility standards as before.[15]

As eligibility restrictions were eliminated, the scope and content of social provisions changed. Social services were originally advanced in 1962 as a way to prevent and reduce dependency—intensive social casework services would presumably *rehabilitate* the poor, changing their behavior in ways that would help them become economically independent.[16] Social services also included other basic forms of provision such as homemakers and foster-home care; however, the essential feature was the provision of social casework. Although this was not specified in the law, "welfare professionals in the Bureau of Family Services knew more or less what they meant by 'services.' At a minimum, it meant casework by a trained social worker."[17]

There is an intangible quality about casework service that makes the exact nature of the provision difficult to specify. This vagueness has led to the cynical observation that such service "is anything done for, with, or about the client by the social worker. If a social worker discusses a child's progress in school with an AFDC mother, a check is made under 'services related to education. . . .' When the discussion turns to the absent father and possible reconciliation, a check is made under 'maintaining family and improving family functioning.'"[18] In a similar vein, Handler and Hollingsworth characterized public assistance services as "little more than a relatively infrequent, pleasant chat."[19]

At its best, social casework is certainly a more skillful and nurturing enterprise than these comments suggest. But large caseloads, the demands of eligibility certification (while trying to establish a casework relationship), the diversity of clientele (many of whom did not need or want casework services but were forced to accept them), and the omnipresent bureaucratic regulations of public assistance were hardly conducive to effective practice.

In any event, whatever its powers and benefits, social casework was not a cure for poverty. The addition of almost one million recipients to the public assistance rolls between 1962 and 1966 dramatically proved this point.

The failure to reduce economic dependency combined with social casework's intangible quality made these services a prime target of congressional disillusion, a disillusion that was reflected in the 1967 Social Security Act amendments, under which casework was deemphasized. The 1967 amendments opened the way for a broader conception of social services. Before, federal grants for services mainly paid the salaries of social caseworkers.[20] In contrast, the 1967 amendments "created such a comprehensive array of specific services that literally almost any service was federally reimbursable."[21] At the same time, greater emphasis was placed on the delivery of services far more tangible than social casework. According to Derthick, "a distinction soon began to develop between 'soft' and 'hard' services. Advice and counseling from a caseworker were 'soft' . . . and presumably less valuable than day-care centers, or drug treatment centers, or work training, which were 'hard,'" and which soon became much more widely available. She continues, "the changed conception and changed social context helped lay the basis for granting funds for a much wider range of activity than the daily routines of caseworkers."[22]

With the passage of the 1974 social service amendments, the movement toward services diversification reached new heights. Under Title XX, each state was free to support whatever social services it deemed appropriate for its communities. The only requirement was that these services be directed to one of five federally specified goals, goals that were so broadly stated as to encompass almost anything the imagination of social service planners could devise. In the first year of implementation, Title XX plans for the fifty states and the District of Columbia specified a total of 1313 distinct services.[23]

The substantive range of services is illustrated in Table 3.1, which shows services grouped into twenty-eight categories devised by the federal government for purposes of tabulation and analysis. Whereas many federal reporting requirements and regulations were eliminated in the 1981 conversion from the "old" Title XX to the "new" Social Services Block Grant (SSBG), there have recently been new requirements mandating annual reports, uniform definitions of services, and specific information on the number of people receiving services, the amount of SSBG funds going for each service, methods of service delivery, and criteria for eligibility. Today, some states offer the full range of services, whereas a few use all of their funds to support just one or two services. Some states have also attempted to mesh Title XX funds with other federal, state, and local social service dollars in order to consolidate their services and budgetary planning.[24]

Along with the increasing emphasis on tangible services and the diversification of social service content, a profound change in the purpose of the social services was taking place. The 1962 services were almost exclusively aimed at reducing poverty; under Title XX there developed a service network of broad scope largely concerned with maintenance and care, directed more at enhancing human development and the general quality of life than at reducing economic dependency.[25] The first major step in this direction was the 1967 divorce of income-maintenance functions from social service functions in the public assistance program.[26] In 1977, this administrative separation was reinforced at the federal level by placing income-maintenance programs under the Social Security Administration and joining social service and human development programs under the Office of Human Development Services. This trend is reflected in Title XX's current emphasis on services that are not associated with notions of personal deficiency or inadequate character, such as transportation and meals-on-wheels for the elderly, homemaker services for the disabled, and daycare for children of all backgrounds.

TABLE 3.1   *Title XX Social Service Categories*

Adoption Services	Housing Services
Case Management	Independent/Transitional Living Services
Congregate Meals	Information and Referral
Counseling Services	Legal Services
Day Care (Adults)	Pregnancy and Parenting
Day Care (Children)	Prevention/Intervention (At-Risk Families)
Education and Training Services	Protective Services (Adult)
Employment Services	Protective Services (Child)
Family Planning Services	Recreational Services
Foster Care Services (Adults)	Residential Treatment
Foster Care Services (Children)	Special Services (Disabled)
Health-Related Services	Special Services (Youth)
Home-Based Services	Substance Abuse Services
Home-Delivered Meals	Transportation

Along with the separation of financial aid from the provision of social services, responsibility for the delivery of services became more dispersed through the increasing use of purchase-of-service arrangements between public agencies and social service providers in the private sector. Under the 1962 amendments, state public assistance agencies were enjoined from using federal funds to purchase services directly from voluntary agencies. It was possible, however, to purchase these services indirectly, with grants to other public agencies, which could then "contract out." Opportunities for purchase of services from private sources were significantly broadened when the 1967 social security amendments authorized purchase arrangements for a wide array of activities. Although the amendments allowed state agencies to purchase services directly from private agencies, private-agency donations could not be used as the states' 25 percent matching share *if* those contributions reverted to the donor's facility.[27] This restriction was lifted in 1974. The growing reliance of voluntary agencies on government funding was seen by some as a trend that robbed the voluntary sector of its traditional independence.

Over the last three decades, Title XX's flexible service delivery provisos generated an enormous expansion in the systematic use of public funds to purchase private/voluntary services. Given the virtual elimination of federal reporting requirements in the 1981 Social Services Block Grant, it is difficult to calculate the precise magnitude of purchase arrangements. It is estimated, however, that federal funds provide about 50 percent of all financial support for services provided by nonprofit agencies.[28]

These changes in the scope and delivery of provisions were accompanied by basic reforms in federal financing. Under the 1962 laws, federal financing was open ended, with the states reimbursed for 75 percent of social service costs to recipients in the four public assistance categories: the aged, the blind, the disabled, and families with dependent children. The 1967 amendments expanded the range of services and clientele that might qualify for federal funds. With this expansion the definitions of "social services" and client-eligibility standards were loosely drawn. Whether a particular service for certain clients qualified for federal reimbursement was dependent in large part on local interpretation rather than on a clearly defined statutory formula. The most enterprising states made the boldest interpretations, claimed the greatest need, and received the largest proportional share of federal grants for social services. In the states' scuffle for federal funds, grantsmanship was the name of the game. Three states—New York, Illinois, and California—were the biggest winners, together receiving 58 percent of federal grants in 1972.[29]

This open-ended approach to financing underwent fundamental revisions with the 1974 Title XX amendments. The new legislation incorporated the social service provisions originally financed under the four public assistance categories (Titles I, IV-A, X, and XIV of the Social Security Act) into a single grant (Title XX) program. With the $2.5 billion ceiling that Congress placed on social services, financing was no longer open ended. This limitation ushered in a change in allocative procedures that tied federal allotments to a formula based strictly on state population. Each state was thereby entitled to a proportional share of Title XX funds, but the receipt of these funds was contingent on meeting certain regulations and supplying a local matching share. When the Social Services Block Grant was enacted in 1981, the local share requirement was dropped along with most other federal regulations. SSBG allocations continue on a population basis, spreading funds in a way that yields a rough form of interstate equalization. However, this mode of finance is not especially sensitive to the greater needs of poorer states.

Application of the Framework

Now let us superimpose the dimensions of choice on the complex social service program changes that have occurred since 1962. Our approach to policy analysis provides a way of thinking about this program that extracts and organizes its major elements, making the whole more readily comprehensible. Using the framework we have outlined, the substance of social service policy may be divided into our four choice categories, which are summarized as follows:

1. *The bases of social allocations: Selective to universal.*

In 1962, eligibility for social services was means-tested, effectively limited to recipients of the four categorical aid programs—Aid to Families with Dependent Children (AFDC), Aid to the Blind, Old Age Assistance, and Aid to the Permanently and Totally Disabled. By 1974, eligibility criteria were broadened by the Title XX amendments to include many middle-income beneficiaries. The Social Services Block Grant, which revised Title XX in 1981, gave the states latitude to impose any eligibility criteria they wished. Because most states continue to employ the limited requirements of earlier years, it would be an exaggeration to say that there is universal access to social services. Nevertheless, there has been a pronounced trend from selective toward universal access.

2. *The nature of social provision: Intangible and limited to concrete and diversified.*

In 1962, social services consisted primarily of social casework to help families improve their functioning and gain economic independence. What these services entailed, beyond some form of psychotherapeutic counseling, was only vaguely defined. More tangible forms of service were established in 1967, emphasizing employment training, daycare, and family planning. Under the 1981 conversion to the Social Services Block Grant, states may offer any kind of social service imaginable. By 1990, diversification of social services had grown to include twenty-five categories of provision.

3. *The delivery system: Public and linked to income maintenance, to public, private, and free standing.*

Up to 1967, social service and income maintenance functions were combined and delivered by the same administrative unit. Caseworkers distributed financial aid and also provided social services. After 1967 these functions were administratively divorced and performed by different workers, with an emphasis placed on hiring AFDC recipients to perform certain service roles related to daycare and eligibility determination. Also, since 1975, an increased reliance on purchase-of-service arrangements by state and local governments has drawn an increasing number of private nonprofits into what was originally a delivery system of public agencies.

4. *Finance: Open-ended categorical grant to fixed-amount block grant.*

In 1962 the federal government reimbursed states for 75 percent of all social service costs for recipients in the public assistance categories. When these services were incorporated into Title XX, a $2.5 billion expenditure ceiling (which slowly rose to $2.8 billion by 1995, declined to $2.4 billion in 1996, and is currently at $1.7 billion) was established with grants allocated to states according to a formula based strictly on population size. To qualify for grants, states were required to supply a 25 percent local match. For all practical purposes, Title XX amounted to a block grant. In 1981, the Social Services Block Grant provided states almost complete discretion in use of these grants and no longer required matching funds or reporting or planning requirements.

In specifying the dimensions of choice—the first step of a two-step process in social welfare policy analysis—we ask these questions: What benefits are to be allocated, and to whom? How are these benefits to be delivered and financed? These questions may be answered without reference to purpose. So now we turn to the second step in the analysis process—the "why" question, addressing the values, theories, and assumptions that inform social choices.

Distributive Justice in Public Assistance

Some answers to the "why" of social choice can be found in the explication of underlying values. Alva Myrdal explains the importance of illuminating the values embedded in policy designs:

> An established tendency to drive values underground, to make analysis appear scientific by omitting certain basic assumptions from the discussion, has too often emasculated the social sciences as agencies for rationality in social and political life. To be truly rational, it is necessary to accept the obvious principle that a social program, like a practical judgment, is a conclusion based upon premises of values as well as upon facts.[30]

The analysis of values and social welfare policy may be approached from at least two levels. At the broader level the analytic focus is on policy in the generic sense. Rather than examining specific dimensions of choice and their accompanying values, this level of analysis addresses broad purposes. Specifically, to what extent does the policy achieve distributive justice? At this level of generality, three core values shape the design of policy: *equality*, *equity*, and *adequacy*. As we will see by examining the changing arrangements for financial aid under public assistance, these values are not always in harmony.

In addition to providing social services, the main function of categorical public assistance programs has been to provide financial assistance to the needy. When these programs were established under the Social Security Act of 1935, three categories of needy people were eligible for aid: the elderly under Title I, Old Age Assistance (OAA); dependent children under Title IV, Aid to Dependent Children (ADC); and the blind, under Title X, Aid to the Blind (AB). A fourth category was added in 1950 under Title XIV, Aid to the Permanently and Totally Disabled (APTD).

In 1961, Aid to Dependent Children was changed to Aid to Families with Dependent Children (AFDC), reflecting an emphasis on maintaining the family unit. Legislation in 1988 required the states to provide financial aid to children of unemployed parents (AFDC-UP).

These four categorical programs were financed by the federal government and administered by the states, with each state contributing a variable matching share, the size of which was based on its wealth. A fifth public aid option, General Assistance (GA), is available for individuals who do not qualify for support under the federally financed programs. Funded entirely by states and localities, General Assistance is usually more parsimonious than the federal categories with regard to the duration and amount of assistance.

In 1965, a broad program of medical assistance for the poor was enacted, unifying the various arrangements for meeting medical costs that existed under the four categorical programs. Known as Medicaid, this program also allows the states to offer payments to the "medically indigent," people whose economic resources are insufficient to pay all their medical costs but who do not otherwise qualify as needy for cash assistance.

Through the early 1970s, Medicaid and the five categorical programs (OAA, APTD, AFDC, AB, and GA), along with food stamps, formed the general core of public assistance in this country. Within the framework established by federal legislation, the states had considerable latitude to design programs according to their own local norms and preferences. One reflection on this policy was the twenty-odd different agency names used by the fifty states to designate the bureaucracies administering their public assistance programs. These included Public Welfare, Social Services, Family and Children Services, Institutions and Agencies, Human Resources, and Economic Security, to name but a few. More profound variations existed with regard to standards of eligibility and levels of assistance. For example, under AFDC, monthly aid payments varied enormously from state to state. At the time AFDC was abolished in the mid-1990s, for example, aid for an average family ranged from $115 in Alabama to $748 in Alaska. In more than half the states, AFDC payments equaled less than the minimum required to meet basic needs according to cost standards that these states themselves had set. Many of these differentials continue today, under the welfare reform legislation enacted in 1996.

The structure of categorical public assistance was dramatically altered by the Social Security Act amendments of 1972 under which Old Age Assistance, Aid to the Blind, and Aid to the Permanently and Totally Disabled were replaced by the consolidated Supplementary Security Income (SSI) program (implemented in 1974). In contrast to the incorporation of the categorical social services under Title XX, which increased state administrative authority, the replacement of the financial aid categories by SSI brought these programs entirely under federal control. Administered by the Social Security Administration and supported totally by federal funds (although states occasionally supplement the payments), SSI provides uniform cash assistance to the needy, blind, aged, and disabled throughout the country. Average federal payments to SSI recipients in 2009 were $674 monthly for an individual and $1011 monthly for a couple.

AFDC, as indicated in Figure 3.3, was not included in the federalization of the 1970s. Until 1996, it continued to be administered by the states under federal regulations and to be jointly financed through open-ended federal matching grants. With the passage of welfare reform, the Personal Responsibility and Work Opportunity Reconciliation Act of 1996, AFDC was replaced by TANF—the Temporary Assistance for Needy Families program. This unprecedented reform, substituting TANF block funding grant for AFDC's open-ended arrangement, effectively eliminated a national entitlement to public assistance—fulfilling President Clinton's campaign promise to "end welfare as we know it," if not exactly along the lines he envisioned.

Under TANF, states receive a fixed level of federal funds to provide income support to poor families with children based on the amount spent on AFDC in 1994.[31] It should be noted that because AFDC caseloads had been declining in most states, the initial post-TANF allocations were higher than the amount states would have received under AFDC.[32] Future prospects, however, are uncertain. During periods of recession, for example, if caseloads rose and states ran out of block grant funds, eligible applicants for public aid might have to be denied assistance unless a state had the political will to commit its *own* funds to the program.

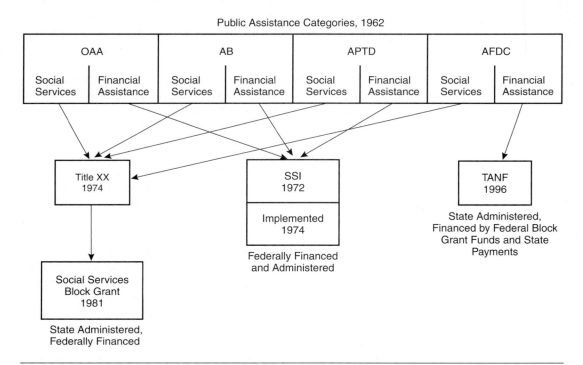

FIGURE 3.3   *Reorganization of Public Assistance: Social Services and Financial Aid.*

Beyond capping the level of federal support that states might draw on to aid needy families, TANF introduced sweeping changes in the essential character of public assistance—among which time-limited welfare was the most radical measure. Under TANF, states are barred from providing federal cash benefits to families for more than a total of five years during their lifetime, although up to 20 percent of recipients may be exempted from the limit due to hardship. States must also develop plans describing how TANF recipients will engage in work activities after being on the welfare rolls for two years.

In allocating financial aid outside of economic markets, public assistance programs like TANF and SSI represent an effort to alter the distribution of resources in society. In this effort one aim of public assistance is to further distributive justice—an undertaking that must come to grips with the values of *equality*, *equity*, and *adequacy*.

Equality

Although it is one of the foundation stones of distributive justice, equality is a value open to interpretation. At least two salient notions were differentiated by Aristotle: numerical equality and proportional equality.[33] These concepts represent the egalitarian and meritarian elements of distributive justice. Numerical equality implies the same treatment of everyone—to all an equal share. Proportional equality implies the same treatment of similar persons—to each according to his or her merit or virtue. These interpretations of equality offer conflicting prescriptions for the treatment of dissimilar persons. With the concept of proportional equality, Vlastos points out, "the meritarian view of justice paid reluctant homage to the egalitarian one by using the vocabulary of equality to assert the justice of inequality."[34] To clarify this distinction and to reduce the definitional awkwardness, we will use the term *equality* in its numerical sense and will subsume the meaning of proportional equality under the value of equity.

Social welfare policy is influenced by the value of equality with regard to the outcome of benefit allocations. Specifically, the value prescribes that benefits should be allocated so as to equalize the distribution of resources and opportunities. In some policies, this value is predominant, as, for instance, in the development of quota hiring plans for the equal allocation of work roles among different groups of people. In a modified version, there are opportunity-oriented policies whereby the equal shares objective is recast in terms of equal opportunity. Fair housing legislation, for example, demands that people, whatever their racial and ethnic characteristics, receive the same treatment in their quest for shelter. It does not, however, ensure equal results for everyone.

In public assistance, the introduction of uniform federal grants under SSI was, in part, a measure to promote greater equality in financial aid across the country. The influence of the equality goal in shaping the design of public assistance is also evident in the extent to which money is shifted from wealthy states and individuals toward those that are poor. Although such redistribution takes place through public assistance, it falls considerably short of creating even a roughly equal share for all because distributive justice is also responsive to other values.

Equity

Equity denotes a conventional sense of fair treatment. There is a proportional quality to notions of fair treatment—if you do half the work, you deserve half the reward. People's deservedness should be based on their contributions to society, modified only by special considerations for those whose inability to contribute is clearly not of their own making. Accordingly, there are many "equitable inequalities" that are normatively sanctioned, as in policies that offer preferential treatment for veterans and in unemployment benefits that vary in proportion to prior earnings.

In public assistance, equity is stressed through the doctrine of "less eligibility," first formulated by the English Poor Law Commissioners in 1834. In the Commissioners' words,

> It may be assumed that in the administration of relief, the public is warranted in imposing such conditions on the individual relieved, as are conducive to the benefit either of the individual himself, or of the country at large, at whose expense he is to be relieved. The first and most essential of all conditions, a principle which we find universally admitted, even by those whose practice is at variance with it, is that *his situation on the whole shall not be made really or apparently so eligible as the situation of the independent laborer of the lowest class.* [Emphasis added.][35]

One reason for the extremely low level of public assistance in most states is the ingrained belief that aid should not elevate the conditions of recipients above those of the poorest workers. Here, the emphasis on equity supports the maintenance of incentives to work. It is interesting to note the historic shift that has taken place in the relation between incentives to work and public assistance as increasing numbers of women have entered the labor force.

In the 1960s and 1970s, policymakers began a serious debate about the right of welfare mothers to collect public aid and remain at home with their children. The issue was not simply whether welfare benefits should be lower than the income one might earn in the paid labor force, but whether active measures should be employed to encourage welfare mothers to work. Reflecting the view that various incentives should be offered to encourage welfare recipients to seek employment, the 1967 amendments to the Social Security Act established the WIN (work-incentive) program to provide training and employment to "all appropriate individuals," which included welfare mothers with young children. Previously, work programs had been available on a much smaller scale mainly to fathers of families receiving aid under AFDC-UP. In addition, the provision of daycare services was authorized so that mothers would be free to work and, for an incentive, the first $30 of monthly earnings plus one-third of the remainder were exempted from determination of continued eligibility for assistance. (In 1981, the "30 plus one-third" earnings disregard was limited to only the first four months of employment, and in 1988, WIN was replaced altogether with the workfare provisions of the Family Support Act.)

Around the same time that the 1967 amendments were being implemented, other proponents argued for increasing the level of AFDC benefits for women who stayed at home. Casting this claim in the name of equity, they did not ask that dissimilar people, those who work and those who do not work, be treated equally and awarded similar standards of living. Rather, the argument was made that motherhood itself should be considered an occupation—one, indeed, that is more trying than most. This view was expressed by a ten-member panel (nine of whom were men) commissioned by the federal government to study the problem of U.S. workers. The panel recommended, among other things, that welfare mothers be subsidized to stay home and care for their children.[36] The case for this policy gains momentum when we calculate the substantial per capita costs of daycare services necessary to allow AFDC mothers the freedom to work.[37]

By 1996, the question of whether the interests of equity were best served by providing public assistance to subsidize the home care of children or by expecting welfare mothers to seek paid employment in the labor market was resolved clearly in favor of the labor market option—welfare became "workfare." Indeed, as noted, the Temporary Assistance for Needy Families program not only expects welfare recipients to seek employment within two years, but also sharply limits the number of years that poor families are eligible to receive public aid during their lifetime. The political consensus that motivated the shift from welfare to workfare was influenced in part by the more general movement of women from the household into the market economy. Steadily on the rise, the labor force participation rate of married women with children under eighteen more than doubled after 1960. By 2005, indeed, nearly three in four married moms with children had jobs. As the vast majority of mothers entered the paid workforce, it became awkward for even the most sympathetic welfare advocates to hold public assistance recipients exempt from the obligation to seek employment.

Adequacy

Adequacy refers to the desirability of providing a decent standard of physical and spiritual well-being, quite apart from concerns for whether benefit allocations are equal or differentiated according to merit. Thus, as Frankena explains, the quest for distributive justice involves

> a somewhat vaguely defined but still limited concern for the *goodness of people's lives*, as well as for their equality. The double concern is often referred to as respect for the intrinsic dignity or value of the human individual. This is not the position of the extreme egalitarian but it is essentially egalitarian in spirit; in any case it is not the position of the meritarian, although it does seek to accommodate his principles.[38]

Standards of adequacy vary according to time and circumstances. In medieval times, serfs were usually provided with the necessities to keep them healthy and productive. At the turn of the twentieth century, $624 a year was estimated as a "living wage" for a family of five in New York City.[39] Today, the most common statistic for defining adequacy is the poverty line, which is calculated annually by the U.S. Department of Labor and adjusted to family size. In 2008, for example, a family of four with an income under the $21,200 poverty threshold was considered poor (i.e., to have a less than minimally adequate income) (see Table 3.2). But this official standard of adequacy, while in widespread use, is considered by many to be seriously inaccurate. One approach to a more realistic standard of adequacy, a "basic needs budget," takes the

TABLE 3.2   *2008 Department of Health and Human Services (HHS) Poverty Guidelines*

Persons in Family or Household	Forty-Eight Contiguous States and D.C.	Alaska	Hawaii
1	$10,400	$13,000	$11,960
2	14,000	17,500	16,100
3	17,600	22,000	20,240
4	21,200	26,500	24,380
5	24,800	31,000	28,520
6	28,400	35,500	32,660
7	32,000	40,000	36,800
8	35,600	44,500	40,940
For each additional person, add	3,600	4,500	4,140

Source: Federal Register, Vol. 73, No. 15, January 23, 2008, pp. 3971–972.

rather straightforward approach of determining just how much the various basics of life (food, rent, healthcare, etc.) cost in various locales, and calculating an adequacy standard on their sum. According to calculations by the Economic Policy Institute, for example, working families with two children needed $48,778 in 2008 to make ends meet. This figure, the nationwide average, ranged considerably by location, chiefly due to variations in the cost of housing and child care. In urban areas, for example, the basic needs figure was $42,106 in Oklahoma City and $71,193 in Nassau/Suffolk, New York. In small towns and rural areas, it ranged from $35,733 in Marshall County, Mississippi, to $73,345 in Dukes County, Massachusetts. The $48,778 average, it is important to note, left nearly a third of all families below the family budget threshold—three times the official poverty rate.[40]

The value of adequacy is expressed rather faintly in public assistance policy honored more in the breach than in reality. Nevertheless, its presence is reflected in the fact that grant levels are not set arbitrarily, but are based on state estimates of the costs of basic needs (even though the grants rarely approach the levels of these estimates).

Overall, as a benefit allocation mechanism, public assistance is more responsive to concerns for equity than for adequacy and equality. This emphasis stems, at least in part, from the broader societal context in which the program operates. In a capitalist society, the value of equity is generally accentuated—those who work hard deserve to be rewarded. According to normative standards, the capitalists are those reaping the just fruits of their labor. Socialist societies theoretically place greater stress on the value of equality. As Marx wrote, "The secret of the expression of value, namely that all kinds of labor are equal and equivalent, because, and so far as they are human, labor in general cannot be deciphered, until the notion of human equality has already acquired the fixity of a popular prejudice."[41] Once the notion of human equality has achieved the status of a "popular prejudice," differential treatment of dissimilar people is significantly reduced if not completely abolished because, judged by the most important of characteristics—their humanness—everybody is the same.

From this somewhat lofty perspective, the "why" of policy design may be analyzed in terms of the quest for distributive justice as it is manifest in the differential realization of adequacy, equity, and equality.[42] Although a policy may emphasize any one of these values, the emphasis is often tempered by the demands of the other two values as efforts are made to approximate distributive justice.

Individual and Community Values in Public Assistance

Moving down a rung, a much larger range of social values enters into the consideration of choice. For instance, the values of privacy, dignity, work, and independence may influence the criteria of eligibility, the forms of social provision, and the design of delivery and finance arrangements. To illustrate, Table 3.3 lists the four dimensions of choice and some of the competing values that influence them. These four value dichotomies are suggestive and hardly exhaust the range of possibilities. They were selected because the range of values represents variations on central issues of policy choice exemplified in the polarity of individualism versus collectivism. These issues concern the ways and extent to which expressions of individual interests are given free rein or are harnessed in the service of the common good. As Marshall explains,

> The claim of the individual to welfare is sacred and irrefutable and partakes of the character of a natural right . . . but the citizen of the Welfare State does not merely have the right to pursue welfare; he has the right to receive it, even if the pursuit has not been particularly hot. . . . But if we put individualism first, we must put collectivism second. The Welfare State is the responsible promoter and guardian of the welfare of the whole community, which is something more complex than the sum total of the welfare of its individual members, arrived at by simple addition. The claims of the individual must always be defined and limited so as to fit into the complex and balanced pattern of the welfare of the community, and that is why the right to welfare can never have the full stature of a natural right. The harmonizing of individual rights with the common good is a problem which faces all human societies.[43]

TABLE 3.3   *Dimensions of Choice and Competing Value Perspectives*

Individualist Perspective	Dimensions of Choice	Community Perspective
Cost effectiveness	Allocation	Social effectiveness
Freedom of choice	Provision	Social control
Freedom of dissent	Delivery	Efficiency
Local autonomy	Finance	Centralization

Cost effectiveness may be applied to each dimension of choice. When applied to the basis of social allocations, it is measured by the extent to which each dollar of benefit is allocated to those most in need—that is, those least able to purchase what they need in the open marketplace. The guiding thought is that there be no waste of resources. With the cost-effectiveness criterion, individual treatment varies according to individual circumstances. Implementing this value requires a high degree of selectivity in determining those who are eligible for benefits. Applied in the extreme, this value can produce invidious distinctions among people, dividing the community into groups of the dependent and the independent, the incompetent and the self-sufficient.

Social effectiveness may take different forms. One way it is measured in allocative decisions is by the extent to which all individuals are treated as equal members of the social body. Here, the notion of effectiveness is related to the fact that nobody who is potentially eligible will feel inhibited about applying for benefits because of shame, stigma, or the organizational rigamarole that is often required to implement selective procedures. Allocations are universal: An individual's special need or defect need not be exposed for scrutiny in order to become eligible for benefits. The "badge of citizenship" is sufficient basis for entitlement. In what was once AFDC and is now TANF, for example, the basis of social allocations—a thorough and probing means test of every applicant—is clearly influenced more by concerns for cost effectiveness than social effectiveness.[44]

Titmuss has observed that the apparent strain between cost effectiveness and social effectiveness may be a function of the short-range perspective of using cost-effectiveness calculations, especially for medical benefits, where policy objectives include prevention as well as treatment. For example, if access to medical care entails a means-test investigation that is demeaning, time-consuming, or otherwise inconvenient, clients may procrastinate about seeking aid until the symptoms are so advanced that they can no longer be ignored. At this stage, the cost of treatment is usually more expensive. In the long run, cost effectiveness and social effectiveness can be brought into harmony when the universal allocation of medical care saves more through prevention than selective allocations save by limiting treatment only to those in dire need.[45]

Freedom of choice is reflected in provisions that offer recipients considerable latitude to exercise their individual preferences. Thus, for example, when social provisions are in the form of cash, a high degree of consumer sovereignty is preserved. Social control, on the other hand, is reflected in provisions that limit individual choice. With in-kind provisions, recipients are limited to whatever specific benefits (housing, medical care, counseling, therapy, advice, information, etc.) are offered. Of course, they have the freedom to take it or leave it, but that is where the choice ends. In some social welfare programs, social provisions are linked so that freedom of choice in one area of provision is bought at the price of social control in another. This is the case in public assistance. In the original AFDC program, recipients were given cash grants and could exercise a degree of choice in meeting their daily requirements. Under the Family Support Act of 1988, AFDC benefits was linked to participation in work training programs, and, in some states, to educational programs as well.[46] By 1996, when AFDC was supplanted by the TANF, cash benefits were tied to a variety of behavioral and labor market expectations such as going to school, living at home (for unwed teenage mothers), identifying the child's father, and, of course, getting a job. These behavioral incentives were strongly advocated and supported by conservatives, despite their traditional disavowal of the collectivists' conviction that government might improve the human condition through social engineering.

Freedom of dissent and efficiency are values that influence whether the delivery system is designed primarily along democratic or bureaucratic lines. Blau states the choice succinctly:

> Bureaucratic and democratic structures can be distinguished . . . on the basis of the dominant organizing principle: efficiency or freedom of dissent. Each of these principles is suited for one purpose and not for another. When people set themselves the task of determining the social objectives that represent the interests of most of them, the crucial problem is to provide an opportunity for all conflicting viewpoints to be heard. In contrast, when the task is the achievement of given social objectives, the essential problem to be solved is to discover the efficient, not the popular, means for doing so.[47]

In TANF, the delivery system is organized primarily along bureaucratic lines. Clients do not vote to establish the level of their grants or eligibility criteria. In other social welfare programs, however, social provision is so loosely formulated that the local delivery system is charged with the dual purpose of deciding on specific objectives and then carrying out those decisions. For instance, the War on Poverty and Model Cities programs of the 1960s required substantial citizen participation in program planning and implementation. These systems thus incorporated democratic as well as bureaucratic elements in their structure. The problem in these systems, it often turned out, is that neither value was served very well.[48]

Local autonomy and centralization are values that find expression in the financing and administration of programs. Strains between these values are most likely to emerge when program costs are shared intergovernmentally or, in the private sector, between nationwide and local voluntary organizations. Cost-sharing arrangements are implemented through federal grants-in-aid that vary along a continuum from broad purpose block grants to special-purpose categorical grants. The block grant is a lump-sum national contribution for local programs. It carries few specifications or requirements on how the money should be spent beyond requirements that it be applied to a general program realm such as health, community development, or education. This ensures a high degree of local autonomy. At the other end of the continuum is the special-purpose grant with detailed standards. Here, local discretion regarding the use of funds is restricted according to precise federal criteria. In most cost-sharing arrangements, the methods of finance fall somewhere midway on the continuum, reflecting the mutual desirability of local autonomy and national planning.

For example, although based on categorical principles, the AFDC program contained elements of both values. The federal funders attached various conditions to these categorical grants concerning citizenship, "statewideness," and the provision of services. Yet local autonomy prevailed in at least two crucial aspects of the program. States were free to exercise broad discretion in defining the criteria of need and the amount of financial assistance that is provided to recipients. The centralist thrust of the program was mitigated in part because, as Burns explains, "to prescribe in the federal act both the standards of need which determine eligibility and the minimum level of living to be assured all eligible applicants raises major issues regarding federal interference in an area which traditionally has been thought of as peculiarly a matter for local determination."[49] When AFDC was supplanted by TANF in 1996, the funding arrangement changed from a categorical to a block grant, giving states much greater latitude to determine how funds are spent. Various conditions, nevertheless, were attached to the block grants concerning citizenship, time limits, and work requirements (see Chapter 8).

Theories, Assumptions, and Social Choice

The subtle and complex relationships between value preferences and social welfare policies offer one level of insight into the "why" of social choice. Another dimension of analysis that has a bearing on this question involves theories and assumptions about how clients, delivery systems, methods of finance, and types of social provisions function, both independently and in concert. Much of this kind of theory-derived knowledge is fragmented and only partially verified. This is not to deny the effect of social science knowledge on choice, but rather than overestimate what is known, we use the term *theory* to cover the influence and support that social science insights render to policy choices. We classify as assumptions those suppositions for which there has been little systematic effort to obtain and codify evidence. In the general sense, the term *assumptions* is used to designate theories "writ small."

To illustrate, let us continue to examine public assistance. At least three assumptions underpinning major policy choices in this program have been seriously challenged by subsequent evidence. First, the 1962 "service" amendments were supported by the belief that the clinical model of casework service would bring about change in the economic dependency of individuals in poverty. Implicit is the theory that poverty is mainly a function of individual deficiencies, deficiencies that can be transformed and alleviated through the casework process. This theory was relatively new. Until the 1950s, assistance recipients were generally considered "victims of external circumstances, such as unemployment, disability, or the death of the family's breadwinner," who "needed to be 'relieved'—not treated or changed."[50]

In 1971, after reviewing studies of casework efforts to treat and rehabilitate those on public assistance, Carter concluded,

> It becomes clear that it is time to reassess the purposes of casework services offered welfare recipients and other low income groups for whom problems identified for alleviation are complex and interrelated with other personal, family, and community or societal problems . . . there are serious questions as to what behavioral changes can be set in motion without provision first being made for a decent level of living and access being provided to a range of social resources within the agency and the community.[51]

Second, the separation of income maintenance from the administration of social services was predicated on the assumption that services would be improved because the caseworker–client relationship would no longer be tinged by the coercive undertones emanating from the worker's discretionary authority over the client's budget. Clients, presumably, would be free to accept or reject services as needed, and caseworkers, released from the task of administering grants, would have more time to engage in a voluntary service enterprise. This is a plausible line of reasoning, but one open to critical examination. Neither the strength of the caseworker's coercive powers, and their effects on relationships with clients, nor the extent of client initiative to seek services when routine caseworker visits were terminated was clearly discernible. It is quite possible, as Handler and Hollingsworth suggest, that the coercion argument was exaggerated and, more important, that in the absence of routine home visits welfare clients would be reluctant to seek help from an unknown official. Thus, "requiring welfare clients to take the initiative may have the effect of cutting off a reasonably valuable service that most clients, in their own words, seem to like."[52] Indeed, research findings on this issue reveal that AFDC recipients made higher demands for services and expressed greater satisfaction when service and income maintenance were combined.[53]

As a final example, we turn to the work-incentive program established under the 1967 social security amendments. The perversely accurate acronym for the Work Incentive Program, WIP, conveys the image of an instrument used to drive beasts of burden. Through some creative bureaucratese it was quickly transformed to WIN (Work INcentive). An objective of the 1967 amendments was to swing AFDC services away from traditional social casework toward more practical and concrete work-oriented provisions. This shift in emphasis from welfare to workfare then reflected, and continues to reflect, two assumptions: (1) that jobs are available for anyone who really wants to work, and (2) that we know how to change deleterious patterns of behavior with voluntary incentives. The problem is primarily seen again as individual deficiency—the lack of skills and adverse attitudes toward work—although of a different nature than those amenable to psychiatric casework. The solution is to equip people for jobs and motivate them to seek employment.

Although facts about WIN are not decisive, what is known suggests that its assumptions were flawed. Levitan and Taggart indicated that of the 167,000 people who enrolled in WIN through March 1970, more than one-third dropped out of the program and, all told, only 25,000 got jobs. Those who moved on to work were "creamed" from the pool of applicants—those moving into jobs were those best prepared for jobs. This group included a high percentage of unemployed fathers receiving AFDC-UP who probably would have found employment sooner or later without social assistance. In light of the program's "conspicuously unspectacular performance," the study observes, "the wisdom of expanding WIN is questionable, and the theoretical arguments for such a move are even more dubious."[54]

A subsequent analysis of the WIN experience suggests that the program's shortcomings endured to the end. In 1982, only 3 percent of the AFDC clients registered for the WIN program in New York State were placed in a job; an additional 5 percent found employment through their own efforts. In a distinct echo of Levitan and Taggart's findings, the 1982 study observed that "those who eventually are served generally represent the easiest to employ—those most likely to get jobs without the help of special services."[55] Although findings on work programs in the five states that formed a model for the Family Support of 1988 were somewhat more encouraging, a substantial proportion (from 40 to 80 percent) of participants remained unemployed after six to fifteen months. The extent to which this type of voluntary program can ameliorate the circumstances of welfare recipients, therefore, remains uncertain.[56]

The two assumptions that have girded workfare policies since the mid-1960s continue to brace the TANF initiatives—a line of reforms aptly characterized by Gilbert Steiner as "tireless tinkering with dependent families."[57] In recent years, however, this "tinkering" has produced unprecedented and significant results. Between 1993 and 2008, welfare caseloads declined by more than 50 percent, with TANF's demanding work-oriented reforms, facilitated by other factors, contributing powerfully to this reduction.

As those recipients most willing and able to leave welfare have been drawn out of the client pool, those remaining present a tremendous challenge to the second workfare assumption—that we know how to address the variety of debilitating individual problems involving a lack of skill, ability, and motivation, to say nothing of substance abuse and domestic violence problems. For example, an analysis of the National Adult Literacy Survey, which tests the ability to apply math and reading skills to everyday situations, indicates that a quarter of all public assistance recipients score in the lowest of five levels of literacy—a level where people are unable to perform tasks such as locating an intersection on a street map, filling out a government benefits application, or totaling the costs on an order form.[58]

Can public policy successfully address these problems? Increasing evidence suggests that various measures can effectively address the employment prospects of the difficult-to-serve. Public employment in protected settings for recipients who cannot function competitively in the normal labor market can be provided. Intense efforts at education and rehabilitation can prepare even the most difficult-to-employ for regular work. In the end, nevertheless, as we shall see in Chapter 8, there is likely to remain a group for whom work-oriented policies are simply not an adequate answer—a group composed of the most vulnerable and least competent, for whom Gilbert Steiner's alternative of "honorable dependency" may be the best arrangement the community has to offer.[59]

CAPSULE 3.2 • *Tireless Tinkering with the Poor*

Unfortunately, the sorry history and limitations of day care and work training as "solutions" to the welfare problem could not be faced by the administration's welfare specialists. . . . But after a few years it will inevitably be discovered that work training and day care have had little effect on the number of welfare dependents and no depressing effect on public relief costs. Some new solution will then be proposed, but the more realistic approach would be to accept the need for more welfare and to reject continued fantasizing about day care and "workfare" as miracle cures.

Gilbert Steiner, *The State of Welfare*, 1971.

Emerging Issues: The Search for Equity

In this chapter, we have outlined an analytic approach to the study of social welfare policy. The essence of this approach may be summarized as follows:

1. Viewing social welfare policy as a benefit allocation mechanism requires four types of choices: those pertaining to allocations, provisions, delivery, and finance.
2. Understanding these four dimensions of choice requires knowing the basic alternatives associated with each.
3. Understanding why given alternatives may be preferred over others requires explicating the values, theories, and assumptions implicit in policy design.

The implication here is not that certain choices are inherently preferable to others. Different preferences will be registered by different planners, depending on the values, theories, and assumptions given the most worth and credence. Our objective in the following five chapters is to take each dimension of choice, delineate the basic policy alternatives, and examine the interplay of values, theories, and assumptions. But first, let us briefly explore one important development in the realm of social values that is currently shaping social policy. While concerns for equity have always been a central value in the design of welfare programs, these concerns have gained increasing momentum as policymakers have sought to balance rights and responsibilities in allocating benefits. Since the late 1980s, the enhanced regard for equity has been particularly reflected in the frequent pronouncement that citizens who "work hard and play by the rules" should be able to support their families above the poverty level.

As the third millennium begins, concerns for equity provide a moral compass from which social polices take their bearings. But, as noted, everyone does not always agree on what is fair. Take the case, for example, of an African American high school senior from a high-income family who, on an affirmative action basis, is admitted to a university over an equally qualified low-income white student. Here, minority status is the criterion that defines the disadvantage being redressed by policy. Some might believe, however, that family income is a more appropriate criterion of deservedness. Questions of this sort gain saliency as the number of minority families in affluent circumstances increases.

In recent years, the substantial increase in the number of working wives has also complicated the search for equity, particularly in regard to dependents' benefits in the social security program. Since social security benefits account for more than half of all direct federal expenditures for social welfare, this is a matter that touches vast numbers of citizens. When the Social Security Act of 1935 was first amended in 1939, the insurance principle of "individual equity"—that retired workers should receive benefits roughly equal to their contributions—was compromised by concerns that benefits should provide an adequate standard of family living.[60] The extension of social security benefits to dependents—spouses and children—was thus enacted to ensure a reasonable standard of adequacy for entire families, rather than simply individuals.

Dependents' benefits, however, create many inequities among married couples with different patterns of work and income, and with the increasing proportion of wives joining the labor force, these patterns of social inequity have been magnified.[61] Although weighted in favor of low-income workers, social security pension benefits rise with wage levels. Thus, in the mid-1990s, a nonworking wife whose husband had earned a $60,600 income was entitled to an annual dependent's benefit of $7470—about $1000 more than an employed wife making $11,400 would be entitled to on her own as a primary beneficiary in a two-earner family with a husband earning $25,000 a year. And it was more than twice the dependent's benefit of $3245, which would be granted to a nonworking wife whose husband earned $11,400. Even though the husband with the higher income paid more social security taxes over the years, the pension benefits for his family (as well as all other families) are partially subsidized by transfers from the next generation of contributors. Estimates by Martha Ozawa suggest similar patterns, with the dependent wife in higher-income families receiving higher benefits than either dependent or employed wives in lower-income families. One might ask whether this arrangement is fair. Why should social policy provide subsidies enabling richer groups to maintain their differential economic advantages in old age?[62]

Another major issue in the search for equity involves "getting the numbers right" in relation to social needs and allocations. An implicit equation of equity is that welfare transfers ought to result in a fair distribution of public resources among competing needs and problems. On one side of this equation, we must calculate the full range of transfers and how they are distributed. On the other side, we must fathom the needs and problems to which transfers are addressed, and how well they help to address them. Recognizing that it isn't feasible to devise a comprehensive measure that equates all the needs, resources, and outcomes of welfare transfers, efforts to achieve equity aim not to produce a precise balance, but rather a reasonable allocation of resources within the limits of knowledge. Fairness here reflects a certain proportionality between needs and the resources necessary to meet them. To make informed decisions in allocating social transfers, policymakers should have data on the scope of problems, what is being spent on them, and the extent to which the problem is being resolved by these efforts.

Getting the numbers right on the expenditure side of social transfers requires going beyond the conventional account of welfare spending. As suggested in Chapter 2, an accurate ledger for social accounting would require taking the full measure of welfare transfers, including indirect tax expenditures (benefiting, for example, homeowners, students, employees, veterans, and farmers) as well as conventional direct social welfare expenditures, be they public or private. Much of the data are available and need only to be drawn together in an inclusive annual report on social welfare expenditures in order to considerably reframe the discussion of welfare spending.

Notes

1. Eveline M. Burns, *Social Security and Public Policy* (New York: McGraw-Hill, 1956), ix.
2. T. H. Marshall, "Value Problems of Welfare Capitalism," *Journal of Social Policy* 1(1) (January 1972): 19–20.
3. For further discussion of social and economic markets, see Neil Gilbert, *Capitalism and the Welfare State* (New Haven, Conn.: Yale University Press, 1983) and Neil Gilbert and Barbara

Gilbert, *The Enabling State: Modern Welfare Capitalism in America* (New York: Oxford University Press, 1989).

4. Robert Reich, *The Next American Frontier* (New York: Times Books, 1983), 247.

5. For a review of these developments, see Alfred Kahn and Sheila Kamerman (eds.), *Privatization and the Welfare State* (Princeton, N.J.: Princeton University Press, 1989) and Norman Johnson (ed.), *Private Markets in Health and Welfare* (Oxford, England: Berg Publishers, 1995).

6. Gilbert and Gilbert, 129.

7. Marshall, "Value Problems of Welfare Capitalism."

8. For example, see Richard Titmuss, *Commitment to Welfare* (New York: Pantheon Books, 1970), 124; and Martin Wolins, "The Societal Function of Social Welfare," *New Perspectives* 1(1) (Spring 1967), 5.

9. Mayer Zald (ed.), *Social Welfare Institutions* (New York: John Wiley & Sons, 1965), 4.

10. Neil Gilbert, *Welfare Justice: Restoring Social Equity* (New Haven, Conn.: Yale University Press, 1995).

11. Lawrence Mead, *Beyond Entitlement: The Social Obligations of Citizenship* (New York: Free Press, 1986).

12. The analytic questions with which we will deal have also been explored by Martin Rein, *Social Policy* (New York: Random House, 1970); Titmuss, *Commitment to Welfare*, 130–36; Kahn, *Theory and Practice of Social Planning*, 192–213; and Gilbert Steiner, *The State of Welfare* (Washington, D.C.: Brookings Institution, 1971), 1–30.

13. This case analysis draws substantially on material originally presented in Neil Gilbert, "The Transformation of Social Services," *Social Service Review*, 51(4) (December 1977): 624–49.

14. Martha Derthick, *Uncontrollable Spending for Social Services Grants* (Washington, D.C.: Brookings Institution, 1975), 8.

15. Alan Pardini and David Lindeman, *Eight State Comparative Report on Social Services*, Working Paper No. 21 (San Francisco: University of California, Aging Health Policy Center, 1982).

16. A prominent example of the extreme faith on which the movement for intensive services by trained caseworkers relied is expressed in the design of a study that compared special intensive services by professional caseworkers with fifty multiproblem families over two and a half years to a control group receiving routine services by staff without professional training. The primary assumption on which the study is based is that some degree of variation in social casework skills can have a significant impact on the severe problems created by economic deprivation. The results of this study showed no significant differences between the two client groups and were deemed inconclusive due to methodological flaws. But it is in the methodological design that faith is revealed. The goals of the service and how workers' activities related to these goals were defined in such general terms as to be unmeasurable. See Gordon E. Brown (ed.), *The Multiproblem Dilemma: A Social Research Demonstration with Multiproblem Families* (Metuchen, N.J.: Scarecrow Press, 1968).

17. Derthick, *Uncontrollable Spending for Social Services Grants*, 9.

18. President's Commission on Income Maintenance, Background Papers (Washington, D.C.: Government Printing Office, 1970), 307.

19. Joel F. Handler and Jane Hollingsworth, *The Deserving Poor: A Study of Welfare Administration* (Chicago: Markham Publishing, 1971), 127.

20. Derthick, *Uncontrollable Spending for Social Services Grants*, 19.

21. Mildred Rein, "Social Services as a Work Strategy," *Social Service Review*, 49 (December 1975): 519.

22. Derthick, *Uncontrollable Spending for Social Services Grants*, 19.

23. Social and Rehabilitation Service, Department of Health, Education, and Welfare, Social Services U.S.A., Oct.–Dec. 1975, Publication No. SRS 76-03300 (Washington, D.C.: National Center of Social Statistics, 1975), 7.

24. *Washington Social Legislation Bulletin*, 31(32) (April 23, 1990): 125.

25. The evolution of caretaking services is discussed in Robert Morris and Delwin Anderson, "Personal Care Services: An Identity for Social Work," *Social Service Review*, 49 (June 1975): 157–74.

26. Gilbert Y. Steiner, *The State of Welfare* (Washington, D.C.: Brookings Institution, 1971), 106–10.

27. There were ways to circumvent this restriction. In practice, for example, it was not uncommon for a donation to be made by a United Fund Organization with the request that the contribution be used to support a particular type of activity in a specified community, one performed only by an agency affiliated with the United Fund Organization. In this fashion, private donations could be covertly earmarked as the local share for a designated agency. See, for example, Booz, Allen, and Hamilton, *Purchase of Social Service—Study of the Experience of Three States in Purchase of Service by Contract Under the Provisions of the 1967 Amendments to the Social Security Act*, Report Submitted to the Social and Rehabilitation Service, January 29, 1971 (distributed by National Technical Information Service, U.S. Department of Commerce), 40–42.

28. Lester Salamon and Alan Abramson, *The Federal Budget and the Non-Profit Sector* (Washington, D.C.: Urban Institute Press, 1982), 64.

29. Derthick, *Uncontrollable Spending for Social Services Grants*, 100–101.

30. Alva Myrdal, *Nation and Family* (MIT Paperback Edition) (Cambridge, Mass.: MIT Press, 1968), 1.

31. More precisely, the block grant allocation was based on the highest level of each state's spending calculated on their AFDC expenditures in 1994, 1995, or the average expenditure from 1992 to 1994. In addition, the Act provided a contingency fund to meet increases in needs experienced by the states.

32. Jocelyn Guyer, Cindy Mann, and David Super, *The Timeline for Implementing the New Welfare Law* (Washington D.C.: Center on Budget and Policy Priorities, 1996), 2.

33. Aristotle, *The Politics* (Modern Library Edition) (New York: Random House, 1943), 260–63.

34. Gregory Vlastos, "Justice and Equality," in Richard Brandt (ed.), *Social Justice* (Englewood Cliffs, N.J.: Prentice Hall, 1962), 32.

35. Cited in Karl de Schweinitz, *England's Road to Social Security* (Perpetua ed.) (New York: A. S. Barnes, 1961), 123.

36. U.S. Department of Health, Education and Welfare, *Work in America* (Washington, D.C.: Government Printing Office, 1972).

37. See, for example, William Shannon, "A Radical, Direct, Simple, Utopian Alternative to DayCare Centers," *New York Times Magazine*, April 30, 1972; and Sheila M. Rothman, "Other People's Children: The Day Care Experience in America," *Public Interest*, 30 (Winter 1973): 11–27.

38. William Frankena, "The Concept of Social Justice," in Richard Brandt (ed.), *Social Justice* (Englewood Cliffs, N.J.: Prentice Hall, 1962), 23.

39. See Robert Hunter, *Poverty*, Peter d'A Jones (ed.) (Torchbook ed.) (New York: Harper & Row, 1965), 51–52.

40. James Lin and Jared Bernstein, "What We Need To Get By—A Basic Standard of Living Costs $48,778, and Nearly a Third of Families Fall Short." *Economic Policy Institute Briefing Paper #224*, October, 29, 2008.

41. Karl Marx, *Das Kapital*, Friedrich Engels (ed.), Vol. 1 (Gateway Edition) (Chicago: Henry Regnery 1959), 33–34.

42. For example, see Richard Titmuss, "Equity, Adequacy, and Innovation in Social Security," *International Social Security Review*, 2 (1970): 250–67.

43. T. H. Marshall, *Class, Citizenship, and Social Development* (Anchor Books Edition) (New York: Doubleday, 1965), 258–59.

44. An analysis of cost effectiveness as it is expressed in different income-maintenance strategies is provided by James Cutt, "Income Support Programmes for Families with Children: Alternatives for Canada," *International Social Security Review*, 23(1) (1970): 100–12.

45. Titmuss, *Commitment to Welfare*, 69–71.

46. "Learnfare: Policy Implications," *Youth Law News*, May/June, 1989, 12–13.

47. Peter Blau, *Bureaucracy in Modern Society* (New York: Random House, 1956), 107.

48. Various studies on the War on Poverty and Model Cities have documented this result. See, for example, Ralph Kramer, *Participation of the Poor* (Englewood Cliffs, N.J.: Prentice Hall, 1969); Neil Gilbert, *Clients or Constituents* (San Francisco: Jossey-Bass, 1970); Neil Gilbert and Harry Specht, *Dynamics of Community Planning* (Cambridge, Mass.: Ballinger, 1977).

49. Burns, *Social Security and Public Policy*, 231.

50. Davis McEntire and Joanne Haworth, "Two Functions of Public Welfare: Income Maintenance and Social Services," *Social Work*, 12(1) (January 1967): 24–25.

51. Genevieve Carter, "Public Welfare," in Henry S. Maas (ed.), *Research in the Social Services: A Five Year Review* (New York: National Association of Social Workers, 1971), 224.

52. Handler and Hollingsworth, "The Administration of Social Services and the Structure of Dependency," 418. For a comprehensive historical review of the issues in "separation of services," see Winfred Bell, "Too Few Services to Separate," *Social Work*, 18(2) (March 1973): 66–77.

53. Irving Piliavin and Alan Gross, "The Effects of Separation of Services and Income Maintenance on AFDC Recipients," *Social Service Review*, 51 (September 1977): 389–406. Also, see Bill Benton, Jr., "Separation Revisited," *Public Welfare*, 38(2) (Spring 1980): 15–21.

54. Sar Levitan and Robert Taggart, III, *Social Experimentation and Manpower Policy: The Rhetoric and the Reality* (Baltimore: Johns Hopkins University Press, 1971), 53.

55. Mary Bryna Sunger, "Generating Employment for AFDC Mothers," *Social Service Review*, 58(1) (March 1984): 32.

56. Judith Gueron, "Reforming Welfare with Work," *Public Welfare* (Fall 1987): 13–25.

57. Steiner, The *State of Welfare*.

58. Alec Levenson et al., "Welfare Reform and the Employment Prospects of Welfare Recipients," *Jobs and Capital*, 6(3) (Summer 1997): 36–41.

59. Steiner, The *State of Welfare*, p. 26.

60. Joseph Pechman, Henry Aaron, and Michael Taussig, *Social Security: Perspectives for Reform* (Washington, D.C.: Brookings Institution, 1968).

61. For a detailed discussion of these inequities, see Neil Gilbert, *Welfare Justice*, 1995.

62. Martha Ozawa, "Who Receives Subsidies Through Social Security and How Much?" *Social Work*, 27(2) (1982): 129–36.

4

The Basis of Social Allocations

> "I suppose you mean that you have no money to pay wages in," said I. "But the credit given the worker at the government storehouse answers to his wages with us. How is the amount of the credit given respectively to the workers in different lines determined? By what title does the individual claim his particular share? What is the basis of allotment?"
>
> "His title," replied Doctor Leete, "is his humanity. The basis of his claim is the fact that he is a man."
>
> Edward Bellamy
Looking Backward, 1888

> From each according to his abilities, to each according to his needs.
>
> Karl Marx
Critique of the Gotha Programme, 1874

In his classic utopian novel, *Looking Backward*, Edward Bellamy views the "good society" as a place where every individual can claim an equal share of the goods and services produced by the nation. Citizens are guaranteed a comfortable standard of living from, as Bellamy put it, "cradle to grave." Entitlement does not depend on being rich or poor, single or married, brilliant or dull, healthy or ill; instead, a person's entitlement is his or her humanity.[1] In Bellamy's vision, social allocations are arranged according to the principle that everyone deserves an equal share, with one exception. That is, Doctor Leete explains, "A man able to do duty [i.e., work] and persistently refusing is sentenced to solitary imprisonment on bread and water 'til he consents."[2] Although this may seem harsh, in Bellamy's society work roles are structured to dignify every task and to allow a choice of occupations broad enough to suit individual preferences. Nevertheless, as an introduction to the allocative dimension of choice in social welfare policy, there is perhaps some small comfort in noting that, even in a utopia of rationality, harmony, and consensus, problems of social allocation are not entirely amenable to neat, unqualified solutions.

Who Shall Benefit?

In the real world, few social welfare policy issues engender more vigorous debate than who shall benefit and the manner in which entitlement is defined. The rules used to determine who benefits from any social welfare policy may be predicated on a wide and diverse range of criteria ranging from the unusual (Native American blood quantum) to the mundane (amount of money earned). We refer to the general principles that underlie these criteria as the bases of social allocations.

Attempts to develop principles of eligibility traditionally begin with the distinction between universalism and selectivity. *Universalism* denotes benefits made available to an entire population as a basic right. Examples are Social Security retirees and public education for the young. *Selectivity* denotes benefits made available on the basis of individual need, usually determined by a test of income. Examples include public assistance and public housing.

The social policy literature contains an ongoing debate between proponents of universal and selective principles.[3] Universalists view social policy as society's proper response to those ordinary life problems faced by all members of the community—not just the poor, the disabled, or those facing special hardships. For universalists, all citizens are "at risk" in the sense that all of us, at one time or another, face a variety of common social needs. The proper aim of the welfare state, accordingly, is to organize broad programs of response, without differentiating among rich or poor, men or women, or other citizen categories.

Young people, for example, need care and education. Those who are ill need health care. The elderly, disabled, and unemployed need income support. Universalists favor public arrangements that address these needs on the basis of a general entitlement, as a social right comparable to the political rights we take for granted. Social insurance, public education, healthcare for the aged—programs available without regard to income—stand as the models for a proper welfare society.

Universalists also emphasize the value of social effectiveness, the need, noted earlier, to preserve the dignity of the individual and the cohesion of society. Programs designed for everyone create an equality that is undermined by restricting elegibility to particular groups. Programs based on economic determinations are especially divisive, accentuating differences in society that frequently take on moral as well as economic meanings. Those who receive benefits often feel *demeaned*, even when their rights to benefits are clear. Receiving food stamps, for example, or being assigned to a special class for the educationally impaired, is for many a sign of failure, an embarrassing, stigmatizing experience. "Invidious rationing for the poor," as Alvin Schorr puts it, "does not seem a sound principle for a welfare state."[4]

Universalists, finally, argue the *political* advantages of social programs based on inclusiveness, citing the strength throughout the world of policies aiding broad populations. Universal programs, admittedly, cost more, but they are far more popular than means-tested programs that focus on marginal social groups. The history of social provision in the United States—AFDC being the most notable example—vividly demonstrates the political vulnerability of programs exclusively for the poor.

Selectivists see the world very differently. They view the appropriate scope of social policy in terms of carefully targeted beneficiaries. Families or individuals demonstrating need, they believe, should have priority for assistance. Rather than sponsoring universally available entitlements, selectivists favor benefits that are restricted. Underlying this perspective is the view that a proper social policy, especially

CAPSULE 4.1 • *Targeting within Universalism*

We can draw two conclusions from the history of social provision in the United States. First, targeted antipoverty efforts have generally been inadequately funded, demeaning to the poor, and politically unsustainable. Second, some kinds of (relatively) universal social policy have succeeded politically. And within the framework of universal programs, less privileged people have received extra benefits without stigma. I call this pattern "targeting within universalism" and suggest it could become the basis for a revitalized strategy against poverty.

Those who want to help the poor should not try to devise new programs finely targeted to low-income people or the "underclass." They should forget about reforming means-tested public assistance programs. Rather, they should aim at bypassing and ultimately displacing "welfare" with new policies that address the needs of the less privileged in the context of programs that also serve middle-class and stable working-class citizens.

Theda Skocpol, "Sustainable Social Policy: Fighting Poverty Without Poverty Programs," *The American Prospect*, 2 (Summer 1990): 59, 67.

in an era of fiscal constraint, must be a limited social policy; that people who can afford to meet their own needs should not receive government handouts; and that taxpayers should focus their help on that margin of the population legitimately unable to fend for themselves.

Means-testing, obviously, is a direct way of confining social benefits. Circumscribing eligibility according to need, selectivists argue, reduces overall spending, overcomes the tendency for welfare to benefit the politically powerful middle class, and ensures that available funds focus on those in the most dire straits. The argument certainly is a reasonable one. If we wish to attack poverty, we must focus on the poor—job training to counter poor employment skills, Head Start to provide educational enrichment, and daycare to enable TANF moms to enter the job market. If we are concerned with effective antipoverty policies, why should money be wasted on people not in great need, or in no need at all?

But neither side is quite satisfied to let the debate rest here. Each lays claim to at least a share of the values claimed by the opposition. Universalists, for example, claim cost effectiveness because broad prevention programs such as comprehensive prenatal healthcare or broad scope preschool programs have the potential to avoid or reduce future problems—and their associated costs—in a way that case-by-case eligibility determination cannot. In the long run, it is argued, "an ounce of prevention" creates economic savings for the larger community. As a bonus, universal allocations are said to be less expensive to administer than selective allocations because they do not require constant screening, checkups, and benefit adjustments to ensure the proper level of assistance.

Universalists also argue that comprehensive policies, properly constituted, can be redistributive, concentrating assistance on those with the greatest needs. This is Theda Skocpol's argument in Capsule 4.1. For example, "tax backs" can be employed to shift the burden of universal benefits to the economically better off. That is, by including the value of universal benefits in taxable income, richer individuals and families wind up supporting a disproportionate part of the costs involved.[5] Many countries, for example, including the United States, include at least a portion of the value of social security benefits in taxable income. And increasing numbers are beginning to tax children's allowances. In this fashion, programs for everyone are substantially financed by those most able to pay.

Universal programs, indeed, especially in the health field, have been forced by financial presures in recent years to forsake their long-standing "equal charge" principle. Medicare, for example, from its inception, imposed the same premium fee on all paticipants, whatever their income level. Since 2003, however, Medicare has moved from "treat everybody the same" toward means-testing. Medicare benefits for drug prescriptions and outpatient care, in particular, now require middle-class and affluent recipients to pay substantially higher program premiums than low-income beneficiaries.

Universal services, on the *outlay* side, can also be adjusted to provide a basic level of assistance to all while concentrating additional help on those in greatest need. In this way, programs for the poor, as Nicholas Lemann states, can "be contained (to some extent camouflaged) within programs to help the middle class."[6] Many countries follow this approach, modifying programs of universal scope to address the needs of the poor. In the United States, for example, recent alterations in the Medicare health insurance program have taken this direction. European welfare states have moved similarly. In Great Britain, public health home visits for new mothers are universal, but additional visits are focused on those mothers, and children, at greater risk. In France (see Capsule 4.2), lone parents, low-income families, and disabled children receive, in addition to the standard family allowance, a special targeted supplement.

Selectivists claim their own version of social effectiveness. If society seeks to move toward greater equality, they argue, offering benefits to the poor alone is bound to be more effective than allocations for everyone. Provisions targeted on the needy—whether through education, healthcare, childcare, or housing—clearly reduce the social and economic discrepancies that produce tension and hostility in our society. Given vast unmet needs, equity would seem to demand that the poor receive first call on scarce public resources.

These are some of the general issues that provide a framework for the universal–selective debate. To place this debate in a substantive context, let us illustrate how the choice between universal and selective principles translates into specific policy proposals. And let us also examine the values and assumptions that underlie these principles when they are applied.

Universality and Selectivity in Income Maintenance

In the decades-long dialogue concerning income maintenance programs, numerous reform measures have been put forth by academicians and politicians.[7] These proposals

CAPSULE 4.2 • *The Fine Feathered (Gallic) Nest*

Scarcely three days old, Thomas Meilleroux slept softly in Paris's Hôpital Saint-Vincent-de-Paul, a pink shell of tiny fist tucked under his head. He had every right to wear an air of blissful unconcern. The moment Christine, his mother, announced her pregnancy, social security mailed a thick folder, the *carnet de maternité*.

It brought medications, exams, childbirth classes, and—from the sixth month—a monthly pregnancy allowance of 812 francs (about $135 U.S.). Afterward: ten visits to a physical therapist to tone the stretch-marked tummy. "They make it so easy, you don't even have to think," says Christine. "I never paid a cent."

Now our little bundle of *joie* is three months old. Young Thomas happens to be a firstborn. If he were a second child, Christine would collect a hundred-dollar-a-month family allowance until his 18th year. Were he the third, she'd pocket $200. For a fourth, $330. Single parents, low-income families, and handicapped children get more.

The goal is to raise the birthrate and ensure a decent living standard. But the biggest benefit of the free care lavished on expectant mothers (and a legally enforced maternity leave of at least 16 weeks at 80 percent pay) is an infant-mortality rate of 7.6 per thousand, among the world's lowest—well below the United States' 10.4.

The basic family allowance is not tied to income. Even the matron who shops for her precious heirs in Christian Dior Bébé collects. After all, *c'est son droit*—it's her right.

In France social welfare is not a charity but a right of citizenship inviolable as the August vacation.

From "The Fine Feathered Nest" by Cathy Newman, *National Geographic*, July 1989. Reprinted by permission of National Geographic Image Collection.

can be analyzed from different perspectives. For example, they can be placed along a continuum of generosity, depending on where they define the poverty level and the proposed amount of financial aid they offer. Alternatively, they can be viewed according to their decision-making structure, varying by the degree to which policy is centralized or localized. Most recently, debate has centered on issues of moral values and reciprocity, with conservatives promoting systems of public aid focusing on jobs, time-limited assistance, and the reduction of teen pregnancy.

In the years of debate over the "proper" basis for allocating cash benefits, a variety of program reforms have been advocated. In the 1960s and 1970s, the choice between universality and selectivity was debated in terms of two broad program options: guaranteed income programs (frequently referred to as negative income taxes) and children's allowances (sometimes called family allowances). Since the 1980s, the nature of the debate has changed as efforts have been made to find compromises between universalism and selectivity, and variant programs such as the Earned Income Tax Credit (EITC) have achieved considerable success.

Guaranteed income programs are defined by two characteristics: the provision of a defined minimum subsidy for families with little or no income and the utilization of a formula to determine how much this subsidy decreases as earnings increase. This formula represents what economists call a negative tax. Most proposals suggest administering the guarantee through the Internal Revenue Service, using the same procedures by which personal income taxes are collected and refunds distributed. Simply stated, the income tax structure would become a two-way operation with money flowing to the government from people with incomes above a certain level and money flowing from the government to people with incomes below that level. In either case, the amount paid in or out would be graduated according to income. An essential feature of the plan is that the allocation of benefits is tied directly to an income test and is thereby based on the principle of selectivity.

Schemes for a children's allowance, on the other hand, usually involve the provision of a *demogrant*, "a uniform payment to certain categories of persons identified only by demographic (usually age) characteristics."[8] More than eighty nations throughout the world, including most of the industrial West (but not the United States), offer some form of children's allowance as an integral part of their welfare system. (The United States, however, provides a dependents exemption within its federal income tax, which achieves some of the same purposes.) The development of children's allowances has achieved widespread support for various reasons, among them the fact that children represent a substantial proportion of the poor and, wherever one places the blame and however one perceives the causes of poverty, children are clearly innocent victims. An essential characteristic of the demogrant is that benefits are allocated to *all* families, regardless of economic circumstances, thereby reflecting the principle of universality.[9] Table 4.1 shows four child-allowance variations.

To illustrate the issues that arise in applying the universal–selective framework, the basic features of two classic income maintenance proposals will be described. The first is the negative tax program tested experimentally in the mid-1970s in Seattle and Denver.[10] The second is the children's allowance proposal developed in 1974 by Martha Ozawa, one of the foremost advocates of this type of program in the United States.[11]

Seattle and Denver Income Maintenance Experiments

The Seattle and Denver Income Maintenance Experiments (SIME/DIME) were the largest and most carefully controlled income maintenance experiments in history. The sample enrollment in the experiment included 4706 families, 44 percent assigned to the control group and the remainder divided among eleven experimental groups. Each experimental group received one of three guaranteed levels of annual income—$3800, $4800, and $5600—and was taxed at varying rates. Four negative tax rates were used: two constant tax rates (one of 50 percent and the other of 70 percent) and two varying tax rates that started at 70 percent and 80 percent and declined as income increased. Using the 50 percent constant tax rate and the $5600 subsidy as an example, a recipient family with no earned income would be paid $5600 a year. For each dollar earned, their grant would be reduced by 50 cents. With this negative tax rate, an income of $11,200 is the "break-even level," the point at which the grant drops to zero.

Children's Allowance

The Ozawa proposal, formulated in 1974, involved an allotment of $60 a month for each child, with payments independent of family income or other eligibility conditions.

TABLE 4.1   *Child Allowance Standards in France, Japan, Sweden, and the United Kingdom, 1995*

France

Age: Under 18 (20 for students, apprentices, vocational trainees, or disabled).

Coverage: Payable monthly to families with two or more children.

Benefit amount: $124 for two children; $159 for third and each subsequent child; plus a $35 increase for each child aged 10–15; and $62 for each child beyond age 15. Young child allowance is $178, payable beginning with the fifth month of pregnancy until the third month after birth without means test, then until age 3 subject to a means test. Additional allowances payable depending on means test, single parenthood, etc.

Japan

Age: First child under 4 and second and subsequent child under 3.

Coverage: Payable monthly to residents with one or more children who meet an income test. Requirements for a family of four: income below $36,540 a year.

Benefit amount: $51 for first and second child; $102 for third and each subsequent child.

Sweden

Age: Under 16 (20 for students).

Coverage: Payable monthly to all residents with one or more children.

Benefit amount: $100 for first child; $200 for second; $326 for third; $479 for fourth; and $598 for five or more children.

United Kingdom

Age: Under 16 (19 for full-time students in nonadvanced education).

Coverage: Payable weekly to residents with one or more children.

Benefit amount: $16 for first child; $13 for each additional child; plus supplement of $10 for the first child of a single parent.

Source: Ilene R. Zeitzer, "Social Insurance Provisions for Children with Disabilities," *Social Security Bulletin,* 58(3), Fall 1995, 32–48.

Under the proposal, the allowance itself constituted taxable income. When translated into dollars and cents, this meant that families of equal size received exactly the same benefits. Depending on their income, however, these families ended up returning different amounts of the allowance to the government through their income taxes. A family with income low enough to fall below the federal tax threshold, for example, would not have its allowance taxed at all, whereas a family in the 15 percent bracket would have a portion of the allowance "taxed back." Households with higher incomes, in higher tax brackets, would find their allowance reduced by greater amounts.

In this fashion, the net gain received by the allowance varies by income. The significance of this arrangement is that it makes the children's allowance a benefit that is universal at the point of distribution, but selective at the point of consumption. This is not an attribute only of children's allowance. When we consider how benefits are financed, some form of selectivity creeps into virtually all universal schemes.

As Reddin has demonstrated, universal benefits are "those in which the universal gene is dominant but where there are also variant forms of 'recessive' selective genes incorporated in the structure."[12]

More recent proposals have suggested repealing the existing federal income tax exemption for children and replacing it with a children's allowance.[13] This would have a decided redistributive impact because the exemption—$3650 per child in 2009—benefits upper-income parents far more than lower-income parents. Parents in the 35 percent income tax bracket in 2009, for example, received tax relief worth $1278 (35 percent of $3650) per child whereas parents in the 15 percent bracket received just $548. And poor parents, those earning so little that they pay no taxes, got no benefit. Eliminating the exemption would save a sum that, transformed into a universal allowance, could provide all parents over a thousand dollars per child per year.

A Negative Income Tax for Workers: The Earned Income Tax Credit

The pros and cons of negative income and child allowance proposals have been strongly argued for some time. Neither plan, however, proved politically popular. Rather than making sweeping comprehensive changes in our system of social welfare, citizens and elected officials have generally been content to live with a variety of separate programs geared to specific needs and segments of the population, and reflecting different principles and values. Although our political system generally avoids grand schemes of comprehensive reform, both the negative income tax and the children's allowance have been incorporated, in modest and camouflaged forms, into our ongoing social policies.

The case of the personal exemption has been noted. Tax-paying families have long received exemptions for each of their dependents, providing a significant form of income support that varies with family obligations. The Internal Revenue Code also incorporates a negative income tax in the form of the EITC. The credit, first enacted in 1974, contains many of the key characteristics of guaranteed income schemes. It provides a basic income subsidy to low-income families, it utilizes a formula to determine how subsidies decrease as earned income increases, and it is administered through the tax code. The EITC is different from a guaranteed income plan, however, in that it covers only part of the population (i.e., low-income wage-earning families). People who don't work are not covered.

Under EITC provisions for tax year 2009, as Figure 4.1 indicates, families earning up to $43,415 are eligible for credits. The credit is greatest—the maximum being $5028—for families with incomes a bit over $20,000. As income rises above this amount, the credit is reduced, ultimately phasing out around $43,000. What makes the arrangement a negative tax is its *refundability*. That is, when the value of the credit exceeds the amount of income taxes owed, the worker receives a cash rebate.[14]

The EITC only covers workers, so, unlike the SIME/DIME demonstration, it has a salutary impact on employment. In this sense, it is akin to a wage subsidy,

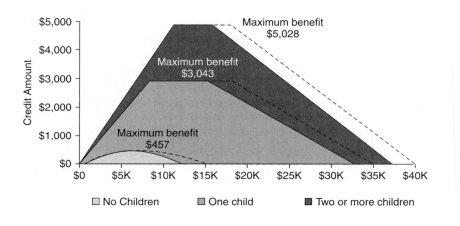

FIGURE 4.1   *The Earned Income Credit, 2009.*

Note: Married couples with income in the phaseout range qualify for a higher credit than single parents—shown by the dashed lines.

concentrating its benefits on those who are poor *even though* they work. Up to a point at least, the more people work, the more they get—quite the opposite of other negative tax and guaranteed income plans. According to David Ellwood, the EITC avoids the "conundrums" of welfare:

> The rewards of work are increased, not diminished. Benefits go only to those with an earned income. People are helped without any need of a stigmatizing, invasive, and often degrading welfare system, and their autonomy is increased, not decreased. Since it truly would be part of the tax system, people would not be isolated. The negative impact on the work effort of the poor is likely to be small if it exists at all, but the benefits to the working poor may be large. And employers would have no reason to change their hiring practices. Their cost of doing business would essentially be unchanged except for slight additional administrative costs for employers who provided negative withholding.[15]

Since it is restricted to working families, the EITC is hardly the broad-brush measure proposed in the 1960s and 1970s by negative tax advocates. Moreover, EITC benefits are more modest than the most proposed negative income tax guarantees. Nevertheless, the EITC exists and the negative income tax doesn't. For all practical purposes, indeed, the negative income tax idea has faded to near oblivion, and is not likely to be revived as part of any income strategy in the near future. Refundable credits on the EITC model, on the other hand, constitute an antipoverty measure with substantial promise. Combined with the income tax exemption, refundable credits offer a mechanism for significant income support—especially for low-wage earners. In 2008, approximately 25 million taxpayers received nearly $50 billion in EITC benefits—a sum considerably larger than the total spent on TANF. Were the EITC further liberalized and tied more firmly to family size, it could go even farther in reducing poverty in this country.

Child Support and Asset Building

Several other income support ideas have also received considerable attention over the past decade, although none with significant legislative outcomes. Scholars like Irwin Garfinkel and John Ellwood, for example, have been articulate proponents of Child Support Assurance, an antipoverty approach aimed at assuring a reasonable level of income to children in single-parent families. Given the difficulty in collecting child support from absent parents, Child Support Assurance would make it the responsibility of government to guarantee such children $2000 to $2500 per year. The U.S. Treasury would distribute these checks automatically, month by month, while at the same time working with the states to make absent parents pay their share. This arrangement would relieve poor moms, in particular, of the difficult, time-consuming, and often futile legal and personal effort to secure child support.[16]

A second proposal, advanced by Bruce Ackerman and Anne Alstott in their 1999 book *The Stakeholder Society*, would provide every young adult a public contribution of $80,000 when they start college, or turn 21.[17] Ackerman and Alstott see such a universal cash grant confronting basic inequalities in America by enabling young people just starting out in life to invest in their futures. The grant—they call it a "stake"—would particularly benefit individuals from poor families, helping them to pay for college, establish a household, and start out successfully on the road to an adult life. (See Capsule 4.3.)

CAPSULE 4.3 • *Stakeholding for Equal Opportunity*

Despite the economic boom, real wages for men have declined, and only the massive entry by women into the workplace has prevented many families from sinking to income levels lower than in the 1970s. Trickle-down economics has failed to trickle.

One way [to address this issue] is to give every young American adult a stake of $80,000 as a birthright of citizenship. The stake should be financed by an annual wealth tax, equal to 2 percent of every individual's wealth in excess of $180,000. Under this "flat tax," the wealthiest 12 percent of Americans will pay 40 percent of the entire bill.

Stakeholders should be free to use their money for any purpose they see fit: to start a business or pay for higher education, to buy a house or raise a family or save for the future. At the end of their lives, stakeholders should repay the $80,000 at death if this is financially possible.

For the rest of their lives, stakeholders will know that their $80,000 contributed to their individual pursuits of happiness. This will prompt a deeper loyalty to the country. The Declaration of Independence's promise of equality and freedom will take on a new meaning, encouraging stakeholders to take their responsibilities as citizens more seriously and make America a better place for their successors.

A similar proposal by Michael Sherraden calls for the establishment of Children's Savings Accounts. The accounts approach is one element in a "social investment strategy" to build the long-term assets of the poor.[18] Sherraden's idea is for the federal government to fund bank accounts for poor children, enabling them to accumulate a nest egg that would ultimately be available for purposes such as college or buying a home.

Investment strategies such as stakeholding and children's accounts focus on the accumulation of resources rather than simple income maintenance. Asset building is viewed as a particularly valuable approach to reducing child poverty. Child savings accounts, for example, would be universal in scope, with every child under 18 receiving annual "deposits" from Uncle Sam and, perhaps, supplemental tax-favored contributions from family members. For Sherraden,

> CSAs [child savings accounts] are consistent with our political values and the imperative to develop the human and social capital of our nation's children. Just as another asset-based policy, the GI Bill, promoted human and social capital in the middle of the twentieth century—with enormous payoffs in educational attainment, increased productivity, and widespread home ownership—a CSA policy would democratize educational opportunity, spread the distribution of wealth, build strong households and communities, and promote economic growth.[19]

To some degree, all three of these proposals have been developed in an effort to stimulate fresh thinking and fresh action about child poverty given the failure of the child allowance movement of the 1960s and 1970s. But whereas Child Support Assurance seeks to provide direct cash aid for immediate needs, asset-building strategies are targeted on long-term goals. And while neither CSAs nor asset approaches have engendered much political excitement, wealth-building programs, especially those operating in a fashion to bolster retirement income and the Social Security system, have recently appeared on the legislative radar screen.

Social Effectiveness and Cost Effectiveness

When the abstract principles of the universal–selective debate are applied to choices among concrete alternatives, such as the income maintenance schemes just described, or to existing programs such as Social Security or public aid, the discussion generally centers on considerations of social effectiveness and cost effectiveness, the definition of these values, and assumptions regarding policy elements that facilitate and impede their realization.

Measures of cost effectiveness in income maintenance are usually determined by comparing the total costs of the alternative schemes, the extent to which the allocated funds fill the poverty gap, and the amount of "seepage" to the nonpoor. Implicit in this is a definition of income maintenance that seeks to improve the lot of the statistically defined poor (those people with annual incomes below the federal poverty line).

On the basis of these criteria, the negative income tax is clearly superior to child allowances or asset programs. That is, benefits such as the EITC provide higher levels of assistance to poor families with only modest seepage to better-off income groups.

The same is true of today's public assistance programs. While universal benefits, available to citizens of all income classes, certainly help to alleviate poverty, they are relatively inefficient in doing so because only a small portion of their overall value assists the poor. This is especially true for children and families. Irwin Garfinkel, for example, found that in the 1990s single-parent families—a group particularly vulnerable to poverty—received a share of universal benefits about equal to their percentage of the overall population. In stark contrast, they received a full 74 percent of targeted, means-tested transfers.[20]

Selecting the poor for benefits, not unexpectedly, is an efficient antipoverty strategy. However, this advantage is hardly impressive if the goal of public policy is to improve the lot of children in general, an important objective given the fact that working and middle-class families, as well as the poor, frequently need help to ensure the welfare of their members. From this viewpoint, cost effectiveness is defined quite differently and universal schemes may be preferable. As Cutt points out,

> Universal schemes may be considered to be redistributive in a horizontal sense—from the childless to those with children—and therefore may be seen as having a broader objective than a selective scheme, specifically the alleviation of need among children in any income group, rather than the more tightly focused alleviation of need in families defined as poor in a statistical sense.[21]

On the other side of the ledger, social effectiveness tends to be identified with the universal approach, although here, too, a definitive case is lacking. Estimates concerning the social effectiveness of income maintenance schemes are based on certain assumptions about the harmful consequences of targeted antipoverty approaches. These consequences include the effects on work, childbearing, family stability, stigmatization, and social integration. To illustrate these factors, let us review some relevant research findings.

Work Incentives

All social welfare benefits, to some extent, provide an incentive for the very circumstances they are established to ameliorate. Unemployment insurance makes it easier to be unemployed. Public assistance makes it easier to support a child without working. In this sense there is a germ of truth in the traditional contention of conservatives that welfare "causes" dependency.[22] To the extent that they eliminate some degree of economic stress, therefore, both SIME/DIME and children's allowances have some negative effect on the incentive to work.

The engineers of welfare reform in the 1960s and 1970s were sensitive to these "perverse incentives" and sought to arrange payments in ways that would minimize them. Since the disincentive to work in a guaranteed income arrangement such as SIME/DIME was great because the basic payment in a zero-work/zero-income situation was high, these programs sought to build in countervailing inducements. As we have seen, this was accomplished by trying to make work attractive by permitting wage earners to keep a significant portion of their income. Rather than reducing their benefits dollar for dollar against their work income, the "tax" on work implicit in the benefit formula was kept low so as not to discourage recipients from getting and keeping jobs.

One of the most perplexing issues in the design of negative income tax schemes is the impact of different tax rates on work incentives. Simply put, how does a 30-, 60-, or 90-cent reduction in grant payments for each dollar of income earned affect a beneficiary's motivation to work? And how do these effects differ for grants offering low and high levels of support? The issue is complex because the lines of influence may flow in both directions. That is, high tax rates may be an inducement as well as a deterrent to greater work effort. The popular belief is that the person who gets to keep only 50 cents on a dollar is less inclined to work than the person who keeps 90 cents. However, assuming the desire for a certain standard of living, an individual who keeps only 50 cents may work harder and longer just to maintain his or her position, whereas the person who keeps 90 cents initially has more money to spend and may opt to enjoy more leisure time rather than supplement his or her income by additional work. That is to say, except for extreme cases where the tax rate approaches 100 percent, the point at which a worker may decide that the additional income is not worth the effort is indeterminate.

Regarding the ordinary federal income tax, for example, there is little evidence to support the belief that high tax rates necessarily have a deleterious influence on work. After reviewing a number of studies, economist George Break concluded that

> neither in Great Britain nor in the United States is there any convincing evidence that high levels of taxation seriously interfere with work incentives. There are, in fact . . . a number of good reasons for believing that considerably higher taxes could be sustained without injury to worker motivation.[23]

In the SIME/DIME experiments, however, the evidence was not quite so encouraging. In the first edition of this book, we reported that the initial findings of one experimental negative tax program showed that "families receiving assistance worked just as hard as ever—and there were even some indications that they had been stimulated to work harder." The early findings also suggested that psychological barriers or disincentives to work were not evident even for those families whose earnings increased to the point where they were no longer eligible for assistance.[24] However, further research revealed that these conclusions were somewhat premature. The preliminary findings reported in the early 1970s were sharply contradicted after a longer period of study of a much larger sample in the SIME/DIME programs.

Findings indicate that, compared to the control group, families receiving the guaranteed-income grant worked significantly fewer hours per year. Although changes in work effort varied with the amount of the grants and the negative tax rates, an estimate of the nationwide effects of a SIME/DIME program suggested that a guaranteed income at 75 percent of the poverty line and a negative tax rate of 50 percent would reduce work effort about 6 percent for husbands, 23 percent for wives, and 7 percent for female heads of families.[25]

There are a number of reasons to believe that these findings underestimate the work reduction that would actually take place. One cannot discount the possibility that simply knowing they were part of an important social experiment may have influenced the participants' behavior. The Hawthorne effect, a well-known phenomenon in social research, suggests that, in the process of becoming actively engaged in an experiment, participants develop a commitment to its success and an inclination to behave in ways that do not disappoint the investigators.[26] Moreover, the limited scale of SIME/DIME could not simulate the effects of a nationwide program with millions of participants who might well organize to lobby for higher benefits. The relatively brief duration of the experiment no doubt inhibited tendencies to reduce work effort and risk losing a job that the participant would need when SIME/DIME grants ended. There is also a reasonable possibility that a guaranteed minimum income would invite early retirements. Compensating for these and other factors that might have biased the SIME/DIME measurements, Martin Anderson estimated that any such scheme, nationally implemented, would result in a minimum 29 percent reduction in the work effort of low-income workers.[27] This means that a guaranteed income for everyone would result in public money replacing a considerable amount of income that recipients would otherwise have earned themselves. This not only makes for a costly program, it makes for a morally questionable one. A society that prizes independent effort and initiative is not likely to value public policy that appears to undermine the work ethic.

Yet questions of the extent to which income guarantees affect work cannot be put to rest on the basis of the findings of a few studies. The economic variables involved in the SIME/DIME experiment must be checked against studies of other programmatic arrangements, different population groups, and varying economic and cultural conditions. Several careful studies have reviewed both the combined and the separate effects on work behavior of welfare benefits, most concluding that significant financial disincentives undermine the work behavior of welfare-eligible adults. Although work may be important to poor families for any number of good reasons—self-esteem and setting a good example for the children, chief among them—it rarely provides a financial advantage (at least in the short run) over welfare. In the 1990s, for example, Kathryn Edin estimated that a working mother would have to earn about $16,000 annually (nearly $9.00 an hour) just to maintain the living standards of a welfare-reliant counterpart.[28] This hardly provides women with limited skills and earnings much

CAPSULE 4.4 • *The Welfare Disincentive*

As with most cash assistance programs, a woman receives maximum AFDC benefits for her family when she doesn't work and has no other income. As she goes to work, her benefits fall as her earnings rise. This process creates a work disincentive. In fact, under the federal mandates that existed through 1995, a woman who had been on AFDC and working for more than four months faced a dollar loss in benefits for every dollar increase in earnings. This is the equivalent of a 100 percent tax rate. . . . A substantial body of research has tried to measure the disincentive effects of AFDC. The results are quite consistent across studies: higher welfare payments discourage work.

Rebecca Blank, *It Takes a Nation*, 1997, 100–101, 146.

encouragement to work. On the contrary, the consensus opinion of social scientists who studied the work–welfare dilemma empirically in the mid-1990s was that the availability of AFDC resulted in women working less.[29] The disincentive effect of welfare, indeed, was one of the primary reasons AFDC was abolished in 1996 in favor of TANF, a program, as we shall see in Chapter 8, that compels work rather than simply encouraging it.

Childbearing

Whereas a guaranteed income can be faulted for sapping the work effort, children's allowances have their own unique set of advantages and disadvantages. At one time, for example, allowances were viewed as having a significant bearing on population size, with critics objecting to allowances on the grounds that they served as "baby bonuses," resulting in excessive procreation, while proponents lauded their effect for increasing the birthrate. More recently, however, the concern has been far more with under- than with overpopulation. Simply put, the crisis in Europe today is one of too few babies. Despite sponsoring a powerful arsenal of family-friendly social policies, far more generous than policies in the United States, most European countries have far lower annual rates of childbearing (and marriage) than rates in the United States. The United States, which is widely castigated for lagging far behind the welfare states of Europe in the development of family-friendly social policies, had a fertility rate in 2005 of 2.08 (close to the replacement rate of 2.1), considerably higher than that of Europe's major rich countries, which are frequently 1.8 or less.

In light of existing evidence, then, assumptions about the effects of children's allowances on family size must be viewed with a healthy skepticism. Even those countries with the most generous family support policies—guaranteed cash allowances plus tax incentives for children plus daycare and job leaves and flexible work scheduling for parents—are facing dwindling birthrates. France, a world leader in public support for larger families—it recently offered women close to $12,000 to have a third child—has a fertility rate of just 1.8. Japan, despite increasingly liberalized family subsidies, is struggling to reduce its record-low 1.3 fertility rate. While public support based on family size undoubtedly provides some people some incentive, to generalize from the few to the many underestimates the complexity of human motivation. Decisions concerning family size reflect fundamental conditions of human existence. In these matters, the influence of aid benefits must be weighed in the larger context of desires for self-betterment and a variety of other social psychological factors (not the least of which is the need to be well thought of by others) that come to bear on people's decisions to have children.

Given the continuing population shortfall throughout Europe and the proven difficulty of influencing birthrates via social policy, be it family allowances or daycare or paid family leave, the debate in many countries has shifted to immigration. That is, the European population deficit, the significant imbalance between the (relatively small) number of workers paying taxes to support social security systems and the (relatively large) number of retirees receiving benefits, has led many to advocate substantial liberalization of the laws regarding the entry of foreign workers. The demographer Wolfgang Lutz has estimated, for example, that allowing one million immigrants per

CAPSULE 4.5 • *Helping Moms, Nudging Babies*

To the dismay of pundits and politicians alike, women in industrialized countries and elsewhere have been bearing fewer and fewer children. While scholars blame several phenomena, including greater access to birth control, later marriage and a drop in what one researcher calls "hopefulness about the future," many researchers agree that at least part of the problem is due to the particular burdens women face in the work force. If becoming a mother requires a woman to take a huge financial and professional hit, the thinking goes, she will be far less likely do it.

Could it be, then, that easing a woman's ability to hold a job and raise children simultaneously will nudge her toward having a bigger family? At least 45 countries are betting on it, having instituted government programs to maintain or raise their fertility rates.

In the European Union, all countries require employers to grant parity in pay and benefits to part-time workers—allowing women more flexibility in their work lives. In Scandinavia, extensive public child-care systems offer a slot to virtually every child under 5 whose parents work.

Accommodating working mothers isn't a new idea, of course. Sweden has offered paid maternity leave since before World War II. And there's also a long history of using public policy for natalist purposes—some of it morally repugnant. Mussolini's government instituted a special tax on bachelors. In the 1980s, Singapore introduced a series of measures to encourage its better-educated citizens to start families, while at the same time discouraging poor and less-educated women from doing the same.

From "The Motherhood Experiment" by Sharon Lerner, *The New York Times Magazine*, March 4, 2007.
© Sharon Lerner. Reprinted by permission.

year into Europe would be the equivalent of every European woman having on average one additional child. While this may make eminent sense for firming up the funding of the social insurances, and for advancing more humane entry policies, it also creates considerable controversy in all those countries, and there are many, where anti-immigration parties have been gaining appeal and where there is a growing sensitivity to "cultural dilution."[30]

The impact of selectivist income maintenance on childbearing, while hotly debated, also remains uncertain. One of the primary critiques of AFDC was that it provided a substantial baby incentive since eligibility was linked to the existence of a dependent child, and the level of benefit was linked to the number of children. Critics like George Gilder—who long has argued that public aid fuels illegitimacy—succeeded in incorporating a "family cap" into welfare reform, disassociating the level of welfare aid from the number of children in the household. Nevertheless, social science research has produced little support for the baby incentive hypothesis. While out-of-wedlock rates have escalated dramatically since the mid-1960s, the availability of welfare payments seems to have had, at most, a negligible effect. (See Capsules 4.6 and 4.7.)

Family Stability

Although children's allowances do not appear to constitute a potent stimulus to procreation, levels of financial support associated with guaranteed-income schemes can

CAPSULE 4.6 • *An Irresistible Offer*

The welfare system makes an irresistible offer to every eligible female over the age of 16. It says to every teenager, "you may be poor, you may have family problems, and you may be discouraged about your future. But if you have a baby right now, we will give you your own apartment, free medical care, food stamps, and a regular income over the next 20 years. If you have another baby soon after, we will increase your allotment."

From "Black Family Agonistes" by William Tucker, *The American Spectator*, July, 1984.

have other effects on family life. There are competing hypotheses about the exact nature of these effects. Because financial stress is one of the major factors increasing the risk of divorce, access to reliable financial aid is likely to help stabilize family life.[31] On the other hand, it has been suggested that providing mothers an assured source of support outside of marriage reduces the material incentives to get or stay married.[32]

These hypotheses were examined in the Seattle and Denver Income Maintenance Experiments, with results that lend credence to the proposition that a guaranteed income decreases marital stability. Overall, the rate of marital dissolution for experimental families was approximately twice that of control group families.[33]

CAPSULE 4.7 • *A Not So Irresistible Offer*

Seventy-nine prominent researchers in the areas of poverty, the labor market, and family structure said today that research does not support recent suggestions by Charles Murray and others that welfare is the main cause of rising out-of-wedlock births. At the same time, the researchers said, there is "strong evidence" that living in poverty harms children and that eliminating welfare for poor children would "do far more harm than good."

According to the researchers, most studies have found that welfare benefits have either no significant effect, or only a small effect, on whether women have children outside of marriage. When inflation is taken into account, they noted, the value of cash welfare benefits such as Aid to Families with Dependent Children has fallen over the past 20 years. At the same time, out-of-wedlock childbearing has increased. If welfare benefits were the main cause of out-of-wedlock births, they said, the decline in benefits should have prompted a decrease or a slower increase in out-of-wedlock births.

The researchers cited several plausible explanations for rising rates of births outside of marriage. Among them are changed sexual mores, decreased economic opportunity for low-skilled workers, more women in the labor market, and deteriorating neighborhood conditions. Rather than denying welfare benefits to poor children, the researchers called for a variety of improvements in programs assisting poor families.

From "Researchers Dispute Contention That Welfare Is Major Cause of Out-of-Wedlock Births" Press Release by Sheldon Danziger, July 23, 1994.

Amid these startling figures, however, there were some anomalies. The marital dissolution rates at the highest support level, for example, were less than those at the lower levels of support. According to theory, the opposite should have occurred. That is, if the degree of economic independence available outside marriage contributes to the risk of divorce, then these risks should increase at higher levels of financial support.[34] Also, although the SIME/DIME findings reflect the short-term consequences of guaranteed incomes, the program's long-term effects on marital stability remain unknown. It is conceivable, for instance, that after the initial round of divorces the remaining pool of married couples and those who remarry would experience lower divorce rates than the current level.[35]

Stigma and Social Integration

One of the most forceful claims for universal schemes is that they avoid stigmatizing recipients. The assumption of the stigmatizing effects of the means test is held so firmly by so many that it has almost come to be considered fact. To achieve selectivity without stigma, Titmuss proposed the elimination of the means test and its "assault on human dignity" by employing, instead, a needs test applicable to specific categories, groups, and geographical areas.[36] To this suggestion, Kahn responded,

> It has yet to be demonstrated . . . that a needs test to open special services to disadvantaged and perhaps socially unpopular groups will not carry some of the consequences of the means test. Nor, apparently, have even the most egalitarian of societies found it financially or politically possible to completely drop means test selectivity.[37]

Precisely what is it about the means test that, presumably, results in an assault on human dignity? Perhaps this result is inferred because means tests are frequently applied to socially unpopular groups such as the poor who may feel stigmatized even before they make an application for benefits. Certainly, college students, a privileged group, appear to carry the means-test burden lightly in applying for financial aid. In some cases, they have been known to express a strong preference for means-tested selection over other bases of allocation. Moreover, average citizens experience a form of means test every year when their taxes are due, without apparent damage to their sense of self-worth. Indeed, the social–psychological effects of the means test may be less inherently painful than is commonly assumed, even for the poor. Several studies have found that the means test per se is not a significant source of irritation to public assistance recipients.[38]

If this evidence is at all persuasive, and we think it is, then why the dogged persistence of this assumption? Why is the means test so often the bugaboo of allocative choices? The answer is twofold. First, discussions of the means test tend to confuse the principle with the practice. Distinctions between the means test as an allocative principle and the actual administration of the means test are important considerations. As we have suggested, the principle may be quite innocuous where worth and self-esteem of individuals are concerned. It is in the application of this principle that the potential for denigration exists. For example, when the methods of determining eligibility include unscheduled home visits at all hours of the day and night, the message conveyed to the recipient is that he or she is untrustworthy and no longer entitled to a private life. Such procedures are clearly damaging to a person's sense of competence and self-respect.[39]

Practices of this nature support the belief in the stigmatizing effects of the means test and create much of the disapproval. However, what is actually at issue in these cases is not the principle but its application. There is no reason why the principle could not be operationally defined according to a simple and dignified procedure whereby applicants declare their needs and resources without fuss and prying. The means test need not be mean-spirited; it need not be administered by hostile bureaucrats; it need not be intimidating.[40] A distinction, for example, can be drawn between the typically probing means test, which demands a complete disclosure of income and assets, and the narrower, more dignified income test, which is concerned only with the applicants' current income, usually verified through their tax returns.[41] Income-tested programs, such as the EITC, apply selectivity without stigma.

The second reason that means-tested schemes frequently are maligned relates to their broader societal effects. By their very nature, means-tested programs divide society into distinct groups of givers and receivers. Although the argument against selectivity usually blends this divisive outcome with the notion that receivers are stigmatized, these effects can be weighed independently. That is, even if stigma did not attach to recipient status, the case remains that selective programs have a divisive influence on the social fabric, fracturing society along sharp lines according to income. The poor become a distinct recipient class, whereas the near-poor, working class, and middle class fall together on the donor side of the transaction. This is an arrangement ill suited to the creation of social harmony. In contrast, universal schemes such as the children's allowance facilitate social integration by emphasizing the common needs families face in a variety of economic circumstances. Of the various issues we have discussed, this integrative function poses one of the most frequently voiced arguments for the social effectiveness of the universal approach to social allocations.

Another Perspective on Allocation: A Continuum of Choice

At the beginning of this chapter, we suggested that the universal–selective dichotomy represents a preliminary effort to analyze the choices related to social allocations. For the remainder of this chapter, we examine social allocations from other perspectives. Our purpose is to expand and refine the analytic concepts that may be brought to bear on this dimension of choice.

Although the universal–selective dichotomy serves as a useful starting point in conceptualizing eligibility, the bases of social allocations are more intricate than these ideas imply. In reality, abstract dichotomies are usually less useful than continua of choice. Thus, there are many policies where benefits are made accessible to people in selected categories, groups, or geographic regions without recourse to an individual means test. Up until now, we have used *selectivity* in the narrow sense to designate

means-tested allocations. Yet, as Titmuss points out, selectivity may be based on differential needs without the requirement of a means test.[42] The dilemma, however, is
that once the concept of selectivity is pried loose from strictly economic means-tested
considerations, its definition may be expanded to cover innumerable conditions, even
some generally interpreted as universalistic, in which case the term's meaning is dissolved. For example, some veterans' benefits, housing-relocation allowances, special
education classes, and employment and college admission preferences involve eligibility standards based on other than means-related criteria. In fact, once we yield to the
broader definition of selectivity, even children's allowances may be included because
they are limited to families with at least one child. To conceive of these as examples of
"selectivity," however, adds little to our understanding.

The problem, then, is to identify a broader range of eligibility alternates than are
provided by "universalism" and "selectivity" (in the narrow means-tested sense) while
still maintaining a degree of abstraction that permits generalizations that tell us something meaningful. Undoubtedly, there are many ways to conceptualize allocative principles. Our view is to consider the different conditions under which social provisions
are made accessible to individuals and groups in society. From this perspective, the criteria for social allocations may be classified according to four allocative principles:
attributed need, compensation, diagnostic differentiation, and means-tested need.

Attributed Need

Eligibility based on attributed need is conditional on membership in a group having
common needs that are not met by existing social or economic arrangements. Under
this principle, *need* is defined according to normative standards. Need may be attributed to as large a category as an entire population, such as in the case of healthcare in
England, or to a delimited group such as working parents, or residents of "underclass"
neighborhoods, or school children with limited proficiency in English. The two conditions that govern this principle are (1) group-oriented allocations that are (2) based
on normative criteria of need.

Table 4.2 identifies several federal policies with eligibility premised on attributed
need. The Family and Medical Leave Act of 1992, for example, ensures workers the
opportunity to attend to the care of a newborn baby or a dependent parent or spouse
without the fear of losing their jobs. The unique nature of HIV/AIDS, and the distinctive circumstances facing its victims, has also resulted in special programs. Federal laws
such as the Ryan White Act, for example, premised on the identity of AIDS as an
"exceptional" disease, provide over a billion dollars yearly for an elaborate network of
specialized local agencies (nearly 2500 at last count) that offer an array of support services from medical treatment and in-home care to tenant counseling and health information lending libraries.

Critics of disease-targeted legislation assert that needy noncovered groups—for
example, cancer patients, people with Parkinson's disease—are shortchanged by these
arrangements. For many years, indeed, the American Heart Association has argued for
funding parity, given that heart disease victims receive fewer research and services dollars per patient than do individuals with AIDS.

TABLE 4.2 *Allocative Principles in Selected Federal Policies*

Conditions of Eligibility	Federal Policy	Eligible Groups
Attributed Need	The Family and Medical Leave Act of 1992	Workers caring for dependents
	Ryan White Care Act	People in metropolitan areas with high AIDS/HIV risk
	Older American Act	The elderly
	Head Start, Legal Aid	Residents of low-income neighborhoods
Compensation	Social Security (OASDI)	Enrolees, with benefits reflecting contributions, with adjustments for low-income status
	Affirmative Action	Minority populations, women
Diagnostic Differentiation	Individuals with Disabilities Education Act (IDEA)	Special needs children (i.e., children with severe disabilities)
	Medicare Nursing Home Care	The functional disabled as measured by impairments in Activities of Daily Living (along with means test)
Means-Tested Need	Supplemental Security Income (SSI)	Elderly and disabled poor
	Special Supplemental Nutrition Program for Women, Infants, and Children (WIC)	Low-income pregnant, nursing, or postpartum women and children nutritionally at-risk

Compensation

Eligibility based on compensation is conditional on membership in groups who have made special social and economic contributions—such as veterans or social insurance contributors—or who have unfairly suffered harm at the "hands of society," such as victims of racism or sexism. The two conditions that govern this principle are (1) group-oriented allocations that are (2) based on normative criteria for equity.

The most controversial compensation-based program—Affirmative Action—which originally was advanced by federal executive action during the 1970s in an effort to compensate for the past exclusion of African Americans from the normal channels of access and opportunity, has evolved into a broad array of race and gender preferences for advancing access to higher education, jobs, and public contracts. While gender or ethnic or racial preferences in the allocation of public services is one of the most divisive issues in American politics, eligibility in many spheres continues to be based on efforts to counter past discrimination. College admissions in many states, for example, utilize affirmative action criteria. Employment and contract opportunities similarly are often "group sensitive," advantaging targeted beneficiary classes. And federal benefits have long been conditioned on race, such as membership in a federally recognized Indian tribe, or possession of a certain "blood quantum."

Affirmative action—preferences—serves a variety of objectives. As a corrective to past racism and sexism, it compensates minorities and women for the legacy of the oppression suffered by their forebears. Affirmative action also seeks to promote diversity in our society and a fair representation of all groups in good jobs and good schools. Opponents of affirmative action not only see preferences as discriminatory against whites and men, they note that its beneficiaries are often middle-class minority students and women, rather than those suffering severe socioeconomic hardships.

The United States isn't the only country with special compensation programs for communities that have faced discrimination. India, for example, provides preferential treatment to those at the bottom of the country's traditional caste system. Half of all new public sector employees must be from the lower castes, and government policy sets college admission quotas favoring untouchables.[43]

Diagnostic Differentiation

Eligibility based on diagnostic differentiation is conditional on professional judgments of individual cases where special goods or services may be needed, as in the situation of the physically or mentally impaired. The two conditions that govern the principle are (1) individual allocations that are (2) based on technical diagnostic criteria of need. Special education services in the public schools, for example, focus on thirteen federally specified disability categories, including mental retardation, autism, visual and hearing impairments, serious emotional disability, and specific learning disabilities. Eligibility for special education is determined solely by authorized professional personnel. In similar fashion, eligibility for mental health services typically requires a determination by an approved mental health professional of the character and severity of a client's disorder.

At the international level, humanitarian aid workers providing relief in famine situations similarly rely on a technical diagnosis of nutritional need to set priorities for food distributions. The typical approach, anthropometric measurement, utilizes criteria such as a person's weight, skinfolds, and body mass to help identify those in greatest need of immediate nourishment.

Means-Tested Need

Eligibility based on means-tested need is conditional on evidence regarding an individual's inability to purchase goods and/or services. The individual's access to social provisions is limited primarily by his or her economic circumstances. The primary conditions that govern this principle are (1) individual allocations that are (2) based on economic criteria of need. While we often think of means-tested programs as a way of providing a safety net for the poor, many public benefits are distributed rather significantly up the income ladder. Low-income public housing, for example, after several decades of focus on the most severely economically distressed—welfare recipients, the homeless, the mentally ill, multiproblem families—broadened its eligibility standards to bring in stable working-class families. Called "deconcentration," this liberalization of the rules was intended to create a mix of economic groups, and with it a mix of "models of behavior," in order to "ward off the social instability that has ruined so many projects."[44] (See Capsule 4.8.)

Similarly, federal health and nutrition programs establish varied income criteria for eligibility, typically related to some proportion of the federal poverty line. The Special Supplemental Nutrition Program for Women, Infants, and Children, better known as WIC, provides food assistance to pregnant women and mothers with young children with incomes up to 185 percent of the poverty threshold. Federal school meals programs are free for children from families under 130 percent of the line and are available at reduced cost for children from families between 130 and 180 percent. Medicaid eligibility is 133 percent for pregnant women, 42 percent for parents, and 74 percent for the elderly and individuals with disabilities. A related program, the State Child Health Insurance Program (SCHIP), was enacted specifically to provide

---

CAPSULE 4.8 • *How Poor for Public Housing?*

While advocacy groups and Federal officials urge that the homeless, the disabled and the poorest of the poor be given priority for scarce public housing vacancies, officials of many large urban housing projects are arguing that they need a broader mix of incomes, including more low-income working families, to insure social stability in their developments.

The debate has sharpened as the Federal Government has reduced its role in providing new housing and the nation's stock of privately owned low-income housing has declined because of gentrification, the demolition of many single-room-occupancy hotels and the conversion of many apartments to condominiums. Meanwhile, the number of low-income households and homeless people has grown, putting more pressure on the nation's existing stock of 1.4 million public housing units as housing of last resort.

The recent trend toward giving preference to those least able to care for themselves has won the support of many advocacy groups for the mentally ill, people with disabilities and the infirm. On the other side are public housing managers and many tenants' organizations, who say they are sympathetic with the shelter needs of the very poor and infirm but believe it is unfair to force public housing communities, many of which are already under extreme pressure because of crime and poverty, to take in even more people least able to help themselves.

Their argument is that public housing's role today should be what it was when it was first created 50 years ago: an agent of social change that provides transitional housing for poor people, including the working poor.

George Sternlieb, a professor of urban affairs at Rutgers University, said the debate over housing policy reflected a clash of conflicting values.

"It's a very difficult dilemma," he said. "If you want to preserve these public housing developments as stable communities, the managers need to be able to control the selection and eviction of their tenants. But we also have to find the room to address today's tragedies—the growing numbers of homeless and people without shelter."

support for children whose parents earn too much for Medicaid eligibility. The fifty states differ in setting SCHIP criteria, some limiting eligibility to families under 185 percent of the poverty line, others setting the standard at 350 percent, thus incorporating many middle class children into the health safety net.[45] The federal government in 2007 reduced state flexibility by imposing a maximum eligibility limit at 250 percent of the poverty line.

Allocative Principles and Institutional–Residual Conceptions of Social Welfare

Before examining these allocative principles further, let us return briefly to an issue raised in Chapter 1 concerning alternative conceptions of the institutional status of social welfare. We reintroduce this issue because the bases of social allocations are closely associated with the institutional and residual conceptions introduced at that time. The purpose of this discussion is to help clarify how these conceptions are linked with policy design.

As noted, the institutional conception posits social welfare as a normal ongoing first-line function of society, whereas the residual view sees welfare as a temporary necessity when the normal channels for meeting needs fail to perform adequately. The fundamental distinctions concern the causes and incidence of unmet needs and problems in society. To what extent do these unmet needs represent a failure of "the system" and to what extent do they represent a failure of those afflicted? To what extent are problems characterized as deviant or special cases rather than as normal occurrences? Answers to these questions are reflected in choices regarding the bases of social allocations as suggested in Figure 4.2. Here, the allocative principles are arranged along a continuum in terms of the degree to which they may be identified with institutional or residual conceptions of social welfare.

Allocations made on the basis of attributed need assume that needs are normal occurrences in society that are attributable to system inadequacies. Under these conditions, eligibility is determined according to an organic status such as citizen, child, working mother, resident, and the like, rather than on the basis of an individual's attributes derived by a detailed examination of physical and psychological disabilities or evidence of special circumstances. Policies designed along these lines exemplify the institutional conception of social welfare in seeking to create stable, ongoing arrangements for meeting normal needs.

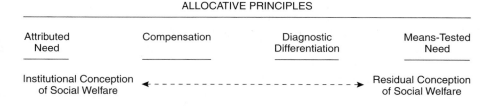

ALLOCATIVE PRINCIPLES

Attributed Need	Compensation	Diagnostic Differentiation	Means-Tested Need

Institutional Conception of Social Welfare ← - - - - - - - - - - - - - - - - - - - → Residual Conception of Social Welfare

FIGURE 4.2   *Allocative Principles and Conceptions of Social Welfare.*

At the other end of the continuum, where means-tested need is the allocative principle, the problem addressed is usually considered a special circumstance arising out of individual deficiency. To be poor is not an organic status defined in terms of an inherent set of rights and obligations, such as those for working mothers, but rather as a relative condition that is determined by calculating all of the income and resources available to an individual against an arbitrary level of economic well-being. Resulting policies exemplify a residual safety-net conception of social welfare that affords temporary support until the individual is "rehabilitated," educated, retrained, or otherwise made self-sufficient.

The principles of compensation and diagnostic differentiation fall midway between the institutional and residual conceptions. The principle of compensation is closer to the institutional view because it implies a systemic failure or "debt." Here, eligibility is determined according to organic status. Diagnostic differentiation is closer to the residual view because it is associated with individual disabilities and requires a more or less mechanical assessment of the applicant's special characteristics for eligibility.

This paradigm suggests that the residual conception of social welfare will persist as long as diagnostic differentiation and means-tested need (i.e., allocative principles that seek to differentiate among individuals) are incorporated in the design of social welfare policies. Under these principles, no matter how benign the operational mechanism for eligibility determination, unmet needs will be attributed more to chance or individual disability than to institutional strains or failures.

There will always be cases, of course, in which it is both necessary and desirable to differentiate among individuals in allocating social welfare benefits. Although the balance, over time, has shifted toward a larger institutional role for social welfare, it is unlikely that the residual functions will ever disappear. However, this does not mean that the negative aspects of the residual functions must endure. If attributed need and compensation are expanded as bases of social allocation, an adequate institutional core of social welfare may emerge. Then, as Shlakman suggests, the residual function becomes smaller and more manageable, and "it has a potential for emerging as the most flexible, most professionally oriented service, providing for the peculiarity of need and exceptional circumstances that cannot be met effectively by programs based on presumed average need."[46]

Operationalizing the Allocative Principles

This fourfold classification of allocative principles simplifies the structure of choice in the interest of order. To compensate for the distortions that occur whenever complex reality is compressed into theory requires at least a brief glimpse at some of the problematic facets of these principles. Differences among the conditions that govern the principles are not always self-evident. For instance, distinctions between normative definitions and technical assessments of need are often clouded. Is the allocation of special education services for learning-impaired students based on valid technical measurements of academic potential, or on middle-class cultural norms? The technical assessment of psychological needs is a sensitive business in which science, art, and prevailing norms intermingle. Operationalizing psychological disorders is particularly uncertain given the ambiguity of diagnostic categories. Special diagnostic handbooks like the *Diagnostic and Statistical Manual of Mental Disorders (DSM)* are widely employed in the mental health field in an effort to make psychiatric diagnoses more objective. And the *DSM*, widely adopted by psychiatrists, psychologists, and social workers, has helped clarify the character of mental disorders resulting in far greater reliability in the diagnostic process.

Yet specifying disability remains an inexact science, and very much subject to professional discretion. Because the diagnosis often determines eligibility for mental health services, what should be a disinterested professional judgment is frequently influenced by factors having only an indirect relationship to the actual symptoms of the client. According to Kirk and Kutchins, for example, the diagnostic process is often determined "not by the clinical needs of the client or the treatment planning activities of the therapist, but by the mental health organizations' need to manage service delivery."[47]

A disability diagnosis, for example, may be the result of an agency's need to regulate the number and type of clients it serves. *DSM* categories, in some cases, are interpreted to give the agency desirable, treatable, or reimbursable clients.[48] (See Capsule 4.9.) A client with a problem that fails to meet the threshold of severity necessary for Medicaid reimbursement, for example, may be "overdiagnosed" to ensure eligibility. In other circumstances, a problem may be deliberately concealed if this is necessary to obtain services for a client. Kirk and Kutchins relate the situation of a mental health

CAPSULE 4.9 • *A Diagnosis for Profit*

In addition to their scientific and clinical uses, diagnoses also have fiscal implications. A formal clinical label is frequently required for reimbursement by third-party insurance companies and government programs. Diagnosis in mental health, more than ever before, is a business act, as well as a clinical one, providing a mechanism for clinicians to be reimbursed and for clients who cannot afford treatment to get the service they need.

But not all personal troubles are equally reimbursable. Reimbursement directly to the client or the agency is tied to particular psychiatric diagnoses, often the more serious ones. Personality disorders, family problems, or routine adjustment difficulties may not be reimbursable. Thus, the acquisition of fiscal resources depends directly on the clinician's decision about the nature of the client's medical disorder.

Mental health practitioners and their agencies are very aware of this connection. More importantly, they admit that it affects their use of diagnosis. There is evidence of widespread overdiagnosis, in which clinicians use more serious diagnosis than warranted in order to qualify the client or the agency for reimbursement. One staff member quipped that a client's *DSM* diagnosis was an "insurance claim."

Stuart Kirk and Herb Kutchins, *The Selling of DSM*, 1992, 233–34.

clinic that refuses to diagnose substance abuse among clients since this would deny them eligibility for subsidized housing.[49]

The principle of compensation is invoked to redress inequities imposed by historical injustices and to reward contributions to society made by individuals and groups. But the restoration of equity to "victims of society" may be deferred because these cases are controversial or simply not recognized by the public. Are inner-city residents entitled to a special travel subsidy if public transportation is not available to their areas of employment because middle-class residents drive to work on publicly subsidized highways? To what extent are the hardships visited on past generations a legitimate debt to present generations? Is it equitable to compensate past inequities through the creation of new inequities? These questions suggest some of the complex interplay among values and social choice that attach to the principle of compensation.

Even the relatively straightforward principle of means-tested need becomes entangled in a web of value-laden choices at the point of application. First, of course, a standard of need must be operationally defined. Here, it is interesting to note how the "iron law of specificity" operates in matters of social policy. The "iron law" holds that policymakers (1) experience discomfort with the uncertainties that attach to broad problems, such as racism, unemployment, and poverty; (2) ease the discomfort by employing arbitrary but plausible surrogates of such problems; (3) treat these surrogates as substitutes for the problem in subsequent policy decisions; and (4) reinforce the surrogates through continued use, ignoring alternative problem definitions.[50]

Consider the notion of poverty and how closely it has become associated with the federal poverty index. The federal government has been publishing poverty statistics since 1964, using a poverty index developed at that time by labor economist Molly Orshansky. Orshansky constructed her poverty "line" by taking the minimum amount of money necessary to sustain a nutritious diet and multiplying that by three, based on the assumption that poor families required one-third of their income for food. The statistic that resulted, adjusted for family size, is increased annually to account for inflation. This provides a social indicator that is concrete, plausible, and convenient to use, but one that overlooks the existential quality of poverty as a condition of life.[51] Compare the poverty index to Robert Hunter's observation, "To live in misery we know not why, to have the dread of hunger, to work more and yet gain nothing—this is the essence of poverty."[52]

Here, we need a major caveat lest the "iron law of specificity" be taken too literally. That is, specificity operates only if the issue of choice is one on which it is possible to achieve fundamental agreement among the parties involved. (It might be the U.S. Congress, a presidential commission, a citizen's organization, or a local social agency board of directors.) More precisely, it must be a question of choice where there is substantial uncertainty. (Such a situation is more likely to involve the definition of a problem such as poverty, crime, or unemployment than the character of its solution.) If the situation is marked not so much by uncertainty as by strongly opposing views, then specification is likely to have the reverse effect, making agreement more difficult to achieve. In these cases, particularly when controversial solutions are being offered, there is a certain expedience to abstraction, which we will discuss in the next chapter.

Once the standard of need has been settled in means-tested allocations, there still remains the problem of determining how individuals measure up to this level. The scope of economic resources that are weighed in eligibility formulas is open to question. Should it include the value of assets as well as income? Should it include items of sentimental as well as economic value (wedding rings, for example)? What about insurance payments, children's college accounts, the value of the tools of one's trade, or the income of relatives (distant or close)? When eligibility determination does include relatives' income as a resource, and the relatives are held liable for support, then in effect they too must be subjected to a means test. Under Medicaid, for example, nursing home eligibility often requires that the value of certain assets be under a certain level. If the assets of the applicant, or the applicant's spouse exceed this limit, then they must be "spent down" to the qualifying level. (Certain property—such as a home, household possessions, and one car—are exempt from the valuation.) For the most part, however, adult children are not legally responsible for their parents, and their own income and assets are not counted in the determination of their parents' aid eligibility.

The question of what resources should be included in a determination of income is one of the essential issues in measuring poverty. Specifically, should the dollar value of in-kind social welfare benefits (such as food stamps and public housing) be counted as a component of income? This issue is important since the proportion of in-kind benefits in the federal budget has more than doubled since the early 1980s. Critics have argued that excluding the substantial value of these benefits in calculating the income of the poor inflates the poverty statistics. Estimates made by the U.S. Bureau

CAPSULE 4.10 • *Out of Line*

The federal government's reliance on the concept of the poverty line distorts the true picture of indigence in our nation. First developed in the early 1960s, the federal poverty line reflects economic and social realities completely different from those faced by families today. For example, the line was calculated on a "Leave It to Beaver" model—the two-parent family with one stay-at-home parent. But that model doesn't accurately describe contemporary families and is particularly off-base for low-income families, where single working parents are common. In nearly two-thirds of two-parent families, both parents work. For them, there are costs associated with employment—such as transportation, child care, and taxes—that the poverty threshold either underestimates or

neglects entirely. And despite all evidence to the contrary, the federal poverty line measurement also assumes that costs are the same across all of the lower 48 states. A family living in Manhattan in New York is expected to spend the same amount of money on food, clothing and shelter as a family in the town of Manhattan in Kansas.

The poverty line is an increasingly irrelevant measure of economic well-being. It's time to accept the fact that it's an anachronism and to adopt a new benchmark. A more realistic measure of poverty will give us a new way to assess the success of social programs—not just whether a family moves a dollar above an arbitrary threshold, but whether it is moving toward self-sufficiency.

From "Really Out of Line," by Deepak Bhargava and Joan Kuriansky as appeared in *The Washington Post*, September 15, 2002. Reprinted by permission of Deepak Bhargava and Joan Kuriansky.

of the Census, for example, indicate that the official poverty rate would be reduced by approximately a quarter if an "expanded" definition of income—one counting not only cash income but also the market value of food stamps, housing, and Medicaid—were employed.[53]

There is, however, another important facet to the issue of specifying poverty. The poverty line, in a very important sense, is a relative measure. That is, people with incomes below a certain level are perceived to be poor relative to those with incomes above that level. If in-kind benefits are to be figured into the incomes of those below the poverty line, then perhaps they should be figured into the incomes of those above the line as well. After all, employer-paid benefits for working people, such as health and dental insurance, contributions to retirement plans, and paid vacations, are substantial portions of the "pay" of regular workers.

Having reviewed some of the problems associated with operationalizing the principles that underlie social allocations, there is one final qualification concerning this dimension of choice. That is, in practice these allocative principles are not mutually exclusive even though their underlying premises may seem incompatible as, for example, in the joint employment of attributed and means-tested need. On the contrary, various combinations of allocative principles are found in the design and application of social welfare policies, reflecting the tug, pull, and eventual compromise over competing values. We will illustrate this point with reference to two rather different types of social welfare programs: Social Security—the Old Age, Survivors, Disability, and Health Insurance program (OASDHI)—created under the Social Security Act, and the Community Action Program, legislated under the Economic Opportunity Act.

In social insurance, eligibility for benefits is predicated on the dual principles of attributed need and compensation. Here, a persistent issue is the balance between adequacy and equity in the benefit-allocation formula.[54] The benefit to which a retiree is entitled under old-age insurance is designed, in part, to replace previous earnings as reflected in the contributions made to the social insurance system. To the extent that benefits reflect past contributions, a degree of equity is introduced into this system—workers who paid in more over the years of their employment are entitled to larger benefits in the years of their retirement. However, eligibility is also based on the principle of attributed need. As Hohaus explains, social insurance "aims primarily at providing society with some protection against one or more major hazards which are sufficiently widespread throughout the population and far-reaching in effect to become 'social' in scope and complexion."[55] In the case of old-age insurance, the attributed need of the retired elderly is for an adequate standard of living.

Thus, although Social Security seeks to compensate retirees in proportion to their contributions, it also seeks to provide a level of adequacy for low-income workers whose contributions were minimal. For this group, strictly applying the principle of compensation would result in benefit levels far below even the meager standards to which the individual was accustomed prior to retirement. In most social insurance programs, the dual allocative principles of attributed need and compensation result in a system in which the relationship between benefits and contributions exists in an ordinal sense, but is limited in a proportional sense, as efforts to express equity are modified by concerns for adequacy.

In the development of the Community Action Program (CAP) during the 1960s, the principle of attributed need was widely employed as the basis for social allocations. Initially, people became eligible for a variety of CAP-funded goods and services by virtue of their residence in designated low-income neighborhoods.[56] Once the program began operating, however, these normative assessments of need were often modified. Levitan documents how CAP-funded neighborhood health centers that intended to provide free healthcare services to all target-area residents eventually incorporated a means test into allocation procedures, as did CAP-funded Neighborhood Legal Aid, Head Start, and employment opportunities programs.[57] In certain instances, neighborhood residents supported means tests as an additional basis for allocations, especially in cases where the services were relatively inelastic. A limited number of slots for Head Start students in a summer program is a good example. Neighborhood applicants included large numbers of both poor and nonpoor residents. The poor were not convinced that attributed need was the most suitable allocative principle under such circumstances. For the CAP, then, attributed need became a preliminary screening device, a necessary but not sufficient condition for determining eligibility.

Despite some of their untidy features, the four allocative principles—attributed need, compensation, diagnostic differentiation, and means-tested need—provide a useful framework for conceptualizing policy alternatives. Consider, for example, the provision of preschool daycare services, a program increasingly demanded by students, lower-wage parents, and women transitioning from welfare to work. To whom and on what basis should these services be available? The four allocative principles offer an orderly framework for conceptualizing alternatives. As indicated in Table 4.3, eligibility at one extreme might incorporate all families with young children, based on a community-felt need for an institutional arrangement to allow fathers and mothers greater freedom during the early years of childrearing. However, such a diminution of childrearing responsibilities is unlikely to receive normative sanction in a child- and achievement-oriented society. A more plausible condition of eligibility might require

TABLE 4.3 *Alternative Criteria for Allocating Daycare Services*

Conditions of Eligibility	Alternative Criteria for Allocations
Attributed Need	All families Single-parent families Families with student parents
Compensation	Minority families Military families Families of workers in specified occupational groups
Diagnostic Differentiation	Families with special needs children Families in short-term crisis situations
Means-Tested Need	Families whose earnings and resources fall beneath a low-income standard

casting attributed need, not into the mold of "untrammeled freedom," but rather in the image of freedom to achieve commonly valued objectives such as a career or an education. In this case, eligibility would be limited to working parents and/or students. Other options might involve daycare entitlements on compensatory and diagnostic bases. Finally, there is the means test, which could be used independently or in combination with any of the other principles to restrict subsidies to low-income families.

Eligibility versus Access

So far, we have focused on a question that receives much attention in the design of social welfare policies: Who is to be eligible for benefits? But there is another side to this issue that is often ignored or misinterpreted by social welfare policymakers: Who *actually* benefits?

In selecting the basis of social allocations, there is a strong tendency to proceed on the assumption that being eligible means being served. But this equation often is far from assured. First, those qualifying for services may be *unaware* of their eligibility. Second, those qualifying for services may be *unable* to benefit. Third, potential beneficiaries may be *deterred* from seeking benefis. And finally, those qualifying for services may be *uninterested* in benefiting.

The first issue, the gap between eligibility and awareness, is often a result of inadequate publicity or ineffective communications. Service bureaucracies, for example, may be unwilling or unable to reach out to eligible populations, especially those who may be "hard to reach" due to cultural or linguistic characteristics. (These service delivery barriers, and others, are discussed in Chapter 6.) It is estimated, for example, that a significant portion of homeless youth with children have no knowledge of or access to public services. While these young parents are among the most vulnerable members of society, often in desperate need of assistance, they are frequently left out of public programs. According to a recent survey, for example, fewer than 40 percent of homeless parenting youth are receiving TANF benefits, with fully half of those who had never applied being unaware of the program.[58]

Many potential recipients may be aware of services but may be unable to participate successfully. Individuals with severe emotional problems, addictive behaviors, or antisocial attitudes, whatever their desires or needs, may be "bad" candidates for assistance because they are not likely to make good use of whatever help is offered. Counseling programs offered in a mental health agency, for example, may simply not be able to meet the intense needs of the severely mentally disabled. Similarly, job training may not work for disturbed or hostile teenagers. Indeed, those with the greatest needs may have the least chance of success, even when significant resources are invested. Considerable evidence has accumulated over the years, for example, that employment programs often have only a minimal impact on the most poorly educated, least job-ready welfare clients.

Those who qualify for services and those whose successful participation is not impaired are typically expected to desire and readily accept the assistance offered. Eligible clients or consumers who don't are often labeled "resistant," and attention may then be directed to developing specially responsive service structures that take account of the "barriers" that impede program participation.[59]

But this assumption of receptivity bears close scrutiny. For a variety of reasons, those eligible for benefits may be uninterested in becoming recipients. They may be hard to reach because they do not want to be reached. The costs of program participation may be perceived as outweighing the benefits. People may be aware of their eligibility but may avoid services they view as demeaning or stigmatizing. They may not wish to reveal information; religious, political, or cultural convictions may inhibit their involvement. People may be uninterested in programs, viewing them as burdensome, complex, threatening, or (whatever the precise measure of eligibility) only for "poor people." The elderly, for example, may refuse services out of pride, seeing safety net programs as demeaning. Immigrant parents may be reluctant to sign up for assistance for themselves or their children for fear (justified or not) that enrolling in programs may categorize them as a "public charge" (that is, likely to become dependent on government), thus jeopardizing their immigration status and their chances for citizenship. Others may simply be intimidated, unwilling to apply due to hostile bureaucrats, overly long and complex application forms, or a discouraging, unfriendly atmosphere.

These factors help explain the steep drop in public welfare participation since the enactment of welfare reform in 1996. As Figure 4.3 indicates, in the years immediately prior to the abolition of AFDC and the creation of TANF, over 80 percent of all welfare-eligible families participated in the program. Since 1997, participation has declined percipitiously, dropping to less than half by 2001. While a variety of theories

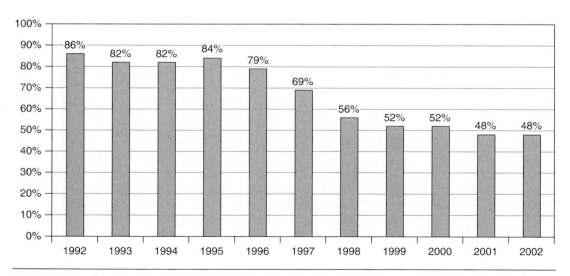

FIGURE 4.3   *Participation in AFDC/TANF by Families That Meet Program Eligibility Requirements, 1992–2002.*

Source: U.S. Department of Health and Human Services, Indicators of Welfare Dependence, 2005.

help explain why so many eligible families no longer seek benefits, one salient factor is the marked change in program atmosphere. Today's message in welfare offices around the country is that TANF is a temporary program, something to help on the way to a job, not a right, not an entitlement. According to the Urban Institute, this new "culture" of welfare, imposed through a variety of formal and informal means, has powerfully diverted thousands of needy famlies from applying for aid.[60]

Finally, it should be noted that eligibility often fails to ensure service because of exclusionary practices on the part of agencies seeking to make the most efficient use of limited budgets. Needing to ration scarce resources, organizations frequently avoid clients who they consider less likely to benefit from their programs. This avoidance of the hard-to-serve is a widespread phenomenon in the social services. For many years, for example, critics charged vocational rehabilitation and job-training organizations with "creaming" their prospective clientele—focusing their efforts on those most likely to succeed while ignoring the least skilled, the least able. The Job Training Partnership Act, for example, legislated in 1982 to assist the economic have-nots, is generally agreed to have mainly served those who were very close to being "job ready," rather than the "hard-core" poor.[61]

Not everyone needing help can be served, of course, and human service organizations must make determinations of how to best employ their limited resources. If an agency's primary mission is to move the homeless to self-sufficiency, it makes little sense to assign one of a very few units of transitional housing to individuals who have little potential for independent living. In fact, providers of transitional housing generally screen for candidates who are likely ultimately to make it on their own—motivated people who will meet with social workers, attend training classes, save money, and seek out jobs and permanent accommodations. Homeless individuals with severe drug,

---

CAPSULE 4.11 • *Participation versus Poverty*

If all eligible families with children participated fully in key federal safely net programs, 3.8 million people could escape poverty. According to a new analysis by the Urban Institute's Assessing the New Federalism project, "if policymakers improved participation in Food Stamps, Supplemental Security Income, Temporary Assistance for Needy Families, and the Earned Income Tax Credit, poverty could fall by 20 percent—extreme poverty by 70 percent."

According to the researchers, the chance to reduce economic hardship for so many provides a strong rationale for improving access to safety net programs by streamlining eligibility, application, and recertification processes. This could be done by implementing such practices as standardizing income eligibility, work rules, asset tests, and client treatment across programs; sharing information across agencies; improving outreach and education; and developing family-friendly offices that accommodate the schedules of working parents.

Sheila Zedlewski et al., "Extreme Poverty Rising, Existing Government Programs Could Do More," reported on in the Urban Institute's *New Federalism—Policy Research and Resources*, Issue 14, The Urban Institute, June 2002.

alcohol, and mental health problems are not likely to be selected even when they possess the interest and motivation to apply for transitional housing. This creates a discouraging irony. Creaming often means focusing on those most likely to benefit, individuals who might very well be able to make it on their own, without help, and ignoring those with the greatest objective needs but the least likelihood of succeeding on their own.

The motivation for targeting the "best" clients may also be based on pecuniary motives. Profit-seeking health and welfare organizations have frequently been charged with "cherry picking" the most potentially lucrative clients. Critics of commercial health maintenance organizations (HMOs), for example, charge that they often focus their membership recruitment on the healthy, studiously discouraging enrollments by the sick and disabled. A recent federal report concluded that HMOs frequently target healthier beneficiaries, marketing their plans in health clubs, resorts, and sports venues while avoiding sites easily accessible by the sick and feeble. One HMO went so far as to locate its offices on the upper floors of elevator-less buildings.[62]

Emerging Issues: Generational Equity

Broad issues of social allocation—frequently described in class, race, and ethnic, or gender terms—are persistent concerns of social policy practitioners and analysts. Each generation defines these issues in its own way, reflecting its own unique demographics, its own economic circumstances, and its own needs and perspectives. For example, the "graying" of America has highlighted issues of eligibility and benefits in terms of "generational equity." While volumes have been written advancing assorted theses concerning the winners and losers in the welfare state, one fact that is abundantly clear is that welfare is not simply a matter of public charity to the poor. Social Security and Medicare—the universal programs that compose the major segment of the U.S. welfare state—principally serve the middle class. Even selective, means-tested programs are distributed broadly, with nearly a quarter of the population receiving cash entitlements at one time or another over a typical decade-long period.[63] As the twenty-first century unfolds, many of the traditional issues of social allocation are taking new shape. Broad controversies over class, racial, and gender fairness continue, of course, but other forms of group distinction are drawing attention as public policy and economic change create new and unfamiliar patterns of wealth and well-being (and poverty and disadvantage) in our society. Questions concerning "who benefits," for example, are frequently being postulated in generational terms, with age group "winners"—the elderly—contrasted with age group "losers"—children and young adults.

Interest in the question of age group—or generational—fairness to a significant degree reflects differences that have occurred in the socioeconomic circumstances of the young and the old. Changes in the well-being of the elderly are particularly dramatic, as Figure 4.4 indicates. Medicare and Medicaid, programs destined to became even larger segment of the federal budget in years ahead, go over whelmingly to older Americans, as does Social Security. These three entitlements, according to the

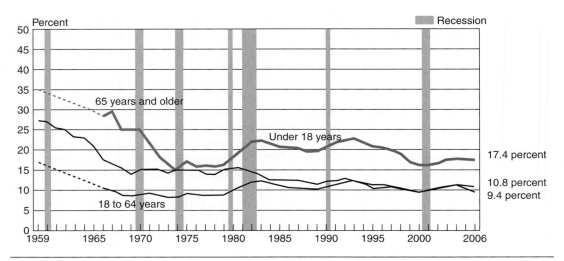

FIGURE 4.4 *Poverty Rates by Age: 1959 to 2006.*

Note: The data points are placed at the midpoints of the respective years.
Data for people aged 18 to 64 and 65 and older are not available from 1960 to 1965.

Source: U.S. Census Bureau, Current Population Survey, 1960 to 2007 Annual Social and Economic Supplements.

Congressional Budget Office, are likely to compose 70 percent of the federal budget by 2030. The results of these investments are clear. For the first time in history, the elderly, as a demographic group, are not economically disadvantaged. For the first time in history, retirement and the end of regular job income does not automatically mean a life of poverty and insecurity.

For many, the resounding success of the elderly is directly correlated with the distressing dilemmas facing children and adolescents. Former Colorado Governor Richard Lamm, for example, has posited a direct trade-off between the welfare of the two groups. "My aging body," he said, in discussing health care costs, "can prevent your kids from going to college. . . . We as a society spend more money turning 80 year olds into 90 year olds than we do 6 year olds into educated 16 year olds. There's something that doesn't build a great nation with that formula."[64]

Others, while acknowledging policy bias in favor of the elderly, reject generational critiques that view the young and the old as competitors for a fixed pot of social resources. It has been pointed out, for example, that in many countries high spending for the elderly is not correlated with low spending on behalf of children, and many analysts of the left, such as Paul Adams and Gary Dominick, interpret public expenditure differences in class rather than age terms. It is the structure of American political and economic life—its capitalist orientation, its lack of a real labor movement—rather than an aging population, in other words, that is said to be the fundamental cause of generational discrepancies.

The contradictory results of American social welfare for young and old, it must be noted, reflect the fundamental bifurcation of income-support policy into universal and means-tested components. Much of the improvement in the lives of seniors reflects seventy years of universalistic public policy that has focused on relieving the hardships of old age. No other social objective, indeed, has received anything close to the same degree of governmental attention or resources. Old age insurance, for example, is the costliest component of the country's costliest program—Social Security. And while the welfare state certainly spends considerably to address other areas of need, the elderly receive top priority. According to economist Lester Thurow, for example, government spends nine times as much per capita on those over 65 as on those under 18.[65]

Covered by old-age insurance and universal medical insurance through Medicare, the material circumstances of the elderly have been substantially bettered. In 1982, poverty rates for the elderly dropped below those for the overall population for the first time in history. And, as Figure 4.4 indicates, they are now below the rate for the working-age (18–65) population. Indeed, counting the value of in-kind benefits, the poverty rate for those over 65 dropped below 6 percent by the late 1990s. For children, however, the scope of poverty has remained substantial over the past decade, with young children the worst off. The 2006 poverty rate for children under 18 was roughly 17 percent. This is why most of the major ideas recently advanced for "generational equity," for improving the life chances of children, have focused on broad and comprehensive programs such as school reform, food programs, an expanded EITC, universal child support, and early childhood education.

Although not all of the dire circumstances facing today's children reflect public policy choices—divorce, unwed parenthood, and unemployment are largely independent factors—choices concerning social allocations and benefit eligibility have been of critical importance. Means-tested benefits are vulnerable to swings in ideological currents and political alignments, as well as constrained federal and state budgets. Critical programs such as preventive health and legal services have been restricted, and the real (spendable) value of TANF payments has dropped in almost all states. Whereas universal programs—programs for the elderly like Medicare and Social Security—have proved largely resilient to program cutbacks, means-tested services for children have not and remain particularly vulnerable. Many commentators, looking forward to the baby boom retirements of the upcoming years, foresee a massive generational transfer of resources from young to old. For Robert Samuelson, for example,

> The aging of America involves a profound transformation of the nature of government: commitments to the older population are slowly overwhelming other public goals; the national goverment is becoming mainly an income-transfer mechanism from younger workers to older retirees. Our children face a future of rising taxes [and] squeezed—perhaps falling—public services.[66]

The issue of how benefits are allocated cannot be carried much farther at this point without some reference to the *substance* of benefits, what it is that clients actually receive. In the next chapter, we turn to this issue and examine the nature of social provisions.

Notes

1. Edward Bellamy, *Looking Backward* (New York: New American Library, 1960), 75. Originally published 1888.
2. Ibid., 95.
3. See the articles by Theda Skocpol and Robert Greenstein in Christopher Jencks and Paul Peterson (eds.), *The Urban Underclass* (Washington, D.C.: The Brookings Institution, 1991), 411–59. See also Irwin Garfinkel, "Economic Security for Children: From Means Testing and Bifurcation to Universality," in Irwin Garfinkel et al. (eds.), *Social Policies for Children* (Washington, D.C.: The Brookings Institution, 1996), 33–82.
4. Alvin Schorr, *Common Decency* (New Haven, Conn.: Yale University Press, 1986), 31.
5. Sheila B. Kamerman and Alfred J. Kahn, "Universalism and Income Testing in Family Policy," *Social Work* (July–August 1987): 277–80.
6. Nicholas Lemann, "Target Practice," *The New Republic* (November 11, 1996), 29.
7. See James C. Vadakin, "A Critique of the Guaranteed Annual Income," *Public Interest*, 11 (Spring 1968): 53–66; Edward Schwartz, "A Way to End the Means Test," *Social Work*, 9(3) (July 1964): 3–12; James Tobin, "The Case for an Income Guarantee," *Public Interest*, 4 (Summer 1966): 31–41; Alvin Schorr, "Against a Negative Income Tax," *The Public Interest*, 5 (Fall 1966): 110–17; Irwin Garfinkel, "Negative Income Tax and Children's Allowance Programs: A Comparison," *Social Work*, 13(4) (October 1968): 33–39; Helen O. Nicol, "Guaranteed Income Maintenance: Another Look at the Debate," *Welfare in Review*, 5(6) (June/July 1967): 1–13; Alvin Schorr, "To End the 'Women and Children Last' Policy," *The Journal of the Institute for Socioeconomic Studies*, IX:2 (Summer 1984): 58–78.
8. Eveline M. Burns, "Where Welfare Falls Short," *The Public Interest*, 1 (Fall 1965): 88.
9. Not all children's allowance programs are universal in the sense that they cover all families in the country. In some countries, such as France, eligibility for the children's allowance is employment related and financed through payroll taxes imposed on the employer, rather than out of general funds.
10. For a description and analysis of these experiments, see Mordecai Kurz and Robert Spiegelman, *The Design of the Seattle and Denver Income Maintenance Experiments*, Center for the Study of Welfare Policy Research Memorandum, No. 28 (Menlo Park, Calif.: Stanford Research Institute, 1972) and Martin Anderson, *Welfare: The Political Economy of Welfare Reform* (Stanford, Calif.: Hoover Institution Press, 1978).
11. For several child allowance proposals, see Alvin Schorr, *Poor Kids* (New York: Basic Books, 1966).
12. Mike Reddin, "Universality versus Selectivity," *The Political Quarterly* (January/March 1969): 14.
13. Daniel R. Meyer et al., "The Effects of Replacing Income Tax Deductions for Children with Children's Allowances: A Microsimulation," *Journal of Family Issues*, 12(4) (December 1991): 467–91.
14. U.S. General Accounting Office, *Earned Income Credit, Targeting the Working Poor,* Report Number GAO/GGD-95-122BR (Washington, D.C.: U.S. Government Printing Office, USGPO, March 1995).
15. David T. Ellwood, *Poor Support* (New York: Basic Books, 1988), 115.
16. Roberta Blank, *It Takes a Nation* (New York: Russell Sage Foundation, 1997), 226.
17. Bruce Ackerman and Anne Alstott, *The Stakeholder Society* (New Haven, Conn.: Yale University Press, 1999).
18. James Midgley, "Growth, Redistribution and Welfare: Toward Social Investment," *Social Service Review*, 77(1), 1999, 3–21.
19. Jami Curley and Michael Sherraden, *The History and Status of Children's Allowances: Policy Background for Children's Savings Accounts*, 1998, Center for Social Development, Washington University in St. Louis, 23.
20. Irwin Garfinkel et. al. (eds.), *Social Polices for Children*, 1996, 38.
21. James Cutt, "Income Support Programmes for Families with Children—Alternatives for Canada," *International Social Security Review*, 23(1) (1970), 104–105.

22. The classic case is Charles Murray, *Losing Ground: American Social Policy 1950–1980* (New York: Basic Books, 1984).

23. George Break, "The Effects of Taxation on Work Incentives," in Edmund Phelps (ed.), *Private Wants and Public Needs* (New York: W. W. Norton, 1965), 65.

24. Fred Cook, "When You Just Give Money to the Poor," *New York Times Magazine*, May 3, 1970, 23, 109–12. A more detailed breakdown of these findings is presented by David N. Kershaw, "A Negative Income Tax Experiment," *Scientific American*, 227(4) (October 1972): 19–25. For a description of the research design used in this study, see Harold W. Watts, "Graduated Work Incentives: An Experiment in Negative Taxation," *The American Economic Review*, 59(2) (May 1969).

25. Michael Keelye et al., "The Labor–Supply Effects and Costs of Alternative Negative Income Tax Programs," *Journal of Human Resources*, 13(6) (Winter 1978): 3–26. See also Henry J. Aaron, "Six Welfare Questions Searching for Answers," *Brookings Review*, 3 (Fall 1984): 13.

26. A description of the Hawthorne effect can be found in almost any textbook on social research methods. This phenomenon derives its name from the study of the Hawthorne Plant of the Western Electric Company in which the effect was first identified. See F. J. Roethlisberger and W. J. Dickson, *Management and the Worker* (Cambridge, Mass.: Harvard University Press, 1939).

27. Martin Anderson, *Welfare: The Political Economy of Welfare Reform* (Stanford, Calif.: Hoover Institution Press, 1978), 104–27.

28. Kathryn J. Edin, "The Myths of Dependence and Self-Sufficiency: Women, Welfare, and Low-Wage Work," *Focus*, 17(2) (Fall/Winter 1995), 4. See also Jason DeParle, "Better Work than Welfare," *New York Times Magazine*, December 18, 1994, 43–49, and Sheldon Danziger and Robert Plotnik, "Poverty and Policy: Lessons of the Last Two Decades," *Social Service Review* (March 1986): 36–50.

29. Blank, 145.

30. Richard Bernstein, "Aging Europe Finds Its Pension Is Running Out," *New York Times*, June 29, 2003.

31. Phillips Cutright, "Income and Family Events: Marital Stability," *Journal of Marriage and the Family*, 33 (May 1971): 291–306.

32. William J. Goode, "Marital Satisfaction and Instability: A Cross Cultural Analysis of Divorce Rates," *International Social Science Journal*, 5 (1982): 507–26.

33. Michael Hannan, Nancy Tuma, and Lyle Groeneveld, "Income and Marital Events: Evidence From an Income Maintenance Experiment," *American Journal of Sociology*, 82 (May 1977): 186–211.

34. Ibid. For additional discussion of the implications of these findings, see Maurice MacDonald and Isabel V. Sawhill, "Welfare Policy and the Family," *Public Policy*, 26 (Winter 1978): 107–19.

35. The short-term versus long-term effects of SIME/DIME on marital stability are analyzed in James W. Albrecht, "Negative Income Taxation and Divorce in SIME/DIME," *Journal of the Institute of Socioeconomic Studies*, 4 (Autumn 1979): 75–82.

36. Titmuss, *Commitment to Welfare* (London: George Allen and Unwin Ltd., 1968), 122.

37. Alfred Kahn, *Theory and Practice of Social Planning* (New York: Russell Sage, 1969), 203.

38. See, for example, Joe Handler and Ellen Hollingsworth, "How Obnoxious is the 'Obnoxious Means Test'? The View of AFDC Recipients" (Madison: University of Wisconsin, January 1969 Institute for Research on Poverty Discussion Paper); Richard Pomeroy and Harold Yahr, in collaboration with Lawrence Podell, *Studies in Public Welfare: Effects of Eligibility Investigation on Welfare Clients* (New York: Center for the Study of Urban Problems, City University of New York, 1968); and Martha Ozawa, "Impact of SSI on the Aged and Disabled Poor," *Social Work Research and Abstracts*, 14 (Fall 1978): 3–10.

39. A penetrating description of the ways administrative practices are used to intimidate and deter public assistance applicants is presented by Frances Fox Piven and Richard Cloward in *Regulating the Poor: The Functions of Public Welfare* (New York: Pantheon Books, 1971), 147–82. Also see Betty Mandell, "Welfare and Totalitarianism: Part I. Theoretical Issues," *Social Work*, 16(1) (January 1971): 17–25.

40. For a discussion of income testing, see Sheila Kamerman and Alfred Kahn, "Universalism and Income Testing in Family Policy: New Perspectives on an Old Debate," *Social Work*, 34(4) (July–August 1987): 279.

41. For example, see George Hoshino, "Can the Means Test Be Simplified?" *Social Work*, 10(3) (July 1965): 98–104.

42. Titmuss, *Commitment to Welfare*, 114–15.

43. Salil Tripathi, "Caste-ing the Net Too Wide," *Wall Street Journal*, May 22, 2006

44. Bob Herbert, "Renovating HUD," *New York Times*, October 16, 1998.

45. The Kaiser Commission on Medicaid and the Uninsured, "Who Needs Medicaid?" April, 2006.

46. Vera Shlakman, "The Safety-Net Function in Public Assistance: A Cross-National Exploration," *Social Service Review*, 46(2) (June 1972): 207.

47. Stuart A. Kirk and Herb Kutchins, *The Selling of DSM*, 1992, p. 229.

48. Ibid., p. 230

49. Ibid., p. 226.

50. The "iron law of specificity" is based on our experiences participating in and observing the behavior of numerous planning and policy-making bodies. To see it operate in a microcosm (for those who doubt its power), we would suggest that at the next meeting in which you participate where a policy decision is pending on a fairly abstract issue, and there is some floundering, deliberately make a proposal that is simply plausible and contains some specification of the issue in concrete units, such as amount of dollars, units of service, numbers of people to be served, and the like. Then mark the time it takes for the discussion to shift from philosophy to considerations of whether the decision should involve a little more or a little less of the concrete units in your proposal.

51. For further discussion of the poverty index, see Mollie Orshansky, "Measuring Poverty: A Debate," *Public Welfare*, 33 (Spring 1975): 46–55; Peter Townsend, *Poverty in the United Kingdom: A Survey of Household Resources and Standards of Living* (Berkeley, Calif.: University of California Press, 1979); The Heritage Foundation, "How 'Poor' are America's Poor," September 21, 1990; Robert Greenstein, "Attempts to Dismiss Census Poverty Data," Center on Budget and Policy Priorities, September 28, 1993; and Constance F. Citro and Robert T. Michael, *Measuring Poverty: A New Approach* (Washington, D.C.: National Academy Press, 1995).

52. Robert Hunter, *Poverty*, Peter d'A. Jones (ed.) (New York: Harper & Row, 1965, originally published 1904), 2.

53. Eleanor Baugher and Leatha Lamison-White, U.S. Bureau of the Census, Current Population Reports, Series P60–194, *Poverty in the United States: 1995* (Washington, D.C.: U.S. Government Printing Office, 1996), xii.

54. See, for example, Richard Titmuss, "Equity, Adequacy, and Innovation in Social Security," *International Social Security Review*, 23(2) (1970): 259–68.

55. Richard Hohaus, "Equity, Adequacy, and Related Factors in Old-Age Security," in William Haber and Wilbur Cohen (eds.), *Social Security: Programs, Problems, and Policies* (Homewood, Ill.: Richard Irwin, 1960), 61.

56. Drawing boundaries is a recurrent problem with this method of allocation. Exactly where any given central city low-income neighborhood begins and ends is a matter that even carefully designed empirical research rarely settles to everyone's satisfaction. For a technical analysis of this issue, see Avery Guest and James Zuiches, "Another Look at Residential Turnover in Urban Neighborhoods: A Note on 'Racial Change in a Stable Community' by Harvey Molotch," *American Journal of Sociology*, 77(3) (November 1971): 457–71. We should add that methodological efforts at boundary definition in most Community Action Programs were superficial.

57. Sar Levitan, *The Great Society's Poor Law* (Baltimore: Johns Hopkins University Press, 1970).

58. Center for Law and Social Policy, *Families on the Edge: Homeless Young Parents and Their Welfare Experiences*, November 20, 2002.

59. For example, see Oliver Moles, Robert Hess, and Daniel Fascione, "Who Knows Where to Get Public Assistance?" *Welfare in Review*, 6(5) (September/October 1968).

60. Greg Acs, et. al., "The Road Not Taken? Changes in Welfare Entry during the 1990s," The Urban Institute, December 2003.
61. Kirk Victor, "Helping the Haves," *National Journal* (April 14, 1990): 898–901.
62. Robert Pear, "H.M.O.s Warned on Recruiting Only Fit Medicare Clients," *New York Times*, June 11, 1999, 1.
63. Howard Chernick, "Wide Cast for Safety Net," Economic Policy Institute Briefing Paper, November, 1995.
64. Quoted in *The New Republic*, July 8, 1996, 17.
65. Lester Thurow, "The Birth of a Revolutionary Class," *New York Times Magazine*, May 19, 1996, 46.
66. Robert Samuelson, "Paying for Baby Boomers" *Newsweek*, August 6, 2007.

5

The Nature of Social Provision

> The only crucial question becomes one of waste or economy. The two alternatives for redistributional reforms, in-cash or in-kind, therefore have to be compared as to their effectiveness in relation to financial outlays. Just because both systems are costly, they must be scrutinized as choices. It would be an illusion to pretend that both lines could be followed. No budget could expand widely in two different directions.
>
> Alva Myrdal
> *Nation and Family, 1941*

The strain between community and individualist tendencies in the welfare state is nowhere more apparent than in choices concerning the forms of social provision. Two forms of provision mark the traditional line of debate in this policy dimension: benefits in-cash versus benefits in-kind. Should needy families be provided a monthly income to cover their basic needs or should help be given as food and fuel, clothing, and shelter? Should children be guaranteed education in the basic public schools or should their families receive cash, or an equivalent voucher, providing them options in the educational marketplace? The choice posed in these questions, although fairly simple to comprehend, is quite another matter to resolve.

Basic Forms: Cash versus In-Kind

One of the earliest arguments in favor of in-kind benefits was advanced in the 1930s by Swedish economist Alva Myrdal in the context of that country's debate over the nature of child welfare provisions. For Myrdal, benefits in-kind were superior to cash children's allowances because of economies of scale. That is, public enterprise, presumably efficient in the manufacture and distribution of mass-produced goods and services, would provide shoes or clothing or similar products at low cost. The alternative—cash grants that could be used to purchase privately produced goods—was viewed as far more expensive. In the state planning perspective of the period, a uniform benefit, mass produced and centrally distributed, was seen as eliminating many of the wasteful, duplicative aspects of competition in the open marketplace.[1]

Myrdal also suggested that assistance in-kind was more effective than cash subsidies because benefits landed squarely on their targets. If the policy goal, for example, was to enhance child welfare, the question of effectiveness becomes, How much of the benefit directly serves this objective?[2] Using this criterion, the drawback of cash is clear—money subsidies cannot be controlled at the point of consumption. There is no way to guarantee that a child's allowance (or any cash subsidy) will not be incorporated into the general family budget and used to purchase a variety of items, only a portion of which may apply directly to the intended purpose.

The argument advanced by the classic theorists of welfare economics, on the other hand, posits that cash provisions are optimal because cash gives its users maximum choice, therefore "maximizing their utility" (i.e., their happiness). Theoretically at least, it can be demonstrated that, given $50 to spend freely, an individual will invariably achieve a higher level of satisfaction ("welfare") than one given $50 worth of goods and services specified by someone else. This position, of course, assumes a consumer who is rational and capable of judging precisely what is in his or her best interest. It further assumes that maximizing the preferences of individuals also serves the good of the broader community—that the choices made by consumers for their own welfare aggregate to advance the common welfare.[3]

The case for the superior effectiveness of in-kind benefits, on the other hand, hinges on their ability to advance specific community concerns. With public control, food, medical care, school lunches, and other common objectives can be distributed directly. Given free choice, recipients of welfare benefits can purchase booze, plasma TVs, or iPhones; benefits in-kind, restricting such "bad" choices, ensure that public judgments about appropriate consumption are advanced.

Some of the hazards of cash benefits are apparent from the results of the Experimental Housing Allowance Program (EHAP) conducted by the U.S. Department of Housing and Urban Development during the 1970s and 1980s. An elaborate social experiment executed over an eleven-year period, EHAP involved 30,000 households in twelve sites across the country. The impact of unrestricted housing allowances on patterns of housing consumption was one of several questions analyzed. In Pittsburgh and Phoenix, the sites chosen to explore the issue, 1800 low-income households, received housing allowance grants over the course of three years. Findings revealed that only very small portions of the allowances were actually spent on housing, just 10 percent in Pittsburgh and 25 percent in Phoenix.[4] For most recipients, the allowances served principally as a general income supplement.

To make sure that social provisions further the purposes for which they are designated, Myrdal called for "increasing control from the consumption side" (i.e., stipulating the forms of public benefits). She posited this kind of "social engineering" as a manifestation of benign social policy based on cooperation and group loyalty. For Myrdal, the in-kind approach rested on "social solidarity and the pooling of resources for common aims" rather than just the "insurance of individual interests."[5]

Hence, the core of the argument—the imposition of social controls to harness individual interests to the collective good. As Holden puts it, "only through in-kind assistance is society able to exercise a measure of control over the final utilization of the tax dollar."[6]

The term *social control*, of course, has a distinctly negative connotation. Critics have always charged that the welfare state is nothing but a device for regulating the conduct of the poor and underprivileged, a repressive mechanism that "keeps people in their place," maintaining conformity to an unjust order. The frequency with which this indictment is made does not constitute proof of guilt. Yet, to be sure, the charge is not without substance, neither today nor 120 years ago. As Briggs notes,

> Many of Bismarck's critics accused him, not without justification, of seeking through his legislation to make German workers "depend" upon the state. The same charges have been made against the initiators of all "welfare" (and earlier, of poor law) policy. Yet it was Bismarck himself who drew a revealing distinction between the degrees of obedience (or subservience) of private servants and servants at court. The latter would "put up with much more" than the former because they had pensions to look forward to. "Welfare" soothed the spirit, or perhaps tamed it.[7]

In general, social welfare professionals find social control a disagreeable element of policy. We mention this because the objectionable functions associated with, and the resistive feelings aroused by, the term should not restrict our faculty to weigh the case for provisions in-kind. Social controls are required to regulate a complex and highly interdependent society. Regulation that replaces the power of the individual with the power of the community, Freud observed, "constitutes the decisive step of civilization."[8] The issue is not whether we will have controls but whether they will be designed to realize our ideals of human dignity and justice or to serve pernicious ends—to soothe or to tame the spirit.

Clearly, Alva Myrdal proposed social controls for estimable purposes. Yet the dilemma of social control exercised through in-kind benefits is that, although such control may facilitate the realization of collective aims, it also restricts the freedom of the consumer, rich or poor. Myrdal recognized these objections. However, she suggested that at least in regard to provisions for children, in-kind benefits posed no constraints on consumer sovereignty because "children rarely have much voice in decisions about the use of the family income."[9] This defense is hardly persuasive, however, especially in the contemporary cash–kind debate. As Nobel economist Milton Friedman pointed out,

> The belief in freedom is for "responsible" units, among whom we include neither children nor insane people. In general, this problem is avoided by regarding the family unit as the basic unit and therefore parents as responsible for their children.[10]

While advocating benefits in-kind, nevertheless, Myrdal's position was less than doctrinaire. And even she was not completely persuaded by her own argument that such benefits didn't limit freedom of choice. Hence her counsel to exercise caution when applying the in-kind principle, especially for inexpensive items that often are imbued with personal meaning:

> Clothing falls in that category and it thus seems to be difficult to subsidize in-kind. Here personal taste is delicate and social prestige has become involved. Even if some class equalization in clothing, especially for children, is judged desirable, it would probably be extremely unwise to force any uniformity on families. . . . It would be cheaper, perhaps extremely rational but still a bit inhuman, to provide layettes, bedding, and

CAPSULE 5.1 • *Cash and Chaos*

Researchers have discovered that government benefit checks to poor minorities are generating accidents, homicides and substance abuse leading to deaths. The evidence lies in the fact that the federal government mails out the checks at the start of every month and deaths from these causes are higher in the first week of each month, compared with the last seven days of the prior month:

- Deaths from substance abuse jump 14 percent during the first week
- Homicides go up 6.2 percent and suicides rise 5.3 percent

- Motor vehicle accidents increase 2.8 percent

According to the study director, David Phillips, "our data raise the possibility that when you try to help by giving money to an addict, you feed the habit instead of the person." Public cash programs can easily be spent on illegal drugs and alcohol.

Phillips suggested that the federal government should consider acting more like a private charity, to keep addicts from binging in the first few days of each month.

From "Study Links Deaths to Timing of Aid Checks" by Laura R. Vanderkam, *The Washington Times*, July 8, 1999. Copyright © 1999 The Washington Times, LLC. This reprint does not constitute or imply any endorsement or sponsorship of any product, service, company or organization.

baby carriages for all newborn children. All these cost items, invested with so much tender care, are certainly not appropriate for communalization.[11]

As a final qualification, Myrdal advised that a serious preference for benefits in-kind should be entertained only *after* an adequate family income was established. In circumstances where it wasn't, she considered cash assistance an "appropriate deviation" from the in-kind principle.

In today's context, many of Myrdal's assertions seem naively quaint. First, the alleged cost savings of publicly produced benefits has been universally challenged. Time and again, state monopolies have been shown to be relatively costly providers of goods and services—be they steel, garbage collection, education, or daycare. And although economies of scale may apply to certain forms of technology, they are certainly questionable in the case of social services such as casework and vocational counseling.[12] This is because social services tend to draw on what Thompson describes as "intensive technology," techniques employed to change and aid the client, with the precise treatment based on constant feedback.[13] This type of technology, tailored to individual cases, substantially hinders standardization.

With social provisions more amenable to standardization, such as clothing, the sacrifice of freedom of choice in favor of a regimented universal product is bound to be discomforting. Moreover, although these benefits in-kind may theoretically eliminate some of the "wasteful" attributes of multiple providers, the market competition associated with cash benefits can generate innovations that result in significant cost reductions over the long haul.

Where economies of scale are not clearly operative, the issue turns on the question of whether cash subsidies and private competition are preferable to provisions in-kind and publicly run bureaucracy. Examining this choice in the context of education, Milton Friedman opted for cash over in-kind provisions because

> [grants] would bring a healthy increase in the variety of educational institutions available and in competition among them. Private initiative and enterprise would quicken the pace of progress in this area as it has in so many others. Government would serve its proper function of improving the operation of the invisible hand without substituting the dead hand of bureaucracy.[14]

The primary appeal of the argument for cash benefits, then, is in its reliance on consumer sovereignty. There is a compelling quality to the argument for an individual's freedom of choice. In essence, it posits the right to self-determination, the right to use one's resources for whatever the psychological or material benefits derived, and, conversely, the right to command one's resources toward whatever future is desired. It is the right of individuals to exercise self-indulgence as well as self-denial.

This viewpoint relies heavily on the faith that the market is responsive to consumer demands. On this point, those favoring collective interventions are not convinced. John Kenneth Galbraith, for example, argued that the consumer "is subject to forces of advertising and emulation by which production creates its own demand." According to this proposition, which he label the "dependence effect," consumer wants are not determined independently. Rather, the producers of goods and services also manufacture consumer *desires*.[15] The counterargument is that producers cannot determine consumer wants; they merely provide information about what is available and endeavor to convince the consumer of its worth and value.[16] Whether or not the "dependence effect" is as consequential as Galbraith would have, his proposition discloses one of the hidden perils of unqualified acceptance of the market mechanism: namely, consumer awareness and skills must be taken into account when considering voluntary exchanges in pursuit of rational self-interest. Rational choices require objective information about the items to be consumed. Such knowledge is often expensive and difficult to obtain. The predicament is more intense for the poor and ill educated. As Rivlin explains,

> Unless he knows what he is buying, a consumer cannot chose rationally. Yet, in the social [welfare] area, it is very difficult for him to find out anything about the quality of service before he uses it. Moreover, the costs of shopping around or sampling the merchandise of a hospital or a school may be prohibitive.[17]

A multitude of studies examining Medicaid, for example, have demonstrated that no-strings cash transfers can hardly optimize the health of socially disadvantaged children. An open-market approach to health services is clearly an insufficient means, by itself, to improved healthcare, because personal factors ranging from a lack of knowledge about healthcare and language problems to an inability to obtain childcare, transportation, or time off from work to keep medical appointments potently deter the full and effective use of healthcare resources.[18]

Other arguments are advanced in favor of cash. Cash, clearly, is convenient to use. Providing cash rather than in-kind benefits saves substantially on administration

CAPSULE 5.2 • *The Case for Cash*

Is the problem that people don't have enough services? Or is the problem that they don't have enough cash? Do poor people need services? Do they need case management? A lot of people say they do. In my own city we have several people that have many case managers. They have a welfare case manager, they have a mental health case manager, they have a foster care case manager, they've got a parole case manager. And so case management, like planning, is one of those ideas that, if you just got enough of it, everything would work out. At least that's what case managers think, and I'm not going to make any comments on case managers because they have needs too.

But if people have a lot of money, they don't need a case manager and they don't need any of your damned services because they just buy them. They buy whatever they want. And that's my first principle—more money is better than less money. What people need is money, and don't call it resources, just call it cash, because you can't beat cash with a stick. Cash is what is required.

Adapted from informal comments by Jerry Brown, Mayor of Oakland, California, to a Brookings Institution National Issues Forum, June 14, 2000.

because it involves little in the way of processing or regulatory costs. Cash is said to remove the stigma attached to in-kind provision, allowing the poor the dignity of managing their own lives. Finally, cash provides the most efficient means of reducing income poverty. Converting all public assistance to the poor to cash would eradicate poverty, at least in terms of its official measure. This is so because in-kind programs— like Food Stamps and social services—don't directly raise the income level of their recipients; their value never directly enters the budget of the poor.

This "efficiency" argument, of course, is somewhat misleading because one's "welfare" demands more than simply an income above the poverty line. If all antipoverty programs were "cashed out" (i.e., converted to their dollar equivalents) and then distributed on the basis of need, we *would* eliminate "official poverty," but we would certainly aggravate the problems that in-kind benefits address—poor health, malnutrition, and inadequate housing. This is because cash means consumer choice, which means people spending their dollars in their own fashion, which means that targeted public interest priorities may not be advanced. It also reflects the fact that cash assistance, even when it brings recipients to income levels near the poverty line, does not provide coverage anywhere near to what in-kind programs—especially medical programs—currently provide. Elderly people in nursing homes, for example, often receive Medicaid benefits at levels many times the poverty line. The acutely ill often receive healthcare benefits worth even more.

Benefits in-kind, then, promote what many view as a more genuine concept of "welfare" than cash alone. Food stamps may not efficiently reduce income poverty, but they may increase a household's food consumption. At the very least, the social control of consumption ensured by the in-kind approach offers a degree of protection to the unwary and the ignorant. From this perspective, it might be said that it is not so much freedom to choose that is reduced by in-kind help as freedom to err or to choose poorly on the basis of limited knowledge. The response to this might be that, without freedom to err, self-determination is a hollow construct. What the collectivist sees as the desirability for social protection, the individualist views as a paternalistic infringement on individual responsibility.

The advocates of the cash option, particularly influential in the 1970s, almost succeeded in getting a negetive income tax enacted as a replacement for welfare. While moribund for the most part in recent years, the cash argument was recently resurrected, not so much as an antipoverty device, but as a way to overhaul the entire apparatus of social welfare—both in its means tested and its universal aspects. The "just cash" banner, hoisted afresh in 2006 with the publication of Charles Murray's *In Our Hands—A Plan to Replace the Welfare State*, which presents the argument for cash in its purest form, as a replacement for the full array of contemporary health, social service, and income support programs.[19] Murray's plan provides an automatic annual grant of $10,000 to every American adult over 21, an amount that would, he calculates, cost considerably less in the years ahead than the price of the status quo. The bulk of Murray's volume is an argument for the beneign effects of "The Plan." It would, he states, eliminate poverty, ensure health and retirement security, and create better citizens by giving people full responsibility for their own lives. At $10,000 per capita, all two-parent families would be guarenteed at least $20,000 a year, an amount that, when suplemented by even modest earnings, would in almost all cases exceed the poverty threshold.

The cash-versus-kind issue, whether couched in terms of a "plan," a negative income tax, a guaranteed annual income, or a universal demogrant, pitches the discussion of social provisions at a fairly high level of generality, a level from which we can observe contending arguments more from a theoretical than from a practical perspective. In the everyday world of policy debate and choice, theoretical justifications often give way to the tug and flow of partisan politics.

Much of our consideration of the cash–kind debate, of course, depends on the degree to which individual freedom and consumer choice are valued in comparison to social justice and community good. Nevertheless, even the most ardent supporters of consumer choice typically bow to the necessity of collective interventions under certain

CAPSULE 5.3 • *Care Not Cash*

San Francisco's Care Not Cash program reached its two-year mark Thursday, eliminating welfare payments in favor of shelter beds, permanent housing, drug treatment, and social services. When the program began in 2004, 2497 homeless people were receiving General Assistance checks of $320 to $390 per month. All of those people have since left the welfare rolls. Over 1300 opted for permanent supportive housing while others left the system altogether. Since the program began, the number of homeless people in the City has dropped 28 percent.

From "Newson Praises Care Not Cash Effort" from *San Francisco Chronicle*, May 5, 2006. Copyright 2006 by San Francisco Chronicle. Reproduced with permission of San Francisco Chronicle in the format Textbook via Copyright Clearance Center, electronic rights used by permission of San Francisco Chronicle.

circumstances, such as providing for the mentally incompetent.[20] When it becomes a voting issue, indeed, as it has in the case of the homeless, voters of all ideological persuasions tend to support policies that replace general cash assistance with concrete food and housing and counseling programs. (See Capsule 5.3.)

And, for the most part, those who advance benefits in-kind are sensitive both to the need for adequate cash support and to the social and psychological benefits of self-expression and autonomy inherent in consumer choice. For them, as Mencher suggests, "the problem is not the potential conflict between individual rights and social controls but the maintenance of maximum opportunity for individual choice as an integral part of the system of government responsibility."[21] To achieve this balance, a mixture of different forms of social provision that offer varying degrees of consumer sovereignty and social control is optimal.

Alternative Forms: An Extension of Choice

We have discussed the nature of social provisions in terms of two basic benefit forms, cash and kind. The forensic utility of this classification affords reasonably firm lines for debate. Yet to think of social provisions in such dichotomous terms oversimplifies the practical realties that policymakers face. Finer distinctions are possible and desirable for analytic precision.

Social benefits may come in a variety of forms, from those that serve to enhance individual power to provisions in the form of concrete goods. Embedded in these varied forms is a dimension of transferability—the extent to which the provision allows for consumer choice. For example, public housing units, cash supplements for housing, and rent vouchers offer varying degrees of freedom of choice to the consumer. Conversely, they ensure to varying degrees that public support will not be used for anything other than its intended purposes. In terms of form and transferability, social provisions may be broadly classified into six categories: opportunities, services, goods, vouchers and tax credits, cash, and power.

Opportunities are incentives and sanctions employed to achieve desired ends. Although this is the vaguest type of direct provision, it is not unimportant; much social policy is concerned with the creation and distribution of opportunities. Unlike goods and services, opportunity benefits involve the provision of civil rights or an "extra chance." Sometimes the extra chance is built into the basis of social allocations, as in the additional points afforded veterans on civil service exams and the special efforts of schools to recruit underrepresented students. In these cases, the nature of the provision considerably overlaps the basis of social allocations. Opportunities ultimately lead to the acquisition of other benefits. However, opportunities have no immediate transfer value inasmuch as they must be utilized within the context that they are offered. A recipient of opportunity X cannot trade it for opportunity Y, or for goods, services, or other social provisions.

Services are activities performed on the client's behalf, such as in-home care, individual counseling, case management, and job training. These provisions are nontransferable in terms of their immediate market value to recipients.

Goods are concrete commodities such as food, clothing, and housing. These benefits have limited transfer value, generally confined to marginal channels of exchange such as pawnshops, flea markets, and informal barter.

Vouchers and *tax credits* are benefits that have a structured exchange value and may be transferred for resources within a delineated sector. Tax credits, for example, can be used to offset daycare expenses; food stamps can be exchanged for a variety of food products. Such provisions offer greater degrees of freedom of choice than goods or services. As a form of social provision, vouchers have special appeal because they preserve a modicum of consumer sovereignty (within a sector) while allowing for the exercise of social control (between sectors). Thus, they attract a range of proponents with both community and individualist predilections.[22]

Cash benefits, programs such as public assistance, children's allowances, and social insurance, provide unrestricted purchasing power. Any tax arrangements that let individuals and families keep more of their own income also qualify, serving as indirect cash benefits. These provisions, of course, all have universal exchange value, offering the most latitude for consumer choice.

Power involves the redistribution of influence over the control of goods and resources. It can be achieved through policies that transfer policymaking authority to a particular group of people. In the 1960s and 1970s, for example, federal policy often required representation of the poor, service consumers, and other disadvantaged people on the boards of agencies that dispensed social welfare benefits, such as the Community Action Agencies established during the War on Poverty. Here, social provisions were incorporated into policy decisions about the structure of the delivery system (which we will examine in Chapter 6). Although such power cannot be "spent" in the same way as cash or credits, it offers a significant degree of latitude to command social and economic choices.

In addition to these forms of provisions, there are social interventions that indirectly assist individuals and groups. A good deal of important social welfare policy, rather than providing tangible benefits to specific individuals in need, establishes institutions that are instrumental in the developing and implementing benefit programs. *Instrumental provisions* are those that encourage more efficient and effective arrangements among agencies that supply direct social welfare benefits.

To illustrate, let us consider Title III of the 1973 amendments to the Older Americans Act, which established more than 600 Area Agencies on Aging (AAAs) throughout the United States. These agencies, which are ongoing, have responsibilities for planning, pooling, and coordinating local resources to produce comprehensive service systems for the elderly. The AAAs also are expected to function as advocates for the elderly, monitoring and evaluating relevant policies and programs. In this fashion, AAAs furnish indirect forms of aid in their jurisdictions.

Although instrumental provisions influence the distribution of social benefits through planning and coordination, there appears to be a tendency among indirect service agencies, such as AAAs, to move into the provision of direct services. There are several reasons for this sort of functional drift, not the least of which is that it strengthens the agencies' ties to the elderly constituents who receive immediate and concrete benefits from the direct services offered.[23]

Vouchers: Balancing Social Control and Consumer Choice

Compared to cash or in-kind provisions, social benefits in the form of vouchers possess a special attraction—they preserve consumer choice while allowing a degree of social control. This ensures that benefits serve a vital public purpose, be it the provision of food, shelter, education, or healthcare.

The food stamp program is the largest and best known voucher arrangement in the United States. In its original form, public assistance recipients and other low-income persons were eligible for paper food coupons with a designated cash value that could be used to purchase food products at supermarkets (see Figure 5.1). Since 2004, benefits have largely been provided as electronic benefit transfers (EBTs), a debit card system that allows recipients to transfer their government food stamp benefits directly to the food retailer. In addition to reducing the stigma of coupons, electronic benefits are far more administratively efficient for markets, banks, and the federal government.

Starting as a pilot project in 1961, food stamps grew at a phenomenal pace after the program went national in 1964. Between 1967 and 1975, the number of participants soared from 1.5 million to 19.3 million, at which time the program came to be

FIGURE 5.1　*The Currency of Food.*

known in Congress as the "food stampede." From 1970 to 2000, program costs rose from 600 million to 18 *billion* dollars. In the period from 2000 to 2009, costs nearly doubled again, to $35 billion.

Perhaps the first *educational* voucher scheme was advanced by Milton Friedman in 1955.[24] Instead of directly financing and operating public schools, he proposed that government should distribute vouchers to parents which could be used to purchase education at the schools of their choice. By introducing the competition of the economic market, school programs would presumably become more innovative and the overall quality of education would improve. It was also possible, of course, that some schools might effectively deny access to the poor by charging more than the cash value of vouchers, by employing admissions tests that reject weak students, or by misleading the unsophisticated consumer about the quality of their programs. Thus, as a safeguard, later voucher plans, such as those developed by Christopher Jencks and his associates in the 1970s, included a series of protective regulations guarding against discriminatory admissions policies and requiring that precise information on educational programs be made available to aid parents in the intelligent exercise of choice.[25]

The first voucher experiment, conducted in the mid-1970s at the Alum Rock Union Elementary School District in northern California, sought to test the advantages of competition and consumer choice in education. When the Alum Rock demonstration was launched, its design was closer to Jencks's regulated plan than Friedman's *laissez-faire* approach. The Alum Rock voucher concept, moreover, was restricted in a number of ways: Choice was limited to the thirteen of the district's twenty-four public schools; enrollment ceilings were used to maintain a degree of balance between demand and supply; and teachers were assured they would not lose their jobs if their school did not attract enough pupils. Despite these modifications, the Alum Rock demonstration enhanced parental choice and promoted a significant degree of competition among schools.[26]

The findings from Alum Rock revealed that although the range of educational alternatives increased, geography was the predominant consideration for most parents—more than 80 percent selected the schools nearest their homes. And choices

CAPSULE 5.4 • *Voucher Pro*

Government could require a minimum level of schooling financed by giving parents vouchers redeemable for a specified maximum sum per child per year if spent on "approved" educational services. Parents would then be free to spend this sum and any additional sum they themselves provided on purchasing educational services from an "approved" institution of their choice. The educational services could be rendered by private enterprises operated for profit or nonprofit institutions. The role of government would be limited to insuring that the schools met certain minimum standards, such as the inclusion of a minimum common content in their programs, much as it now inspects restaurants to see that they maintain minimum sanitary standards.

Milton Friedman, *Capitalism and Freedom*, 1962, 89.

CAPSULE 5.5 • *Voucher Con*

Though voucher advocates argue that competition would inevitably lead to the triumph of good schools over bad because of the "magic of the marketplace," this seems far from obvious. The success or failure of a given public school program is very difficult to quantify objectively, and most working parents cannot devote endless time to researching the matter.

In fact, it is easy to imagine that the schools that would win the competitive struggle for parental dollars would be those that invested most heavily in advertising and public relations and least heavily in academic content. The actual physical content of most colas or sneakers is almost indistinguishable, but Coke and Nike reign supreme because of massive spending on public image-making and celebrity endorsements. Although fine for the soft drink industry, this is not a desirable model for our public education system.

The gravest danger for widespread school choice is rarely explicitly raised by either side of the debate. Unlike most other nations around the world, which are relatively homogenous in culture and race, we have just a few social institutions that bind our diversity together, and one of the most important has been a unified public school system. Under vouchers, there is a very real possibility that substantial portions of our most vulnerable populations will be drawn into Nation of Islam schools or a variety of ethnic-nationalist ideologies, which could have a lethal effect upon our already fraying social cohesion.

From "Voucher Veto" by Ron K. Unz. Reprinted with permission from the May 3, 1989 issue *The Nation*. For subscription information, call 1-800-333-8536. Portions of each week's Nation magazine can be accessed at http://www.thenation.com.

made among different miniprograms *within* schools favored traditional over new, experimental modes of education.[27] On the matter of educational quality, data from several studies found no significant differences among the academic test scores of students from voucher and nonvoucher schools.[28]

In 1990, Milwaukee, Wisconsin, adopted the nation's first district-wide school voucher program, providing tax-free tuition vouchers enabling low-income children—almost entirely African American and Hispanic—to select either public or private (secular) schools. In 1995, vouchers worth $3600 were provided and over 1000 low-income students, 1 percent of the district student body, were participating. "Low income" was defined as households with incomes below 1.75 times the federal poverty index.

Despite considerable evaluative attention, the results of the Milwaukee experiment are ambiguous. John Witte, a researcher at the University of Wisconsin, has generally given the voucher plan poor grades, concluding that participating students scored about the same as other students in math and reading performance. Voucher advocates, however, argue that the Milwaukee experiment proved that school choice results in higher parental satisfaction, better retention rates, and higher test scores.[29]

The most recent voucher findings, drawn from massive experimental studies conducted in New York City, Dayton, Ohio, and Washington, D.C., appear to show a pattern of academic benefit to African American participants, revealing that after two to three years, African American students in the voucher programs scored significantly higher than their public school peers; the scores of non–African American students, however, did not differ significantly from those of their peers.[30]

While the voucher idea originated on the *laissez-faire* right, the concept has gained support across the political spectrum. African American advocates in several large cities have embraced vouchers as a way to improve ghetto education by providing alternatives to what are perceived as inadequate, unresponsive public schools. Sectarian groups promote the idea as a way to assist parents who wish to send their kids to parochial schools. And many families—apolitical but education minded—see vouchers as a device to gain more influence over the substance of the schooling their children receive.

Although public policy has become more amenable to vouchers—and to other kinds of educational options—the overwhelming majority of U.S. schoolchildren remain in their local public schools, partly because of the inertia of entrenched arrangements and partly out of a very real fear that vouchers would significantly undermine public schools, resulting in even worse education for many children. Against those who see school choice as the means for innovation, efficiency, and consumer empowerment, these critics fear the creation of fragmented, divisive educational systems segregated by income and ideology and the destruction of one of the few institutions in our society that brings together children from different backgrounds and promotes a measure of social integration.

It is important to note that the appeal of educational vouchers isn't limited to the United States. School choice has been embraced in a number of welfare states, including some of those with the strongest social democratic traditions. In Sweden, for example, families are able to select public *or* publicly funded private schools for their children. Since 1991, the number of independent schools has quintupled, nearly all of them funded equally with government "municipal" schools. Most of the independent schools are run by nonprofits, many by churches.[31]

In the *housing* field, conservatives have long argued for vouchers that would allow low-income people to find their own housing in the private market. The federal Section 8 program, enacted during the Nixon administration, was the first significant voucher program to this end. Operating through local housing authorities, Section 8 provides eligible low-income renters a certificate that they can present to any landlord willing to take part in the program. Tenants then pay 30 percent of their monthly income toward the rent, with the federal government making up the rest. In return, landlords agree to federal guidelines that set limits on overall rental charges.

Programs such as Section 8 have many appealing features. They give renters a choice; vouchers can be used anywhere, enabling poor people to blend into ordinary communities. They expand opportunities for decent, appropriate housing. One commentator remarked that they turn "low-income renters into an army of deputies who monitor government spending. Their collective, self-interested discretion amounts to an invisible hand that decides whether the housing needs of the poor are most cheaply met through new construction, existing units, moderate rehabilitation," or other alternatives.[32]

The idea of housing vouchers has a special appeal given the disappointing record of federal housing policy over the past half century. Government public housing strategies—especially inner-city megaprojects—have often been fiascos, and HUD bureaucracy has been prone to inefficiency and scandal. Nevertheless, housing vouchers, though they serve 3.5 million poor U.S residents, remain limited in scope for one important reason: cost. A universal voucher system covering a major portion of the population currently in inadequate housing would be enormously expensive.

Substance of the Social Provision

Our categorization of benefit types in terms of form and transferability permits useful insights into the nature of social provisions, particularly for cash, vouchers, and goods that are fairly concrete. A broad variety of options are possible within each of these categories. For example, the provision of goods may include food commodities, clothing, and shelter; cash may be provided in modest or generous amounts; and vouchers may be designed to cover part or all of the costs of different goods and services. Despite the many alternatives, there is a palpable quality to these types of provisions that makes them readily comprehensible. The substance of these provisions is evident; most of the relevant qualities of the benefit become known as soon as the amount of cash, type of good, and credit or voucher sector are specified.

Consider, again, the school voucher. We can specify a cash value that can be exchanged only to pay for designated educational programs. Different programs might be housed in a single local public school, spread out among a few local public and private schools, or encompass all accredited schools in the country. The point is that once the value of the voucher and the sector in which it can be used are identified, the nature of the provision is substantially clear. It should be noted that with both cash and vouchers, our analysis of social provisions ends at the point that recipients obtain benefits. Subsequent choices concerning how these benefits are utilized involve individual transactions. What is ultimately purchased becomes a matter of individual choice much like any other.

For the other benefit categories—opportunities, services, and power—the substance of the social provision is more abstruse. To understand what is provided requires some probing. Consider a proposal to provide family counseling services. The type of service has been designated—counseling—but the substance of the provision remains ambiguous. It may emphasize information giving, insight therapy, behavior modification, or the alteration of environmental contingencies. It may center on couples, parents and children, or groups. It may be short or long term. And it may be conducted by personnel with a variety of backgrounds and training who base their practice on alternative theories of diagnosis, assessment, and change.

Likewise, daycare may involve a range of services, from bare-bones custodial care to comprehensive child development, depending on staff–child ratios, staff qualifications, program content, and available equipment. Opportunity benefits in the area of employment may range from traditional systems of access to affirmative preferences to quotas. In college admission, there is considerable debate regarding the substance of affirmative action provisions. While the Supreme Court, in 2006, approved the use of race as one element in the admissions process, affirmative action procedures vary widely in their weight and in their character, running the gamut from special recruitment efforts to the modification of admission standards. The redistribution of power in various settings may cover a spectrum of influence, from that exercised by a citizens' advisory committee to community control of local institutions. Without clarifying the substantive aspects of services, opportunities, and power, we are severely limited in understanding precisely what it is that social programs provide.

Expediency of Abstraction

To prescribe that policy analysts should strive for precision in defining the nature of social provisions is not to deny the political function of abstraction. Although our major concern is with comprehending social welfare policy by dissecting the various dimensions of choice, we allow ourselves a momentary detour because, in the real world of policy choice, ambiguity in the design of social provisions serves an important purpose. This is critical to note, if for no other reason than to balance the analytic impulse to dissect social choices with the wisdom of practical experience.

The advantages of leaving the nature of the social provision vague when strong contending views prevail concerning policy specifics. One is that doing so allows those who formulate policies to secure broader support. When social provisions are defined at a high level of abstraction, different parties may read into them what they please, making agreement easier to reach. Upon implementation, additionally, there is greater flexibility and potential for experimentation. Once vague provisions are operationally transformed, of course, former advocates may find themselves startled at the substance of their creation, and may even end up seeking its undoing. Hence, there is a fragile quality to the political expedience of abstraction; it can smooth the way for passage of legislation without necessarily developing the commitments required to support a program over the long haul.

The classic example, the Community Action Program of the Economic Opportunity Act of 1964, spearheaded the War on Poverty under President Johnson. It took approximately six months for this program to move from the drawing board to enactment. John Donovan indicates that few single pieces of domestic welfare legislation of comparable importance had ever moved through Congress with such ease and rapidity. He also observes, "there were only a few people in Washington early in 1964 who had any very clear notion of what community action in fact was."[33]

According to the bill presented to Congress, Community Action would

1. mobilize and utilize, in an attack on poverty, public and private resources of any urban or rural, or combined urban and rural geographical area, . . . including but not limited to a state, metropolitan area, county, city, town, multicity unit, or multicounty unit;
2. provide services, assistance, and other activities of variety, scope, and size to give promise of progress toward elimination of poverty through developing employment opportunities, improving human performance, motivation, and productivity, and bettering the condition under which people live, learn, and work;

3. be developed, conducted, and administered with the maximum feasible participation of residents of the areas and members of the groups [served] . . . ; and

4. be conducted, administered, or coordinated by a public or private non-profit agency . . . broadly representative of the community.[34]

This statement is seemingly innocuous, in part because of the legal syntax, but also because its deft phrasing is general enough to allow different minds to draw different conclusions. The task force responsible for drafting the antipoverty bill viewed community action as a mechanism for increasing the participation and power of the poor in the political life of the community. Daniel Moynihan notes, "The observation that Community Action Programs are a federal effort to re-create the urban ethnic political machines that federal welfare legislation helped dismantle would not misrepresent the attitudes of the task force."[35]

During the Congressional hearings, there was little explication of the idea that community action was intended to transfer power to the poor. One notable exception was Attorney General Robert Kennedy, who pointed out that the poor were powerless to affect the institutions that served them, and that community action could change this pattern.[36] New York City Mayor Robert F. Wagner opposed the provision giving decision-making power to the poor. He stated, "The sovereign government of each locality in which a Community Action Program is proposed should have the power of approval over the makeup of the planning group, the structure of the planning group, and over the plan."[37]

What emerged from the hearings were a number of interpretations, many of which implied that community action would provide primarily instrumental, opportunity, or service benefits.[38] Stressing the instrumental provision, Marion Crank, Speaker of the Arkansas House of Representatives, told the subcommittee, "The important new feature of Title II is that it will encourage a coordinated effort toward solving some of the serious problems in our area."[39] Emphasizing service provision, Robert C. Weaver noted, "The Community Action Programs will focus upon the needs of low-income families and persons. They will provide expanded and improved services and facilities where necessary in such fields as education, job training and counseling, health, and housing and home improvement."[40] But the nebulous quality of the provision was typified by comments of one Representative who referred to Title II as the "community facilities provision."[41] Under the circumstances, it is not surprising that the requirement for "maximum feasible participation," soon the *bête noire* of local politicians, slipped through the hearings virtually unquestioned.

Thus, depending on viewpoint and preference, it was assumed that community action would be an instrument to coordinate the planning and delivery of local services, an expansion in the level of services for the poor, or an increase in the decision-making powers of the poor to formulate and administer their own local programs. Community action was defined broadly enough to encompass all these interpretations. But two things were left unclear. The first was the order of priority. The possibility that the provisions might be mutually inconsistent was largely overlooked. No one, for example, dealt with the possibility that transferring power to the poor might mitigate against the increase of goods and services and impede efforts at coordination. No guidelines were offered for trade-offs among different objectives. More significantly, there was little probing of the substance of these various social provisions. What *types* of services did the poor need and want? How *much* power and influence did "maximum feasible participation" imply? Did "participation" mean that the poor were to be advisors or to have a controlling vote? Serious consideration of these choices would, no doubt, have delayed passage of the legislation. Instead, it sailed through Congress in a haze of abstraction.

When it came to implementation, and efforts were made to specify and operationalize "maximum feasible participation," the program encountered heavy resistance. By 1965, when the first guidelines for involvement of the poor were issued, local mayors were already expressing considerable displeasure with the program and were demanding that local governments be given greater control.[42] The Bureau of the Budget also reacted by suggesting that the poor should be involved less as policymakers and more as community action personnel.

In 1966, Congress imposed its own restrictions on the use of community action funds, and by 1967 the Economic Opportunity Act was amended to clarify the substance of "maximum feasible participation." These amendments gave states, counties, and cities the power to incorporate local Community Action Agencies within their own governmental structures, or to designate other groups to fill this role. Although very few local governments chose to exercise this option, the amendments symbolized and reaffirmed the fundamental authority and control of local governments. In addition, these amendments limited the composition of Community Action Agency boards to no more than one-third poor people, with the remaining membership divided equally between public officials and representatives from the private sector. When the dust had settled, the definition of "maximum feasible participation" as power allocated to the poor had been carefully limited.

In 1974, the scale tipped even farther in a conservative direction. The Office of Economic Opportunity (OEO), which financed and coordinated the Community Action Agencies, was dismantled. With its removal, control of the Community Action Program was transferred to a new Community Services Administration (CSA), and its financial base experienced a precipitous decline.

Social Provisions as Reflections of Policy Values

As noted, choices concerning the form of social provision can largely be understood in terms of individualist and community values, with individualists disposed to consumer sovereignty and communitarians disposed to social direction. Although this perspective affords a general level of explanation, particular social provision choices often get rather complicated.

Social provisions, for example, often directly reflect policy objectives. To fully comprehend why a policy design contains specific provisions requires insight into the assumptions that underlie policy objectives. Such insight requires that we understand policy objectives not simply as ends, but as means–ends relationships. That is, objectives articulate how the cause-and-effect relationships of social problems are perceived. They reflect, in essence, the theoretical outlooks of those involved in policy formulation.

In practice, of course, policy objectives are rarely stated in theoretical terms because that would tend to make decision makers appear unsure. The notion that "objectives are only theories" does find its way into many research and demonstration programs. But on the whole, program objectives are put forth with emphatic assurances that they provide valid solutions to clearly understood problems. To do otherwise—to candidly and skeptically advance programs as hypotheses—is to invite the wrath of advocates and to undermine the confidence of potential allies. If policymakers are tentative about a program, the public is not likely to be supportive. On the other hand, if their confidence is misplaced, and results are disappointing, they can lose credibility.

Although planners, administrators, and policy analysts may sympathize with the plight of elected officials, it is not their own. To be effective in what they do, they need a clear grasp of the theoretical quality of policy objectives. Moynihan's charge that the failure of professionals in developing the War on Poverty "lay in not accepting—not insisting upon—the theoretical nature of their propositions" may be inflated, but it underscores the point.[43] That is, professional obligation entails the critical examination of the theories and assumptions that support the choice of different social provisions. As Suchman explains,

> [T]he process of seeking to understand the underlying assumptions of an objective is akin to that of questioning the validity of one's hypothesis. Involved is a concern with the theoretical basis of one's belief that "activity A will produce effect B." Such concerns are the earmark of professional growth. So long as one proceeds on faith in accepted procedures without questioning the basis for this faith, one is functioning as a technician rather than a professional. The future development of the various fields of public service as science as well as art will depend to a large extent upon their willingness to challenge the underlying assumptions of their program objectives.[44]

With this in mind, let us take a final look at the Community Action Program. We have noted that its major thrust was posited in the form of instrumental, service, and power provisions, depending on the different perspectives involved. These different viewpoints did not derive from whim; in most cases, they reflected certain theories and assumptions about the causes of and remedies for poverty.

There are many intricate theories of poverty, but the purpose of this discussion is to illustrate how theory applies to the analysis of social provisions. Rather than present the details of these theories, we will consider three independent variables around which many are organized: *resource deficiency*, *individual deficiency*, and *institutional deficiency*.[45]

From the viewpoint of resource deficiency, the lack of basic material resources such as healthcare, housing, and income is the primary characteristic of poverty and a major factor contributing to its development and perpetuation.[46] Simply put, this is a formal expression of the conventional assumption that "to get, you must first have." To the extent that Community Action Program provisions were concentrated on special kinds of services, such as neighborhood health centers and daycare, program objectives were based on the proposition that poverty could be reduced by changing the circumstances under which people live.

The theory of individual deficiency, in its most primitive form, reflects the Social Darwinist view that poverty results from personal defects—some are simply less fit and less adaptable than others. A less invidious version of the theme focuses on the "culture of poverty"; poverty is explained in terms of a debilitating cultural and environmental milieu that incapacitates the poor. The defect is not biological; rather the values, norms, and behaviors of the poor are at fault. In either case, this perspective leads to the conclusion that poor people themselves must be changed.[47] To the extent that Community Action Program provisions were concentrated on counseling, job training, and educational services, program objectives were based on the proposition that reducing poverty required changing skills, values, and behaviors.

Alternatively, poverty may be explained in terms of institutional deficiency. The basic assumption here is that social welfare institutions not only fail to function properly, they operate in ways that sustain poverty.[48] This perspective finds expression in two provisions of the Community Action Program. The objective of the instrumental provision, with the Community Action Program serving a coordinating and planning function, was to improve institutional performance by increasing the rationality, efficiency, and comprehensiveness of service provision. The institutional deficiency, here interpreted as a technical problem, is addressed through administrative channels. The provision of power, on the other hand, views institutional deficiency as a political problem. The objective, then, is to make social welfare institutions more responsive to the poor, not through technical rationality, but by increasing the political capacity of those in poverty to influence these institutions. To the extent that the Community Action Program was interpreted in these terms, program objectives were based on the proposition that reducing poverty required change in the institutional structures that contribute to poverty's maintenance.

Which are the best or the preferred interpretations of the Community Action Program? On this question, the analysis sheds little light. An explication of the theories and assumptions that underlie the choice of different social provisions does not create the rules for choosing. However, it does help to clarify *what* we are choosing. First, it offers a basis for making judgments about the coherence of policy design in terms of the complementarities of social provisions. Many social welfare policies have multiple objectives, requiring the delivery of more than one type of provision. In some cases, these objectives are incompatible because of their underlying assumptions. For instance, it has been suggested that the service and power objectives of the Community Action Program were contradictory. This can be explained by the different assumptions underlying each objective. To put it bluntly, if the poor suffer mainly from individual deficiencies (their need for services, for example), then increasing their power vis-à-vis service-giving agencies is tantamount to placing the healer in the arms of the lame. However, if institutional deficiency is seen as the major problem, then offering increased services only buffers and protects the status quo.

The second function of this analysis is to specify the major independent variables on which we are putting our money, so to speak. Clarification of this point provides guidelines to assemble empirical data that bear on the validity of the assumptions and also furnishes referents for future policy evaluation. Social welfare policy is rarely based on evidence that is so clear and overwhelming as to be determinate. Nevertheless, it is pertinent to inquire about evidence that clearly ties a given provision to a specified outcome. Faith may be a potent sedative for uncertainty, but it is insufficient for the thoughtful design of social provisions.

Yet the influence of sheer faith in underlying theories and assumptions cannot be ignored; although we emphasize empirical grounding, choices regarding social provisions are, often as not, light on evidence. A prominent example is cited by Connery and others in discussing the major assumptions supporting the development of federal community mental health programs:

> In 1963, when the basic legislation was being considered, it was noted that there were no American studies demonstrating that, when the quality of care was held constant, community-based treatment facilities functioned any better than those located in large hospitals. If this is valid, it would appear that the nature of mental health services and the investment of hundreds of millions of dollars throughout the country was substantially shaped on the basis of firmly held and persuasively argued beliefs that lacked a substantial empirical base.[49]

We introduced this section by suggesting that understanding specific choices concerning social provisions required a grasp of the theories and assumptions underlying policy objectives. At this point we advise that a distinction be drawn between theories and assumptions (along the lines noted in Chapter 3) with theories deriving largely from empirical insights and assumptions being based on faith and ideology. Obviously, this distinction is often difficult to make and is always relative. Yet heightened sensitivity to the "why" of social choice is enhanced by considering not only the cause-and-effect relationships that underlie policy objectives but also the degree to which these relationships are informed by theory or assumption—by the tenets of evidence or faith.

Cash, Kind, and the Cycles of Public Assistance

The tension between cash and kind in all its practical and philosophical dimensions has been persistently illustrated in the evolution of U.S. public assistance. Should government provide direct cash aid to needy families, or should cash be accompanied (or replaced) by programs and regulations advancing community values? Should poverty be addressed by giving poor families money sufficient to ensure the satisfaction of their basic material needs, or should cash benefits be conditioned by a variety of obligations, making assistance a "social contract" with "personal responsibility" for jobs, education, and moral conduct the quid pro quo for aid?

What is interesting is that the responsibility theme, at various times, has been embraced by both the left and the right. In the early 1960s, for example, welfare reform was staunchly tied to the provision of social services. Social workers and their allies argued that providing AFDC without supportive counseling and other social services was a shortsighted, unrealistic way to attack poverty. Social work leaders, led by the National Association of Social Workers, believed that welfare recipients faced human problems that required more than just cash assistance; the forces undermining self-sufficiency could not be addressed by the simple expedient of supplying money.

Money was important, but it took face-to-face counseling and attention to individual client circumstances to produce long-term positive results.

In 1962, as we have discussed, Congress endorsed this theory, and social services for the first time were legislated as a major strategy for welfare reform. Rehabilitation was the key word, and social services were funded to strengthen welfare families, reduce dependency, and help the poor gain the knowledge and skills necessary to adapt to the mainstream.

With the demise of the services approach of the Great Society, welfare reform in the late 1960s and early 1970s turned toward cash strategies. Negative income approaches, first promoted by Milton Friedman in his conservative manifesto *Capitalism and Freedom*, in 1962, were endorsed both by the left and right, and Richard Nixon nearly succeeded in having his Family Assistance Plan (guaranteed annual income) enacted in 1970. Although social services were scarcely defunded, their value as an instrument for relieving poverty was deemphasized. In the legal theory of the decade, cash assistance increasingly was seen as a right, akin to a property right or a civil right, and any insistence on social work services, jobs, or counseling was perceived as demeaning, even exploitative. And although the left viewed cash as a basic right of citizenship, the right saw it as a way to disentangle AFDC from the welfare bureaucrats. As Richard Nixon stated, "People should have the responsibility for spending carefully and taking care of themselves. Patronizing surveillance by social workers

CAPSULE 5.6 • *"Where Have You Gone, Florence Crittenton?"*

Before the government offered cash payments to unmarried mothers, hundreds of private maternity homes provided vital services in every major city. These important institutions cared for tens of thousands of endangered women and children by building confidence, inculcating healthy new habits, actively discouraging illegitimacy, and working to integrate endangered families back into mainstream society.

Within two years of AFDC's enactment, the number of individuals receiving government public assistance had more than doubled, including lots of unmarried mothers. Maternity homes went into eclipse. Institutions that expected behavioral reform could not compete with no-strings checks.

It is time we fixed [this] error. Unwed motherhood should no longer generate entitlement to public cash aid or be perceived by teenage girls as the road to economic independence.

Young unwed mothers as a class should be viewed as persons peculiarly in need of supervision, education, discipline, and reform, and not as appropriate beneficiaries of unconditional cash payments. Group homes can play an extremely useful role in this area. They are a way for communities to provide care in the critical months before and after birth, and to instruct new mothers in childcare and the responsibilities of parenting. They can assist placements for adoption. And they can be the means by which the community discourages further out-of-wedlock births.

From "Back to the Maternity Home" by George Liebmann, *American Enterprise*, January/February, Vol. 6, No. 1, 1995. Used by permission of The American Enterprise Institute for Public Policy Research, Washington, D.C.

makes children and adults feel stigmatized and separate. What the poor need to help them rise out of poverty is money."[50]

With the election of Ronald Reagan in 1980, the pendulum once again swung toward services—but services of a very specific type. With the increasing expectation that able-bodied recipients of aid should be required to work, or at least trained for work, the AFDC amendments of 1988—the Family Support Act—created the Job Opportunities and Basic Skills Training (JOBS) program to transform welfare into a transitional program geared toward jobs. Although JOBS funded a broad range of job-related services and created minimum requirements for caseload participation, its achievements have been unimpressive. By 1994, for example, only 13 percent of all AFDC adults were involved in JOBS programs, and most of these involvements were related to education, without a strong employment focus.[51]

By the mid-1990s, skepticism about cash welfare had become a paramount theme of the right. Abandoning the consumer-choice pro-cash orientation of their conservative forebears, Congressional Republicans crafted new welfare measures that harkened back to a Victorian paternalism in their emphasis on work and responsibility. The enactment of welfare reform in 1996 set into motion a significant shift away from the cash approach to helping the poor. Given the substantial emphasis in the new welfare legislation on moving recipients into the workforce, most states adopted "work first" approaches in the late 1990s, requiring participation in short-term work search and job readiness and skill-building activities, and then supporting employment with childcare services and medical assistance. As time went on and policymakers increasingly realized that "hard to employ" clients faced exceptional difficulties in getting or keeping jobs, greater emphasis was given in most states to intensive and longer-term supportive services as a means of ensuring progress from welfare to a steady job.

Transportation assistance, for example, has been provided in many communities. According to William Julius Wilson, the "spatial mismatch" between city residents and suburban jobs has been a particular barrier for African Americans "because they have less access to private automobiles and do not have a network system that supports organized car pools. Accordingly, they depend heavily on public transportation and therefore have difficulty getting to the suburbs, where jobs are more plentiful."[52]

In addition, TANF programs invested in postemployment services and social work–oriented approaches such as drug and alcohol treatment and services for the victims of domestic violence. A related necessity, of course, has been for helpful, knowledgeable welfare staff able to effectively connect clients to available resources. The first years of welfare reform made evident the great need for caseworkers who could address the multiple needs of the least employable, most troubled families by following up on clients, providing encouragement and advice, and assisting with the all-too-common problems of domestic violence, ill health, and substance abuse.

Federal data dramatically portray the shift from cash to services. While cash assistance made up more than three-quarters of all TANF spending in 1997, it composed just over one-third in 2004.[53] Many of those receiving TANF support today are not even on the welfare rolls, since the official tally of those "on welfare" only counts individuals who are receiving monthly cash aid. So while fewer and fewer people are getting monthly welfare checks (as we shall see in Chapter 8), more and more are getting childcare and vocational training and other help designed to promote work.

When we examine the *overall* public assistance caseload, furthermore, the proportion of recipients relying on cash aid is also far lower than in the past. At the same time that the number receiving cash aid through TANF and other cash programs has been plummeting, *non*cash benefits through Medicaid, social services, and food stamps have grown. In 2008, for example, the Medicaid rolls exceeded 25 million beneficiaries while 29 million received food stamps. Just 14 million, by comparison, were on cash welfare.

Emerging Issues: Choice for Whom?

While the nature of social provision remains one the most controversial areas of welfare debate, the specific issues at the focus of political contention have changed significantly over the past generation. In the 1960s and 1970s, many advocates of reform on both the left and the right saw income transfers as the best way to confront poverty. For conservatives, cash payments would maximize choice and remove the inefficiencies of bureaucracy-heavy service programs. For progressives, guaranteed income would incorporate the poor into the mainstream—the poor, after all, were just like everyone else, they just lacked economic resources.

For over a decade now, the cash approach to solving the *general* problem of poverty has been in disfavor. While one particular cash strategy (the earned income tax credit) has successfully lifted many low-income *workers*, and their families, above the poverty line, cash per se is no longer viewed as a reasonable policy for addressing the needs of the large number of working-aged adults who are *apart* from the labor market. The disincentives of "free cash," once a topic of debate among economists, have become a primary element in the mainstream critique of welfare. And the public increasingly sees poverty as a psychological or cultural phenomenon, rather than as purely an economic one. Troubled, addicted, illiterate, or mentally disordered individuals clearly need more than simply a check. While a basic level of money support may be necessary to alleviate material disadvantage, jobs and supportive services are broadly viewed as critical if the goal is to enable individuals to achieve self-sufficiency, and therefore prevent poverty in the long term. Cash by itself can't create job skills, teach someone to read, improve parenting skills, or motivate good (or impede bad) behavior.

Much of the new emphasis on services, as noted in Chapter 4, is directed at the behavior of the poor, and a good part of this emphasis is expressed in service programs that are morally prescriptive in the sense that they promote not only regular employment but also family obligation, sexual responsibility, and sobriety. Paul Starobin calls this new governmental model the "Daddy State":

> For decades, the Nanny State has been the Right's term of opprobrium for the liberal approach to social welfare problems. But now, a provocative new approach is gaining ground. Introducing the Daddy State, an emerging tough-love strategy for treating such festering maladies as unwed parenthood, street crime, and drug abuse. Government acts

not as a compliant supplier of personal needs, but as a demanding, if caring, enforcer of civic responsibility. Nanny Staters are interested in social justice; Daddy Staters in public order.[54]

And it is this "moralized" model, of course, which was incorporated so dramatically into the welfare reform legislation of 1996.

While all but a small faction of libertarians have come to reject the cash-only approach to antipoverty policy, there is a contrary call—for consumer power, consumer choice—in other social welfare fields. At the same time that welfare recipients are having their choices curtailed, for example, there is a potent movement in favor of privatization—whether it be through a modification of social security to permit individual investment accounts or through school reform by giving parents more control over their children's education. Voucher advocates, for example, argue that education can only improve when parents are "empowered" by having a choice among various school providers. Voucher opponents, for their part, see education undermined by commercial values, by the parochialization of the schools, and by a diversion of funds from those public institutions that exist to serve poor and vulnerable students. As Ron Unz argues (Capsule 5.5), school vouchers weaken our civil society and foster separate and unequal systems of education.

Schools and welfare represent divergent trends in the evolution of the national debate on the proper nature of social provisions. As welfare becomes more intrusive, education becomes more *laissez-faire*. As choices for welfare recipients narrow, parents of schoolchildren enjoy a broadening array of options. The explanation for the difference, of course, is that people on welfare are viewed as only partially competent. The coercion we deplore in governmental policy for most citizens is considered justifiable, if not long overdue, for the poor.

Notes

1. Alva Myrdal, *Nation and Family* (Cambridge, Mass.: MIT Press, 1968), 133–53. A similar position is offered in Charlotte Whitton, *Dawn of Ampler Life* (Toronto: MacMillan of Canada, 1943). For a utopian proposal where benefits in-kind are employed more generally as the foundation of a guaranteed standard of living, see Paul Goodman and Percival Goodman, *Communitas*, 2nd ed., rev. (New York: Vintage Books, 1960), 188–217.
2. The question of how directly the objective is served can be asked apart from the issue of how well the objective is served. The former involves effectiveness in terms of impact, the latter in terms of performance or ultimate outcome.
3. For further discussion of this assumption, see James Buchanan, "What Kind of Redistribution Do We Want?" *Economia*, 35 (May 1968); and Martin Rein, "Social Policy Analysis as the Interpretation of Beliefs," *Journal of the American Institute of Planners*, 37(5) (September 1971). These assumptions are critiqued in Gunnar Myrdal, *Value in Social Theory*, Paul Streeten (ed.) (London: Routledge and Kegan Paul, 1958), 137.
4. Raymond J. Struyk and Marc Bendick, Jr. (eds.), *Housing Vouchers for the Poor* (Washington, D.C.: Urban Institute Press, 1981).
5. Myrdal, *Nation and Family*, 151.
6. Gerald M. Holden, "A Consideration of Benefits In-Kind for Children," in Eveline M. Burns (ed.), *Children's Allowances and the Economic Welfare of Children* (New York: Citizen's Committee for Children of New York, 1968), 151.

7. Asa Briggs, "The Welfare State in Historical Perspective," in Mayer Zald (ed.), *Social Welfare Institutions* (New York: John Wiley & Sons, 1965), 62.

8. Sigmund Freud, *Civilization and Its Discontents*, James Strachey (trans. and ed.) (New York: W. W. Norton, 1962), 42.

9. Myrdal, *Nation and Family*, 150.

10. Milton Friedman, "The Role of Government in Education," in Robert Solo (ed.), *Economics and the Public Interest* (New Brunswick, N.J.: Rutgers University Press, 1955), 124.

11. Myrdal, *Nation and Family*, 150.

12. See, for example, Shirley Buttrick, "On Choice and Services," *Social Service Review*, 44(4) (December 1970): 427–33; and Anthony Pascal, "New Departures in Social Services," *Social Welfare Forum* (New York: Columbia University Press, 1969), 75–85.

13. James Thompson, *Organizations in Action* (New York: McGraw-Hill, 1976), 17–18.

14. Friedman, "The Role of Government in Education," 144.

15. John K. Galbraith, *The Affluent Society* (New York: Mentor Books, 1958), 205.

16. See Friedrick Hayek, "The Non Sequitur of the 'Dependence Effect,'" in Edmund S. Phelps (ed.), *Private Wants and Public Needs* (New York: W. W. Norton, 1962), 37–42.

17. Alice M. Rivlin, *Systematic Thinking for Social Action* (Washington, D.C.: Brookings Institution, 1971), 137–38.

18. See, for example, Peter Marquis et al., "Barriers to Child Health Care," *Archives of Pediatric and Adolescent Medicine*, 149 (1995): 541–45.

19. Charles Murray, *In Our Hands—A Plan to Replace the Welfare State* (Washington D.C.: AEI Press, 2006).

20. A more detailed discussion of these conditions is presented by Milton Friedman, "The Role of Government in a Free Society," in Edmund S. Phelps (ed.), *Private Wants and Public Needs* (New York: W. W. Norton, 1962), 104–17.

21. Samuel Mencher, *Poor Law to Poverty Program* (Pittsburgh: University of Pittsburgh Press, 1967), 336.

22. For example, see Friedman, "The Role of Government in Education"; Buttrick, "On Choice and Services"; and Christopher Jencks, "Private Schools for Black Children," *New York Times Magazine*, November 3, 1968.

23. Neil Gilbert and Harry Specht, "Title XX Planning by Area Agencies on Aging: Efforts, Outcome, and Policy Implications," *The Gerontologist*, 19(3) (June 1979): 264–74; Stephanie Fall Creek and Neil Gilbert, "Aging Network in Transition: Problems and Prospects," *Social Work*, 26(3) (May 1981): 210–16.

24. Friedman, "The Role of Government in Education," 128.

25. Christopher Jencks et al., *Education Vouchers: A Report on Financing Elementary Education by Grants to Parents* (Cambridge, Mass.: Center for the Study of Public Policy, 1970).

26. Paul Wortman and Robert St. Pierre, "The Educational Voucher Demonstration: A Secondary Analysis," *Education and Urban Society*, 9 (August 1977): 471–91.

27. David Cohen and Eleanor Farrar, "Power to Parents? The Story of Education Vouchers," *Public Interest*, 48 (Summer 1977): 72–97.

28. See, for example, D. Weiler (ed.), *A Public School Voucher Demonstration: The First Year at Alum Rock* (Santa Monica, Calif.: Rand Corporation, 1974); Wortman and St. Pierre, "The Educational Voucher Demonstration"; and R. Crain, *Analysis of the Achievement Test Outcomes in the Alum Rock Voucher Demonstration, 1974–75* (Santa Monica, Calif.: Rand Corporation, 1976).

29. See Paul Peterson, Jay Greene, and Chad Noyes, "School Choice in Milwaukee," *The Public Interest*, 125 (Fall 1996): 38–56.

30. William Howell and Paul Peterson, *The Education Gap: Vouchers and Urban Schools* (Washington, D.C.: Brookings Institution, 2002).

31. Robert Holland, "Voucher Lessons from Sweden," The Heartland Institute, Document #11451, 2003.

32. E. G. West, "Choice or Monopoly in Education," *Policy Review*, 15 (Winter 1981): 103–17.

33. John C. Donovan, *The Politics of Poverty* (New York: Pegasus, 1967), 40.

34. U.S. House of Representatives, A Bill to Mobilize the Human and Financial Resources of the Nation to Combat Poverty in the United States, 88th Cong., 2nd session, March 1964, H.R. 10443, 17–18.

35. Daniel Moynihan, "What Is 'Community Action'?" *The Public Interest* 5, Fall, 1966, 7.

36. U.S. House of Representatives, *Economic Opportunity Act of 1964, Hearing before the Subcommittee on the War on Poverty Program* (Washington, D.C.: Government Printing Office, 1964), Part I, 305.

37. Statement of Robert F. Wagner before the Ad Hoc Subcommittee on the Poverty Program of the House Education and Labor Committee, April 16, 1964, 3–4 (mimeographed).

38. For a more thorough discussion of these various interpretations, see Moynihan, "What Is 'Community Action'?"

39. Statement by the Marion H. Crank, Speaker of the Arkansas House of Representatives, before the Ad Hoc Subcommittee on the Poverty Program of the House Education and Labor Committee, April 10, 1964, 3 (mimeographed).

40. Statement of Robert C. Weaver before the Ad Hoc Subcommittee on the Poverty Program of the House Education and Labor Committee, April 16, 1964, 12 (mimeographed).

41. Quoted in Elinor Graham, "Poverty and the Legislative Process," in Ben B. Seligman (ed.), *Poverty as a Public Issue* (New York: Free Press, 1965), 251–71.

42. For example, see Advisory Commission on Intergovernmental Relations, *Intergovernmental Relations in the Poverty Program* (Washington, D.C.: Government Printing Office, 1966); and William F. Haddad, "Mr. Shriver and the Savage Politics of Poverty," *Harpers* (December 1965): 43–50.

43. Daniel Moynihan, *Maximum Feasible Misunderstanding* (New York: Free Press, 1969), 188–89.

44. Edward A. Suchman, *Evaluative Research* (New York: Russell Sage, 1967), 41.

45. Martin Rein, *Social Policy* (New York: Random House, 1970), 417–45.

46. For a classic example of this perspective, see Alvin Schorr, *Slums and Social Insecurity* (Washington, D.C.: U.S. Government Printing Office, 1963).

47. See Michael B. Katz, *The Undeserving Poor*, 1989, especially 9–36; and Isabel V. Sawhill, "The Behavioral Aspects of Poverty," *The Public Interest* 153, Fall, 2003.

48. See, for example, Frances Piven and Richard Cloward, *Regulating the Poor* (New York: Random House, 1971); and Ian Gough, *The Political Economy of the Welfare State* (London: Macmillan Press, 1979).

49. Robert H. Connery et al., *The Politics of Mental Health* (New York: Columbia University Press, 1968), 478.

50. Richard Nixon, quoted in Edward Berkowitz, *America's Welfare State from Roosevelt to Reagan*, 1991, 128.

51. U.S. General Accounting Office, *Welfare to Work: Most AFDC Training Programs Not Emphasizing Job Placement*, GAO-HEHS-95-113, May 19, 1995.

52. William Julius Wilson, "Work," *New York Times Magazine* (August 18, 1996): 52.

53. U.S. Government Accountability Office, *Welfare Reform: Better Information Needed to Understand Trends in States' Use of the TANF Block Grant*, GAO-06-414, March 3, 2006.

54. Paul Starobin, "The Daddy State," *National Journal*, March 28, 1998, 678–83.

6

The Design of the Delivery System

"You're very strict," said the Mayor, "but multiply your strictness a thousand times and it would still be nothing compared with the strictness that the Authority imposes on itself. Only a total stranger could ask a question like yours. Is there a Control Authority? There are only Control Authorities. Frankly, it isn't their function to hunt out errors in the vulgar sense, for errors don't happen, and even when once in a while an error does happen, as in your case, who can say finally that it's an error?"

Franz Kafka
The Castle, 1930

When Kafka's hero wanders through a bureaucratic maze, continually confounded in his attempts to make sense of the system, his fictional world is not far removed from the real-life experiences encountered by many applicants for social welfare benefits. The system for delivering benefits is closed to certain applicants; others enter it only to find themselves shuffled from agency to agency without ever receiving appropriate help. And many will ask in despair for a "control authority" through which to seek redress for their grievances. At times, the answer they receive closely approximates the quote from Kafka.

This situation does not necessarily arise out of authoritarian mentalities or bad intentions. Indeed, there is no way to avoid some measure of bureaucracy in structuring services. Organization, to a considerable degree, requires bureaucracy. But there are important choices to consider in designing organizational forms, choices that provide policymakers and planners with opportunities to avoid some of the more Kafkaesque aspects of service delivery. In this chapter, we will examine some of the choices and uncertainties involved in the design of social services delivery systems.

The delivery system, as noted in Chapter 3, refers to the organizational arrangements that exist among service providers and between service providers and consumers, in the context of the local community. We focus on "the local community" because this is where providers and consumers usually come together.[1] Service providers may be individual professionals, self-help associations, professional groups, or public and private agencies acting separately or in concert to provide services in venues such as private homes and offices, community centers, residential facilities, emergency shelters, welfare or mental health departments, clinics, or hospitals.

The number of choices involved in designing delivery systems is large. Consider, for example, the following seven options (which by no means exhaust the possibilities). Providers may

Be administratively centralized	or	Be decentralized
Combine services (e.g., health, probation, income support)	or	Offer single services
Be located under one roof	or	Maintain separate facilities
Coordinate their efforts	or	Operate independently
Rely on professional employees	or	Employ consumers or paraprofessionals
Delegate authority to service users	or	Concentrate authority in the hands of "experts"
Control costs by inhibiting supply	or	Control costs by inhibiting demand
Be public administrators	or	Be private contractors

Through the early 1980s, most of the literature on the design of social service delivery systems focused on the first six options, choices that concern structural arrangements to promote services' coherence and accessibility. Since then, a new literature has emerged that is centered less on structural arrangements and more on questions related to cost-control and service delivery under public or private auspices. In examining choices in the design of delivery systems, we will begin with the selection of administrative auspice—one of the most pressing issues in the planning and politics of services organization.

Privatization and Commercialization in Service Delivery

Analyses of auspice tend to focus on two levels of choice: (1) the broad issue of privatization, which addresses the alternative of having a service delivered directly by a public agency or indirectly through contracting with a private provider (voluntary and for-profit agencies); and (2) the narrower issue of commercialization, which addresses the choice between for-profit and nonprofit providers.

Privatization and the Future of Public Social Services

Since the early 1980s, there has been considerable growth in third-party purchase of service arrangements, through which public funds are used to pay for services delivered by private agencies.[2] This trend is expanding under welfare reform, with community organizations, often faith based, receiving preference as TANF contract agencies.

Today's degree of enthusiasm for privatization represents a level of commitment to community-based agencies that has not been seen since the community action movement of the mid-1960s. It is an enthusiasm inspired by the convergence of two popular assumptions—one suiting the free-market ideology of the right, the other satisfying the citizen participation/empowerment objectives of the left. Privatization is therefore linked both to the presumed advantages of the competitive marketplace and to the failings of public bureaucracies. Private agencies perform well, it is said, because they offer the most efficient approach to the production and delivery of social services.[3] Public bureaucracies perform poorly, the argument continues, because they enjoy a monopoly in their areas of service; public consumers, a captive audience, must take what is offered.[4]

Although a competitive market *does* provide strong incentives to adopt cost-effective practices, the efficiency assumption nevertheless bears scrutiny. This is because the market metaphor does not exactly apply in the realm of social services contracting where the forces of competition responsive to consumer choice are undermined by third-party purchase of service arrangements.[5] Under purchase of service contracts, the entire transaction is perceived neither by the individual consumer, who does not pay for the service, nor the purchasing public body, which does not receive the service. Moreover, social service consumers are often vulnerable—children, elderly, and poor—and less than well informed. In the absence of the market discipline imposed by knowledgeable consumers who pay for what they get, third-party contracting does not operate in the kind of environment that secures the cost and quality of services being delivered, a problem Hansmann describes as the "contract failure theory."[6]

CAPSULE 6.1 • *The Privatization Nostrum*

Today, government is beset with cynicism, conservatism, and libertarianism. "Privatization" is the magic nostrum to cure our public ills and two administrations have been industriously, if not always coherently, engaged in dismantling the structure they were supposed to be managing. "Bureaucracy" and even "government" have become pejoratives instead of descriptive terms. . . .

The pendulum has swung before and it will swing again. The attractions of libertarianism, which views each human being as ensconced in a shell of isolation, will fade in the face of the world's great social problems of population, of environment, of energy, and the establishment of peace. We will learn again that we must live together, all jostled up on this little planet; and we will learn that government plays an essential and honorable role in the endeavor.

From "Public Administration Revisited" by Herbert A. Simon and Victor A. Thompson, *Society*, 28(5), July/August 1991. Used by kind permission of Springer Science and Business Media.

CAPSULE 6.2 • *Public Service, Noble Purpose*

The monopoly provision argument assumes that public organizations have no ways to call forth good performance from employees other than the incentives typically available to private firms. This view ignores the role that the larger and—I do not hesitate to use the word—nobler purposes of many public endeavors can play in spurring employees to better performance. For example, the vast majority of people in our society who risk their lives on behalf of others in the regular course of their jobs are government employees—police officers, fire fighters, soldiers, foreign service officers. Certainly not every public employee is motivated by saintly purposes, nor does every government agency have a large public purpose. But where public purpose draws people into government in the first place, it should be nurtured and consciously be made part of a strategy for public management, not dismissed as something for snickers or sarcasm.

Steven Kelman, "The Renewal of the Public Sector," *The American Prospect*, no. 2 (Summer 1990): 53.

Competitive bidding for third-party contracts has been used in efforts to address the problem of contract failure, which stems from the absence of competition and consumer choice. Evaluations of the competitive bidding mechanism in several service areas, however, suggest that the results neither reduce costs nor enhance quality.[7] "Proxy shopping," another method recommended to introduce the discipline of market competition into purchase-of-service arrangements, involves contracting only with service providers who can attract paying customers (who serve as proxy-shoppers for public agencies). The reasoning here is that, if consumers who have shopped around with money in their pockets are willing to pay for the service, the cost and quality should be competitive with that of other providers.[8] Still, there must be enough suppliers to form a competitive market, which is often not the case when dealing with community-based agencies.

Even if competition can be introduced into purchase-of-service arrangements, the problem remains that the transaction costs of contracting are quite high; these costs include complicated measurements to determine the price of units of service being purchased and expensive procedures to then monitor the quality of what is delivered (these costs of holding providers accountable are discussed in more detail in the next chapter).[9] One answer to this criticism is that the transaction costs of purchasing services from private agencies may be mitigated by contracting with community-based agencies. Why? The reasoning goes that community-based agencies will be accountable and responsive to their local consumer constituency; these agencies are in essence local groups organized to serve their own communities. Thus, even though the consumers do not pay for the services they are receiving, they are nevertheless in a strong position to influence the quality of these services, often participating on the boards of local agencies. Under these circumstances, the transaction costs of contracting can be reduced because monitoring for quality would be conducted by the consumers who have the power to influence their local organizations.

Contracting, then, can be promoted not only as a method for efficient and effective delivery of services, but also as a mechanism for advancing the democratization of social services. Community-based agencies are "mediating" institutions. Local, private, and responsive to the people served, they provide a cushion of civil society between the individual and the state. Seen in this light, minimizing the role of government in the delivery of social services gives private institutions "the space to flower, reclaiming their rightful place at the center of a revitalized civil society."[10] In the mid-1990s, this "civil society" theme engendered considerable discussion about ways to reinforce local community structures to build the "social capital" necessary to promote democracy, local networks, and responsive helping systems.

CAPSULE 6.3 • *The New Parlance of Community*

Civil Society

An intellectual revolution is underway concerning the nature of our social crisis. It is no longer credible to argue that rising illegitimacy, random violence, and declining values are rooted in the lack either of economic equality or of economic opportunity. These positions are still current in our political debate, but they have lost their plausibility.

America's cultural decay can be traced directly to the breakdown of certain institutions—families, churches, neighborhoods, voluntary associations—that act as an immune system against cultural disease. In nearly every community, these institutions once created an atmosphere in which most problems—a teenage girl "in trouble," the rowdy neighborhood kids, the start of a drug problem at the local high school—could be confronted before their repetition threatened the existence of the community itself.

When civil society is strong, it infuses a community with its warmth, trains its people to be good citizens, and transmits values between generations. When it is weak, no amount of police or politics can provide a substitute. There is a growing consensus that a declining civil society undermines both civility and society.

—Senator Dan Coats

Social Capital

By analogy with notions of physical capital and human capital—tools and training that enhance individual productivity—"social capital" refers to features of social organization, such as networks, norms, and trust, that facilitate coordination and cooperation for mutual benefit. Social capital enhances the benefits of investment in physical and human capital.

Our political parties, once intimately coupled to the capillaries of community life, have become evanescent confections of pollsters and media consultants and independent political entrepreneurs—the very antithesis of social capital. We have too easily accepted a conception of democracy in which public policy is not the outcome of a collective deliberation about the public interest, but rather a residue of campaign strategy. The social capital approach, focusing on the indirect effects of civic norms and networks, is a much-needed corrective to an exclusive emphasis on the formal institutions of government as an explanation for our collective discontents. If we are to make our political system more responsive, especially to those who lack connections at the top, we must nourish grass-roots organization.

—Robert Putnam

Senator Dan Coats, "Can Congress Revive Civil Society?" *Policy Review*, no. 75 (January/February 1996): 25. Robert D. Putnam, "The Prosperous Community: Social Capital and Public Life," *The American Prospect*, no. 13 (Spring 1993): 35, 41.

There is, however, another less sanguine view of the value and the potential of community-based agencies. Abstract discourse on civil society, local responsiveness, social capital, and citizen empowerment tends to ignore the harsh fact that there is often a dense concentration of social problems in communities with the highest proportions of residents in need of social services. Fred Wulczyn, finding that one out of eight children born in some of New York's poorest neighborhoods are admitted to foster care as infants, estimates that the cumulative rate of foster care placement in these communities may be approaching 20 percent.[11] Plagued by high levels of child abuse, family disorganization, and crime, these communities not only have few natural "civic" resources, they would be extremely difficult to organize for constructive local agency participation.

Effectiveness and local responsiveness aside, however, the plain fact is that community-based agencies often deliver social services for lower costs than public bureaucracies. They deliver services for less because they *pay* their workers less. Public bureaucracies, after all, represent one of the last strongholds of the union movement in the United States. Community-based organizations can also often rely on volunteers, keeping their personnel costs down.

Ironically, efforts to revitalize civil society through support of geographically based mediating institutions are being promoted at the cost of functionally based communities of organized labor, which *also* constitute powerful mediating institutions of civil society. Indeed, in his classic analysis, Emile Durkheim noted, "A nation can be maintained only if, between the State and the individual, there is intercalated a whole series of secondary groups near enough to the individuals to attract them strongly in their sphere of action."[12] With organizations based on territorial divisions (villages, districts) becoming less important, Durkheim envisioned occupational groups emerging to fill the void and re-create a sense of social solidarity.

Philosophical arguments about the place of geographic- and functional-community institutions in civil society will not mitigate the increasing fiscal pressures on state public assistance agencies to contract out the delivery of services under TANF block grants. As policy analysts consider the shift from the public social services to community-based delivery structures, the assumptions underlining privatization should be carefully examined and the trade-offs should be made explicit. Private services may be less costly, but whether community-based agencies are more *effective* in delivering social services isn't at all certain. To date, research findings on the effectiveness of social services delivered under public and private auspices haven't yielded a definitive answer.[13] As Kamerman and Kahn observe, the evidence runs both ways, "varying with field, time, context, and scale."[14] Although private community-based agencies reside close to the people being served, are less bureaucratic, and are more responsive to local influences than public bureaucracies, this does not guarantee greater effectiveness in service delivery.[15]

Faith-Based Services

Religious institutions—nearly half a million churches, synagogues, and mosques in the United States today—constitute the largest component of the American voluntary sector, and a critical element in our civil society. Yet the role of religion in social welfare has always been an ambiguous one, and subject to great controversy.

CAPSULE 6.4 • *Faith Societies*

There is no country in which the people are so religious as in the United States. . . . The great number of religious societies existing . . . is truly surprising: there are some of them for everything; for instance, . . . to convert, to educate and civilize; . . . to take care of widows and orphans; to endow congregations and support seminaries; . . . to prevent drunkenness.

Achille Murat, *The Principles of Republican Government*, 1832.

In the early years of the American welfare system, religious institutions played dominant roles. Much of the urban antipoverty effort of the late nineteenth century, for example, was founded on religious conviction. While usually operating informally, through personal charity and volunteer do-gooding, a number of formal organizations were vital to the social health of the cities. Urban missions such as the Salvation Army, for example, addressed slum conditions and alcoholism and destitution via the Bible and material relief. Catholic and Protestant hospitals and orphanages and old-age homes evolved to serve society's dependents.

With the rise of the welfare state, the role of religion in social welfare declined. Early proponents of public welfare were aggressively secular, viewing religious helping as parochial, amateurish, and moralistic. And while religious agencies continued to provide valuable services, they increasingly operated much like any other kind of voluntary nonprofit—as formal 501(c)3 agencies with professional staffs and broad nondenominational missions. Catholic Charities USA, for example, became a billion-dollar enterprise serving the broad community and receiving most of its funding from government contracts.

Today's faith-based organizations—the term developed in the mid-1990s—have been undergoing a significant renaissance since the enactment of welfare reform in 1996. A provision in that legislation authorizing "charitable choice" permitted states to contract with religious agencies to assist welfare clients. This was a significant break with previous practice that largely prohibited contracting with organizations that were overtly religious—organizations, for example, that displayed religious symbols or used religious criteria in selecting employees. Under TANF, not only would secularized agencies like Catholic Charities be eligible for support, but also more overtly faith-oriented groups.

President George W. Bush, recalling his own alcohol problems as a young man, frequently touted the importance of faith, of divine inspiration, in addressing substance addiction and other social problems. One of Bush's first initiatives as president was to embody his philosophy of "compassionate conservatism" in new initiatives to promote the welfare efforts of religious and community organizations. Believing that the faith community had been improperly inhibited by bureaucratic red tape and funding restrictions, new Centers for Faith-Based and Community Initiatives were established in seven federal cabinet agencies to make sure that local faith organizations could compete on an equal footing for federal dollars, receive federal technical advice and support, and face fewer bureaucratic barriers.

As a result, significant numbers of churches and associated bodies were recruited to provide job training, literacy development, abstinence promotion, prison-based reentry counselling, fatherhood programs, drug and alcohol treatment, and residential programs for unmarried mothers. So long as they do not actively evangelize or discriminate against nonbelievers, these agencies can receive state funding. While these limitations do not satisfy strict "separationists" who view "charitable choice" as a dangerous violation of the First Amendment boundary between church and state, a broad coalition has come to view faith organizations as valuable instruments for social welfare, either as partners with government (the view from the left) or as substitutes for government (the view from the right). While liberals and conservatives increasingly recognize the importance of adding a spiritual dimension to social service programs, liberals see government and religious charities coexisting in the promotion of a welfare-sensitive civil society while conservatives see religious agencies based on morality, private charity, and direct compassion replacing bureaucratic, inefficient public programs.[16]

Commercialization: Services for Profit

Prior to the 1960s, social services were delivered almost exclusively by public and voluntary nonprofit organizations. When they were considered, questions of auspice

---

CAPSULE 6.5 • *Taking Faith Seriously*

In recent years there has been an explosion in empirical research on faith-based social programs. Most studies, including the most scientifically rigorous, find that faith moves social and civic mountains.

Consider the latest scientific literature on religion and crime. A 1997 study by Byron Johnson, director of the Center for Research on Religion and Urban Civil Society, reports that New York State prisoners who participated intensively in Bible studies were less likely to be rearrested:

> Participants were only a third as likely to be arrested a year after release as otherwise comparable prisoners who did not participate.
>
> On average, eight years after release, the Bible studies participants remained arrest-free over 50 percent longer than the parolees in the comparison group.

Likewise, in a study of a faith-based program in a Texas prison, Johnson reports:

> Two years after release, participants were less likely to be arrested than inmates paroled early from the program and than otherwise comparable inmates who did not participate in the program.
>
> Only 8 percent of the Prison Fellowship program graduates, versus 20 percent of the matched comparison group, were incarcerated within two years after being released.

So, whether with respect to reducing recidivism rates, improving public health outcomes, accelerating volunteer mobilization, or other objective measures, the empirical evidence has become weighty enough for numerous top scientific organizations to begin taking religion seriously.

From "Not a Leap of Faith" by John J. Dilulio, Jr., *Weekly Standard*, June 30, 2003. Reprinted by permission.

addressed the relationship between public and voluntary nonprofit providers.[17] With today's increasing involvement of commercial agencies in the delivery of social services, new questions have emerged concerning how well social welfare objectives can be served by providers motivated by profit.

Social welfare advocates view the emergence of profit-oriented agencies with a jaundiced eye.[18] There is a strong suspicion that the profit motive is not morally compatible with the ethos of social provision. Yet moral objections would be difficult to sustain if it could be shown that profit-oriented agencies were the most effective and efficient means for delivering social services. If, on the other hand, profit-oriented agencies are less efficient and effective than nonprofit providers, moral objections would be unnecessary to deter the privatization of services. Assessing the efficiency and effectiveness of social services, however, is a complex business. Service objectives are often multiple and vague. They are no less important for these qualities, but they frequently defy precise measurement.[19]

Despite the difficulties of empirical measurements, there is a body of research comparing the relative effectiveness of profit versus nonprofit providers.[20] Some studies reveal that nonprofit providers are more sensitive to client needs; others show service areas in which profit-oriented agencies do the best job; still others find no significant differences between profit and nonprofit agencies. On the whole, findings on the relative merits of for-profit and nonprofit service providers, like comparisons between public and private providers, are indeterminate.

In the absence of decisive empirical evidence, theoretical analyses of the distinguishing features of profit and nonprofit organizations offer a variety of guidelines for choice. Theoretically, nonprofit organizations have greater public accountability than profit-oriented organizations because their structure of governance requires boards of directors composed of people who are expected to promote the broad interests of the community. In contrast, the directors of profit-making agencies are expected to protect the financial interests of owners. In nonprofits, therefore, there is less temptation to exploit vulnerable service consumers for material gain. Finally, there is a charitable ethos associated with nonprofits that is at variance with the capitalist spirit of profit-making enterprises.[21]

These differences suggest several practical conclusions for choosing between profit-making and nonprofit providers[22]:

1. *Standardization of service.* Services that involve uniform procedures and standard products, such as public health vaccinations, readily lend themselves to the economic planning skills and business initiative of profit-making organizations. At the same time, the uniform character of these services allows the purchasers to monitor their delivery for potential abuses more easily than services that require a technology that is custom tailored to each case (such as therapy).
2. *Client competence.* Many social services deal with client groups that are highly vulnerable to exploitation. Children, the mentally retarded, and confused and emotionally upset people do not have the ability to hold service providers accountable for the quality of their services. To the extent that public accountability and the charitable ethos influence the behavior of nonprofit agencies

more than that of profit-making agencies, the nonprofit form is preferable for delivering services.

3. *Coerciveness of service.* Services invested with coercive powers, such as protective services for children and work with parolees, pose a significant threat to personal liberty. In these cases, the service provider's degree of public accountability is of foremost importance. With the clients' freedom at stake, the lack of public accountability of profit-making organizations would not seem to offer the most adequate form of protection.[23]

4. *Potency of the regulatory environment.* Profit-oriented and nonprofit providers would seem equally preferable in delivering services that are under sufficient public regulation to ensure the maintenance of standards and client protection. We should note, however, that the scope and potency of regulatory activity in the social services are limited.

Although these conditions tend to favor nonprofit agencies, there are clearly service areas where this general proposition does not hold, such as transportation for the handicapped and elderly. In choosing between profit and nonprofit providers, the essential issue is not to seek the universally superior form of organization, but to determine the particular conditions under which profit- or nonprofit-oriented agencies may best serve social welfare clients. In assessing these conditions, we must consider not only the points noted, but also the nature of the purchase-of-service arrangement, especially the extent to which funding agencies can design grant requirements to ensure compliance with their objectives (an issue that will be addressed in Chapter 8).

CAPSULE 6.6 • *Profit versus Nonprofit*

Patients enrolled in profit-making health insurance plans are significantly less likely to receive the basics of good medical care—including childhood immunizations, routine mammograms, pap smears, prenatal care, and lifesaving drugs after heart attacks—than those in not-for-profit plans, says a new study that concludes that the free market is "compromising the quality of care."

The research, conducted by a team from Harvard University and Public Citizen, an advocacy group in Washington, is the first comprehensive comparison of investor-owned and nonprofit plans. The authors found that on every one of 14 quality-of-care indicators, the for-profits scored worse.

"The market is destroying our health care system," said Dr. David Himmelstein, the study's lead author. "We have had a decade or more of policies aimed at making health care a business, and they have failed."

Promoting Coherence and Accessibility: Service Delivery Strategies

Whether social services are provided under public or private auspices, issues remain about how to structure the delivery system in ways that foster coherence and accessibility. Broadly speaking, efforts to promote coherence and accessibility address three kinds of questions concerning the structural arrangements for service delivery: (1) Where shall authority and control for decision making be located? (2) Who will carry out the different service tasks to be performed? and (3) What will be the composition (the number and types of units) of the delivery system?

Attempts to answer these questions often stir controversy as they respond to the tug and pull of conflicting social values. In addressing questions about where authority should be vested, for example, the value of consumer participation may be emphasized regardless of its impact on the efficiency of service delivery. Issues having to do with efficiency compete with other values that may be equally important to society, such as providing jobs for low-income people or ensuring equity in the geographic distribution of services.

In the heat of controversy, criticisms of service delivery intensify. Such criticism tends to focus on the characteristic failings of local service delivery systems, particularly *fragmentation*, *discontinuity*, *unaccountability*, and *inaccessibility*. These problematic facets of service delivery have been amply documented and analyzed.[24] Plans to reform the organization and the delivery of social services usually concern one or more of them.

For a description of these problems, consider the following hypothetical circumstances: An unemployed single mother with a cocaine problem drops off her daughter at a daycare center and then goes to receive treatment at a substance abuse clinic, after which she spends her day in a TANF work-support program. If the daycare center, clinic, and work-support program are in different parts of town, operate on different schedules, and provide overlapping services, that's fragmentation. If there is no convenient means of transportation among these three organizations, no referral between the clinic and the work-training program, and no TANF subsidies to help pay for the daycare, that's discontinuity. If the client is not admitted to the treatment or training program because of her place of residence, lack of medical insurance, or the like, that's inaccessibility. When any or all of these circumstances exist and the client has no viable means of redressing her grievances, the delivery system suffers from unaccountability.

These problems have many facets, are interconnected at some points, and span a broader range of issues. Problems of *fragmentation* concern organizational characteristics and relationships, especially coordination, location, specialization, and duplication of services. (Are services available in one place? Do agencies mesh their activities? Are they aware on one another's existence?) Problems of *accessibility* concern obstacles to a person's entering the network of local social services. (Do eligibility standards based on income, age, success potential, or other characteristics exclude certain persons from service?) Problems of *continuity* concern obstacles to movement through the network of services and the gaps that appear as agencies try to match resources to needs. (Are there adequate channels of communication and referral?) Problems of *accountability* concern relationships among persons served and service decision-makers. (Are those needing help able to influence decisions that affect their circumstances? Are decision makers unresponsive to client needs and interests?)

Phrased as policy issues, these problems confront policy planners and administrators with choices that, although conceptually distinct, are confounded in practice. That is, an ideal system of services is one in which services are integrated, continuous, accessible, and accountable. Taken separately, however, each of these elements strains against one or more of the others. We may summarize some of the service delivery choices as follows:

1. Reduce fragmentation and discontinuity by increasing coordination, opening new channels of communication and referral, and eliminating duplication of services (possibly increasing unaccountability and inaccessibility).
2. Reduce inaccessibility by creating new means of access to services and duplicating existing service efforts (possibly increasing fragmentation).
3. Reduce unaccountability by creating a means for clients and consumers to have input into, and increased decision-making authority over, the system (possibly increasing fragmentation and discontinuity).

CAPSULE 6.7 • *The Services Tangle*

Case 1: Working Poor Purgatory

Since making the leap from welfare to work two years ago, Tami Buddi has put a lot of miles on her aging family sedan. To collect child-support payments from her former boyfriend, she drove to the county courthouse in a nearby suburb of Minneapolis. To keep appointments with her job counselor, she drove to a second county office. To apply for subsidized health insurance, she drove to a third site, clutching a thick application and a sheaf of payroll stubs. No one told her about federal training grants, so she found a night school on her own, which meant more time behind the wheel every week. All this while working full time as a bill collector and raising a 10-year-old daughter by herself.

"It's like they sat down and tried to make it complicated," she says with a cynical chuckle.

This fragmentation helps explain why millions of poor Americans never receive the benefits that Congress created for them, benefits that were supposed to express society's support for the ideal of work. Economists estimate that about 80 percent of eligible workers collect the Earned Income Tax Credit (EITC), a refundable credit for the working poor. But only 51 percent of eligible adults receive Medicaid, and only 41 percent collect food stamps. An even smaller fraction receives child-care subsidies. And—maybe most troubling for its long-term implications—only about 200,000 adults receive job training in a typical year through the main federal workforce statute, even though perhaps 20 million low-wage workers are struggling along with a high-school diploma or less.

In the past, a local welfare office was the main portal to government benefits such as Medicaid and food stamps. But, since 1996, when Congress passed a landmark overhaul of public assistance and made welfare contingent on work, the number of families applying for cash support has plummeted. The number of working poor has risen sharply, meanwhile, but these adults are mostly disconnected from social services.

CAPSULE 6.7 • *The Services Tangle* ***(continued)***

Case 2: Red Tape 9-11

Across metropolitan New York, bereaved spouses armed with spreadsheets, fax machines and stacks of application forms are pursuing what some call their new full-time jobs and what others resentfully refer to as a form of professional begging: asking charitable organizations for help.

Families that have lost loved ones in the World Trade Center attack say they have often been utterly overwhelmed by the multiplicity of charitable funds, aid organizations and government agencies. In dozens of interviews, widows and widowers described days spent bouncing from one bureaucracy to the next, struggling to navigate a maze of confusing rules, deadlines and requirements.

"We have to make five and six calls to each of these agencies to get someone who knows what they're doing," said Liz McLaughlin, 34, a mother of an infant son who lost her husband, Robert, a Cantor Fitzgerald trader.

Another woman, who did not want to be identified for fear of offending charity groups, said she had dealt with at least nine different United Way representatives who conducted three separate interviews involving the same basic set of questions.

"I was turned into a widow on September 11 and a single mother, and now they're turning me into a beggar," she said.

Problems in service delivery do not exist because there is a shortage of ideas about how to improve the situation. On the contrary, the technical repertoire of planners and managers includes a wide range of strategies for effecting the delivery of local services. Much of the problem is simply the piecmeal nature of our welfare state. Historically, policymakers have addressed needs one by one. Problems are identified and legislation is enacted. In this fashion, benefits and services evolve one program at a time, with their associated professionals, rules and regulations, and service delivery and funding patterns. Each of these programs is necessary, of course, but so are arrangements to create the interconnections necessary to avoid the problems dramatized in the capsules.

To create integrated and responsive service arrangements, issues of choice and uncertainty need to be resolved. We approach this task in the following sections by identifying choices among service delivery strategies, analyzing the types of systemic changes related to different strategies, suggesting what needs to be known about the effects of these strategies.

Proposals for reform invariably accompany critical analyses of service delivery. Although specific proposals for service delivery reform contain considerable variation, most correspond to one or another of six general strategies, each of which addresses at least one of the service delivery questions mentioned earlier:

1. Strategies to restructure policy-making authority and control:
   a. Coordination
   b. Citizen participation
2. Strategies to reorganize the allocation of tasks:
   a. Role attachments
   b. Professional disengagement
3. Strategies to alter the composition (i.e., number and types of units) of the delivery system:
   a. Specialized access structures
   b. Purposive duplication

Each of these strategies seeks to restructure local service systems to enhance service delivery. Coordination and citizen participation both impinge on the bureaucratic hierarchy of the system. Role attachments and professional disengagement alter the roles and status characteristics of actors in the systems. Specialized access structures and purposive duplication change the substantive composition of the elements in the system.

Strategies to Restructure Policy-Making Authority

Coordination.   Social workers and social planners are quick to declare their faith in the generic, the whole-person, and the comprehensive approach to service. They recognize the complexity of social causation and the interdependencies among the mental, physical, and environmental factors that influence clients' functioning and life chances. At the same time, policy is a particular thing, with legislation generally focused on the specific, rather than the comprehensive. The thrust of agency practice, as a consequence, is directed toward specialization, with agency professionals looking at problems in terms of their own training and technical expertise. In one sense, then, the function of services coordination is to mitigate the strains created by the juxtaposition of specialization and the comprehensive approach in the professional value structure.

Coordination is a strategy aimed at developing an integrated and comprehensive social service system. Whereas innumerable arrangements have been suggested and tested for bringing some coherence to the natural fragmentation of services, three approaches capture most of the possibilities—centralization, agency co-location, and case-level collaboration. These models are exemplified in different approaches to the organization of local social services in England and the United States.

The structure of the British system is rooted in the 1970 Local Authority and Social Services Act, which prescribed a major reorganization of local service agencies. The staffs and functions of children's and welfare departments, community development services, home-help services, and other local agencies were centralized under the auspices of newly created Local Authority Social Services Departments (LASSD). In turning to the LASSD as a mechanism for centralization, the British utilized what Simon recommends as being among the most powerful of coordinative procedures.[25]

At the same time that increased coordination through administrative unification offers a remedy for service fragmentation, it also gives rise to potentially dysfunctional consequences. For instance, services centralization tends to increase the organizational distance between clients and decision-making authorities. Centralization may lead to an internalization and perhaps heightening of what were previously interorganizational strains. The potential for intraorganizational conflict is especially sharpened when a variety of heretofore autonomous agencies with different aims, technologies, and perceptions are cast into a unitary organizational mold, as in LASSD.[26]

In addition, the consolidation of services under one administrative structure can limit service accessibility. While administration may be centralized in a single authority, service delivery may in fact occur in a number of locations dispersed throughout a community. It is "centralization" only in the sense that it functions according to the rules and regulations of a unified administrative structure, with intake into the services network concentrated in the hands of a relatively few gatekeepers. Such a "single door" can serve as a mechanism to rationalize service delivery from the standpoint of case referral and continuity, or it can act as a barrier to service for those who, inadvertently or by design, do not fit the administrative criteria for eligibility.

FIGURE 6.1   *One-Stop Service Center, Borough of Hornsey, Crouch End, London.*

CAPSULE 6.8 • *One-Stop Shop*

Welcome to the San Diego Family Justice Center's Web site. The center is the most comprehensive "one-stop shop" in the nation for victims of family violence and their children. Victims of domestic violence can now come to one location to talk to an advocate, get a restraining order, plan for their safety, talk to a police officer, meet with a prosecutor, receive medical assistance, counsel with a chaplain, get help with transportation, and obtain nutrition or pregnancy services counseling.

Our center is a unique, special, safe place where victims of domestic violence are our highest priority. We are committed to providing victims and their children with the help they need to break the cycle of family violence that so often damages and destroys families.

From San Diego Family Justice Center web site, www.nfjca.org, April, 2003.

The second major approach to the coordination of services is co-location, which typically involves the geographic centralization of different agency resources but not their administrative unification. Since the 1960s and 1970s, continuous efforts along these lines have been made under federal sponsorship through neighborhood service centers (developed by the Community Action Program of the War on Poverty), City Demonstration Agencies (organized by the Model Cities Program), focal-point agencies (authorized in the 1978 amendments to the Older Americans Act), and one-stop job centers (mandated under the Workforce Investment Act of 1998).[27]

Co-location structures encompass a variety of more or less formal and binding arrangements. This variability is usually expressed by reference to the degree of resources, administrative integration, and decision making authority invested by member organizations in the joint enterprise.[28] Some involve agency collaboration with a degree of joint decision making; others are more *ad hoc* with no sharing or modifications of component agency decision-making authority.

Co-location arrangements may require organizations to pool to some degree their staff skills and knowledge, intake and recordkeeping, and decision-making. In such circumstances, the costs to member agencies may in fact be less than the benefits of coordination.[29] By and large the goals and policies of local service agencies are not like interlocking pieces of a big jigsaw puzzle that, given time, patience, and a constructive mentality, can be neatly fit into the frame of a common cause. The fit, of course, can be accomplished but with costs to autonomy that many organizations are disinclined to pay. Thus, co-location often result in agencies working in a common place but failing to integrate their efforts in any more meaningful fashion.

In comparing centralization and co-location strategies, the crucial distinction resides in the different control mechanisms employed in each. Co-location involves voluntary collaboration of autonomous agencies: cooperation is based primarily on reciprocity, and the units involved are not bound to a formal hierarchy of positions, as they are under a centralized administration such as Britain's LASSD. Compared to bureaucratic authority, of course, reciprocity is a tenuous mechanism of control. It is operative, as Dahl and Lindblom note, "provided that the people have the same norms and conceptions of reality."[30]

This is why co-location frequently occurs among agencies trying to achieve a common goal. In this era of welfare and work, for example, services in a number of states and counties around the country have come together, co-located, to "make work pay." One notable example is Dayton Ohio's Montgomery County Job Center, a large warehouse "megamall," where several dozen community nonprofits and public agencies provide cash welfare, food stamps, housing aid, employment counseling, health insurance, childcare subsidies, legal services, and mental health services.

Beyond simply providing single-door convenience, the Center has helped reduce

the intimidation and stigma associated with traditional welfare offices. Clients enter through a pleasant, tiled lobby where a receptionist hands out color coded cards that guide them to the right department—yellow for child care, for example, of blue for housing. A client who simply wants to find work can step directly to a bank of computers retrofitted with the nation's top-rated employment database. A really troubled family can see a team of job counselors, eligibility experts, and social workers. The center is on a major bus line and, because many of its clients already hold jobs, stays open until 6:30 p.m. on Tuesdays and Wednesdays.[31]

Case-level collaboration, the third coordinative model, involves decentralized interactions among service agencies and services personnel, rather than formal structured patterns of services unification or co-location. Lacking a system of coordination from above, it is often the ground-level services worker who is responsible for connecting the diverse components of the helping network. Such coordination from below is nothing new, of course. Service workers have traditionally had to ensure that clients with multiple problems receive the various services they need, but the complexity of today's service delivery system increasingly demands caseworkers who have the sophistication and knowledge and the mandate to link clients to services in a timely and efficient manner.

Over the past several decades, for example, interagency agreements in the child and family field have frequently been created to ensure the coordination of services for multiproblem clients.[32] Collaboration among child welfare and mental health agencies, in particular, has become increasingly important as growing numbers of troubled children and adolescents have been placed in foster care and other types of out-of-home arrangements. Working together, mental health and child welfare officials have established compacts identifying their joint responsibilities, creating wrap-around and cross-system program models, pooling funds for common clients, cross-training personnel, and obligating ground-level staff to collaborate in a variety of specific situations.[33]

Case management is the best-known method for planning and delivering services to people who require assistance from several different sources. The case manager, a designated agency representative with cross-organizational responsibilities, works with clients in an ongoing relationship to develop a suitable service plan, to facilitate access to services, to monitor service delivery, and to evaluate service outcomes and client progress. Although "linkage" is clearly the key component, case managers must often serve as advocates and resource developers as well in order to ensure appropriate services. The model is particularly suitable for vulnerable clients who, on their own, are unable to maneuver in the service network.[34]

Case management is a primary element under welfare reform.[35] It is also employed in complex agency systems such as child welfare where children are subject to fragmented services provided by schools, mental health services, juvenile courts, departments of social services, and other child- and youth-serving organizations. Such organizational fragmentation is often aggravated by the differing orientations of service workers, health personnel, and judges, each of whom may deal with problems such as abuse and neglect by using their own theories and solutions. Pediatricians, for example, are mainly interested in the physical health of the abused child, whereas the emphasis of the caseworker is on adjudicating the child's dependency status. Similarly, the child welfare worker may find that the reluctance of some physicians to report findings of abuse obtained during physical exams undercuts their ability to investigate and prosecute child abuse.

As a coordinating mechanism, case management facilitates access to services. Although it often raises costs, especially if the case manager is effective in lobbying on behalf of clients, this approach can be viewed as cost effective because it leads to early identification of problems when they are, presumably, easier to treat. Moreover, case management can ensure greater efficiency in the use of services by eliminating duplication. In several welfare reform demonstrations, case managers serve a gatekeeping function, helping to focus limited services, such as childcare, on those participants in greatest need.[36]

Citizen Participation. Unlike coordination, in which new relationships are forged among agencies, citizen participation strategies are aimed at redistributing decision-making power between agencies and clients. The rationale for citizen participation is that clients will receive responsive and effective services only if they have genuine influence. Neither professional good will, nor professional ethics, nor bureaucratic rationality are considered sufficient to ensure that recipients' needs are met since both professionals and organizations have multiple objectives, their own survival being foremost.

The redistribution of authority through citizen participation is distinguished according to different levels and types of participation. For example, Arnstein identifies nine levels of participation ranging from manipulation to citizen control.[37] Spiegel discusses types of citizen participation from the point of view of the level of government involved, the functional area in which decisions are made, and the degree of technicality involved in the decision.[38] Kramer approaches the analysis of this strategy by focusing on the functions and purposes of different types of citizen participation, which he describes as ranging along a continuum from receiving information, to advising, to planning jointly, to having complete control.[39]

Ignoring the various nuances, three modal types tend to emerge. First, there is *nondistributive participation* or pseudoparticipation. This, for example, may involve therapy or education; in any case, there is no perceptible change in the established pattern of authority. The second is *normal participation* (tokenism to some critics), in which citizen influence on decision-making authority is clear and present but to a degree that makes only modest differences in final outcomes. The third type is *redistributive participation*. Here, the shift in authority is such that citizen participants are able to exert substantive influence on service delivery decisions.

Citizen participation is a strategy where *means* represent a value in their own right, with that value being democracy. The basic assumption is that democratic services will be more responsive than a system in which decision making is solely the prerogative of professionals. It is possible, of course, that a democratized system, a client- or community-run system, can suffer deterioration in the quality of service delivery. In such cases, the strategy might be valid for broader political reasons, but not for the objectives being considered here.

Although participatory democracy connotes the idealized New England town meeting where everybody had a right to vote (except, of course, women, slaves, and those too poor to own land), in practice citizen participation invariably requires the election or appointment of representatives. People simply do not have the time or the inclination to participate in every decision that affects them. This strategy, then, must come to grips with the notion of representation and the concomitant issues of which citizens will participate, on whose behalf, and how they will be chosen.

Participation was a prominent service delivery theme during the 1960s when the involvement of poor people became an intrinsic element of varied radical movements to organize the disadvantaged for social change (i.e., "power to the people"). Its legislative equivalent—"maximum feasible participation"—became not only a standard for the organization of Community Action Boards under the War on Poverty, but also the ethos for redistribution of bureaucratic and political power in the broader society. The participation ethos joined neighborhood activists, civil rights advocates, and cultural radicals in a short-lived movement for change that sought to bring the disenfranchised into positions of genuine inclusion in society.

At the level of service delivery, maximum feasible participation sought to decentralize decision making by requiring elections in low-income neighborhoods to select the boards of directors of the War on Poverty's Community Action Agencies. The resulting experiences, however, suggest some of the problems of the participation strategy. Neighborhood elections were conducted in several communities around the country, but turnouts were always disappointing, always far below voter participation in municipal, state, and federal elections. In Pittsburgh, for example, less than 2 percent, and in Philadelphia less than 3 percent, of eligible residents participated in community board elections.[40] Kramer reports that "the numerous neighborhood elections in San Francisco and Santa Clara can best be described as pseudo-political processes."[41]

In the post–War on Poverty era, participation models took more conventional forms. Many of the block grants enacted since the 1970s promote civic mechanisms to encourage the involvement of the poor in service programs affecting their communities. The Community Development Bloc Grant, for example, provides for advertised public hearings, and many communities have established elaborate procedures involving advisory boards, need surveys, and service evaluations to ensure client participation.[42] In addition, several pieces of major legislation have incorporated provisions to stimulate the involvement of service users. Federal child welfare legislation, for example, emphasizes opportunities for the participation of natural parents in deliberations concerning the legal status of their children. More recently, federal housing policies have been reformulated to involve tenants more fully in the management of public housing. Harking back to earlier community action models, HUD (Housing and Urban Development) has established alliances with nonprofit tenant associations, bypassing the traditional power centers of municipal housing professionals.

Strategies to Reorganize the Allocation of Tasks

Role Attachments.　To a significant degree, social services are provided by middle-class professionals. Although services are offered to the entire community, a disproportionate segment of those in need come from lower income groups. The class chasm between servers and the served, according to role-attachment strategy, can interfere with a client's movement into and through the service delivery systems. On the one hand, middle-class professionals may not understand, respect, or be sensitive to their clients' outlook on life, behavior patterns, language or dialect, or cultural values. Perhaps inarticulate by middle-class standards, clients may be perceived as unengaged, recalcitrant, or even threatening. The norms of professional objectivity and impersonal treatment, on the other hand, prescribe behavior that may be perceived by clients as patronizing, unfriendly, or officious. Given these mixed perspectives, problems of access and discontinuity may reflect social stratification, rather than simply organizational structure.[43] The case is stated succinctly by Miller and Riessman:

> Agencies must take upon themselves the responsibility for seeing that the individual patient gets to the service, or gets from one service to another. Without the assumption of this responsibility, the concept of continuity of care or services will become a meaningless programmatic shibboleth. Nor can these problems be resolved through administrative improvements alone. *A human link is needed.*[44] [Emphasis added.]

Some argue that this linkage is performed best by paraprofessionals, who compose an ever-increasing portion of direct service workers in all welfare states. In the United States, there are currently between two and three million paraprofessionals in human service fields like education, juvenile probation, substance abuse services, and services for the disabled and the frail elderly. In long term care nursing home aides, home helpers, personal care attendants, and daytime chore workers provide 80 percent of all paid care. Most paraprofessionals are women, a third are women of color, and nearly two-thirds are between 25 and 54 years old. Earnings are generally below ten dollars an hour.[45]

Paraprofessionals, peer counselors, attendants, and aides are an established part of today's human services, and it is generally recognized that nonprofessionals, by virtue of their experience and special skills, have a significant potential to bridge the gap between bureaucratic, professionalized agencies and their clientele. Paraprofessionals seem particularly adept at establishing rapport with clients, with providing information, with connecting clients to complimentary services, and with providing emotional support.

Not all are enamored with the paraprofessional paradigm, however. The employment of nonprofessionals, it is argued, may result in clients receiving services that are amateurish or low quality. Teachers' aides, for example, may be poorly educated, barely literate themselves, or unable to provide children the help they need in reading and math. And there are significant empirical questions concerning the assumption that paraprofessionals, as indigenous community members, are especially effective in engaging clients in the services endeavor.

Finally, even when nonprofessionals are effective in linkage roles and are integrated into the service delivery structure, the latter may vitiate the former. The effectiveness of the nonprofessionals can wane under pressures to resolve the strains between bureaucratic conformity and what may be their more freewheeling style. Examining the integration of nonprofessionals into agency structures, Hardcastle concluded, "the diminution of the non-professional's indigenous qualities—the emphasis on primary role skills, extemporaneousness, and lower-class behavior and communication patterns—appears inevitable because of the essentially bureaucratic nature of the organization."[46] In addition, it is not surprising to find that once on the job, many nonprofessionals bend their efforts toward becoming professionals. They seek the financial and status rewards accruing to those who achieve higher degrees of usable knowledge and skill.

TANF case managers, for example, frequently former welfare recipients themselves, may be sympathetic to program participants and sensitive to the challenges they face in childcare, health care, transportation, and the like, but as agency employees they must carry out agency policy, policy that is often punitive and harsh. One recent article about Florida's business-oriented TANF model focused on the dilemmas faced by these case managers: "They believe that they're hurting children with sanctions; many are deeply religious people who feel terribly guilty about that; a number of the women we interviewed broke down and cried."[47]

CAPSULE 6.9 • *Leaving Blackness at the Door*

Jennifer Powell is one of the 500 community development workers the English government pledged in 2003 to recruit as part of its five-year Delivering Race Equality in Mental Health programme. Although Powell and her colleagues work closely with local communities on improving mental health, they avoid using a medical approach with clients. "In south Asian communities there is no word for depression so we talk to people about their lives and their experiences and how they are feeling." This approach has made it easier for Powell to make connections with local communities, although it took time to gain their trust and respect. "I love working with minority communities because I'm working with my own communities. It is diversity in its truest sense because we work cross-culturally with different sexualities and abilities." However, this wasn't always the case during her time in mainstream mental health services. Powell says: "Sometimes black staff felt we couldn't work in our true manner because it [wasn't] understood or deemed appropriate; it's like we [had] to leave our blackness at the door when we came to work."

From "A Late Delivery" by Anabel Unity Sale from *Community Care*, November 9, 2006, http://www.communitycare.co.uk. Used by permission.

While paraprofessionals naturally hope to rise along a career ladder, gaining skills, responsibilities, and pay, the opportunities for advancement are often modest. Even when they exist, paraprofessionals are often too ensnared in their own personal dilemmas to take advantage of them. Paraprofessionals are themselves often safety net recipients, getting food stamps, daycare, and earned income tax credits, and subject to many of the same social and health problems that plague their low-income clients.

While the literature on cultural factors in service delivery emphasizes the need for services personnel to be ethnically and culturally sensitive, this does not necessarily require that they be the same race or class or culture of those they help. Peer counselors in the substance abuse field, for example, whatever their race or ethnicity, may be able to build constructive relationships with clients simply on the basis of having "been there, done that" themselves. On a broader level, a review of the literature by Snowden and Derezotes points out that while the utilization of minority staff may be associated with an increased number of minority clients, cross-race pairings can be, and often are, effective. Indeed, in certain cases they may be preferable to same-race pairing. When they go wrong for reasons related to race, this usually occurs in the early phases of the relationship.[48] While the literature on service delivery, therefore, continues to emphasize the need for personnel to be ethnically and culturally sensitive, this is hardly a panacea.

Professional Disengagement.   Although the imperative of bureaucratic conformity may cramp the style of nonprofessionals, forcing them to adopt a professional or quasi-professional *modus operandi*, it has been observed that the same imperative operates to inhibit *professional* functioning. For example, Levy described a public welfare setting where the discrepancy between the needs of administration and those of clients posed an acute moral dilemma for many workers.[49] He suggests that the high turnover rate in this setting was related to difficulties professionals had in reconciling their inner feelings with the stringent logic of welfare administration. Piliavin states the case more generally:

> Social work has acquired many of the earmarks of a profession, including a professional association that has developed and promulgated standards, goals, and an ethical code for those providing social services. The members of this association and other social workers guided by its framework of values encounter a dilemma unknown to their early predecessors; they find agency policies and practices frequently in conflict with avowed professional norms.[50]

To enhance service delivery, then, some may feel that they can only be effective if they disengage from the bureaucracy, rather than try to reform it. That is, professionals may be tempted to undertake fee-for-service private practice in order to circumvent the constraints posed by agency policies. In so doing, of course, they change their role from *bureaucrat* to *entrepreneur*. Recognizing that many people who use social services can't afford to pay for them, those favoring private practice options often propose that the financial base for implementing this strategy be furnished through government vouchers that give clients the opportunity to select the service provider of their choice.

CAPSULE 6.10 • *Trust and the Paraprofessional*

The types of benefits most often noted by paraprofessionals revolved around the close and trusting relationships formed between paraprofessional and client. There was agreement among two-thirds of the paraprofessionals interviewed that spending time with the client was the primary contributor to improved client trust. Peer workers explained that they have more time than other program staff to spend with clients, and therefore are able to build a relationship before making suggestions or taking actions. As one paraprofessional commented, "It takes a long time, six or eight weeks, just to know someone before you can start to take action, and the case coordinator comes right in and tells them what has to be done." In order to ensure that peer workers have sufficient time to develop these critical relationships with clients, it is suggested that small caseloads (4–13 clients) be maintained.

Peer workers also stressed the importance of soliciting clients' self-identified needs and addressing those needs, in addition to the explicit program objectives. . . . Paraprofessionals acknowledged that social workers have a different role in the program and often have many more cases and pressing objectives to accomplish.

From "Perspectives of Paraprofessionals: A Survey of AIA Peer Workers" by Kathleen O'Brien, *The Source*, Vol. 4, No. 2, Fall, 1994. Used by permission of National Abandoned Infants Assistance Resource Center, University of California.

Even assuming that government financing through such arrangements could somehow be accomplished, the private practice strategy has certain limitations. Private practitioners may have expertise in public welfare, corrections, relationship counseling, family services, school social work, services to the aged, and the like, but they cannot possibly be specialists in all of them. In this sense, the private practitioner is subject to the same professional myopia as the agency-based worker, except that agencies may be able to incorporate a variety of specialists. Just as in the bureaucratic delivery of services, there is little to prevent private practitioners from imposing their particular brand of service—insight therapy, behavior modification, or some other technology—rather than dealing with the recipient's unique needs. And even for the least avaricious, the tendency to interpret client problems in terms of one's own expertise is reinforced under a fee-for-service arrangement. As a means of increasing accessibility to and coherence of the delivery system, the entrepreneurial model is likely to be less effective than agency-based practice.

Although there is little empirical evidence to support the presumed virtues of the entrepreneurial model, private practice continues to be popular among professional social workers. According to a 2002 survey of National Association of Social Workers (NASW) members, about one in five reported working in either solo or group practice. (Many of these also held down an agency job.)[51]

The major assumption underlying this strategy is open to question. Although some professionals may function poorly in organizational settings, it is not necessary to conclude that organizational demands inherently limit professional functioning. Reasoned arguments can be made that there is greater latitude for individual discretion to

CAPSULE 6.11 • *The Lure of Private Practice*

Social workers enter private practice today for the same reasons that they have been attracted to the private practice of psychotherapy since the 1920s: to obtain more autonomy over their practice and to earn more money. The findings of a recent study of the goals of private practitioners in New England upon entering private practice bring the priorities of these social workers into stark relief. The most important goals indicated by the survey respondents, in decreasing order of importance, were to "do direct counseling," "maximize professional autonomy," "grow professionally," "be my own boss," "set my own hours," and "earn money." The least important goals indicated, in decreasing order of importance, were "help solve society's problem," "become more politically involved," "help economically disadvantaged people," and "work with ethnic minorities." It is important to note that these people had been well socialized into the social work profession; they had an average of ten years of post–MSW social work experience prior to entering private practice.

Harry Specht and Mark E. Courtney, *Unfaithful Angels: How Social Work Has Abandoned Its Mission*, 1994, 125–26.

negotiate the constraints and opportunities of organizational life than many professionals exercise, mainly because they lack the expertise required to be effective in their roles as bureaucrats. Most professionals prefer to identify themselves as helpers and service givers, and training is consciously sought to prepare for these roles. They tend to ignore or downplay the bureaucratic role that they must carry.[52]

Furthermore, it is possible to design agency-based practice in ways that tap the energies and resources associated with entrepreneurial activity. In the Kent Community Care Project, for example, British social workers were given a budget they could spend according to the needs and circumstances of each frail elderly client. The objective was to create a local network of supportive services that would allow the frail elderly to remain living in the community rather than being institutionalized, and at a lower cost to the public than would result from an institutional placement.[53]

Strategies to Alter the Composition of the Delivery System

Specialized Access Structure.   The objective of this strategy is neither to change the combination of roles in the service delivery system nor to change authority relationships through centralization or co-location. Its advocates believe that specialized professional–bureaucratic services perform important functions despite their weaknesses as delivery mechanisms. Instead of changing roles and the like, they want to change the composition of the delivery system by adding a new element, one that acts on other service agencies, prying open their entry points, and ensuring that proper connections are made by clients. In a word, *access* is to be provided as a social service.

Traditionally, the provision of access was considered a marginal function carried out by agency staff rather than a separate function around which to organize a distinct set of services. As a marginal function, access is unduly restricted by the narrow perspectives of agency specializations, perspectives relating primarily to an agency's core function instead of the particular problems brought by clients. This phenomenon is a by-product of neither incompetence nor malice. It is a normal structural reality of specialized service organizations.

To facilitate client access to services while maintaining a relatively high degree of specialization, it has been proposed that a "professionally unbiased doorway" be added to the service delivery system in the form of a special agency offering case-advocacy, advice, information, and referral services that help clients negotiate the bureaucratic maze.[54]

Although in some respects a persuasive idea, having special access agencies may be problematic. From the client's perspective, one effect of this strategy may be *increased* service fragmentation and complexity. Further, whereas access services are increasingly important in urban societies, they are rather intangible. Thus, the access agency may be perceived by clients as merely another bureaucracy to negotiate, another base to be touched before the proper resources are matched to their needs.

The existence of access agencies, of course, may also result in other community agencies diminishing their *own* access services. For instance, there is likely to be reduced pressures on these agencies to perform outreach or to make referrals to clients they are unable to serve. The extent to which the creation of the access agency lessens traveling time, expense, or confusion in the client's search for service is presently unclear. Moreover, the separation of assessment and diagnosis (access) from treatment (services) that occurs from this strategy may prove rather clumsy in practice.

A note must be added about online service provision, a relatively new method of service delivery that employs computer technologies to help individuals secure assistance with a variety of problems and concerns. Pioneered in the health field, where the term *telemedicine* is commonly employed, e-mail, teleconferencing, and webcam techniques are equally useful in social work. According to McCarty and Clancy, "nearly anything a social worker does face-to-face could theoretically be done online."[55] While something may be lost in the absence of direct personal contact, there already exists a rather extensive online fee-based counseling and "teletherapy" industry. Informal online forums also exist, often on a peer advice basis, with people helping others in circumstances similar to their own. And for individuals in remote locations, computer connections may often be the only convenient way to connect and communicate with social service and health providers.

Purposive Duplication.   Purposive duplication entails re-creating in a new agency any or all of the services available in the existing system. Purposive duplication is advanced in two forms that have a surface resemblance but are dissimilar enough to warrant distinction—*competition* and *separatism*.

Competition involves the creation of duplicate agencies within the existing delivery system to compete with established agencies for clients and resources. This strategy increases choice. More important, competition is expected to have an invigorating effect on agencies and professionals, sensitizing them to client needs and producing greater enterprise and creativity. The consequences of this strategy, however, are not always compatible with its motives. Instead of a healthy competition for clients and resources, internecine conflict may ensue between powerfully entrenched agencies and new agencies scraping for a foothold in the system. The outcome of such conflict is reasonably predictable.

The duplication of services to stimulate competition may be achieved through *direct* or *indirect* methods. The direct approach involves the restructuring of the delivery system with the creation of new agencies. Community Action Agency funds, for example, were often provided during the War on Poverty Era to develop new agencies that offered daycare, counseling, and community organization services to a community rather than to expand the service offerings of existing agencies. The indirect approach involves changing the form of social provision, such as by distributing social provisions to consumers in the form of vouchers. The experience with educational vouchers and charter schools, for example, has shown the significant impact such "choice" mechanisms have on increasing the supply and variation of providers.

Separatism differs from competition in both the systemic location of new structures and their purposes. In the separatist design, new agencies are created and organized outside the established delivery system, which they do not seek to enter. Competition is likely to be an inadvertent and unplanned by-product of separatism, more so for resources than for clients. The intention is to form an alternative network that will serve certain disadvantaged groups who, because of their race, ethnicity, gender, sexual orientation, or socioeconomic status, are served poorly or not at all by the existing system.

While offering direct aid to clients neglected by the existing network of services, alternative agencies also perform other functions. As Miller and Philipp point out, they engage in unorthodox activities that help to clarify legal issues, offer a theoretical critique of conventional service paradigms, and provide a community of interest for new, often unpopular, client groups.[56] In recent years, for example, independent community-based services networks have developed for battered women, the LGBT (Lesbian, Gay, Bisexual, and Transgender) community, persons with AIDS, and newly arrived immigrant groups. Proponents of separatism emphasize that this strategy contains social and political values for disadvantaged groups that transcend the enhancement of service delivery.

Duplicate strategies, in either form, are expensive. The money may be well spent if the new agencies become a dynamic force for desired changes in the delivery system and reach those who are excluded from services. Weighing against these benefits are the risks of expending scarce resources to produce fruitless conflict and to create even greater program fragmentation.

Unsettled Questions

We have identified six major strategies to foster social service coherence and accessibility: changing patterns of authority by coordination and citizen participation, altering roles and status by role attachments and professional disengagement, and changing substantive composition by development of specialized access structures and purposive duplication. We have analyzed each to find their expected benefits and to discover how they may exacerbate difficulties in other directions. All of these strategies are plausible ways to develop more effective service delivery; yet each has limitations and latent dysfunctions. And although some strategies may be complementary, others are just as clearly contradictory.

Before we can accurately judge the efficacy of any of the reform strategies, certain empirical questions must be answered. We will not attempt to detail all of these questions, but rather to identify several key issues requiring more investigation.

Coordination

Within what range and mix of services does coordination operate most effectively? At issue here are the criteria for selecting the number and types of services to be incorporated within a coordinating structure to produce minimum strain and maximum productive collaboration. There is substantial evidence, for instance, that certain service functions (such as social action and direct services) create disharmony and strain when joined.[57] We have little evidence, however, of what the optimal mix of services is and whether coordination is more likely to improve service integration when organized around a geographic base (all services in a designated neighborhood), a clientele with special demographic characteristics (such as the aged, adolescents, lone parents, or ethnic groups), functional areas (such as homelessness and housing), or combinations thereof.

In addition, it is difficult to gauge what, if any, cost savings are achieved through coordination. So far, the evidence is sparse and tentative. The following conclusions, however, drawn from a study of thirty service-integration projects, illustrate some of the variables that enter into the measurements.

> It may not be possible to justify services integration strictly in terms of total dollar savings. Centralized/consolidated operation of core services, recordkeeping, joint programming, joint funding, joint training, and/or central purchase of service arrangements on behalf of a number of service providers promote economies of scale, and coordinated staff utilization, funding, planning and programming, and evaluation help reduce duplication. Although there are some cost savings resulting from economies of scale and reduction of duplication, they do not appear (at least in the short run) to equal the input costs of administrative and core service staff required to support integrative efforts. However, if one includes protection of public investment in services as a measure of efficiency, then a stronger case can be made for service integration on grounds of efficiency. If the public investment in one service (job training, for example) is to have lasting benefit only if another service (a job placement service, for example) is also provided, the cost involved in assuring that the client gets the job placement services as well as job training may be justified in terms of protecting the investment in job training.[58]

Purposive Duplication

Under what circumstances do the savings that accrue to a large-scale organization make the duplication of services practical? The research required to answer this question involves cost–benefit analyses of social service programs. A major argument against purposive duplication and in favor of coordination is the increased efficiency attributed to the latter. However, the gain in efficiency may vary from one type of service to another.[59] At the same time, coordination or administrative unification is usually achieved at the expense of diversity. Ultimately, value judgments will be made concerning the relative desirability of efficiency versus diversity in the delivery of social services. The more information available regarding the economic costs and social benefits of duplication, the better informed these value judgments will be.

Access Agencies

To what extent does the creation of an access agency facilitate entry into social services? One issue already suggested is that the addition of an access agency to the local service system may have the unanticipated effect of decreasing the net amount of information and referral provided within that system (because other agencies may diminish similar services they previously offered). This question remains open to direct empirical investigation. Another line of study involves an analysis of the percentage of those seeking assistance who actually receive services. It would be useful to know how many bases these persons touch before they receive help, and how this varies in the presence and absence of access agencies.

Role Attachments

What types of local nonprofessional workers are best suited to withstand the strains inherent in the performance of linkage functions between professional workers and the community served? At issue here is the fact that the term *indigenous nonprofessional* is applied to a variety of people with diverse values, commitments, aspirations, and reference groups. Workers in this category are likely to possess different capacities for coping with pressures toward bureaucratic conformity and professionalism. Accordingly, a useful line of investigation suggested in an exploratory study develops a typology based on the differences among nonprofessional workers.[60] It was found that certain types of nonprofessional staff members appear better suited than others to perform tasks such as outreach. Further investigation is needed to extend and substantiate these tentative findings.

Professional Disengagement

How does the move from agency-based to private practice affect access to and continuity of services offered? Although the disengagement strategy assumes that the delivery of social services will improve when the professional worker is freed from bureaucratic restrictions, little evidence exists either way. A line of inquiry might involve selecting a few cities for study in order to evaluate the effects of having similar services offered by private practitioners and agency-based practitioners with regard to the characteristics of the persons served, the percentage of referrals made, the percentage of follow-ups, and the like.

Citizen Participation

To what degree does substantive citizen participation in agency decision making increase accountability to those being served? As indicated, election and selection procedures for citizen participants are frequently such that those who actually participate are not accountable to the service users they ostensibly represent. We lack careful comparisons of the decision-making behavior of citizen participants and the expressed wishes and interests of the people they serve as well as delineation of selection procedures that produce participants with a high degree of accountability. One issue for further investigation involves the extent to which elected representatives (on a block, neighborhood, and city-wide basis), appointed representatives, and volunteer (or self-selected) representatives differ in their accountability.

Each of these unsettled questions contributes to the uncertainty that surrounds policymakers who are concerned with selecting the right strategy to improve the delivery of social services. To conclude that more research is needed (which it is) is the unblemished mark of academicians (which we are). To this advice, practitioners may nod abstractly in agreement while they continue to design and implement the policies that govern service delivery. This means that policy choices regarding service delivery may eventually benefit from future investigation, but they will not await the results; choices will be made based on the knowledge we possess, imperfect as it is.

Controlling Costs: Services Rationing and Managed Care

Many of the service delivery strategies we have described were formulated in the 1960s and 1970s, an era of notable expansion in social services. The presumption of growth, as Glennerster puts it, was deeply imbedded in the intellects of social welfare planners.[61] When social services expenditures were curtailed in the 1980s and political support arose for meeting service needs through the market economy, several new issues of choice surfaced. Along with the privatization/contracting option, already described, a variety of efforts to contain costs emerged, many of which involved designs for the rationing of services through managed care.

When social service budgets are restricted through legislative cutbacks, the burden of implementation falls on the organizations and professionals responsible for service delivery. At the juncture where clients' needs intersect with social service resources, a frequent challenge is making do with less.

To some extent, of course, agencies have always engaged in service rationing. Resources are always limited; social needs are always substantial. But during periods of economic expansion, there is less pressure for careful thought about and stringency in expenditures. It is in periods of fiscal difficulty that choices addressing rationing, cost controls, and cutbacks become pivotal.

Services rationing may be accomplished through several processes. Ellie Scrivens, analyzing the dynamics of rationing, divided them into two broad categories: demand inhibitors and supply inhibitors. Strategies that act to reduce the *demand* for

CAPSULE 6.12 • *The Supreme Word on Managed Care*

Traditionally, medical care in the United States has been provided on a "fee-for-service" basis. A physician charges so much for a general physical exam, a vaccination, a tonsillectomy and so on. The physician bills the patient for services provided or, if there is insurance and the doctor is willing, submits the bill for the patient's care to the insurer, for payment subject to the terms of the insurance agreement. . . . In a fee-for-service system, a physician's financial incentive is to provide more care, not less, so long as payment is forthcoming. The check on the incentive is the physician's obligation to exercise reasonable judgment and medical skill in the patient's interest.

Like other risk-bearing organizations, H.M.O.s take steps to control costs. At the least, H.M.O.s will in some fashion make coverage determinations, scrutinizing requested services against these contractual provisions to make sure that a request for care falls within the scope of covered circumstances, or that a given treatment falls within the scope of the care promised. They customarily issue general guidelines for their physicians about appropriate levels of care. . . .

These cost-controlling measures are commonly complemented by specific financial incentives to physicians, rewarding them for decreasing utilization of health care services, and penalizing them for what may be found to be excessive treatment. . . . No H.M.O. could survive without some incentive connecting physician reward with treatment rationing.

David H. Souter, writing for a unanimous Supreme Court in the case of *Pegram v. Herdrich*, June 12, 2000.

services erect physical, temporal, and social barriers to service. On the deterrence of physical barriers, Scrivens cites a report on the British social services in which it was observed that some of their facilities were "forbidding with reception arrangements not such as to encourage anyone, let alone anyone in distress, to approach them."[62] Temporal barriers can be raised in the form of waiting lists, time-consuming application procedures, remote service locations, and inconvenient office hours. Clients also may be put off by social barriers that involve embarrassing eligibility requirements. The failure to communicate relevant information to clients about available services is another effective deterrent.

On the other side of the ledger, strategies that reduce the *supply* of services include restriction and dilution. With a restrictive strategy, eligibility criteria are tightened so that fewer clients needing services can actually qualify. This goal is accomplished by narrowing the rules governing eligibility and stringently applying professional discretion in interpreting the rules. Strategies for diluting services decrease the amount and quality of provisions by cutting time spent with clients, prematurely terminating cases, lowering the qualifications of professional staff, and substituting volunteers for professionals.[63]

As long as demand exceeds supply, there will be some form of rationing in service delivery. Thus, we must ask, "On what grounds might one choose among the various strategies outlined in this chapter?" Some of these strategies are objectionable because of their furtive character. They amount to what Lipsky calls "bureaucratic disentitlement," where service delivery is curtailed not by transparent and formalized policy

CAPSULE 6.13 • *Managed Care—Pro and Con*

Pro

What makes the assault on managed care so peculiar is that Americans are healthier than ever. It's one thing for the public to loathe an industry whose performance is declining, but the health care business is losing stature at a time when its performance is improving. By almost all measures, U.S. public health gets better every year. Almost every health trend has been positive during the decade of managed care. And, after rising at a frightening pace for most of the 1980s, the cost of health care has stabilized.

Gregg Easterbrook, "Managing Fine," *The New Republic*, March 20, 2000, 21.

Con

Most of the country understands that an unconscionable obsession with the bottom line has resulted in widespread abuses in the managed-care industry. Simply stated, there is big money to be made by denying care. It is now widely known that there are faceless bureaucrats making critical diagnostic and treatment decisions, that some doctors are being retaliated against for dispensing honest advice, that women have had an especially hard time getting the care they need, and that patients have died because they were unable to gain admittance to emergency rooms.

choices but rather by "low-level marginal decisions or non-decisions of low visibility."[64] The problem, as Lipsky sees it, is that through obscure actions and inactions, social service agencies may devise allocative policies that are not open to public inspection. In choosing among rationing strategies, those based on explicit procedures open to public scrutiny, such as tightening formal eligibility requirements, offer greater protection to the public than veiled activities designed to discourage consumption and dilute services.

While rationing strategies generally evoke hostile and negative responses, they have been successfully implemented—either in explicit or furtive forms—in many human services fields. One rationing strategy that has received a significant amount of attention is managed care, and the common use of arrangements to "manage" the utilization of health and mental health, and other forms of service, has heightened sensitivity to costs and promoted a more considered, a more conservative use of resources.

Managed care is basically a form of human services organization that is designed to improve the efficiency of care and treatment by increasing the attention given to costs when making service decisions. It is a form of organization that has become institutionalized in the health care economy, where around two-thirds of all Americans are now enrolled in networks of health care providers that contract with managed care organizations and abide by managed-care rules. These rules have created an apparatus of incentives, procedures, and structures that revolutionized the nature of American health care, fundamentally altering relationships among doctors, hospitals, drug and insurance companies, and employers, and putting cost considerations front and center in the decision-making process.

Cost considerations, of course, were never absent from health care, but the dominance of public and nonprofit auspices in the field, and the powerful centrality of the medical profession, traditionally limited the intensity of budget-oriented thinking. Under traditional fee-for-service medicine, the primary model of health care finance until the 1990s, doctors and hospitals largely determined overall costs by the fees they charged. These fees, pretty much taken as a given, were paid automatically and without question by third-party insurance companies and by public agencies. But in the last two decades, with remarkable swiftness, this automatic payment, fee-for-service model has disintegrated, supplanted by managed medicine and its rationalizing cost–benefit techniques. Chief among these techniques are gatekeeping, utilization management, and provider cost control incentives.

Gatekeeping controls access to services—especially to high cost services—by giving a central authority the power to influence fundamental decisions about the level and nature of services. In health care settings, the gatekeeper, typically a primary care physician, is the initial contact for the patient. It is usually this physician who directs and coordinates care and who is responsible for authorizing prescriptions, referrals to specialists, or hospital care.

Utilization management, the second cost control device, establishes another level of screening. The health provider in managed care often must apply to a utilization manager for approval to initiate a particular treatment regimen. This oversight by external cost-oriented monitors diminishes the degree of autonomy exercised by professionals and may also erode the professional's ability to maintain client confidentiality because contractual agreements between managed care companies and service providers often contain a clause allowing the organization access to whatever patient record information is necessary to make sound decisions concerning access to service.[65]

The final cost-control mechanism—physician cost incentives—rewards doctors who restrain the utilization of health care services, and often attempts to limit what the managed care company may consider excessive treatment. Since managed-care physicians are often "capitation" funded, receiving one annual lump sum per enrolled patient, they have a financial incentive to impose their own rationing on patient care. The more they can restrain patient costs, the more they can earn.

For managed-care advocates, these various rationing arrangements provide a rational, coordinated approach to medicine, an approach that enhances services and encourages prevention while restraining unnecessary costs. Under fee-for-service medicine, it was clearly in the financial interest of the care provider to offer more care, not less, whatever the actual circumstances of need. Doctors and hospitals, automatically paid their "prevailing" charges by third-party insurers, had few reasons to limit care—no matter how unnecessary or redundant it might be. This perverse incentive to oversupply care and treatment—an excess of care and treatment that bore no relation to good health—is precisely what sustained the great health care inflation of the 1980s and early 1990s and resulted in the cost pressures that managed care set out to, and in fact did, stabilize. Health maintenance organizations (HMOs), for example, one common form of managed care provider, reduced hospital stays by 30 percent between 1992 and 2000, without any detriment to health.

Managed-care critics, on the other hand, provide an arsenal of dramatic horror stories about inappropriate restrictions, or denials of care, with which to argue the incompatibility of cost containment and good health care. For the critics, managed care doesn't rationalize care, it inappropriately withholds it by creating an unconscionable conflict of interest between the practitioners' obligation to their clients and their obligation to their employers. As Strom-Gottfried and Corcoran explain, competitive pressures in the managed care environment have resulted in "financial incentives to limit treatment or referrals, pressures to 'skim' populations for healthier clientele, and the risk of sanctions should one advocate for improved patient care."[66]

Emerging Issues: Culturally Competent Service Delivery

After the mid-1980s when the era of rapid growth in the welfare state came to a close and political support arose for market alternatives, the discourse of service delivery shifted to services rationing, voucher and choice strategies, privatization, the contracting out of services, and, recently, a reliance on faith-based organizations to organize and delivery social programs. Along with these developments came an increasing sensitivity to the challenges of successfully engaging ethnic and cultural minorities in service delivery. As we noted in Chapter 4, many needy people who are officially eligible for social benefits fail to receive them. Others receive services, but fail to benefit from them. While the "disparities" problem has been best documented in the health field, the gap between white and minority service outcomes is pervasive in the broad range of the human services, from education to criminal justice to child welfare.

Often, the service delivery gap results from a lack of knowledge—people may simply be unaware that useful services are available, or that they may be eligible. In other situations, those who know they qualify for services may be unable or unwilling to apply for them. This may result from fear, disinterest, pride, antigovernment attitudes, misunderstanding, religious or cultural perspectives, or any number of other factors. Many Latino families, for example, find the idea of nursing homes, of strangers caring for their relatives, unacceptable, while American Muslims may perceive such homes as a violation of the *Koran*, which obligates families to care for their own elderly relatives. Some Latinos, citizens or legal residents, may fear being perceived as undocumented immigrants when applying for services. Still others, limited in their English fluency, may find service personnel and agency forms and documents unintelligible.

In recent years, considerable attention has been focused on issues of underutilization, culture, and diversity. While the social work profession, from its beginning, has emphasized the importance of assessing problems, formulating services, and delivering programs in a fashion that engages the reality of their clients' world, today's parlance is increasingly presented in terms of overcoming "barriers," be they impediments of language or culture or class.

A significant number of service delivery strategies have been implemented to bridge the gap between social service organizations and the "socially excluded." We have already discussed the use of paraprofessionals and services duplication as a vehicle to engage hard-to-reach populations. While it is generally acknowledged that practitioners who speak the same language as their clients, and have an awareness of their culture, can facilitate access to services, there remains a significant scarcity, especially in mainline social service organizations, of such staff.

Professionals themselves, of course, have adapted to the increasingly diverse communities in which they work. Aware of the difficulty newcomer and minority populations often encounter in their dealings with public and voluntary agencies, and committed to the idea that culturally competent services can overcome barriers to care and well-being, professional schools have modified their instructional programs. At the same time that they have endeavored to enroll more minority students, for example, schools of social work have incorporated coursework that both facilitates an awareness of cultural patterns and develops skills for successful practice with diverse populations. Coupled with traditional social work skills—empathy, acceptance, respect for the client, individualized treatment, technical competence—these skills can lead to more effective services for underserved racial and ethnic populations.

Direct service practitioners, for example, are increasingly trained to be sensitive to cultural variations in social problems and to identifying appropriate methods of communication and intervention. Administrators and policymakers, for their part, recognizing the many ways in which communication affects success, are implementing new service strategies to better engage their clients.

Some agencies try to bridge the language gap by encouraging limited English proficiency (LEP) clients to provide their own interpreters. Sometimes minor children play this role, or friends and neighbors. Such an approach can be useful in an absence of alternatives, but it may also present significant problems when the untrained interpreter either inhibits or obstructs communications, as in cases where confidential or embarrassing material is presented, or else fails to accurately understand and translate agency terminology.

Other agencies rely on paraprofessionals, often hiring minority staff to serve as grassroots liaisons to assess community attitudes, disseminate information, and, hopefully, foster trust. The New York City Police Department, for example, has hired community affairs officers in each precinct of the city as well as special outreach staff for immigrant and gay/lesbian/transgender populations. The City also recently hired Muslim civilians for outreach purposes and to help train police officers in matters of culture, language, and tradition.

Similarly, localities and states have hired outreach and community development workers to better relate to immigrant and minority populations, to increase goodwill, and to better engage citizens in the business of government. In other instances, local governments have encouraged the development of ethnic-specific agencies to improve service delivery to underutilizing populations. In the San Francisco Bay Area alone, for example, there are contract agencies for Native American child welfare (The American Indian Child Resource Center, Oakland), Latino mental health (Clinica de la Raza, Oakland), Asian elders (On Loc Senior Services, San Francisco), and African

CAPSULE 6.14 • *Ethnics and Ethics*

(a) Social workers should understand culture and its function in human behavior and society, recognizing the strengths that exist in all cultures.

(b) Social workers should have a knowledge base of their clients' cultures and be able to demonstrate competence in the provision of services that are sensitive to clients' cultures and to differences among people and cultural groups.

(c) Social workers should obtain education about and seek to understand the nature of social diversity and oppression with respect to race, ethnicity, national origin, color, sex, sexual orientaiton, marital status, political belief, religion, and mental or physical disability.

NASW Code of Ethics. Copyright © 1999, National Association of Social Workers, Inc. Used by permission.

American youth development (Bayview Hunters Point Foundation for Community Improvement). These agencies, and the many others that exist in almost all urban centers today, not only provide a friendly front door for services, they also frequently serve as intermediaries for clients who deal with county and state child welfare, mental health, public health, and education agencies.

For agency managers, one of the essential keys to effective service delivery is ensuring meaningful communication channels for people with limited English-speaking abilities. In this respect, language is obviously a primary area of concern. As the number of residents with limited English proficiency has risen, effective communication has become an essential issue. A lack of language understanding can be a significant barrier to service, either excluding eligible foreign language speakers from services, or delaying their access to services, or providing less than optimal services. Language barriers are especially problematic in fields that depend on complex client–professional communication, as with doctors and nurses in health care or with social workers in child protection or mental health counseling.

A recent article, for example, described a young Latino man who presented himself in the emergency room as feeling "intoxicado" (i.e. "nauseated') before collapsing. The physician on duty interpreted this as meaning "intoxicated" and ordered emergency treatment for a drug overdose. In the meanwhile, the patient had a brain aneurysm resulting in quadriplegia and, later, a $71 million settlement against the hospital after legal action.[67] In another case, a Spanish-speaking mother reported that her young two-year old had fallen off her bike and "hit herself." The resident taking the report misinterpreted this as child abuse, contacted Child Protective Services, resulting in the mom having to relinquish both of her children.[68]

Language access can be facilitated in a variety of ways. Interpreter services can be provided. Bilingual frontline as well as professional staff can be hired. Computer technology can provide information in multiple languages, as can forms and information packets. Non-English telephone helplines can expand services coverage.

National social policies in many welfare states have contributed to the effort for culturally and linguistically responsive services. In England, a five-year program, Delivering Race Equality in Mental Health, funded the creation of 500 community development workers to improve ethnic minority access to public services.[69] In Australia, federal initiatives have been operating to overcome the long history of discrimination against the aboriginal peoples.

In the United States, federal civil rights legislation since the 1960s has required states and local health and service organizations to ensure access to services for individuals who don't speak or understand English. Under Title VI of the 1964 Civil Rights Act, for example, states and localities must provide equal access to services to a variety of racial, ethnic, and national origin groups. Under this last category, those with limited English proficiency must be provided fair, nondiscriminatory access to all federally funded programs. Specifically, all governments or organizations receiving federal funds must ensure that individuals receive, free of charge, the language assistance necessary to ensure their equal access. Under these laws, and their elaborating regulations, culturally competent services are a fundamental civil rights issue, not merely an issue of culturally competent practice.

State and local health, mental health, welfare, and child protection authorities, as well as private contract agencies, have responded to the Title VI mandate in a variety of ways. Some mental health agencies, for example, have implemented "threshold language" policies that specify a number or proportion of foreign language speakers that, when exceeded, requires special steps to be taken to ensure "linguistic access."[70] Schools, for their part, are obligated to provide special language supports when a critical mass of English language learning students is present.

But while federal legislation mandates services like interpretation and translation and provides some limited funding under Medicaid, Food Stamps, and the State Children's Health Insurance Program (SCHIP), many providers still lack the resources to engage effectively many of their clients. Language requirements are often viewed as onerous "unfunded mandates," unfairly dictating federal priorities to state and local agencies, rather than as supports for improved equality and effectiveness in service delivery.

Notes

1. Whereas most services are designed for delivery (i.e., policy implementation) at the local level, designing and planning activities may or may not occur at the local level. Frequently, program designers and planners may be several steps removed from the local community, located at the State house or the White House. The location of the program planners is a factor of major significance in policy development.
2. Alfred Kahn and Sheila Kamerman (eds.), *Privatization and the Welfare State* (Princeton, N.J.: Princeton University Press, 1989); Neil Gilbert, *Capitalism and the Welfare State* (New Haven, Conn.: Yale University Press, 1983); Congressional Research Service, Privatization and the Federal Government, December 28, 2006.
3. E. S. Savas, *Privatization: The Key to Better Government* (Chatham, N.J.: Chatham Publishers, 1987); Neil Gilbert and Barbara Gilbert, *The Enabling State*: *Modern Welfare Capitalism in*

America (New York: Oxford University Press, 1989); Ken Judge and Martin Knapp, "Efficiency in the Production of Welfare: The Public and Private Sectors Compared," in Rudolph Klein and Michael O'Higgins (eds.), *The Future of Welfare* (Oxford: Basil Blackwell, 1985).

4. Robert Bellah, "Community Properly Understood: A Defense of Democratic Communitarianism," *The Responsive Community* (Winter 1995/96), 49–54; Peter Berger and Richard Neuhaus, *To Empower the People: The Role of Mediating Structures in Public Policy* (Washington, D.C.: American Enterprise Institute Press, 1977); Harry Specht and Mark Courtney, *Unfaithful Angels: How Social Work Has Abandoned Its Mission* (New York: Free Press, 1994), 152–76.

5. Burton Weisbrod, *The Nonprofit Economy* (Cambridge, Mass.: Harvard University Press, 1988); Susan Rose-Ackerman, "Social Services and the Market," *Columbia Law Review*, 8(6) (1983): 1405–38.

6. Henry Hansmann, "Economic Theories of Nonprofit Organization," in Walter Powell (ed.), *The Nonprofit Sector* (New Haven, Conn.: Yale University Press, 1987), 29–32.

7. Mark Schlesinger, Robert Dortwart, and Richard Pulice, "Competitive Bidding and State's Purchase of Services: The Case of Mental Health Care in Massachusetts," *Journal of Policy Analysis and Management*, 5(2) (Winter 1986): 245–64; David Young, "Referral and Placement in Child Care: The New York City Purchase of Service System," *Public Policy*, 12(3) (Summer 1974): 293–328.

8. Rose-Ackerman, "Social Services and the Market."

9. Rosabeth Kanter and David Summers, "Doing Well While Doing Good: Dilemmas of Performance Measurement in Nonprofit Organizations and the Need for a Multiple-Constituency Approach," in Walter Powell (ed.), *The Nonprofit Sector: A Research Handbook* (New Haven, Conn.: Yale University Press, 1987), 154–67.

10. Charles Krauthammer, "A Social Conservative Credo," *The Public Interest*, 121 (Fall 1995): 16.

11. Fred Wulczyn, "Status at Birth and Infant Placements in New York City," in Richard Barth, Jill Berrick, and Neil Gilbert (eds.), *Child Welfare Research Review 1* (New York: Columbia University Press, 1994).

12. Emile Durkheim, *The Division of Labor in Society*, George Simpson (trans.) (New York: The Free Press, 1933), 28.

13. See, for example, Neil Gilbert, *Welfare Justice* (New Haven, Conn.: Yale University Press, 1995), 135–37; Neil Gilbert and Kwong Leung Tang, "The United States," in Norman Johnson (ed.), Private Markets in Health and Welfare (Oxford: Berg Publishers, 1995).

14. Kahn and Kamerman, *Privatization and the Welfare State*, 262.

15. As Peter Blau observed long ago, bureaucracy and democracy are different modes of social organization for decision making and implementation that are effective for different ends. See Peter Blau, *Bureaucracy in Modern Society* (New York: Random House, 1956).

16. See John J. Dilulio Jr., *Godly Republic*, 2007, for a review of political and legal issues surrounding federal faith-based initiatives.

17. See, for example, Ralph Kramer, "Public Fiscal Policy and Voluntary Agencies in Welfare States," *Social Service Review*, 53 (March 1979): 1–14, and Alfred Kahn, "A Framework for Public–Voluntary Collaboration in the Social Services," *Social Welfare Forum 1976* (New York: Columbia University Press, 1976), 47–62.

18. Kurt Reichert, "The Drift Toward Entrepreneurialism in Health and Social Welfare: Implications for Social Work Education," *Administration in Social Work*, 1 (Summer 1977): 129. See also Mimi Abramovitz, "The Privatization of the Welfare State: A Review," *Social Work* (July/August 1986): 257–64.

19. For further discussion of problems in this area, see R. M. Kanter, "The Measurement of Organizational Effectiveness, Productivity, Performance and Success: Issues and Dilemmas in Service and Non-Profit Organizations," Program on Non-Profit Organization Working Paper 8, Institution for Social Policy Studies, Yale University, 1979.

20. Richard Titmuss, *The Gift Relationship* (New York: Pantheon, 1971); Cynthia Barnett, "Profit and Non-Profit Distinctions in Theory and in Fact: The Lack of Fit Between Theory and Empirical Research in Health Care Organizations," 1982 (mimeographed paper); Lenard Kaye, Abraham Monk, and Howard Litwin, "Community Monitoring of Nursing Home Care: Proprietary and Non-Profit Association Perspectives," *Journal of Social Service Research*, 7(3) (Spring 1984): 5–19; Catherine Born, "Proprietary Terms and Child Welfare Services: Patterns

and Implications," *Child Welfare*, 62(2) (March/April 1983): 109–18; Stephen Shortell, "Hospital Ownership and Nontraditional Services," *Health Affairs* (Winter 1986).

21. For elaboration on this point, see Neil Gilbert, *Capitalism and the Welfare State* (New Haven, Conn.: Yale University Press, 1983), 17–19.

22. Ibid. Also see Neil Gilbert, "Welfare for Profit: Moral, Empirical, and Theoretical Perspectives," *Journal of Social Policy*, 13(1) (January 1984): 63–74.

23. This concern, it appears, is not always decisive. For example, in recent years federal and state agencies have contracted with profit-making corporations to run prisons. See Harry Hatry et al., "Comparison of Privately and Publicly Operated Corrections Facilities in Kentucky and Massachusetts," The Urban Institute, August 1989.

24. Harry G. Bredemeier, "The Socially Handicapped and the Agencies: A Market Analysis," in Frank Riessman, Jerome Cohen, and Arthur Pearl (eds.), *Mental Health of the Poor* (New York: Free Press, 1964); Richard Cloward and Frances F. Piven, "The Professional Bureaucracies Benefit Systems as Influence Systems," in Murray Silberman (ed.), *The Role of Government in Promoting Social Change* (New York: Columbia University, School of Social Work, 1966); Alfred J. Kahn, "Do Social Services have a Future in New York?" *City Almanac*, 5(5) (February 1971): 1–11; Irving Piliavin, "Restructuring the Provision of Social Service," *Social Work*, 13(1) (January 1968); William Reid, "Interagency Coordination in Delinquency Prevention and Control," *Social Service Review*, 38(4) (December 1964); Martin Rein, *Social Policy: Issues of Choice and Change* (New York: Random House, 1970); Gideon Sjoberg, Richard Brymer, and Buford Farris, "Bureaucracy and the Lower Class," *Sociology and Social Research*, 50(3) (April 1966): 325–37.

25. Herbert H. Simon, *Administrative Behavior*, 2nd ed. (New York: Free Press, 1965), 238.

26. Peter Townsend et al., *The Fifth Social Service: A Critical Analysis of the Seebohm Report* (London: Fabian Society, 1970).

27. See, for example, Neil Gilbert and Harry Specht, *Coordinating Social Services* (New York: Praeger Publishers, 1977), and Stephanie Fall Creek and Neil Gilbert, "Agency Network in Transition: Problems and Prospects," *Social Work*, 26(3) (May 1981), 210–15.

28. James D. Thompson, *Organizations in Action* (New York: McGraw-Hill, 1967); and Reid, "Interagency Coordination in Delinquency Prevention and Control."

29. Reid, "Interagency Coordination in Delinquency Prevention and Control."

30. Robert A. Dahl and Charles E. Lindblom, *Politics, Economics, and Welfare* (New York: Harper & Row, 1953), 238.

31. David Hage, "Purgatory of the Working Poor," *The American Prospect*, September 2004, A4.

32. Mary Richardson et al., "Coordinating Services By Design," *Public Welfare* (Summer 1989): 31–36.

33. Jane Knitzer and Susan Yelton, "Collaboration between Child Welfare and Mental Health," *Public Welfare* (Spring 1990): 24–33.

34. Karen Orloff Kaplan, "Recent Trends in Case Management," *Encyclopedia of Social Work*, 18th ed., 1990 Supplement (Silver Spring, Md.: National Association of Social Workers, 1990), 60–77.

35. Denise Polit and Joseph O'Hara, "Support Services," in Phoebe Cottingham and David Ellwood (eds.), *Welfare Policy for the 1990s*, (Cambridge, Mass.: Harvard University Press, 1989), 191–92.

36. Ibid., 193.

37. Sherry Arnstein, "A Ladder of Citizen Participation," *Journal of the American Institute of Planners*, 35(4) (July 1969).

38. Hans B. C. Spiegel et al., *Neighborhood Power and Control: Implications for Urban Planning* (New York: Columbia University, Institute of Urban Environment, 1968), 157.

39. Ralph M. Kramer, *Community Development in Israel and the Netherlands* (Berkeley: University of California Press, Institute of International Studies, 1970), 127.

40. Gilbert, *Clients or Constituents* (San Francisco: Jossey-Bass, 1970), 145; and Arthur B. Shostak, "Promoting Participation of the Poor: Philadelphia's Antipoverty Program," *Social Work*, 11(1) (January 1966).

41. Ralph M. Kramer, *Participation of the Poor* (Englewood Cliffs, N.J.: Prentice-Hall, 1969), 127.

42. George Peterson et al., *The Reagan Block Grants: What Have We Learned?* (Washington, D.C.: Urban Institute Press, 1986).

43. Sjoberg, Brymer, and Farris, "Bureaucracy and the Lower Class."

44. S. M. Miller and Frank Riessman, *Social Class and Social Policy* (New York: Basic Books, 1968), 207.

45. The Aspen Institute, *Direct-Care Health Workers*, January, 2001, 1–2.

46. David A. Hardcastle, "The Indigenous Non-Professional in the Social Service Bureaucracy: A Critical Examination," *Social Work*, 16(2) (April 1971): 63.

47. "Schram to Explore Punitive Welfare Policy," *Bryn Mawr Now*, June 28, 2007.

48. Lonnie Snowden and David Derezotes, "Cultural Factors in the Intervention of Child Maltreatment," *Child and Adolescent Social Work*, 7(2) (April 1990).

49. Gerald Levy, "Acute Workers in a Welfare Bureaucracy," in Deborah Offenbacher and Constance Poster (eds.), *Social Problems and Social Policy* (New York: Appleton-Century-Crofts, 1970); see also Harry Wasserman, "The Professional Social Worker in a Bureaucracy," *Social Work*, 16(1) (January 1971): 89–95.

50. Piliavin, "Restructuring the Provision of Social Service," 35.

51. National Association of Social Workers, Practice Research Network, "What is NASW's Practice Research Network?" February 6, 2003.

52. Robert Pruger, "The Good Bureaucrat," *Social Work*, 18(4) (July 1973): 27.

53. Results of the project are reported by Bleddyn Davies and David Challis, "Experimenting with New Roles in Domiciliary Service: The Kent Community Care Project," *Gerontologist*, 20 (June 1980): 288–99.

54. Alfred J. Kahn, "Perspectives on Access to Social Service," *Social Work*, 15(2) (March 1970): 99.

55. Dawn McCarty and Catherine Clancy, "Telehealth: Implications for Social Work Practice," *Social Work*. April, 2002, 47:2, 153.

56. Henry Miller and Connie Philipp, "The Alternative Service-Agency," in Aaron Rosenblatt and Diana Waldfogel (eds.), *Handbook of Clinical Social Work* (San Francisco: Jossey-Bass, 1983), 779–91.

57. Edward J. O'Donnel and Marilyn M. Sullivan, "Service Delivery and Social Action through the Neighborhood Center: A Review of Research," *Welfare in Review*, 7(6) (November/December 1969): 95–102; and Neil Gilbert and Harry Specht, *Coordinating Social Services*.

58. Marshall Kaplan, Gans, and Kahn, and The Research Group, Inc., *Integration of Human Services in HEW: An Evaluation of Services Integration Projects*. An Executive Summary of a Study for the Social and Rehabilitation Service of the Department of Health, Education, and Welfare (1972), 11.

59. For an insightful analysis of the vital functions that may be served by duplication within systems, see Martin Landau, "Redundancy, Rationality, and the Problem of Duplication and Overlap," *Public Administration Review*, 29(4) (July/August 1969): 346–58.

60. Philip Kramer, "The Indigenous Worker: Hometowner, Striver or Activist," *Social Work*, 17(1) (January 1972).

61. Howard Glennerster, "Prime Cuts: Public Expenditure and Social Service Planning in a Hostile Environment," *Policy and Politics*, 8(4) (1980): 367–82.

62. Ellie Scrivens, "Towards a Theory of Rationing," *Social Policy and Administration*, 13(1) (Spring 1979): 53–84.

63. For more detailed discussions of these strategies, see Abraham Deron, "The Welfare State: Issues of Rationing and Allocation of Resources," in Shimon Spiro and Ephraim Yuchtman-Yaar (eds.), *Evaluating the Welfare State: Social and Political Perspectives* (New York: Academic Press, 1983): 149–59; and R. A. Parker, "Social Administration and Scarcity," *Social Work Today*, 12 (April 1967): 9–14.

64. Michael Lipsky, "Bureaucratic Disentitlement in Social Welfare Programs," *Social Service Review*, 58(1) (March 1984): 20.

65. For a discussion of this issue, see Barry Rock and Elaine Congress, "The New Confidentiality for the 21st Century in a Managed Care Environment," *Social Work*, 44(3) (May 1999): 253–62.

66. Kimberly Strom-Gottfried and Kevin Corcoran, "Confronting Ethical Dilemmas in Managed Care," *Journal of Social Work Education*, 34(1) (Winter 1998): 109–19.

67. "Language a Widening Barrier to Care," www.forbes.com, July 19, 2006.

68. Ibid.

69. Delivering Race Equality in Mental Health Struggles to Recruit Workers," www.community-care.co.uk/articles/2006/11/09/102085.html, posted November 9, 2006.

70. L.R. Snowden, M.C. Masland, R. Guerrero, "Federal Civil Rights Policy and Mental Health Treatment Access for Persons with Limited English Proficiency," *American Psychologist*, February/March, 2007.

7

The Mode of Finance: Sources of Funds

> The Congress shall have power to lay and collect taxes on incomes, from whatever source derived, without apportionment among the several States, and without regard to any census or enumeration.
>
> *16th Amendment to the U.S. Constitution,*
> February 25, 1913

> Taxes are a changing product of earnest efforts to have others pay them.
>
> Louis Eisenstein,
> *The Ideologies of Taxation, 1961*

People don't much care for paying taxes. Although Supreme Court Justice Oliver Wendell Holmes might have considered taxes "what we pay for a civilized society," most Americans view them, at best, as a burden to be reluctantly endured. Taxes may constitute the basic foundation for health, education, and welfare policies, but they aren't likely to ever place high in the public's regard.

Likeable or not, taxes—along with philanthropy and other sources of revenue—provide the essential fuel for social welfare endeavors. Our objectives in this chapter and the next, therefore, are to examine the process of revenue raising in the United States, to explore some of the basic policy choices involved in financing the welfare state, and to identify the implications of different funding sources and different systems of funding transfers. In social welfare, the things that money can do are substantially influenced by how that money is obtained.

Questions about the mode of finance interest policymakers, managers, and planners more than they do direct practitioners. Managers and planners are concerned with securing resources to sustain their programs. They need to understand the kinds of activities funders will support. Funders, whether they're legislators, foundation trustees, or executives of agency federations, are concerned with making choices among competing interests and programs to achieve *their* goals. In negotiations for program support, both funders and fund seekers address the questions of the previous chapters: Who is eligible for help? What will they receive? How will service delivery be organized?

The direct service practitioner is usually less attentive to questions of finance than to other dimensions of policy choice. This is because financing choices appear remote from the exigencies of day-to-day practice, and their effects on client welfare are typically indistinct. Funding decisions for almost any kind of social welfare program—whether mental health, housing, or AIDS counseling—are likely to involve "big government" somewhere along the line. Because most programs of significance require the money, sanction, or surveillance of one or more levels of government, direct practitioners are likely to consider funding questions outside of their influence. This view, certainly, is not entirely unrealistic. Funding arrangements *are* complex, and final program decisions are frequently made by individuals and groups many steps removed from actual service delivery.

Nevertheless, it is critical that professionals concerned with social welfare have a working knowledge of the major issues, concepts, and values involved in the mode of finance. While tax matters tend to be viewed with extreme disinterest by many, few areas of social policy have more direct and immediate impact on the everyday lives of low-income and working-income families.

Although the vast majority of professionals may not participate directly in allocation decision making, they can, in their role as citizens, members of professional associations, and agency employees, affect how decision makers think and act. It is not unreasonable, then, to expect professionals, regardless of their specific job, to be able to respond thoughtfully to questions such as these: Should a public agency "purchase" services by entering into a contract with a voluntary or for-profit agency? If so, under what circumstances? Are block grants preferable to categorical funding? What are the constraints of voluntary financing? What assumptions support the use of contributory schemes and fee-charging arrangements? What are the distributional implications of different tax sources?

Two interrelated sets of choices are fundamental to the financial dimension of policy design. These choices pertain to

The source of funds. Should financial support be derived from recipients in the form of user charges, from taxes that make up general revenues, from some form of social insurance, from voluntary contributions, or from some combination of these?

The system of transfer. What arrangements should govern the flow of money from the level of government where it is raised to the level where it is used, the different levels of review between funders and providers, and the conditions placed on the transfer of funds?

We will discuss choices that inform the design of transfer systems in the next chapter; here we will examine alternative sources of funding and their implications.

Sources of Funds

Funds to pay for social welfare benefits are obtained in three fundamental ways—through taxes, through voluntary giving, and through fees. *Taxes* are compulsory and governmental. They constitute public levies on citizens and businesses, and they are the primary source of support for public social welfare activities. *Voluntary giving* involves private contributions. Whether described as charity (which connotes giving for the poor) or philanthropy (which connotes giving for a broader range of health, research, civic, and religious activities), contributions represent voluntary, uncoerced, donations. *Fees* constitute the charge for social welfare goods and services on the open market. The providers of these goods and services may be entrepreneurs who are selling products or nonprofit agencies that are requiring user fees in order to cover their expenses. In a few instances, public institutions (chiefly colleges and universities and hospitals) also impose charges.

In the actual conduct of the welfare state, these three funding sources often are intermixed. That is, the budgets of social welfare agencies and organizations frequently include revenues deriving from taxes, voluntary giving, *and* fees and charges. Although public agencies, for example, tend to be funded with tax dollars, they may rely on user fees (e.g., tuition) or private giving (e.g., PTA fund-raising). Similarly, private nonprofit agencies increasingly depend on tax support, supplementing their private revenue sources with contract funding from government. And profit-making organizations, like commercial hospitals, frequently rely on payments from third-party insurers, public or private, for their income.

The pluralistic funding patterns of the welfare state—often described as the mixed economy of welfare—can create terminological confusion. To clarify the terrain a bit, the distinctive characteristics of the major social welfare auspices must be specified. In our discussion, *voluntary* agencies refer to charitable, nonprofit organizations that are financed, at least to some extent, with voluntary contributions. These organizations devote their resources to education, science, religion, art, culture, and social service and are therefore commonly perceived as serving a public, or community, interest. In this sense, voluntary agencies may be conceived of as privately administered public-interest institutions.

Public agencies, established by law, and directly accountable to elected officials, are supported by governmental funds. Their programs are often referred to as "statutory" or "legislative."

For-profit organizations, a relatively new phenomenon in many sectors of the U.S. welfare state, are providers that operate on an entrepreneurial basis, like any commercial business. The role of these organizations remains controversial despite the strong ideological and legislative support harnessed on behalf of "privatization" since the Reagan years.

The Philanthropic Contribution

There are presently close to a million nonprofit agencies registered under federal tax code section 501(c)(3) as charitable organizations. The 501(c)(3) designation, synonymous with tax deductibility, covers a broad range of nonprofits, from traditional social service agencies to arts, environmental, health, educational, and religious bodies.

Charitable organizations vary in their reliance on voluntary contributions. Although religious congregations depend almost entirely on private giving, for example, hospitals rely on charity for less than 5 percent of their funding. In the social services, private giving provides about a fifth of total revenues. Although much of the support provided voluntary agencies is not of private origin, philanthropy remains the irreducible private core of private agencies.

As Table 7.1 indicates, philanthropy provided $306 billion in 2007 for community purposes, with three-quarters of this amount coming from ordinary individuals. Some donations are organized through the annual fund-raising activities of federations such as the United Way and the United Jewish Appeal, "umbrella organizations" that collect on behalf of member agencies. The United Way, for example, collects around five billion dollars annually through its 1350 local affiliates, chiefly through workplace giving campaigns. Alternatives to the United Way—federations representing social action, environmental, ethnic, and women's causes—raise over $200 million annually in their own fund-raising drives. Overall, however, these federations tap only a small portion of individual giving. Most people contribute directly to the charity of their choice, and most of these contributions go to religious groups. The very rich give heavily to universities and hospitals although, as Table 7.2 indicates, human services donations are not insignificant.

After individual giving comes corporate and foundation donations and bequests. Corporations gave $15.7 billion to philanthropy in 2007, about 5 percent of overall giving.[1] Although corporate giving aids the spectrum of nonprofit activities, elementary and secondary schools have been a major priority since the mid-1980s, reflecting

TABLE 7.1   *Sources and Recipients of Philanthropic Contributions, 2007 (in Billions of Dollars)*

Sources		
Foundations	$38.5	12.6%
Corporations	$15.7	5.1%
Individuals	$229.0	74.8%
Bequests	$23.2	7.6%
Total	$306.4	100.0%
Recipients		
Religion	$102.3	33.4%
Education	$43.3	14.1%
Human Services	$29.6	9.7%
Health	$20.0	6.9%
Foundations	$29.5	10.0%
Arts, Culture	$13.7	4.5%
Unallocated, Misc.	$53.2	22.2%
Total	$306.4	100.0%

Source: Giving USA Foundation, *Giving USA*, 2008.

TABLE 7.2   *Notable Giving for Human Services Since 1995*

Andre Agassi
$1 million to the Las Vegas Boys & Girls Club

David Geffen
$2.5 million to New York's Gay Men's Health Crisis

Paul Newman
$2 million to establish the Barretstown Gang Camp at Barretstown Castle, Ballymore Eustace, in County Kildare, Ireland

Henry and Lucy Moses Fund
$2 million to four New York City hospitals to help pay for uninsured patients

New York Times Neediest Cases Fund
Annual Christmas fund raises about $5 million for human services charities in New York City

Edna McConnell Clark Foundation
$5 million to the Harlem children's Zone

Century 21 Real Estate
$5.8 million to the National Easter Seal Society

Reader's Digest Association, Inc.
$1 million to the Boys and Girls Clubs of America

Ronald MacDonald Children's Charities
More than $1.1 million to 45 children's organizations

George Soros
$50 million to create the Emma Lazarus Fund to help immigrants become U.S. citizens

Donald L. Saunders
$7.5 million to Combined Jewish Philanthropies, Mass.

Ford Foundation
$9 million to Oxfam America

Frankie and Stan Harrell
$4 million to Metropolitan Ministries, Tampa, Florida, for Project Uplift, to provide care for homeless and at-risk families and individuals

Theodore Forstmann and John Walton
$50 million for a scholarship program to help 50,000 inner-city school children attend private schools

Robert and Mary Pew
$25 million to improve public education for poor children in Florida

Joan Kroc
$80 million for a Salvation Army community center in San Diego

Source: The 2007 Slate 60, February 22, 2008.

businesses' concern with the capacity of U.S. workers to compete in the global market-place. Although education has received the largest portion of corporate giving every year since 1978, the portion going to colleges and universities has been diminishing.

Private foundations are voluntary funding entities that primarily exist to give money to other nonprofit organizations. There are approximately 75,000 grant-making foundations operating today, holding nearly $500 billion in assets and annually awarding $38 billion for social welfare, scientific, and cultural activities. Private foundations, a unique creation of U.S. capitalism, were originally built on the fortunes of late-nineteenth- and early-twentieth-century tycoons such as Andrew Carnegie, John D. Rockefeller, and Henry Ford. In the modern era, media and computer entrepreneurs such as Ted Turner and Bill Gates are renewing the philanthropic tradition, using a portion of their great wealth to advance health and educational and social service causes. The largest American foundation, the Bill and Melinda Gates Foundation, which held $35 billion in assets at the end of 2007 gives away more than two billion dollars a year, chiefly for public health–related programs, much of it focused on the nations of the developing world.

Voluntary Financing: Not Entirely a Private Matter

Reflecting an individualistic orientation, the United States is unique among all welfare states in the elaborate development of its voluntary and for-profit welfare sectors. The parallel development of the voluntary and the public sectors, furthermore, has created a social welfare system that is distinctly bifurcated—a system that is dynamic in its ability to change and innovate, yet difficult to manage and control. One critical aspect of this dual system lies in the nature of its funding. "Voluntary" financing of social welfare services is not really as private or as philanthropic as one might think. This is because money contributed to nonprofit organizations engaged in health, education, welfare, religious, scientific, or cultural activities reflects not only private generosity but also public policy. Most notably, private contributions are untaxed—and have been since 1915 when Congress sought to promote philanthropy by making donations tax deductible. Private generosity, in this sense, is partially private altruism, partially a tax break.

One study of the relationship between tax exemptions and voluntary giving, for example, estimated that 96 percent of large-sum donors would substantially reduce their contributions if tax benefits were removed.[2] Because "tax deductions are a monetary ointment to salve the strains of charity," they provide an indispensable incentive for individuals to support the nonprofit services of their choice.[3] Little wonder that attempts to limit the deduction are always greeted with fierce denunciations by the beneficiaries of philanthropic *largess*—most notably, universities, art museums, and scientific research institutions.

In addition to questioning the charitable impulse behind philanthropic giving, one should also question how "voluntary" contributions are in the first place. Community pressures to give, for example, whether at the office or elsewhere, can exert sufficient social coercion so that a choice *not* to give may be available only at great cost to the individual's prestige and social position. Such pressures, of course, do a disservice to the idea of voluntarism.

CAPSULE 7.1 • *Ted's Excellent Idea*

That list [the *Forbes* magazine annual list of wealthiest Americans] is destroying our country. These new super-rich won't loosen up their wads because they're afraid they'll reduce their net worth and go down on the list. That's their Super Bowl.

Why isn't it better to be the biggest giver rather than the biggest hog? What difference does it make if you're worth $12 billion or $11 billion? With a billion dollars you can build a whole university. They are fighting every year to be the richest man in the world. Why don't they sign a joint pact to each give away a billion and then move down the Forbes list equally?

These big billionaires are busy letting go middle managers in their 50s, the day before their pension plans kick in. We're getting to be like Mexico and Brazil, with the rich living behind fences, like they do in Hollywood. The Federal Government, the state government, the municipal government—they're all broke. All the money is in the hands of these few rich people and none of them give any money away. It's dangerous for them and for the country. We may have another French Revolution and there'll be another Madame Defarge knitting and watching them come in little oxcarts down to the town square and BOOM! Off with their heads!

From "Ted's Excellent Idea" by Maureen Dowd, *The New York Times*, August 22, 1996. © 1996 The New York Times. All rights reserved. Used by permission and protected by the Copyright Laws of the United States. The printing, copying, redistribution, or retransmission of the Material without express written permission is prohibited. www.nytimes.com.

Functions of Voluntary Services

Ideally, philanthropic incentives encourage the development of pluralism in community services and provide opportunities for the religious, ethnic, and cultural interests of individuals and groups to flourish. Ralph Kramer classifies this as the "value guardian" function of voluntary agencies, which allows for the expression of particularistic and sectarian values in social welfare.[4] In its role of value guardian, the voluntary organization is one of the major social devices for mitigating many of the strains that exist in U.S. political life. The history of successive waves of ethnic and racial minorities who have been assimilated into U.S. society, indeed, can be written as a biography of their organizational lives.[5]

Writing in 1895, Charles Henderson characterized voluntary organizations as social units that are less permanent and rigid than formal institutions, and thus better able to meet the needs of particular classes or social groups. Of course, many voluntary organizations evolve into large bureaucratic agencies, a phenomenon of interest in the study of social movements.[6] But Henderson's comments on the functions of voluntary associations are still quite relevant:

> [Voluntary associations] may be compared to the tenders which ply between the port and the great ships which are more at home on the deep sea than in the shallow harbor or to the skirmish lines which are thrown in advance of the main army. . . . It is said that these societies dissipate social energy, rival the home, sap the resources of the church, and multiply like a plague of locusts. Unquestionably, the objection is partly justified by

facts. There are too many societies, especially too many bad ones. They overlap, duplicate, and interfere with each other. Some of them seem to be organized simply to
advertise the benevolence of the executive secretary. . . . But the severest judgment of an
abuse leaves the normal use untouched. The voluntary associations require criticism
and regulation but the principle of their life is legitimate.[7]

In addition to supporting diversity and pluralism in community life, voluntary services provide an important vehicle for implementing new and possibly unpopular ideas.
The flexible and changing characteristics of some voluntary agencies make them uniquely
suited to this "vanguard" function.[8] This function was exemplified in the early 1960s by
the Ford Foundation's sponsorship of the Grey Areas Projects, the demonstration program that paved the way for the President's Committee on Juvenile Delinquency, the
Economic Opportunity Program, and Model Cities.[9] It occurred again in the 1980s when
local voluntary agencies in cities such as New York and San Francisco took the initiative in
confronting the AIDS epidemic. This is not to imply that governmental agencies are inca-
pable of innovation and experimentation. On the contrary, most of the funds used for
research, experimentation, and innovation in social welfare services come from public
sources. Nevertheless, voluntary agencies often are able to pursue ideas and initiatives that
would be far too unpopular to secure government sanction.

Voluntary agencies also may function as "improvers" and "supplementors" of
public services. They can serve as vigilant critics, ensuring the quality of public services. And, finally, they can support programs to meet needs that public agencies are
unable or unwilling to undertake.[10]

The case of the Family Service Association of America (FSAA) provides a good
illustration of the supplementary function performed by a voluntary agency.[11] The
FSAA was founded in 1911 as the National Association for Organizing Charities
(NAOC), an outgrowth of the Charity Organization Societies of the late 1800s. The
primary function of NAOC was to coordinate the work of community agencies
involved with charitable giving.[12] The organization was opposed to public relief giving.[13] In the first decades of the twentieth century, NAOC dropped its coordinating
functions, concentrating instead on the rehabilitation of distressed families. In 1919, it
became the American Association for Organizing Family Social Work, using the combined methods of relief giving and social casework.

When the Social Security Act was passed in 1935, the federal government under-
took substantial relief for special categories of the needy. The FSAA responded by
abandoning the "quantitative" job of providing income relief in favor of the "qualitative" task of providing family casework. By 1953, FSAA had developed a "family-
oriented" casework approach for dealing with social problems and, for a while, the
difference between public and voluntary services seemed clear. But with the 1956
amendments to the Social Security Act, public welfare itself took on a family orientation and states were encouraged to grant assistance and "other services" to needy children, parents, and relatives "to help maintain and strengthen family life." The 1958
and 1962 amendments to the act further strengthened this orientation. By the mid-
1960s, therefore, agencies such as FSAA once again began to reassess their functions
vis-à-vis public services. While, no doubt, there were many other reasons for the

CAPSULE 7.2 • *Philanthropic Correctness*

In the decades following the Second World War, foundations served as leading instruments of the liberal consensus, using their position at the intersection of the elite worlds of government, politics, academia, and the press to remake America in their own progressive image. Foundations funded, in whole or in part, the early expansion of our system of public libraries, Jonas Salk's discovery of the polio vaccine, the writing of Gunnar Myrdal's *An American Dilemma*, the Public Broadcasting Corporation, the "Grey Areas" project that led to Model Cities, and the Michigan study that yielded Head Start.

What was striking about the foundations of the 50s and 60s, however, was not so much the merit of their ideas as the extent of their influence. John Gardner, president of the Carnegie Corporation from 1955 to 1965, served as Lyndon Johnson's Secretary of Health, Education, and Welfare, taught at Harvard and MIT, worked at the FCC and founded Common Cause. McGeorge Bundy, president of Ford Foundation from 1966 to 1979, was a former dean of the faculty of arts and sciences at Harvard and national security adviser under Kennedy and Johnson. With years of experience and contacts throughout interlocking worlds of the elite, Gardner and Bundy conveyed their ideas to academics, editors, members of congress, and presidents and, in many cases, saw them enacted into law.

From "Philanthropical Correctness" by David Samuels as appeared in *The New Republic*, September 18 and 25, 1995. Reprinted by permission of David Samuels.

change, in 1971 the Community Service Society of New York City abandoned its long tradition of family casework and took up a strategy of community organization for neighborhood self-improvement.[14] In 1973, member agencies of the FSAA in Chicago and Minneapolis also began to emphasize social advocacy. In the 1980s, family service agencies returned to their historic services-focused mission and in 1998 FSAA merged with the National Association of Homes and Services for Children to form a new Alliance for Children and Families, representing more than 350 child and family organizations serving more than five million individuals through a wide assortment of programs. The San Francisco Family Service Agency, for example, provides daycare, residential care, HIV/AIDS supports, Foster Grandparent, and drug and alcohol services, along with conventional family counseling.

Voluntary agencies increasingly serve another important function, one not noted in Kramer's system of classification, and that is their role as protector of the poor in an era of diminishing welfare state spending. When federal policy, in particular, threatens significant cutbacks—as occurred during the Reagan era in the mid-1980s, the Contract with America campaign in the mid-1990s, and the great recession beginning in 2008—national attention turns to nonprofit organizations to protect the country's most vulnerable citizens. Nonprofits, presumably more efficient, more sensitive, and more effective than their public counterparts, would step into the breach, offset public cuts, and rescue the poor.

The problem, however, is not only that public cutbacks *impair* private action—the first thing state and local governments frequently do is to pass their federal cutbacks along to private charities by reducing their contracts—but that the magnitude of government reductions simply overwhelms any potential remediation by community agencies. In 1995, for example, Lester Salamon and Alan Abramson estimated that balancing the proposed Contract with America cuts would require a doubling in private charitable contributions in a six-year period, not a likely scenario.[15]

Problems and Issues in Voluntary Financing

Even without such emergency demands, several problems arise in financing voluntary social welfare services. First, there is the fundamental question of the public–private relationship. Are there some community activities that should be *exclusively* private and voluntary? Are there others that should only be public? And if public financing of private endeavors is appropriate, how should we balance cultural pluralism and social equality? Should contributions to ethnically or religiously exclusive educational, health, and social welfare agencies, for example, be tax exempt? Should governments provide *direct* support for faith-based agencies (such as Catholic schools) if they meet community requirements and standards? Does such support violate constitutional guarantees separating church and state? These issues become difficult to untangle complex when there is a "mixing" of voluntary and public funds.

Public support for voluntary agencies occurs in a variety of forms. The *tax deductibility* of charitable contributions has been noted. Direct *public subsidies*, largely unconditional lump-sum grants to voluntary agency programs, although uncommon today, were at one time quite the norm. They have come to be considered poor public policy, however, because, as an essentially "agency-oriented" means of financial support, they commit government to supporting *all* of the goals and purposes of an organization. *Purchase of service contracting*, a newer option, is an arrangement whereby governments buy specific services, such as foster care, job training, or respite services. In some cases, governmental units may even contract with private agencies to perform "indirect" activities such as program development, social planning, eligibility determination, and services evaluation.

The Mixed Economy of Welfare

As discussed earlier, government provides a major part of the funds expended by voluntary agencies. Catholic Charities USA, one of the country's largest charities, receives nearly two-thirds of its income from government. The Planned Parenthood Federation relies on public support for one-third.[16] In the overall social services arena, indeed, half the budget comes from public funds, as Figure 7.1 indicates. It is estimated, for example, that more than half of all Title XX social services funds are spent on services purchased from voluntary and for-profit organizations. Considering these trends, Ralph Kramer has stated, "It is ironic that a national coalition of nonprofit organizations chose as its name 'The Independent Sector' when its constituents had become, more than ever, dependent on government."[17]

One major virtue of these subventions is that they enable governments to start programs quickly, utilizing the existing capacity of voluntary organizations while avoiding the rigidities of civil service and bureaucracy. Also, as noted earlier, contracting

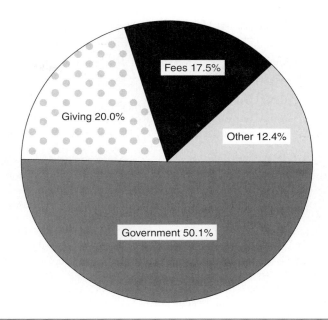

FIGURE 7.1   *Sources of Funding for Human Service Nonprofits, 1995.*

Source: AAFRC, *Giving USA 1996*, 39.

reduces the costs of having to pay civil service salaries and being restricted to negotiating with public services unions. This is especially advantageous for experiments and demonstrations. Contracting also permits public officials to tailor programs to the special circumstances of hard-to-reach or minority populations. Relying on the access and expertise of existing community-based agencies, governments can be far more responsive to special population groups than if they tried to provide services in-house.

For the voluntary agency, the obvious advantage of purchase arrangements is access to the public coffers as additional sources of income. But they pay a price. To the extent that voluntary agencies are supported by government funds, they forfeit some degree of autonomy. Consequently, the ability of these agencies to function as agents for the expression of new or unpopular ideas, as critics of public services, and as the guardians of pluralistic values may be limited. Family-planning clinics funded with federal grant-in-aid funds, for example, are prohibited from providing information about abortion, a severe limitation on their ability to provide their clients a comprehensive set of options. In the extreme, voluntary agencies may simply become an instrument of government policy. The degree to which governmental constraints may be imposed, of course, depends in part on the method of financing that is employed. Indirect subsidies through tax deductions and vouchers are relatively benign and *laissez-faire*, whereas direct contracting through purchase of services arrangements hold the potential for considerable intrusiveness.[18] In the view of some, when voluntary agencies accept funds from government, they should be treated no differently

CAPSULE 7.3 • *Charities on the Dole*

Those who expect America's charities to replace government as a provider of social welfare ought to look a little closer. They will find that the so-called independent sector, which receives between one-quarter and one-third of its funds from taxpayers, isn't so independent after all.

In fact, many social-service agencies actually receive most of their funding from government. Save the Children owes 60 percent of its budget to the generosity of taxpayers, Catholic Charities 65 percent, CARE 78 percent, and the United Cerebral Palsy Association more than 80 percent. Topping this list is the ineptly named Volunteers of America, which receives 96 percent of its $51-million budget from government sources. There are, of course, many small, innovative, and values-driven grass-roots charities that are addressing human needs much more efficiently than failed federal programs and social-service agencies. These groups mostly avoid government money, because they know that government support comes with strings attached. . . .

These strings involve more than just paperwork and regulations. Government support also changes charities' incentives, giving them reasons to keep caseloads up instead of getting them down by successfully turning around peoples' lives. It distorts their missions. It turns lean, cost-effective organizations into bloated bureaucracies and dilutes their spiritual or religious message. In instances where the Salvation Army decided to accept government funds (which constitute about 15 percent of its revenues), it stopped requiring church attendance as a condition of its assistance. Unfortunately, this experience is all too common. The charity that stays genuinely independent from government is still the exception.

Although charities are supposed to offer an alternative to government provision of social welfare, they have become so dependent on and aligned with government that they no longer represent a way out of the welfare state. If we place our faith in private non-profits as they are currently organized, we are in for a big disappointment. Before we can rely on charities to help us dismantle government, they must wean themselves off the dole.

From "Charities on the Dole" by Kimberly Dennis, *Policy Review*, 5, March/April 1996. Used by permission of Policy Review.

than any other agency of government. According to Glasser, for example, the private agency that accepts public funds *should* forgo privileges of autonomy.[19]

Accountability

The issue of governmental support places voluntary agencies in a paradoxical situation. Government controls are seen as undesirable, as contrary to the independence and the special role of voluntary agencies. On the other hand, reasonable controls must protect the use of public dollars. Government policymakers, under law, must be prudent in their use of tax revenue, and prudence demands reasonable mechanisms for accountability.

Even before the modern era of massive contract financing, charitable trusts were held to be "in the public interest" and therefore subject to a degree of government regulation.[20] It is on this basis that voluntary funds have been restricted and some degree of public control exercised. Tax-exempt organizations must be chartered by state governments, and the states may require various kinds of accounting procedures and impose standards of practice. One important limitation is that "no substantial part" of the voluntary agencies' activities may consist of efforts to influence legislation.[21] This restriction accounts, in part, for the reluctance of many voluntary welfare agencies to become engaged in political action.

Public concern regarding the accountability of voluntary organizations, particularly philanthropic foundations, found legislative expression in the Tax Reform Act of 1969. Although not as severe as many critics of voluntary organizations desired, the act imposed several important limitations on voluntary organizations. Almost one-third of the act concerned foundations, establishing policies regarding the investment of funds, public reporting, and the amount of income that could be received on assets. In addition, the act required foundations to pay a 4 percent excise tax on their income and to dispose of at least 5 percent of their capital annually.[22]

The problem of establishing accountability for voluntary agencies can be understood in relation to a much older and more general notion known as "charitable immunity." Originating in centuries-old English law, this concept holds that charitable trusts cannot be held responsible for derelictions of duties to clients (negligence and neglect, for example) because, without such immunity, government intervention might eventually violate the intentions of the donors and limit the functions of voluntary charity.[23] The questions of charitable immunity and the extent to which bequests may be altered by action of government is significant.

For many years, charitable bequests and legacies have been protected by this concept of immunity (sometimes referred to as "the dead hand") and have been allowed to follow donors' original purposes, even when some of these appear frivolous, discriminatory, or otherwise socially harmful. Whimsical examples from recent history include a trust fund for Christmas dinners ("one bushel of oats or a half bushel of corn chops") for hungry horses in Kansas City, a trust fund establishing "marriage portions" for poor young women about to be married, and a legacy providing "a baked potato at each meal for each young lady at Bryn Mawr."[24]

CAPSULE 7.4 • *Fatal Embrace*

How [can we] protect [voluntary institutions] from the fatal embrace of government regulation? The problem . . . grows immensely when tax funds are channeled to them—in the name of accountability, equity, or whatever moral principle is supposedly to govern the expenditure of public money. . . . When such institutions are first "discovered" and then funded by government, the very vitality that originally distinguished them from government agencies is destroyed. Indeed, they *become* government agencies under another name.

Peter Berger and Richard John Neuhaus, "Response," in Michael Novak (ed.), *To Empower People: From State to Civil Society,* 2nd ed. 1996, 150–51.

A more serious illustration is the case of Girard College. In this instance, the U.S. Supreme Court decided that the charitable bequest involved could not be used for tax-exempt purposes if the activities of the enterprise conflicted with the public interest by supporting discrimination against minority groups.[25] Here, the grip of "the dead hand" was loosened by another important legal concept, the *cy pres* (i.e., "as near as may be") doctrine, which holds that courts may modify bequests to be "as near as" possible to the original intent of the giver in light of social changes that have taken place in the community.[26]

Another case of this kind involved the Buck Trust controversy. This case provides an interesting test of the strength of the "dead hand" in respect to community definitions of "social need." In 1973, Mrs. Buck, following her husband's wishes, willed her estate, valued at that time at $10 million, to Marin County, California, "to be used exclusively for nonprofit charitable, religious, or educational purposes in providing care for the needy." However, when Mrs. Buck died in 1979, her estate had vastly increased in value; by 1984, it was worth $360 million and was producing approximately $20 to $25 million a year. The San Francisco Foundation, the administrators of the trust, challenged the "Marin only" provisions, arguing that the county (one of the wealthiest in the United States) was not able to make use of the funds. Marin County, ultimately supported by the courts, argued for a strict construction of the will and its clear geographical limitation. Despite the fact that Marin County, by all statistical measures, had only a small amount of need—and a small population of the needy—the court decided that the definition of "need" was fundamentally subjective. Marin residents perceived of themselves as needy, the Buck instructions were clear, and the trust would not have to be shared with neighboring communities.

The vast increase in purchase-of-service contracting since the 1960s has made the accountability issue especially critical for state and local governments. Several billion dollars worth of public services are purchased annually, providing government policy-makers a flexible tool for delivering community services in a cost-efficient, responsive manner, often engaging clientele groups that might be reluctant to deal directly with public bureaucrats. But clearly, contracting brings with it accountability issues with respect to both fiscal and program standards. The typically diffuse goals and objectives of contract agencies, for example, make it difficult to determine effectiveness.

Public policymakers address accountability through the contract document itself, negotiating funding agreements that set forth the ground rules for the purchase of service. As in all contracts, there must be "consideration"—in exchange for a budgeted allocation, provider agencies agree to deliver a specified quantity of services of a particular sort to an identified target group. Public control is then exercised through a variety of monitoring and evaluating procedures—audits, site visits, agency program reports, and the like.

"Accountability," of course, is a rather ambiguous term. And the conventional dichotomy of autonomy versus accountability—the need of private agencies for independence versus the need of public bodies to ensure the proper use of tax dollars—often generates more heat than light. Nevertheless, it poses a real dilemma in today's mixed economy of welfare, a dilemma that typically is answered more on ideological than on technical grounds.

Conservatives and Voluntarism

Voluntarism involves more than money—whatever its source. Classic voluntarism, the voluntarism of Tocqueville, of the Victorian Lady Bountiful, of today's weekend or spring break volunteer, involves action, good works, and civic engagement. More than the citizens of any other advanced industrial nation, indeed U.S. residents donate money *and* time. They give to charitable organizations and they join churches, help with the local PTA, and serve on the boards of directors of local social services agencies.

For many conservatives, volunteer civic responsibility is the best way to approach social provision, representing a humane and effective alternative to an inefficient, bureaucratic, and bloated welfare state. This view, advanced since the 1980s by an influential body of literature from the political right, has found voice—and expression—in national developments.[27] Conservative regimes, such as the Reagan–Bush administrations in the United States and the Thatcher government in the United Kingdom, advanced the view that a large part of the welfare system *should* be the domain of the voluntary sector. Under Reagan, it was declared policy that public sector welfare activities should be substantially privatized, absorbed by "the voluntary spirit." More recently, advocates of "compassionate conservatism" called for greater use of faith-based organizations.

Voluntarism *is* an enticing idea: get government off our backs and neighbors will help neighbors, families will pitch in, and church and civic agencies will roll up their collective sleeves and get the job done. The only thing wrong with this idea is that it doesn't work. The readiness of Americans to volunteer, as Figure 7.2 indicates, is extremely impressive in the international context. However, the welfare state developed because, in modern society, neighbors, friends, family, and local communities—the entire "thousand points of light" celebrated by the first President Bush in 1989—were *unable* to provide for contemporary social needs. That is not to say that public agencies and social welfare professionals can disregard private support systems and community groups. There is clearly major work to be done to better articulate the functions of human service professionals and the natural helping networks and voluntary activities of communities. But, it is quite another thing to reach into the dustbin of our Victorian past for discarded ideas as solutions to contemporary social problems.

Liberals and Voluntarism

The spirit of service—to neighbors, community, nation, or humankind—is far from a conservative monopoly. Tocqueville's pattern of voluteerism has been a U.S. phenomenon, across the spectrum, from the start. But whereas conservatives tend to view private action as an alternative to public responsibility, liberals promote volunteer effort as a way to advance national goals. It was this spirit that framed John Kennedy's famous injunction, "[A]sk not what your country can do for you—but what you can do for your country."

Since the Kennedy years, Democratic presidents have promoted public efforts to stimulate individual volunteering. Lyndon Johnson initiated VISTA, (Volunteers in

Percentage of Population Volunteering, 1993

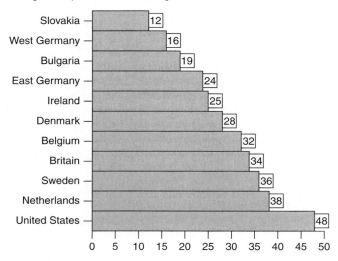

FIGURE 7.2   *National Volunteers.*

Sources: A New Civic Europe? A Study of the Extent and Role of Volunteering. Volunteer Centre U.K.; *Giving and Volunteering in the United States,* Independent Sector, in *Giving USA,* 1996, 162.

Service to America), an effort to replicate the Peace Corps on the domestic scene. In the 1970s and 1980s, new programs enlisted older citizens (RSVP) and young teachers. And in 1993 Congress and President Clinton created Americorps, the largest community service program since the Great Depression. Run by a federal Corporation for National and Community Service, Americorps has engaged close to 50,000 young citizens in service jobs that are part volunteer, part student aid. Participants earn a $4725 scholarship for each year of service, a modest room and board allowance, and healthcare benefits, while working for charitable purposes ranging from the Red Cross and Habitat for Humanity to jobs as teachers' aides in disadvantaged inner cities.

Contributory Schemes and Fee Charging

Those receiving social benefits may be asked to finance them in two ways: through "contributions" to statutory (i.e., public) social and health insurance programs and through fees paid for services. Public social security programs, although somewhat akin to private insurance, do not operate according to general marketplace rules of exchange. Rather, the conditions of exchange are regulated by government, reflecting recipient need as well as recipient contribution. And private profit, of course, is not allowed.

Social Security, officially Old Age, Survivors, Disability, and Health Insurance (OASDHI), is the outstanding example of a contributory system in the United States. Its basic principle is that all those eligible for benefits at the time they withdraw from the labor force will have paid insurance-like "contributions" during their working years. Like any other insurance system, their investments "earn" entitlements to benefits. Social Security, of course, is not like "any other" insurance system. First, despite the euphemism, "contributions" constitute a tax on both earnings (for employees) and payrolls (for employers); both workers and employers, therefore, are obligated to support the system. In 2008, approximately 98 percent of the U.S. workforce was covered by a combination of Social Security and other governmental retirement systems. Second, unlike private insurance, OASDHI benefits are not paid on the basis of a written contract. Although there is a universally understood obligation for government to stand by its commitments, the exact nature of Social Security taxes and benefits are determined by Congress and change from time to time. And while there is an important relationship between contributions and benefits, Congress awards benefits on the basis of need as well as on the basis of contributions.

Fee charging, although associated with the buying and selling of goods found in the commercial marketplace, is not at all uncommon among voluntary, commercial, and, often, public organizations. Health care, notably, is primarily fee-for-service care, with payments provided by consumers in the form of insurance premiums, deductibles, co-shares and co-payments. As a result, of course, the affluent receive excellent health care in the United States, whereas the less affluent—especially those having to rely on public assistance, or having no insurance at all—get less.

The high cost of health care contributes in a major way not only to the significant percentage of uninsured Americans, but also to the increasing reluctance of businesses to offer health insurance to their employees. In 2008, firms paid $9325 in family health premiums for each insured worker with workers contributing an additional $3354.[28] One consequence of these steep and increasing costs is a decreasing number of companies offering health benefits. Since 1999, the percentage of firms providing health policies to their workers has dropped from 66 percent to 63 percent. At the same time, more and more workers have been opting out of their employer's plans. Even though they only pay a portion of the total cost—around 25 percent on average—their premiums are often too high to afford.[29]

In the social services, fees, of necessity, are less common. While daycare and private schools rely heavily on user fees, agencies serving the poor must rely on subsidies from charities, foundations, and government. Nevertheless, even programs serving the disadvantaged often utilize fees and charges to cover part of the cost. Under these arrangements, fees may be calculated on a graduated "sliding scale" according to the user's economic circumstances. Rarely covering the entire cost of the services rendered, these fees subsidize poorer clients, and no one is turned away due to an inability to pay.

Sliding scale fees, for example, have long been used by family service associations, with charges for counseling sessions ranging from zero to over $100 an hour, according to income. Mental health agencies similarly rely on payments, depending on the caseworker to negotiate an appropriate fee with the client. According to one analysis of fee-setting procedures, payment schedules generally "attempt to resolve the tension between consumers' expectations of paying fees for service, their ability to pay, the true cost of the service, and an agency's need to raise additional revenue."

Fee charging is also frequently introduced into public contributory programs. Medicare, the health insurance program for the aged under social security, gives beneficiaries an option to participate in a Supplementary Medical Insurance Program (Part B) that covers physicians' fees. In 2009, about 97 percent of all eligible beneficiaries elected Part B, paying $96.40 per month for coverage. In addition, there is an annual deductible for physician's care plus a 20 percent co-payment above that amount. There is also a deductible for hospital insurance under Part A (which means that the recipient must pay this amount of the bill first before the program covers any costs) and an additional co-payment for hospital days sixty-one through ninety. In some health plans (such as Britain's National Health Service), members may be required to pay a fee that covers part of the cost for each episode of care, be it a visit to a dentist, prescribed medication, or a hospital stay.

Assumptions about psychological and behavioral dynamics underlie much of the debate concerning the use of contributory and fee-charging schemes. From the psychological point of view, it is argued that recipients are less likely to feel stigma or shame when they pay their own way, even if they are still partially subsidized. At the same time, the act of contributing is believed to enhance the individual's sense of social responsibility. This has been one of the major arguments for operating Social Security on a contributory basis. The behavioral rationale for contributory schemes and fee charging, as applied to service-giving programs, is that user payments restrain overutilization. That is, even small fees for doctor or therapist visits, or for prescriptions, are said to discourage unnecessary or excessive care.

There is a limited amount of empirical evidence addressing these psychological and behavioral arguments. Recipients of Social Security benefits appear to feel a greater sense of entitlement to benefits than do recipients of other programs, but what part of this is due to having made contributions and what part is due to general public acceptance of the program is not clear. There are other well-accepted programs where beneficiaries do not make direct contributions (such as unemployment insurance, public education, and veterans' services) yet seem to develop the same sense of entitlement as OASDHI recipients.

A sense of entitlement can be based on factors such as compensation or general public commitment to the program. Supplementary Security Income recipients receive better benefits, feel more entitled to them, and are socially perceived as being more deserving than recipients of TANF. Although contributory schemes may have some effect on the sense of entitlement, they are by no means determinative.

Similarly, it is not clear whether contributions and user fees reduce the excessive consumption of benefits or whether they act as a barrier to needed services. User fees, even when nominal, can be a significant burden for people who are having a difficult time making ends meet. Given difficult choices that have to be made between spending for different necessities, for example, health insurance may often give way to immediate food, daycare, and housing needs. In Medicare, co-payments of $3 on prescriptions can add up quickly for the elderly needing multiple medications, resulting in people foregoing some of the drugs necessary for their health. Similarly, in private agencies, the contribution required for programs under sliding-scale arrangements may not be affordable for those already living at the margin. This cost barrier also explains, in part, why many workers decline to participate in employer-sponsored insurance coverage.[30] In private-managed-care plans, several studies have found that even modest copayments for office visits significantly reduce the use of primary care services, although they appear to have no impact on visits to medical and surgical specialists.[31]

Public Financing: Not Entirely a Public Matter

Despite the importance of private and voluntary welfare, the essence of today's welfare state is principally one of public provision and public finance. Government remains the major source of funds for health, education, income maintenance, and welfare services, and the primacy of public financing means that social welfare policy choices are fundamentally matters of politics rather than matters of consumer choice or voluntary philanthropy.

In the same way that voluntary financing is not completely a matter of private philanthropy, public (or governmental) financing of social welfare services is not quite as public a business as it may initially appear. In the broadest sense, taxation is a central instrument regulating the interaction between government and the private economy. The core ideological debate between redistribution and social justice on the one hand, and the need for profit and economic efficiency, on the other, clearly comes into play here. In a narrower sense, tax policy directly impacts the private, nonstatutory realms of social welfare. Tax exemptions for charitable contributions illustrate one way in which government uses its taxing powers to subsidize private welfare—the exemption provides a substantial public incentive for private generosity. Other incentives—including the federal income tax deductions for catastrophic medical expenses, home mortgage interest, and child and dependent care expenses—all influence private activity in publicly specified ways. All of these represent private "welfare" elements in the public finance systems.

In Chapter 2, we introduced the concept of "tax expenditure" to denote those special tax features that are designed to encourage certain kinds of behavior. Whether called tax credits, deductions, or exclusions, these provisions constitute a system of welfare that parallels regular social welfare spending. Although they are analogous to normal expenditures in that they represent a decision by government to direct resources to particular objectives, they are far less visible. Often, indeed, they are not identified and reviewed regularly as part of the regular (expenditure) budget.

The purpose of tax expenditures is not to finance government but rather to encourage different kinds of valued activities. But while regular benefits—such as Social Security, TANF, or highway outlays—are cash outlays, allocated through the annual budget process, tax expenditures occur when government *doesn't* tax at the level it normally would. They are, basically, targeted tax cuts. To subsidize childcare for working families, for example, Congress authorizes direct spending in the form of cash payments to eligible families and also utilizes tax deductions and credits to help families with childcare expenses.

The use of the tax code as a system of special benefits has long been derided as welfare for the rich. And tax loopholes, many extraordinarily complicated, *do* frequently advance the interests of people with high incomes. This is because almost all tax breaks are linked to tax brackets, meaning that earners in higher brackets receive more of a reduction for each dollar deducted than do those in lower brackets. A 35-percent bracket taxpayer gets back 35 cents per dollar deducted; a 15-percent taxpayer gets back 15 cents; those paying no taxes get back nothing.

In the federal system, nevertheless, two of the most significant tax expenditures—exclusions for income-transfer payments and employee fringe benefits—serve distinctly social objectives. The income tax exclusion granted public assistance and Social Security payments derives from the simple logic of protecting the limited income of the poor. It hardly makes sense, after all, to provide income support with one hand while taxing it back with the other. The exclusion, however, is not absolute. Because Social Security beneficiaries are often reasonably well-to-do, federal policy does tax a portion of the Social Security payments of the better-off elderly.

Employee fringe benefits—compensation received in the form of health and pension plans, special housing allowances, and employee-assistance services such as counseling, daycare, and the like—are *doubly* benefited under the federal tax code. First, the cost to employers of these benefits constitutes a deductible business expense. As such, they can be deducted from taxable income, appreciably lowering the taxes owed by a firm. Second, employees benefit because compensation in the form of wages and salaries is taxed but compensation in the form of fringe benefits is not. This means that a valuable and costly form of remuneration is given to employees on a tax-free basis.

These provisions have been enormously successful in broadening our system of private welfare. Tax expenditures have promoted pension plans by making them less costly for employers to sponsor. The pension deduction—the second largest of the over one hundred items listed in the most recent federal tax expenditure budget (some of which are enumerated in Table 7.3) provides a huge tax savings for businesses,

CAPSULE 7.5 • *Health Care By Loophole*

The tax code is intrinsically linked to the nation's system of health care. Since 1860, when railroads, then lumber and mining companies, first hired doctors to keep their workers healthy and on the job, employers have been the primary providers of the nation's health care protection. That approach flourished during World War II when wages were frozen and businesses offered free health benefits to attract workers. Today, employer-financed insurance covers about 160 million Americans—and provides a $140 billion tax deduction for businesses. Workers save another $200 billion a year because they continue to get this insurance tax-free.

From "Health Care Loophole" *AARP Bulletin*, March 2007, p. 3. Reprinted by permission of AARP.

TABLE 7.3   *Revenue Losses from Major Social Welfare Tax Expenditures in the Federal Individual Corporation Income Tax, Fiscal Year 2009 (in Billions of Dollars)*

Tax Expenditure	Revenue Loss
Social Security (OASDI) exclusion	$24.5
Retirement 401(K) plans	$51.0
Employer pension plans	$45.7
Exclusion of employer contributions for medical insurance and care	$168.5
Child and dependent care credit	$1.7
Charitable contributions	
for education	$5.3
for health	$5.3
for other purposes	$47.0
Earned Income Credit	$5.4

Source: U.S. Budget for Fiscal Year 2009, Historical Tables, Analytic Perspectives, Table 19-3. Figures are estimates.

important benefits for employees, and, of course, corresponding losses to the Federal Treasury.

Similarly, private health plans have been encouraged. Today, employers provide health insurance for over 150 million employees and dependents, deducting some $300 billion for these benefits, resulting, as Table 7.3 indicates, a $168 billion loss in tax revenue. Once again, in addition to providing a major business deduction, fringes provide an enormous break for employees. Because health benefits are tax free, they constitute a favorable alternative to regular, taxable in wages. Workers furnished with $8000 a year in medical coverage, for example, receive the full benefit value. If the $8000 were provided in the form of salary, however, that would buy only $5760 worth of insurance for a worker in the 28-percent income tax bracket.

The overall cost to the government of tax expenditures is considerable—well over $700 billion annually, an amount equivalent to approximately one-third of all federal revenues. In some areas of activity, the magnitude of tax expenditures approaches and even exceeds that of direct spending. In the federal budget category "education, training, employment, and social services," for example, direct outlays are just barely ahead of the amount given up in tax expenditures. In the housing field, homeowner deductions for mortgage interest, property taxes, and capital gains exemptions on home sales cost the federal government about five times the amount spent for low-income housing programs like Section 8.

Public objectives, it is clear, can be advanced by *both* tax expenditures and regular outlays. As noted, daycare is a major area of federal and local activity under spending programs such as Title XX, the Elementary and Secondary Education Act, and Head Start, as well as under *tax* programs such as the dependent care credit, and the employer provided childcare exclusion. Although spending programs generally provide revenues directly to program and agency providers, tax credits and deductions give consumers additional purchasing power for use in the marketplace. In this way, they resemble vouchers, providing substantial freedom of choice to their users.

Are tax expenditures a good thing? Do they, on balance, help the poor? The answer to these questions is complex. Some tax expenditures clearly aren't redistributive. For one thing, only taxpayers benefit from them; if one's earnings fall below the tax threshold, then no benefits are generally available. Even socially oriented tax expenditures—such as those for day care, charitable contributions, and health plans— often wind up providing the most to those with the fewest needs. The dependent care credit, like the others, is tilted upward, with much of its benefits going to middle- and upper-income families. Health plan tax expenditures also vary considerably in their impact because younger workers, women, minorities, and unorganized workers, as a group, are less likely to be covered than older workers, men, whites, and union members. In addition, the benefits of those who *are* covered are likely to be far broader for the second group.

The prevailing view is that the overall system of tax expenditures is regressive. One calculation estimates that at least half their total benefits goes to the richest fifth of the population.[32] According to Isabel Sawhill, moreover, few tax subsidies are targeted so as to help those who need them most. They "neglect the housing, health care, and income security needs of low-income families while simultaneously providing billions to assist the affluent and the middle class."[33] This kind of "welfare for the rich" clearly diminishes the overall progressivity of the income tax. It accounts, in addition, for the fact that although income taxes remain the most redistributive form of taxation, *real* rates vary only moderately among income groups. (Real, or "effective," rates refer to actual taxes as a proportion of overall income.) Despite the nominal 35-percent federal income tax bite on the marginal income of the rich, the top one percent of taxpayers actually pay a bit less than one-fifth of their income to Uncle Sam.[34]

Tax expenditures have other weaknesses. First, they are a relatively hidden form of public support, which means that they generally avoid the review and scrutiny afforded direct spending. Many states and localities, for example, fail to identify tax expenditures in their annual budgets, and most exert little fiscal control over them in their committee deliberations. For the most part, tax expenditures are a form of entitlement, continuing unexamined from year to year to qualifying taxpayers.

CAPSULE 7.6 • *The Leaky Bucket*

The idea among tax theologians is that the income tax on individuals and corporations— before deductions, exclusions, and the like are factored in—represents a sort of ideal tax structure. The revenues due the Treasury under this ideal structure are like water that flows into a bucket. The deductions and exclusions are represented by holes punctured in the bucket. The holes have become quite large.

Paul Starobin, "Washington Update," *National Journal* (August 21, 1993): 2087.

A second problem is their impact on the tax base. By their very definition, tax expenditures remove funds from the public coffers. It is estimated, indeed, that federal tax loopholes reduce almost by half the amount of income subject to taxation.[35] This means that taxes that in many instances would have been paid by the better-off are forgone. With less income taxed, less revenue is provided, reducing funds available for tax-supported programs—social programs in particular. A substantial portion of the present deficit problem, for example, is clearly the result of fewer dollars being available for public support. In recent years, indeed, there has been an enormous increase in the number and size of tax expenditures, resulting in a substantial gap between forfeited receipts and taxes actually collected, and an ever greater abandonment of the implication of the Sixteenth Amendment to the U.S. Constitution that federal taxes be paid on income from *all* sources.

The erosion of the tax base, in addition to reducing government revenues, also impacts differently on different groups. The charity deduction, for example, not only results in the federal government giving up many billions a year in revenue, it also draws resources to the particular charities—culture and research in particular—favored by the biggest givers. Without attempting to judge the relative value of differing nonprofit endeavors, it is clear that when J. P. Getty willed his fortune for a new

FIGURE 7.3 *Helping the Rich Along.*

Source: Tom Toles, Universal Press Syndicate.

museum of art in Los Angeles, everybody paid for the project indirectly because of the taxes forgone. It is not the case, though, that everybody will benefit equally from what Getty's gift produced. In quite the same way, all citizens make up the taxes lost through the billions of dollars deducted for donations to religious institutions.

Tax Types, Tax Burdens

Taxes make up a very substantial part of all welfare economies. Among the wealthy industrial nations of the world, the United States, often described as a welfare "laggard," is, and has been, one of the least taxed. Just 28 percent of the U.S. gross domestic product goes to taxes, compared to 33 percent in Canada, 37 percent in Great Britain, 44 percent in France, 49 percent in Denmark, and just over 50 percent—half the economy—in Sweden.[36]

Taxes provide the wherewithall for a country's spending and affect the distribution of nation's resources just as much as direct allocations do. Redistribution is therefore a double-edged sword, achieved by both financial and expenditure measures. We have discussed the expenditure side of the equation in the chapters dealing with the basis of allocation and the nature of provisions. In the remaining part of this chapter, we intend to look at some of the essential choices confronting social finance, especially choices concerning the fashion in which taxes are levied.

In the United States, as in most other industrial countries, taxes are imposed in a variety of ways. Most importantly, taxes are levied on income, both on individuals, through personal income taxes, and on businesses, through corporate income taxes. In the United States, individual income taxes make up the largest single source of federal income, 46 percent of the total, with corporate income taxes providing an additional 10 percent. Taxes are also levied on the costs of things that people buy (sales taxes), on earnings and payrolls (Social Security "contributions," or taxes), on the value of things people own (property taxes), and on estates and gifts.

One way to distinguish among types of taxes is to consider their fairness, the relative burdens they impose on different income groups. At the progressive end of the continuum are levies that are proportionally higher for the wealthy than for the poor. The federal personal income tax, the most progressive tax in the United States, is an example, being levied in accordance with the "ability to pay." As income rises, in other words, so does the tax rate.

Most poor families are actually *exempt* from the federal income tax. Many, in fact, as we indicated, receive a tax *credit* (the Earned Income Tax Credit), which offsets a good part of their Social Security payroll taxes as well. According to the *nominal* rates, i.e. not taking into account exemptions, credits, or deductions, families are taxed at 10 percent to about $16,000. As income increases, so does the marginal rate, from 15 percent (at about $16,000) to 25 percent (at about $68,000) to 28 percent (at about $137,000) to 33 percent (at about $209,000). The top rate, 35 percent (levied on incomes over $373,000), has dropped considerably in recent decades. It stood at 91 percent in 1960, 70 percent in 1980, and 50 percent in 1986.[37]

These, of course, are the *official*, or *nominal*, rates; in the actual world, as we have seen, these rates are lessened by the significant variety of tax expenditures that reduce

TABLE 7.4   *Real Tax Burden of Major Federal Taxes by Income Group, 2007*

Income Group	Personal Income Tax Burden (%)	Social Security Tax Burden (%)	Corporate Income Tax Burden (%)	Total Federal Tax Burden (%)
Bottom Fifth	−5.0	7.3	1.2	3.4
Lower-Middle	−2.8	8.9	1.1	7.3
Middle	2.8	10.7	0.9	14.4
Upper-Middle	6.8	10.8	1.2	18.8
Top Fifth	14.5	6.9	4.2	25.9
All	10.2	8.3	3.0	21.7
Top 1 Percent	19.4	1.7	9.9	31.2

Source: Urban Institute—Brookings Institution Tax Policy Center, June 25, 2007, www.taxpolicycenter.org/taxfact

taxpayer's obligations. After all of the various tax expenditures are factored in, the *real* rates of federal income taxation are a good deal less than the nominal rates.

The overall impact of the personal income tax, nevertheless, still favors poorer families. As Table 7.4 indicates, the top 20 percent of the population wind up paying roughly 15 percent of their total income in income taxes, while the poorest 40 percent pay nothing at all. In fact, as a consequence of the Earned Income Tax Credit (combined with the Federal Child Tax Credit), low- and lower-middle-income individuals and families often receive a *rebate*, what we earlier characterized as a negetive tax. While the rate progressions indicated in Table 7.4 may not be as steep as many would desire—both for the income tax and for the totality of federal taxes—higher income groups clearly pay higher rates.

Another way of illustrating the redistributive effects of federal taxation is to examine the share of national income accruing to different income groups *before* and *after* taxes are applied. In 2005, poor families—those constituting the bottom fifth of all households—held 4.1 percent of the nation's income before taxes and 4.9 percent after. The richest household quintile, on the other hand, had their income share reduced from 53.5 percent to 50.1 percent. The richest of the rich—the top 1 percent—had their income share reduced from 16.3 percent to 14.0 percent. In considering federal taxes, then, it is fair to conlcude that some income redistribution favoring those in need occurs, although not a very impressive amount. And, clearly, the main instrument of that redistribution is the federal income tax.[38]

Taxes that disproportionately *burden* the poor are called *regressive*. In the United States, a primary example is the sales tax. Levied by most states on most purchases, the sales tax is fixed—everyone pays the same rate. When buying a computer, for example, the consumer, rich or poor, pays the same sales tax percentage. In some states, the sales tax is as low as 2 percent, in others as high as 8 percent. While the tax is fixed, however, the resulting burden isn't, as it takes a greater proportion of the incomes of those on the low end of the income scale than it does from those with higher incomes.

CAPSULE 7.7 • *Code of Good Conduct*

The tax code has become the lawmaker's code of good conduct. Way back during the reigns of FDR, Kennedy, Johnson, and, yes, even Nixon, if the government wanted to support some worthy purpose, it funded a program—along with some (often inadequate) mechanism for administering it and judging its success. But that was before "spending" became a curse and "tax cuts" a blessing. Spending has been deemed woefully inefficient, resulting in large, unresponsive government bureaucracies that consume much of their money in overhead and redundant activity. Tax cuts, by comparison, are simplicity itself—the money stays right in your pocket, and you can spend it as you please, with maximum flexibility and efficiency. So these days if politicians want, for example, to increase the supply of affordable, quality day care, they don't fund and license day care centers. Instead, they give parents a tax credit so that they can make arrangements on their own.

From "Go Figure" by Jodie Allen as appeared in *The New Republic*, July 31, 2000. Reprinted by permission of Jodie T. Allen, a senior editor for the Pew Research Center.

Most taxes fall somewhere between the extremes of progressivity and regressivity. The payroll tax that finances Social Security is a good example. In 2009, all workers paid the same 6.2 percent of their earnings up to $106,800, with earnings above this limit untaxed. Thus, workers who earned $106,800 a year paid the same annual tax ($6622) as those earning $200,000, or $10 million, a year—clearly, regressivity at work. Nevertheless, Social Security is generally perceived as redistributive on its *allocative* dimension since the benefits provided to those earning the smallest amounts are more generous, proportionately, than to those who earned at higher levels. At present, for example, retired low-wage earners receive 58 percent of their former monthly wages, whereas average earners receive 44 percent and high-income earners receive 22 percent. The Social Security system is also redistributive *between* generations because payments to the presently retired come from the Social Security Trust Fund, which is supported by the current generation of workers.

When we examine the actual burden of the Social Security tax on different income classes, as we do in Table 7.4, it is clear that the wealthy, who could afford the most, are taxed the least. While the *overall* impact of the Social Security tax on all workers is 8.3 percent, for the top fifth of taxpayers, it is just 6.9 percent.

The regressive features of Social Security make it considerably less effective than the income tax as a means of redistribution. While the income tax is progressive because it exempts low-income people and has a progressive rate structure (10 to 35 percent), the Social Security tax clicks in at the first dollar earned and exempts *high* incomes—incomes over the $106,800 wage base are not taxed. Second, the Social Security tax burdens ordinary taxpayers who rely on their wages and salaries for a living since it is levied only on payrolls (i.e., earned income) and therefore exempts income from other sources, like investments. While this is in line with the program's character as "insurance" against interruptions in work-related income, it results in full taxation for working people and only partial taxation for those who are wealthy

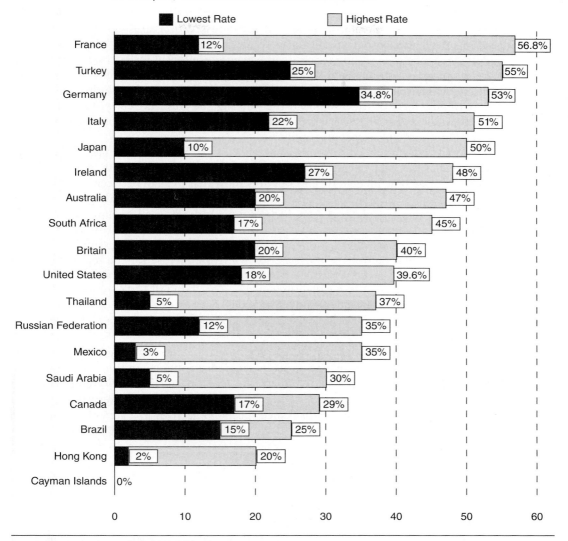

Range of personal income tax rates for single individuals in selected countries, as of Sept. 1, 1996. Local and other taxes are excluded.

FIGURE 7.4   *Around the World in Brackets.*

Source: Ernst & Young.

enough to get income in other ways. The more affluent—those who typically enjoy nonwork income such as capital gains, dividends, and significant family gifts—pay no Social Security taxes on that income. Tax experts point out, finally, that the employer's contributions to Social Security taxes are substantially passed on to consumers (through higher prices) and employees (through lower wages), further aggravating the regressive aspect of the program.[39]

So far, we have been examining federal taxation. But what is the impact of the *overall* tax system—the impact of federal *and* state *and* local taxes—on the distribution of income? Although economists have long debated this question—and the methodologies appropriate to answering it—the general consensus is that, on the whole, it is mildly progressive, due mainly to the very powerful impact of the federal income tax. As the federal tax burden on the rich has declined, however, first during the Reagan supply side years of the 1980s and then during the Bush tax cut years of the early 2000s, and as regressive taxes have increased, particularly state and local sales taxes, the overall tax burden has become significantly less progressive.

Studies by the Congressional Budget Office (CBO), for example, that track tax impacts have found a decided pro-rich trend in effect since the 1980s, and a resulting increase in income inequality. CBO figures show that the gap between rich and poor, and between the *very* rich (top 1 percent) and everyone else, is now larger than at any time since the eve of the Great Depression. And while all groups have enjoyed increased real incomes since the Reagan years, incomes have grown fastest for the affluent. The income of the poorest fifth of American families, for example, increased by just 4 percent between 1980 and 2003 while the incease for the top income fifth rose 54 percent. For the *very* affluent, the picture was even more dramatic. The top 1 percent of all households saw their incomes increase by a full 129 percent.[40]

Social Earmarking

A broad body of policy analysis has examined social welfare financing in terms of "fairness," that is, in terms of issues of equity, redistribution, and antipoverty. More recently, the role of tax policy in influencing *other* aspects of social welfare has drawn considerable interest. Tax laws have been examined as a form of intervention ("social engineering" to critics) that can advance specific objectives in a variety of ways. The way taxes affect individual as well as organizational behavior, for example, has been increasingly recognized. So too has the way tax systems focus revenues on special social needs.

Tax revenues can be designated for either general or specific purposes. "General revenues," such as those provided by federal and state income taxes, finance the broad range of governmental operations. Special-purpose taxes, often called "earmarked" or "dedicated" taxes, are restricted to narrowly specified activities. The Social Security payroll tax is the best-known example, although in recent years, policymakers at all governmental levels have enacted numerous self-financing programs (i.e., programs that provide their own revenues).

Pairing new taxes with new spending has been popular because it permits programs to be adopted or broadened without increasing budget deficits (at the federal level) or threatening spending limits (in the states). Earmarking, in addition, makes clear the connection between dollars raised and services provided. Taxpayers can see where their money is going, something that isn't possible with general taxes. Experience with Social

Security—as well as excises such as gasoline taxes that are linked to road improvements—indicate that such designation, especially in times of fiscal austerity, may be one of the few ways available to expand governmental activities.

An increasing number of designated taxes have been earmarked for social welfare. Many states utilize alcohol beverage taxes for social programs, especially education. Some have financed programs for the blind with amusement taxes. And in several, alcohol and tobacco taxes support prevention and treatment efforts. California voters, for example, passed Proposition 10 in 1998, increasing tobacco taxes to provide significant new revenues—currently about $700 million annually—to help expand early childhood programs and to improve the availability of health and developmental services for the state's young children and their families. More recently, California voters passed an initiative imposing a "millionaires tax" earmarked to improve services for the mentally ill.

Gambling taxes, lotteries, and other quasi-tax measures similarly focus revenues on particular social ends. Since 1980, for example, a majority of the states have raised fees on marriage licenses, birth certificates, and divorce decrees to create Children's Trust Funds to support programs to prevent abuse, neglect, and family violence.[41]

At the local level, cities such as San Francisco and Boston have required commercial developers to put money into low-income housing and childcare trust funds on the principle that new office buildings create social needs. Other communities have added surcharges to property and sales taxes to support libraries and programs to serve the homeless, or have created special taxing districts to finance programs for children. Although not dissimilar in their legal structure from school districts—and other special purpose districts—these taxing entities expressly generate revenues for health and social services. Palm Beach County voters, for example, created an independent taxing district in 1986 establishing a Children's Services Council to plan, coordinate, fund, and evaluate programs for children. Among the priorities defined by the Council in its first year of operations were substance abuse prevention, childcare, and teen-pregnancy programs.[42]

Earmarking places the burden of program support on a clearly identifiable source of payment. We have noted some of the general implications of this arrangement for contributory programs, where the taxpayer is also the recipient of benefits, as in Social Security. In programs where taxpayers *don't* benefit directly, earmarking may elicit less popular support, although creatively linking taxes and programs can substantially allay taxpayer resistance.

Attaching revenues to programs, however, can be hazardous if it undermines the ability of policymakers to utilize revenues flexibly for priority needs. Linking programs to special taxes makes an overall, integrated, planning, and budgeting process difficult to maintain. Earmarking, in addition, is not likely to help disadvantaged groups with poor reputations, or unpopular causes—voters are hardly likely, for example, to target taxes for welfare payments or affirmative action. Finally, the automatic nature of earmarking means that the magnitude and character of program spending may be driven by the amount of money generated, rather than by changing needs.

Taxes and Behavior

Traditionally, public policy attention has focused on the ways taxes influence economic (particularly saving and investment) behaviors. But taxes also affect important *social* behaviors, such as when people retire, how much they save for it, whether they have children or care for dependent relatives, their philanthropic activity, and so forth. In contrast to regulatory legislation (such as Prohibition) that directly outlaws certain kinds of behavior, taxes influence how people act through economic incentives. Certain activities are discouraged by making them costly; others are encouraged by making them inexpensive.[43] Activities that are socially detrimental can be reduced by heavy taxes; desirable behaviors can be promoted by light taxes, or no taxes at all.

Taxation, for example, has been used internationally as a means of population policy. Along with children's allowances, tax policies can reward larger families. In France and the Netherlands, most notably, tax rates at all levels of income are negatively correlated with family size.[44] Even in the United States, the federal income tax provides a modest reward for extra children through the personal exemption, child tax credit, and childcare tax deduction. Although taxes can attempt to advance "populationist" policies, of course, they can equally try to promote "reproductive nonproliferation." In 1979, for example, China enacted its first baby tax on couples having three or more children, imposing wage reductions up to 10 percent for the birth of a third child and as much as 20 percent for a fifth child. Small families, conversely, were rewarded with low taxes *and* preferential treatment with respect to pensions, housing, jobs, and schooling.[45]

Income tax deductions can be used to encourage families to care for ill or dependent relatives. Long-term care is an overriding need of many older people. Although programs such as Social Security, Title XX, and Medicaid provide important public support, many families caring for their parents, or other relatives, still face enormous financial and emotional burdens. In recent years, the magnitude of these costs, and the belief that home care is better than institutional care, has resulted in many tax proposals. But only a few have been enacted. Most notably, Congress changed the childcare credit in 1971 into the dependent-care tax credit to encourage at-home care. Several states also give tax relief to families caring for elderly relatives.

Tax policy can encourage other salutary behaviors. California, for example, permits taxpayers to deduct child adoption expenses that exceed 3 percent of their adjusted gross income; this limitation is waived for families adopting "hard to place" (disabled or older) children. Work behavior is frequently encouraged by making different kinds of work-related expenses deductible. And several states have devised tax schemes to help parents save for their children's college educations.

Just as tax policies encourage some activities, they discourage others. Sales (or excise) taxes, in particular, are widely used to control behaviors that are viewed as harmful. In the United States, for example, excises on cigarettes and alcohol are levied at federal, state, and local levels. Although such taxes are often simply a way of raising additional revenue, or "punishing" people for bad conduct (thus the phrase "sin tax"), they also serve as a behavioral disincentive, rewarding those who eschew an undesirable, socially damaging product. In recent years, for example, many states have considered

CAPSULE 7.8 • *Wine for Welfare*

Senator Strom Thurmond, R-S.C., introduced legislation yesterday that would raise excise taxes on wine to what they are for distilled spirits, which would double or triple the rate, depending on the alcohol content. "Generally I do not favor increased taxes," Thurmond said, "but in this era of shrinking budgets, the only way in which we will be able to finance adequate, impartial and trustworthy research into alcohol-induced diseases such as hypertension, breast cancer and birth defects is to generate a new revenue flow that will be used specifically for investigating such killers."

"fat taxes" on soft drinks and fast foods, both to raise revenues for health programs and to encourage consumers to shift their eating choices toward healthy alternatives.

Alcohol and tobacco "sin taxes" have been a major source of revenues throughout the world for many years. Beverage taxes are used worldwide to control alcohol consumption, and Finland, the Czech Republic, France, Norway, Sweden, and Switzerland all explicitly utilize excises to reduce drinking. Furthermore, in these countries and others, beverages are taxed so that those having the highest alcohol content are subject to the heaviest levies, this presumeably an effort to shift consumption from hard liquor to beer and wine.[46]

In the United States, the federal government has levied alcohol excises since the 1790s. Prior to the imposition of the federal income tax in 1913, alcohol excises constituted the federal government's main revenue source, supplying nearly two-thirds of all Treasury receipts. In recent years, given the clear evidence of a positive correlation between social costs and drinking behavior, taxes have increased. While it is true that drinking habits are not easily changed, data suggest that alcohol taxes *do* have an impact on sales and use. While federal tax charges on beer, wine, and hard liquor haven't changed (meaning that they have been falling in inflation-adjusted terms) in over a decade, state and local rates have. As a result, consumption has been reduced and, concurrently, so have alcohol-related problems such as auto fatalities and cirrhosis mortality. The reductions, so far, have been modest but real.[47] Although critics argue that alcohol demand is relatively "inelastic"—that is, not responsive to price, especially for heavy users—support for tax increases continues to grow.

Other detrimental behaviors can also be restrained. Cigarette taxes have increased as the association between tobacco and disease has become known. Between 1982 and 2006, the federal excise tax on a pack of cigarettes increased from 8 cents to 39 cents. And all fifty states tax cigarettes, with the rate per pack ranging from a low of 7 cents (South Carolina) to a high of $2.58 (New Jersey). In addition, nearly 400 local governments levy cigarette taxes.[48] In Norway, taxation is near draconian, with 85 percent of the price of a pack of cigarettes composed of taxes and fees. In Canada,

CAPSULE 7.9 • *Birthdays and Taxes*

Many American women, mindful of the requirements of the tax code, choose to deliver their babies in time to enjoy a tax benefit. Specifically, they use cesarean section or induced labor to assure birth in the last week of December-rather than the first week of January.

• A child born on December 31 allows the parents to enjoy all the tax benefits of being born anytime during that year—while a child born one day later, in the next calendar and tax year, provide no tax benefits for the previous year.

• Statistics show that the number of births in the last week of December is greater than those in the first week of January.

The tax benefits to parents of December births take three forms: the personal exemption, the earned income tax credit, and the standard deduction.

From "Of Taxes and Birthdays" Macroscope, *Investor's Business Daily*, July 1, 1999.

the price per pack is approaching $7 in some provinces.[49] The effects in all countries have been dramatic—since 2000, for example, tobacco sales in the United States have dropped 15 percent. According to the Coalition on Smoking and Health, every 10 percent increase in the price of cigarettes decreases cigarette consumption among young people by about 4 percent.

Taxes on alcohol, cigarettes, gambling, and junk food are often attacked for their regressive nature, and it is undeniable that they do impose a far greater burden on people with lower incomes. It is estimated, for example, that alcohol taxes absorb five times as much of the income of households with incomes under $15,000 than they do of over-$50,000 households. Nevertheless, it is shortsighted to dismiss the social value of excise taxes. First, these taxes can be enacted as part of broader tax packages that include balancing progressive measures. Second, excise taxes can themselves be progressively structured—alcohol taxes, for example, can be linked to the price of the beverage so that, for example, drinkers of an expensive scotch such as Chivas Regal pay higher rates than those imbibing Bud Lite. Finally, although sin taxes may fall disproportionately on poor and middle-income U.S. residents, these groups make up most of the victims of cigarettes and liquor. Increased taxes *may* be burdensome; more importantly, however, they save suffering and lives.

Emerging Issues: Financing Social Security

No twenty-first century social policy issue is more contentious, and more important, than the financing of Social Security, America's largest social program, and one that directly affects nearly all of us, either as taxpayers who fund the program or as recipients who benefit from it. Since its inception in 1935, employers and employees have paid more than $4.5 trillion in employment (payroll) taxes into the Social Security Trust Fund, and more than $4.1 trillion have been paid out in benefits.

CAPSULE 7.10 • *Boomer Files*

The nation's first Baby Boomer, Kathleen Casey-Kirschling, today filed for her Social Security retirement benefits online. Ms. Casey-Kirschling, who was born one second after midnight on January 1, 1946, will be eligible for benefits beginning January 2008. As the nation's first Boomer, Ms. Casey-Kirschling is leading what is often referred to as America's silver tsunami. Over the next two decades, nearly 80 million Americans will become eligible for Social Security benefits, more than 10,000 per day.

Social Security Administration, News Release, October 15, 2007.

Social Security's financing dilemma is the actuarial certainty that the program's tax revenues, large as they are, will not be sufficient to pay all promised benefits. While there is currently a $2 trillion surplus in the Social Security accounts, the long-term picture is bleak. This is because revenues over the next decades will increase far less rapidly than spending. Ultimately, unless changes are made, annual expenditures will exceed annual revenues, and the Trust Fund will be diminished as it is called upon to cover the difference. Around the year 2041, according to the best predictions, available revenues will not be enough to cover the full cost of benefits.[50]

This long-term funding shortfall, in part, reflects the growing longevity of the elderly, who are living an increasing number of years after retirement. It also reflects the overall size of the baby-boom generation, that enormous cohort of post–World War II babies who are just starting to leave the workforce. A large number of new retirees, of course, would not be a problem if the growth in their numbers was paralleled by growth in the number of working taxpayers. Unfortunately, the ratio between those workers *paying* into Social Security and those retirees *receiving* benefits from it is ever the more "adverse." The ratio, indeed, called the "social security dependency ratio" by economists, will be just 2.1 to 1 in 2030, meaning that only slightly more than two taxpayers will be available to support each beneficiary. The ratio is more than 3 to 1 today. And it was approximately 5 to 1 back in 1960.

Fixing the long-term financing gap has engaged the interest of a large number of policy analysts and during the administration of George W. Bush raised the perennial battle between left and right on the role of private markets versus government. To simplify a complex debate, reformers on the right generally have viewed Social Security's salvation in privatization—in transforming the program from a public tax-financed operation to one based on private investment—while liberal and progressive reformers see the need to retain Social Security's basic features while broadening its funding base, either through higher taxes, or better public investment of Trust Fund assets, or through some subsidy from the general federal budget.

As with welfare reform, the radicals in the Social Security debate have conservatives who, in this case, called for replacing "Social Security as we know it" with a marketized pension system, a system that would permit citizens to divert all or part of their social security taxes into "personal retirement accounts." Instead of a universal

CAPSULE 7.11 • *Privatizing Social Security*

Private accounts offer every single working American a piece of the American Pie.
> —Senator Rick Santorum, R-Pa., December 1, 1998

We condemn those who would turn Social Security over to Wall Street. This isn't a debate over how to reform Social Security. It's a face off over whether Social Security should exist or not exist.
> —John Sweeney, President, AFL-CIO, December 2, 1998

Under privatization, individuals would be at the mercy of forces beyond their control, such as the hazards of the market. While it is true that stocks tend to bear high returns over the long run, this fact would not help the unfortunate souls whose portfolios take a dive right before they retire. . . . Shrewd and fortunate investors end up with enough to buy a powerboat; foolish or unlucky ones wind up gleaning the early-bird special at Denny's.
> —Jonathan Chait, "Security Risk," *The New Republic*, January 18, 1999

Social Security Trust Fund incorporating everybody's taxes and invested in U.S. Treasury Bonds, citizens could invest their tax dollars in whatever manner they choose. They would *have* to invest for retirement; the accounts are mandatory, but they would choose the kind of investment to make.

This form of privatization, it must be noted, is different from the kind described earlier in this text, in Chapter 6. Traditionally, the term *privatization* has referred to government utilizing a private agency or company to carry out public business—contracting with a community agency, for example, to deliver meals on wheels to the homebound elderly, or selecting a private school to provide special education to needy children. Privatizing Social Security is different. Rather than relying on private organizations to administer programs for the public, it entails giving workers choices to control their own social security investments.

The primary argument in favor of private investments has been that it would provide citizens a far better rate of return on their money than Social Security. Given the robust growth over much of the past fifty years in private investments such as those in the major stock market funds, privatization advocates—at least until the market crash of 2008—considered a reliance on Social Security to be an anachronism. Young people, in particular, it was argued, were being cheated by a system that provides them very modest returns on their tax dollars.

The argument *against* privatization was that it is *risky*—no one is guaranteed a fixed benefit—and is far less *fair*, since private accounts give no special attention to the needs of vulnerable groups. As the severe economic downturn of 2008–09 has made clear, Wall Street investments can rise as significantly as they can fall. For advocates of the *status quo*, moreover, privatization represents a dangerous abrogation of the fundamental principles that made Social Security such a successful instrument of income security over the years. While it is acknowledged that modifications will have to be made in order to assure Social Security's long-term fiscal health, supporters of the present system call for reformist, incremental change. It has been proposed, for example, that the retirement age be raised, as well as the level of wages on which taxes are paid. Some have called, in addition, for small increases in the tax rate or a recalculation of the cost-of-living formula to reduce future benefits or for *public* authorities to invest part of the Social Security Trust Fund in private stocks and bonds, much like many states do when investing the assets of their public employee retirement funds.

The major points of contention between partisans of privatization and those who support the basic features of today's Social Security program reflected radically different visions of what social welfare ought to be in a modern capitalist economy. As in other areas of debate, a fundamental clash exists between individual and welfarist values, between private action and public responsibility, and between redistribution and individual equity. While proponents of private accounts relied on the marketplace ethos that benefits should be calibrated to one's acumen in choosing wise investments, partisans of the present system see the "social" component of Social Security as its essential, primary, *raison d'être*. Social Security *guarantees* security, promising a basic level of support for all workers in their old age as well as a measure of redistribution to help women, minorities, and low-wage earners in general. For liberals and progressives, a *social* retirement system is not principally a matter of pension benefits commensurate with previous earnings or stock market investments, but rather a matter of furnishing a pension adequate to meeting old people's basic needs. Social Security taxes, in this way, express society's collective responsibility while Social Security benefits express society's common commitment to decency for the elderly.

To use insurance terminology, Social Security pools risks and responsibilities across the workforce and over the generations. Taxes go into a national fund—the Social Security Trust Fund. They are protected against the vagaries of the stock market. And they fund benefits utilizing a statistical algorithm that provides for "social adequacy," that is, that provides higher retirement returns to lower-income earners. The basic benefit formula, in other words, incorporates a community safety net—Social Security payments correlate not only to contributions (the taxes paid in), but *also* to need.

How significant is the need element in the benefit formula? It is very important. Low-income workers, to use the technical term, receive a specially high "replacement ratio." As already noted, low-income earners receive retirement benefits worth more than half the amount of their previous income, whereas high-income earners—those who paid in at the maximum tax level—receive a return of just 22 percent. This produces a major degree of redistribution clearly differentiating Social Security from the individualism embodied in individual accounts. Social Security, indeed, because of its magnitude, is the largest program of income redistribution in the United States, and a far more significant antipoverty program for its recipients than public assistance.

A core issue separating right and left, therefore, is the degree to which Social Security should be retained as an instrument of redistribution. Under privatized financing, benefits would reflect the return on one's own chosen investment; participants make individual choices and benefit or suffer accordingly. Under government financing, participants share important obligations to one another as part of a group, receiving benefits based not on the success of their individual portfolio, but on the basis of the overall program. Under government financing, a safety net is insured for the poor, with much of the money that high earners pay into the system transferred to low earners.

As the Social Security debate has emerged into the broad political realm, the harder edges of the controversy have been somewhat muted. Privatization advocates have recently stressed the compatibility of private and public programs. Denying a wish to abolish Social Security, many have called for "partial privatization," for keeping the payroll tax largely intact but permitting perhaps 1 or 2 percent of the current 6.75 percent to be shifted to private investments. Such a two-tiered system, it is argued, would in the future secure the advantages of the stock market while still protecting everybody's basic retirement nest egg. For opponents, though, even a partial diversion of tax funds constitutes a dangerous "slippery slope," easily leading to the ultimate dismantling of a guaranteed retirement income.

One thing is clear. Privatization represents a dominant theme in the "do it yourself" social policy of recent decades that elevates individual responsibility and market values over social rights and community mindedness. Like school voucher plans, retirement privatization, whatever its dimensions, is likely to have very different results for different people. While it could provide some Americans expanded resources in their old age, it could also erode the retirement incomes of those lowest on the income ladder. The precipitous decline of stock values in 2008 indeed, has taken much of wind out of the sails of privatization—at least for the time being.

Whatever its merits or dangers, the privatization is hardly a solution for Social Security's fiscal woes. The Social Security "crisis" is basically a financial crisis, and if Social Security taxes—fully or partially—are shifted to private accounts, then the gap between future program income and future program expenditures *increases*. However well individuals may do with their private accounts, the financial basis of the *common* fund is depleted unless some special arrangements are made to replenish it with new taxes, or unless benefits are cut to bring them in line with decreased revenues.

Notes

1. Giving USA Foundation, *Giving USA* 2008 (New York: AAFRC), 37.
2. Gordon Manser, "The Voluntary Agency—Contribution or Survival?" *Washington Bulletin*, 22(20) (October 1971): 10; Voluntary Giving and Tax Policy (New York: National Assembly for Social Policy and Development, 1972).
3. William S. Vickrey, "One Economist's View of Philanthropy," in Frank G. Dickinson (ed.), *Philanthropy and Public Policy* (New York: National Bureau of Economic Research, 1962).
4. Ralph Kramer, *Voluntary Agencies in the Welfare State* (Berkeley, Calif.: University of California Press, 1981), 193–211.
5. For example, see Oscar Handlin, *The Uprooted* (New York: Oxford University Press, 1964).
6. For example, see C. Wendell King, *Social Movements in the United States* (New York: Free Press, 1957).
7. Charles Richard Henderson, "The Place and Functions of Voluntary Associations," *American Journal of Sociology*, 1 (November 1895): 334–39.
8. Kramer, *Voluntary Agencies in the Welfare State*, 173–92.
9. Peter Marris and Martin Rein, *Dilemmas of Social Reform: Poverty and Community Action in the United States* (New York: Atherton, 1967). For a dramatic account of how foundations undertake

projects that the government may abjure because of political considerations, see Thomas C. Reeves, *Freedom and the Foundation: The Fund for the Republic in the Era of McCarthyism* (New York: Alfred A. Knopf, 1969).

10. Kramer, *Voluntary Agencies in the Welfare State*, 242–47.
11. This example is based on the article by Herman Levin, "The Future of Voluntary Family and Children's Social Work: An Historical View," *Social Service Review*, 38(2) (June 1964): 164–73.
12. Salvatore Ambrosino, "Family Service Agencies," *Encyclopedia of Social Work*, 17th ed. (New York: NASW, 1977), 429.
13. Herman Levin, "Voluntary Agencies in Social Welfare," *Encyclopedia of Social Work*, 17th ed. (New York: NASW, 1977), 1574.
14. "Social Work Unit Changing Tactics," *New York Times*, January 29, 1971, 1.
15. *Giving USA 1996*, 36.
16. *The NonProfit Times*. The NPT 100—America's Biggest NonProfits, 1999.
17. Ralph Kramer, "Voluntary Agencies and the Personal Social Services," in Walter W. Powell (ed.), *The Handbook of Non-Profit Organizations* (Cambridge, Mass: Yale University Press, 1985).
18. Elizabeth Wickenden, "Purchase of Care and Services: Effect on Voluntary Agencies," in *Proceedings of the First Milwaukee Institute on a Social Welfare Issue of the Day* (Milwaukee: School of Social Welfare, July 1970).
19. Ira Glasser, "Prisoners of Benevolence: Power vs. Liberty in the Welfare State," in Willard Gaylin, Ira Glasser, Steven Marcus, and David I. Rothman, (eds.), *Doing Good: The Benefits of Benevolence* (New York: Pantheon Books, 1978), 110.
20. Austin W. Scott, "Charitable Trusts," *Encyclopedia of the Social Sciences*, Vol. III, Edwin R. A. Seligman et al. (eds.) (New York: Macmillan, 1937), 338–40.
21. The Tax Reform Act of 1969 made the prohibition on social and political action even more stringent for organizations classified as "private foundations" by removing the qualifying word *substantial*.
22. See General Explanation of the Tax Reform Act, 9162, H. R. 13270, Public Law 91-1972 (Washington, D.C.: Government Printing Office, 1970), 48–49.
23. For a detailed discussion of the concept of charitable immunity, see George W. Keeton, *The Modern Law of Charities* (London: Sir Isaac Pitman and Sons, Ltd., 1962).
24. Warren Weaver, *U.S. Philanthropic Foundations* (New York: Harper & Row, 1967), 11, 23; see also Julius Rosenwald, "Principles of Giving," *Atlantic Monthly*, May 1929; and Wilmer Shields Rich, *Community Foundations in the U.S. and Canada* (New York: National Council on Foundations, 1961).
25. For a detailed history of the Girard College case, see Milton M. Gordon, "The Girard College Case: Desegregation and a Municipal Trust," *Annals of the American Academy of Political and Social Science* (March 1956): 53–62.
26. For further discussion of *cy pres*, see Keeton, *The Modern Law of Charities*, and Edith L. Fisch, *The Cy Pres Doctrine in the United States* (New York: Matthew Bender, 1950), 141–42. On the general controlling legal principle as applied to Girard College, see "Validity and Effect of Gifts for Charitable Purposes Which Exclude Otherwise Qualified Beneficiaries Because of Race or Religion," in 25 ALR 3d 736 (1969).
27. See, for example, the articles in Michael Novak (ed.), *To Empower People: From State to Civil Society*, 2nd ed. (Washington, D.C., AEI Press, 1996). Also see Marvin Olasky, *Compassionate Conservatism* (New York: Press, 2000).
28. Kaiser Family Foundation, *Employer Health Benefits, 2008 Summary of Findings*, p. 1.
29. Ibid, p. 3
30. Sharon K. Long, *Hardship among the Uninsured: Choosing among Food, Housing, and Health Insurance*, The Urban Institute, B-54, May 2003.
31. Daniel Cherkin, "The Effect of Office Visit Co-Payments on Utilization in a Health Maintenance Organization," *Medical Care* (July 1989).
32. Daniel Weinberg, "The Distributional Implications of Tax Expenditures," *National Tax Journal*, XL(2) (June 1987): 237–54.
33. Isabel Sawhill, quoted in Urban Institute, *Policy and Research Report* (Winter/Spring 1990): 28.

34. See Table 7.4, p. 217.

35. Taxable income constitutes about 55 percent of total personal income. See U.S. Advisory Commission on Intergovernmental Relations, *Facts and Figures on Government Finance*, Table C41, 1990, 130.

36. Organization of Economic Cooperation and Development (OECD), *Revenue Statistics, 1965–2006*, 2007, p. 19.

37. www.about.com:taxplanning.u.s.taxes.about.com/od/2008taxes/at/2008_tax_rates.htm

38. U.S. Congressional Budget Office, *Historical Effective Federal Tax Rates: 1979 to 2005*, December 2007.

39. Joseph Pechman, *Social Security: Perspectives for Reform* (Washington, D.C: Brookings Institution, 1968). Eveline M. Burns, *Social Security and Public Policy* (New York: McGraw-Hill, 1956); Richard M. Titmuss, *Essays on "The Welfare State"* (London: Allen & Unwin, 1958).

40. Center on Budget and Policy Priorities, *New CBO Data Indicates Growth in Long-Term Income Inequality Continues*, January 30, 2006.

41. Thomas Birch, *Children's Trust Funds: An Update*, National Committee for Preventing Child Abuse, 1984. See also Ronald K. Snells, "Earmarking State Tax Revenues," *Intergovernmental Perspective*, 16(4) (Fall 1990): 12–16.

42. Healthy Children Report, *Special Taxing Districts for Children*, Harvard University Division of Health Policy, 1988.

43. Charles Lindblom refers to "tax inducements" and "tax punishments." See his "The Market as Prison," *Journal of Politics*, 44(2) (May 1982).

44. Harvey E. Brazer, "Income Tax Treatment of the Family," in Henry J. Aaron and Michael J. Boskin (eds.), *The Economics of Taxation* (Washington, D.C.: Brookings Institution, 1980), 223.

45. Matt Rosenberg, China's One Child Policy, About.com: Geography, geography.about.com/od/populationgeography/a/onechild.htm. Posted June 18, 2008.

46. Mavis M. Brown, Margo F. Dewar, and Paul Wallace, *International Survey of Alcohol Beverage Taxation and Control Policies*, 5th ed., Brewers Association of Canada, November 1982, 378.

47. Philip J. Cook, *Paying the Tab: the Economics of Alcohol Policy*, Princeton University Press, 2007.

48. Donna Rosato, "Thank You for Smoking," *Money Magazine*, September 2007, 20.

49. Ibid.

50. U.S. Department of the Treasury, *Social Security Reform: The Nature of the Problem*, Issue Brief No. 1, September 2007.

8

The Mode of Finance: Systems of Transfer

We are committed to getting power back to the states, we are committed to breaking out of the logjam of Federal bureaucrats controlling how we try to help the poor, and we believe you can trust the 50 states and the 50 state legislatures to work together on behalf of the citizens of their states.

Newt Gingrich,
House Welfare Debate, August 1, 1996

Subsidiarity [decentralization] enthusiasts are often quite two-faced. When there is a social problem they really think is pressing, they tend to lose their enthusiasm for turning it over to the states. Although crime is traditionally a matter for state and local governments, politicians in Washington compete vigorously to federalize the most categories of criminal behavior and spend the most out of the federal Treasury to build prisons. . . . Don' t get me wrong. The states are nice to have around. I live in one myself. But "turn it over to the states" is a trivial answer to any policy puzzle—even when it happens to be correct.

Michael Kinsley,
Time, January 16, 1995

The political system of the United States divides power in two major ways—horizontally, among the executive, legislative, and judicial branches, and vertically, among the different levels of government. In this chapter, it is the *vertical* dimension that is of primary concern because financing the U.S. welfare state is substantially a matter of national, state, and local relationships. And although the federal level, given its national scope and institutional authority, is certainly preeminent among the three, jurisdiction over the public programs and services that meet this country's social needs is broadly distributed. Some programs are exclusively the responsibility of one level. Social Security, Medicare, and veterans' programs, for example, are entirely federal in their funding and operations, whereas General Assistance, libraries, and education are almost fully state and/or local. Other programs operate *intergovernmentally*, under combined authority. States, for example, share substantial authority with the federal government in Medicaid and child welfare whereas federal–city partnerships govern programs for housing and the homeless.

The balance of authority over social welfare programs typically parallels the balance of financial responsibility. Although numerous arrangements exist for transferring funds from their source of origin—the governmental unit collecting revenues—to the point of service delivery—the governmental unit spending them—it is usually the primary funder that exercises primary control. "He who pays the piper calls the tune" is quite the appropriate aphorism.

Two major questions of finance that are paramount in structuring intergovernmental arrangements for social welfare are how money flows and how money is conditioned. The question of *flow* deals with the fashion in which public moneys are transformed from being revenues to being outlays. This is often described in terms of funding streams. The question of *conditions* deals with the priorities, stipulations, and regulations that are placed on the flow of money from one governmental level to another.

Before one can understand the nature of these fiscal choices, however, their ideological context must be considered.

Centralization, Decentralization, and Their Ideologies

Given the size and diversity of our federal system, the balance between centralization (power concentrated nationally) and decentralization (power devolved to state and local governments and institutions) is a perennial issue. In the design of social welfare policy, the values and assumptions related to decentralization and centralization are generally expressed in choices concerning pluralism versus uniformity, small versus large. In the past twenty-five years, ideals of decentralization have been ascendant. Since the Reagan era, in particular, important service responsibilities have been returned to the level of the states and localities. Although these units have been generally eager to increase their program authority, their record with respect to social investment and social sensitivity has been mixed. While the consequences for the poor of reduced federal control are far from uniform, the combination of decentralization and funding restriction has often been detrimental for those dependent on public assistance and social services.

This is not to deny the values of decentralization. Local governments are often more knowledgeable than large centralized units about problems in their areas and more responsive to the special needs of their constituencies. In addition, small units can more easily experiment, and if they fail, the scope of the consequences is limited. Indeed, losses suffered through the failure of one unit's experiment may be compensated for by the lessons of successful alternatives. Finally, there is a metaphysical quality about small localities that is appealing. They lend themselves more readily to visions of the *gemeinschaft* marked by warm, meaningful relationships and a sense of belonging to a vibrant, caring, manageable civic community. As Richard Thompson Ford has stated,

Local and state governments can be more innovative, daring, and proactive—in short, more progressive—than even the liberal Congresses of distant memory. A growing number of state legislatures have pioneered public-school finance reform, working to ensure that kids from poor neighborhoods are not stuck in inferior schools. Many states have civil rights guarantees that are stronger than those under federal law, especially with respect to sexual orientation discrimination.[1]

Conservative theorists, in Europe and America, have articulated thoughtful visions of the role localities can play in the modern welfare state. The idea of "subsidiarity" has gained particular attention in Europe as social policy there has evolved into a three-tiered system of governance with new powers given to Europe-wide institutions such as the European Union. Subsidiarity refers to the principle that although different public functions are appropriate for different governmental levels, action should be carried out at the lowest level where it can be performed effectively.

The devolution argument, as we have seen, is advanced not only by federalists who wish to see more authority given to states and localities but by conservatives who extol the responsiveness and efficiency of *private* institutions—individuals, families, voluntary associations, and the marketplace. Libertarian theorists, for example, often call for limitations on *all* levels of government through tax limits and privatization. Both versions of decentralization see bigness as the enemy; both view society's smaller, more "organic" units as natural reflections of the true public interest.

Although many of these arguments are cogent, they often ignore the limitations of decentralization. As Chapter 2 indicated, the national welfare state emerged as a result of the incapacity of local institutions—public and private—to address twentieth-century problems of poverty and insecurity. In the United States, the federal government—not states, localities, private charities, or the marketplace—responded to the crisis of the Great Depression, securing broad economic gains for ordinary citizens. And it was the federal government again, in the 1960s, that advanced civil rights and social protections for the impoverished and the excluded.

National action has been necessary for many reasons. For one thing, localism can be parochial and oppressive. Privacy and freedom may shelter more securely in the cold impersonality of large centralized units. As McConnell argues,

> Impersonality is the guarantee of individual freedom characteristic of the large unit. Impersonality means an avoidance of arbitrary official action, the following of prescribed procedure, conformance to established rules, and escape from bias whether for or against any individual. Impersonality, and the privacy and freedom it confers, may be despised, and the human warmth and community concern for the personal affairs of individuals characteristic of the small community preferred. Nevertheless, the values involved are different, and are to a considerable degree antagonistic.[2]

The defense of minority interests and civil rights within small units is often more difficult to achieve than within larger units. In small units, it is easier to weld a cohesive majority that may disregard the interests of others or that bring great pressure for conformity to bear. "States' rights" ideologies, for example, long justified the powers and privileges of whites in the South. Through the 1970s, "states' rights" remained the battle cry of segregationists such as George Wallace, Orval Faubus, and the racist

White Citizens' Councils. Up until the present, African American and other minority communities—whether based on ethnicity or sexual preference or disability status—have looked to the federal government not only to support their rights against hostile or indifferent states and localities, but also to promote programs of social and economic assistance. In the American experience, larger centralized units have been decidedly more progressive and reformist.

National units, moreover, command greater resources; some problems are simply beyond the scope of secondary bodies. State and local revenue systems are often deficient. Constrained by regressive tax systems, the fear of losing businesses and affluent taxpayers to rival low-tax jurisdictions, and an increasing proliferation of spending limits, they lack the wherewithal to address pressing needs. Their technical and administrative capacity, despite vast improvements since the 1960s, are often inadequate, with poorly trained and badly paid personnel as much the rule as the exception. State and local units, by their very nature, can do little to affect problems of national scope. Redistributive programs, for example, must be financed by progressive taxes levied by large governmental units. Only the federal government can levy taxes in all jurisdictions at once, so only the federal government is able to bring about significant redistribution in income or services.

The decentralization of authority also results in a troubling degree of variation in local social welfare efforts. Having significant diversity in state and local activities may reflect a salutary degree of pluralism, but it also blocks a national approach to problems and can result in substantial discrepancies in benefit arrangements from place to place. Perhaps the most dramatic example of this is the variation in welfare payments. Over the past twenty-five years, for example, maximum benefits for needy families in Alaska have been five times the level in Alabama, which, in part, reflects different costs of living. Although the federal government modifies this discrepancy a bit through the food stamp program, which has uniform nationwide eligibility and benefit standards, the gap between high-payment and low-payment states in TANF, and other program areas, remains dramatic.

The more general critique of decentralization is that it tends to reduce the emphasis on helping the poor. Historically speaking, in this country, and in others, it has been national leadership that has evidenced the greatest degree of concern with society's disadvantaged and vulnerable. Although it is difficult to characterize the multitude of state and local policies with glib generalizations, it is certainly clear that, for the most part, they have often been less than willing, and perhaps financially less than able, to undertake an effective social agenda.

How the Money Flows

How, exactly, *should* the United States face the question of dividing political, administrative, and fiscal powers and responsibilities among governments at different geographical levels? Should policymakers rely heavily on national decision making, or should regional and local control be the rule? Can a system somehow combine the best features of both arrangements?

CAPSULE 8.1 • *Failing Grades on Child Protection*

Not a single state has passed a rigorous test of its ability to protect children from child abuse and to find permanent homes for kids who often languish in foster care. The 32 states evaluated so far could lose millions of dollars from the federal government if they fail to fix problems within a few years. The problems of child abuse get periodic attention, usually following the tragic death of a child. The new Child and Family Service Reviews are the first time federal officials have tried to measure how well children are faring across state systems designed to protect them—but that often fall short.

The reviews ask whether children are bouncing from one foster home to the next, never able to put down roots; whether siblings taken from their parents are kept together; whether it takes a state too long to finalize adoptions or to send children back to their biological parents . . . The reviews merge dozens of questions into seven "outcome" measurements. Fourteen states have failed all seven; an additional 14, plus the District of Columbia, have failed six of the seven. No state passed more than two. . . .

After the first round of reviews, states must write improvement plans. A second round of tests will determine if states made promised changes. If not, they could lose some of their federal child welfare money.

From "States Failing New Test of Child Welfare System" by Laura Meckler, The Associated Press, August 19, 2003. Copyright © 2003 The Associated Press. All rights reserved. The information contained in the AP News report may not be published, broadcast, rewritten or redistributed without the prior written authority of The Associated Press. Used by permission.

In establishing its own system of differentiation, the United States devised a unique answer to the question of structure and balance—American federalism. The federal division of powers between the national capital and the states, formulated in the Constitution in 1789, has remained the fundamental legal framework of local–national relations. The concept, of course, has evolved considerably over the years. At first, it referred to an arrangement of "dual sovereignty" in which the different levels of government operated more or less separately, each with a large amount of autonomy. Today, federalism is characterized by a substantial measure of cooperative activity. Indeed, when we speak of federalism nowadays we are really speaking of *intergovernmental relations*, of different levels of government jointly formulating, operating, and financing domestic policies. The foremost instrument of modern federal relations is the intergovernmental grant-in-aid, commonly known as federal aid.[3]

Federal grant programs express the common interest of localities, states, and the national government in addressing common purposes in a cooperative fashion. The federal government, taking financial leadership, provides money to states and localities for the conduct of particular types of programs. In this fashion, federal aid is both a fiscal and a policy device for collective decision making. The *purpose* of aid programs is defined by Congress, often in very broad terms, whereas actual program *implementation* is the responsibility of states and localities. And because states and localities run the programs, and often share in their financing, they have a great deal of influence over their character. State and local participation, it is important to note, is fully voluntary. The core of the federal relationship, in other words, is built on cooperation, not coercion, in preserving local diversity within a framework of nationally shared values.

Although federal cash grants to states date back to 1879, their importance as a basic organizing instrument for social welfare didn't emerge until the New Deal. When the Social Security Act became law in 1935, for example, all but two of its dozen or so programs were organized and financed through grants-in-aid. Aid to Dependent Children, Aid to the Blind, and Old-Age Assistance, the three programs that established the United States' basic public assistance system, were all formulated as grants-in-aid. Other titles of the Act provided aid to states for maternal and child welfare services, for crippled children, and for vocational rehabilitation.

In the 1960s, the second major era in the development of the U.S. welfare state, Congress again relied on the grant-in-aid principle. Except for Medicare, all the principal social programs enacted as part of the Great Society followed the federal format—financial aid from Washington in exchange for program commitments by states and localities. Lyndon Johnson, like Roosevelt before him, used federal money to promote national purposes by enlarging and diversifying the scope of state and local programs. During the 1960s, however, greater stress than before was focused on antipoverty and urban programs, and more and more federal dollars went *directly* to cities rather than (as before) almost exclusively to states. In some instances, indeed, such as the Community Action Programs of the War on Poverty, aid was funneled to *private* nongovernmental community organizations at the neighborhood level, bypassing both states and cities.

Today, the vast majority of America's social programs are multilevel partnerships. Only in a few areas of social welfare policy (mainly social insurance, programs for Native Americans, and veterans' affairs) does the national government have sole responsibility. States, for example, are the responsible program partner in mental health, social services, and Medicaid. Local governments take principal responsibility for operating aid programs in elementary and secondary education, community development, urban mass transit, and employment/training. State programs are generally administered at the federal level by the Department of Health and Human Services, whereas city and county programs are generally administered by the Department of Housing and Urban Development.

As Table 8.1 indicates, grant policy has evolved somewhat fitfully over the past fifty years. During the years of the Great Society, the number, size, and relative importance of federal grants grew rapidly, with outlays more than tripling in the 1960s,

CAPSULE 8.2 • *The Decentralization Amendment*

The powers not delegated to the United States by the Constitution, nor prohibited by it to the States, are reserved to the States respectively, or to the people.

10th Amendment to the U.S. Constitution, December 15, 1791.

TABLE 8.1   *Federal Grants-in-Aid, Selected Years*

	Amount (billions of dollars)	As % of Federal Outlays	As % of GDP	Number of Grants
1950	$ 2.3	5	1.1	60
1960	$ 7.0	8	1.4	130
1970	$ 24.1	12	2.4	400
1980	$ 91.4	16	3.4	540
1990	$135.3	12	2.4	450
2000	$285.8	16	2.9	640
2008	$466.6	17	3.1	814

Source: Budget of the U.S. Government, FY 2009, Historical Tables, 233.

making state and local governments increasingly dependent on federal aid as a source of revenue.

Today, while the grant economy seems relatively steady, both as a portion of welfare state spending and state and local outlays, it is actually in significant decline. This is because, for several years now, total intergovernmental spending has been powerfully influenced by Medicaid, by far the largest grant program. So while the magnitude of grant expenditures seems relatively steady, the story *excluding* Medicaid is not so rosy. When Medicaid is deleted from the overall data, the federal grant portion of GDP and state and local spending has been dropping since 1978.

While the level of grant support has waxed and waned, the principle of federal–state–local partnerships has never been stronger. Given the fundamentally centralizing trends that characterize modern society, this is surprising. The endurance of the states is *particularly* surprising, given the many predictions over the course of the last hundred years that their days as viable units of government were numbered. In 1933, for example, Luther Gulick, an eminent scholar of government, wrote,

> Is the state the appropriate instrumentality for the discharge of . . . important functions? The answer is not a matter of conjecture or delicate appraisal. It is a matter of brutal record. I do not predict that the states will go. I affirm that they have already gone.[4]

Gulick's view represented a dominant theme of the Great Depression years, one that found the states unprepared to deal with the enormous economic and social problems facing the nation. The states, primarily rural-oriented, did not seem to have the financial, administrative, or leadership powers required to deal with the effects of the Depression, which fell most heavily on urban areas. And the centralization of power that occurred under Roosevelt, and later Johnson, *did* significantly change U.S. politics, for a while at least, making "the White House, not the State House . . . the fountainhead of ideas, the initiator of action, the representative of the national interest."[5]

Transfers and Politics

The power to implement and administer programs, it must be noted, carries with it not only a degree of control over major policy dimensions—the nature of provisions, the bases of allocations, and the systems of service delivery—but also political power. The transfer of program funds confers the ability to dispense benefits to a constituency, to hire and appoint staff, and to award contracts. Apart from programmatic choices, therefore, the transfer of funds among governmental units represents the exchange of important political resources.

The Great Society, revenue sharing, and block grants all illustrate how political coalitions are a consideration in transfers. Both the War on Poverty and Model Cities, directed at urban areas, enhanced big-city mayors and their constituencies. In the War on Poverty, particularly its Community Action component, the system of transfer reflected the desires of the Democratic Party to link itself with newly developing voting blocks in the cities, particularly with minority groups. Model Cities, a variation on this theme, pushed the development of new coalitions between low-income and minority residents and city hall.

Revenue sharing and block grants, although not ignoring cities, usually had little in the way of a special urban emphasis. The term *general revenue sharing* refers to arrangements where the federal government makes grants to lower units of government with virtually no strings attached, whereas block grants are federal aid programs that place only limited conditions on recipient units. The development of both kinds of programs during and after the Nixon era offers another example of how the system of transfer reflects political coalitions.

Since the 1970s, decentralization has been a clear political priority of Republican national administrations. The Republicans inherited a vast conglomeration of categorical programs from their Democratic Great Society predecessors. Because these programs were established in law, tradition, and experience and were supported by an elaborate organizational and institutional apparatus, the Republicans had to live with them temporarily while attempting to contain and modify them with an eye to their reduction, and, at least in some cases, their ultimate elimination. Low-income and minority groups in urban areas did not represent a major segment of the Republican constituency. State governments were more likely to reflect Republican interests and to represent important parts of the Republican constituency. Therefore, transferring power to the states was of greater interest to Republicans than to Democrats.

CAPSULE 8.3 • *The New Division of Labor*

The feds have the money,
The states have the power,
And the localities have the problems.

—Contemporary Aphorism

Transfers and Policy Analysis

Although political considerations may influence choices concerning the governmental units to which funds will be given, some degree of scientific analysis also enters into these decisions. That is, technically, there are some identifiable characteristics that can be utilized in selecting the unit most appropriate to receive funds. These characteristics include the degree of expertise and resources required to administer a program, the appropriate governmental size given the substantive nature of the program, and the nature of the problem for which a programmatic solution is being sought. However, application of these technical considerations requires the utmost care and scrutiny. Often, for each logical reason given to vest a program in one unit ("They will be more efficient" is one example) another equally compelling reason can be found to vest it in another unit ("They are more committed to the policy goals," or "They are closer to the problem").

Daniel Patrick Moynihan's observations on a report by the Task Force on Jurisdiction and Structure of the State Study Commission for New York City illustrate how technical considerations apply to the allocation of program responsibility. Regarding the allocation of services, the Task Force suggested that rat control services be a central function, whereas service centers to provide information on poison control should be a local responsibility. In both cases, Moynihan argued the reverse arrangements to be technically superior. As for rat control services, he noted,

> Given stable food and harborage, the model urban rat lives and dies in an area extending at most a few hundred feet. . . . [T]he urban rat is preeminently a neighborhood type, preferring when possible, never even to cross the street. As for rodent control, opinion is universal (as best I know) that the fundamental issue is how humanoids maintain their immediate surroundings. I cannot conceive a municipal service more suited to local control, nor one which more immediately calls on those qualities of citizenship which the Task Force describes as constituting in some degree a "quasi-governmental responsibility" toward the community. It comes down, alas, to the question of keeping lids on garbage cans. What better issue for Neighborhood Service Representatives to take up?[6]

On the other hand, poison control centers provide services that require great knowledge about the chemical nature of different substances that people might ingest as well as possible antidotes in cases where the chemicals are poisonous. Quick access by day or night to a tremendous bank of information is required. In light of these requirements, Moynihan suggested,

> At the very least it should be a city function, although a good case could be made for making it regional, or perhaps national: one telephone number anywhere in the nation, putting the doctor through to a laboratory/computer facility that would provide the information fastest. The idea that such a function could be broken down into thirty to thirty-five separate centers, in New York City alone, each to be manned day and night is . . . not persuasive.[7]

Finally, a major consideration in the flow of funds is whether lesser jurisdictions should operate programs for which they have no financial responsibility. Here, the issue is how careful a unit will be in spending funds that it does not have to raise, and whether it will act in the financial interests of the granting authority. For example, one general critique of current Medicaid financing is that the federal government gives almost a blank check to the states by paying for a program in which the basic determinants of costs—the number of recipients and the type and level of benefits—are decentralized.

How Transfers Are Conditioned

Conservatives favor localism in the allocation of government funds. This is the heart of the devolutionary strategy that has dominated federal domestic policy since the 1980s. For conservatives, it is the states and localities that should have primary responsibilities for directing and administering social programs, not "big government" in Washington.

Devolution—in theory and in practice—is a reaction to the centralizing trend of earlier grant-in-aid policy. Beginning in the 1930s, the focus of federal aid moved increasingly toward establishing national standards in the provision of income support and social services. In the 1960s, the Great Society established a nationally directed urban-focused system of social welfare provisions that utilized grant funds as primary instruments for social reform. Great Society programs not only expanded the total sum of grant aid available, they also ushered in new goals and procedures that significantly altered the character and balance of intergovernmental relations.

In terms of ultimate purpose, the programs of the 1960s sought to guarantee minimum levels of opportunity and well-being throughout the nation. Comprehensive (if not precise) statements of national welfare goals were incorporated in a framework of grant-funded services for the disadvantaged, especially the urban disadvantaged. Although the Great Society recognized the importance of utilizing community organizations as program partners in the planning and delivery of services, these new programs incorporated extensive and detailed federal regulations and substantial program monitoring and oversight.

The ideology underpinning the aid transfer programs of the Great Society generation was decidedly centralist. Program direction as well as program finance shifted to Washington. The nation's obligation to eliminate poverty was asserted. Administrative procedures were formulated to ensure that national purposes were properly carried out. Presidents Kennedy and Johnson both knew how very easily social programs could sway off target when carried out by states and localities that were not fully committed to social objectives. Memories of Jim Crow and anti-urban policy biases were still fresh in the minds of Washington policymakers. Grant policies were therefore carefully formulated to ensure that benefits were effectively routed to the needy. Controls and guidelines were highly detailed.

By the mid- to late 1970s, the Great Society era had run its course. Although the programs it spawned were maintained, for the most part their underlying spirit, along with their substantial reliance on federal leadership, faded away. Confronted with a series of major managerial problems and a new farther-to-the-right philosophical *zeitgeist*, federal policies acquired a different face. Federal control and program expansion were replaced by "devolution, disengagement, and decremental budgeting."[8] The Great Society was replaced by the New Federalism.

The New Federalism of Richard Nixon and Ronald Reagan initiated a transfer system that was far more heavily reliant on states and localities. Whereas Great Society programs expressly advanced specific national purposes, New Federalism grants were formulated as a means of helping state and local government accomplish *their* objectives. Federal interventionism was abdicated in favor of decentralized policymaking. Federal spending, federal control, and federal regulation were all sharply reduced.

The contrast between Great Society centralization and New Federalism devolution can be clearly seen in the basic components of the intergovernmental transfer of funds. Financial transfers, whatever their philosophical rationale, always impose a set of reciprocal relationships—aid is never provided without conditions. The conditions that are required—often called "strings" or "controls"—govern how the aid can and cannot be used.

There are four fundamental types of federal aid conditions: *program conditions*, which define the purpose of the grant; *financial conditions*, which govern the dollar-matching arrangements; *beneficiary conditions*, which determine who is eligible to be assisted; and *procedural conditions*, which specify planning, administrative, and reporting procedures. In each area, the character of grant policy has changed markedly over the past thirty-five years as the respective roles of federal, state, and local governments have been redefined.

Program Conditions

Federal aid laws generally specify the kinds of activities they are intended to support. We therefore have grants for nutrition, mental health, runaway centers, drug and alcohol abuse, special education, homelessness, foster care, medical care, cash support for the poor, and so on. Historically, the great majority of grant-in-aid programs have been defined rather narrowly, which is why they are often referred to as *categorical* (i.e., targeted on specific issues or population groups). Despite the recent emphasis on program flexibility, the overwhelming majority of all federal aid programs remain categorically specific.

Programs are categorical when their basic purposes are specified in detail. Categorical grants specify *who* is to be served, *what* benefits they are to receive, and *how* the delivery system is to be organized. For this reason, AFDC was frequently identified as the prototype categorical program, although the term applied to many others. Categorical programs may specify any number of conditions, including requirements regarding certification and licensing of personnel, how recipients are to be interviewed, and appeals machinery to handle client complaints. Categorical funding ensures that the unit of government providing revenue substantially controls its expenditure.

Since the Great Society, the federal aid system has become somewhat less categorical. This shift is in keeping with the conservative critique of the welfare state, which supports a reduction in the scope of big government. For conservatives, big government, especially centralized government, threatens democracy and efficiency because basic decisions are made in Washington rather than in local communities where, it is said, the problems "actually are." For devolutionists, categorical aid is wasteful, supporting programs in which there is no compelling national interest, and creating excessive red tape, paperwork, and regulation.

One major objection to the categorical system has been managerial: the great number of specific programs are often difficult to administer effectively at the local level. It has been said that, although individual programs make individual sense, the aggregate of programs produce administrative overload. Each program is usually separately administered. Coordination is absent. In many cases, mayors or governors may not even be aware of all the programs serving their jurisdiction. When they are aware, they often find themselves powerless to make the system work as a whole.

To deal with these concerns, Republican presidents since the 1970s have sought to *decategorize* federal aid. When Ronald Reagan took office in 1981, a major plank in his domestic platform was to consolidate multiple, detailed, categorical grants into a limited number of broadly formulated "block" grants. Though many of Reagan's proposals weren't accepted by the Congress, seventy-seven categorical grants-in-aid were collapsed into nine block grants in 1981. For example, ten separate grants that addressed alcohol, drug abuse, and mental health problems were combined into one new block grant, streamlining administration, reducing paperwork, and giving the states increased discretion to define programs as they chose.

These new block grants defined goals broadly, giving local officials significant discretion within functional areas such as community development, employment and training, and social services. Although the federal government continues to provide some general direction on spending, recipients have considerable leeway in specifying program priorities as well as administrative and service-delivery arrangements. These features, of course, marked a significant retreat in federal intervention, with a commensurate increase in the role of states and localities.

Under Title XX, for example, about $1.7 billion a year in federal money is currently available to the states for "social services." Title XX is a block grant because these services aren't defined in programmatic terms. Instead of specifying money for family planning, homemaker services, marital counseling, daycare, child abuse prevention, or any other specific activity, Congress simply requires priorities to be set by the states. Similarly, the Community Development Block Grant provides support for "community development," a term that can encompass anything from street repair to daycare services to low-interest facility loans for neighborhood nonprofits.

A more radical devolutionary reform—but one not nearly as successful as block grants—was General Revenue Sharing (GRS). Initiated in 1972, GRS constituted a major break with the categorical tradition in that it provided, for the first time, federal aid without any specification of program priority. In other words, revenue sharing was unconditional with regard to function. Depending on their preferences, localities or states could develop new programs, use the money for tax relief, or build new facilities. If they decided to develop new programs or expand old ones, they could invest in health, recreation, police, sanitation, or code enforcement. For over a decade, GRS provided more than $6 billion a year—one-third to the states, two-thirds to local authorities—for their unhampered use.

The program, despite its appeal to conservatives, was abolished in 1987, as part of the effort to trim the federal deficit. This is rather ironic, given the Reagan administration's commitment to "returning power to the people," but it indicates the political vulnerability of grants that lack a clear program and client focus. GRS was extremely popular among state and local elected officials. It was, after all, money for nothing, grant aid for free. But revenue sharing was never terribly appealing in Washington.

While "decentralization" has been a defining characteristic of conservative social policy, it remains the case that in several important policy areas, catergorial specification remains as powerful as ever. In child welfare policy, despite several abortive efforts to block grant federal aid, national accountability standards have become stronger over time. The increase in child welfare funding since 1997, for example, has been accompanied by new federal mandates regarding permanency planning, child safety, program monitoring, and outcome accountability. In this last regard, the federal government now requires states to provide detailed information concerning child and family outcomes as part of its periodic Child and Family Services Reviews. Other recent child welfare legislation requires states to provide services such as education, housing, Medicaid coverage, and training support for "aging out" 18- to 21-year-old youth.

Financial Conditions

The second major type of federal control relates to financing. In general, aid recipients must be willing to put up what is called a "local match." That is, states and localities must be willing to pay a share of program costs if they desire federal aid.

Matching serves a variety of purposes. For one thing, it reduces the cost burden on the providing unit. Equally important, matching helps to ensure cooperation and efficient program management. A state or locality putting up its own resources is more likely to take its administrative responsibilities seriously than when simply using somebody else's funds.

Matching is also used to influence policymaking. Federal funds offer an important "carrot" by providing incentives for state and local involvement in particular programs. Because states and localities, through long periods of U.S. history, were reluctant to take on social responsibilities, federal aid was one of the major tools available to Washington to promote social welfare initiatives. States and localities are less likely to move into new areas of activity if they must pay the entire cost for such programs. But federal aid in the form of 50-percent, 75-percent, or even 100-percent grants may be difficult to turn down. The offer of ten federal dollars for just one raised locally is very enticing.

Different cost-sharing formulas apply to federal aid programs. In most cases, especially in the older categorical programs, the state/local share ranges from 10 to 50 percent. Under the Maternal and Child Health Act, for example, states contribute $3 for every $4 they receive from the federal government.

Over time, however, state and local contributions have been diminishing. In the 1960s, to ensure state and local participation in new social efforts, the federal government "sweetened the pot," offering higher and higher payment shares. The War on Poverty, for example, was 90 percent federal, 10 percent local. Public housing and

TABLE 8.2 *Mode of Finance: Systems of Transfer*

Funding Arrangements	Specification of Purpose	Role of States/Localities
Categorical grants	Specified narrowly	Strictly implementing federal policies and procedures
Block grants	Specified broadly	Establishing and implementing policy within a given functional area
General Revenue Sharing	Unspecified	Independent policymakers

Elementary and Secondary Education Act Title I grants were 100 percent federal, with recipient governments required to pay only the administrative costs. Food stamps operated the same way. Had Congress demanded more, full national coverage could not have been achieved, given the reluctance of many jurisdictions to contribute even small amounts to social programs.

The trend to minimize the local share continued under the New Federalism. GRS required no local share—it was "free" money. Block grants, for the most part, are the same. Title XX initially required a 25 percent state match, but that was eliminated in 1981. Most block grants currently operating require no state or local funds.

Beneficiary Conditions

A third area of federal control concerns the definition of the beneficiary. Federal aid is often conditioned both with respect to the units of government and the individuals who are eligible funding recipients. Both conditions are often described in terms of targeting.

The simplest way to distribute federal aid among the states is proportionally, strictly in terms of population. Title XX Social Services operate this way. California, with about 13 percent of the national population, gets about 13 percent of the available funds. Every other state also gets funds proportional to its population. Clearly, there is no targeting in this procedure, no special effort to focus help on those states with the greatest needs for services.

When the federal government desires to target aid to reflect need, it utilizes allocation formulas based on various social indicators. HUD housing grants, for example, frequently focus on municipalities with the worst housing stock. Education aid, such as No Child Left Behind, provides support to "districts serving areas with substantial concentrations of children from low-income families." Other programs concentrate on jurisdictions with high poverty, high unemployment, or low per capita incomes.

Targeting not only focuses aid on particular jurisdictions, it also sets conditions with respect to particular populations groups. Many federal programs, for example, require means tests to determine client eligibility. Public assistance programs, by definition, are targeted on the poor. Other federal aid programs, such as Food Stamps, are "assistance linked," meaning that eligibility is may be restricted to individuals eligible for various welfare programs.

The State Child Health Insurance Program (SCHIP) has been particulary controversial in this regard. Originally intended to supplement Medicaid for children slightly above the poverty line, amendments over the years extended eligibility considerably up the income ladder, a phenomenon sometimes referred to as "eligibility creep."

Procedural Conditions

In addition to financial, program, and beneficiary conditions, aid legislation frequently contains a variety of *procedural* conditions relating to planning, personnel, reporting, contracting out, client rights, and the like. Some of these standards are "cross-cutting," meaning that they apply to all aid programs. All programs, for example, prohibit discrimination in hiring personnel and allocating benefits to clients. These civil rights requirements were expanded in the 1970s and 1980s to prohibit discrimination against, among other groups, racial and ethnic minorities, language minorities, women, the disabled, and the aged. Other cross-cutting requirements exist for environmental protection, labor standards, merit personnel systems, and disclosure of information to the public.

Many conditions, however, apply only to specific programs. Some, for example, require citizen participation—the Community Action Programs of the 1960s, for example, mandated "maximum feasible participation" of the poor in formulating and running antipoverty programs. Under Model Cities, municipalities had to undertake a "comprehensive" planning process that involved community residents and public officials in producing detailed analyses of community needs and in describing one- and five-year plans of action. The McKinney Homeless Assistance legislation requires jurisdictions to submit comprehensive homeless-assistance plans that include statements of need, inventories of existing services and facilities, and remediation strategies that take account of the needs of the homeless mentally ill, families with children, the elderly, and veterans.[9]

Some grants require procedures to ensure that funded activities are coordinated with related programs. Others call for appeal procedures for applicants who are denied benefits, for strict confidentiality standards, or for hiring employees with particular kinds of education. No Child Left Behind, for example, requires that all teachers be "highly qualified, while community mental health legislation, for many years, only permitted psychiatrists to head up clinical programs. In the early years of federal child welfare, the federal government strongly promoted the use of social work professionals. A similar emphasis was incorporated within the federal social services legislation of the early 1960s.

There is a large and varied body of regulation governing recordkeeping and program reporting. The federal government generally specifies report standards concerning expenditures and clientele. These demands may be relaxed or they may be rigorous. Probably no other grant condition excites more disquiet and resentment than these accountablity requirements. Detailed report forms submitted in "octuplicate" on a monthly basis may often be a fact of bureaucratic life, but that hardly makes them palatable to state and local practitioners.

Devolving Public Welfare

David Ellwood described the 1996 welfare reform legislation as a compromise among four distinct strands of conservatism. *Work-oriented reformers*, emphasizing the critical importance of jobs, sought to build on earlier welfare legislation by strengthening work requirements and supportive services. *Ideological critics*, seeing dependency and immorality resulting from misguided government programs, emphasized the importance of behavioral incentives—ending support for teen motherhood and out-of-wedlock births while encouraging school attendance, sexual responsibility, and other positive behaviors. *Budget cutters*, the third group of reformers, viewed the welfare problem as one of excessively generous support and therefore favored program cuts, time limits, and other measures to reduce spending. *Devolvers*, finally, saw the welfare problem in terms of excessive federal "command and control," with red tape and regulations impairing the ability of the states to create welfare solutions crafted to their own circumstances. For devolvers, welfare reform required sorting out federal and state roles, assigning to Washington resource allocation, broad oversight, and central information gathering, while making the states responsible for programmatic substance.[10]

Several of these themes have already been discussed: the conservative critique of public welfare in Chapter 1, the "perverse incentives" of income transfers in Chapter 4, and the role of services as an alternative to cash support in Chapter 5. The devolution theme, however, the centerpiece of the 1996 welfare enactment, needs some elaboration.

Welfare reform, that is, the Personal Responsibility and Work Opportunity Reconciliation Act of 1996 (PRWORA), as amended in 2006, addressed a range of low-income programs, from food stamps and daycare to child welfare, Title XX, and cash assistance to poor families with children. Its most dramatic element, Title I, transformed AFDC into a new block grant, Temporary Assistance for Needy Families (TANF), providing the states broad powers to adopt welfare plans suited to their own circumstances. While far from eliminating federal influence over the welfare system, TANF incorporates a sweeping decentralization of authority.

In some respects, the "devolution revolution" of 1996 was hardly a radical departure from previous arrangements. AFDC, for example, had *always* followed a markedly decentralist orientation. As a grant-in-aid program, it was based on state action. States were never compelled to participate. If they did, they retained broad power over benefit levels and eligibility. The federal role wasn't inconsequential but it was largely that of financier: AFDC committed the national government to match state spending for programs the states devised and operated. Federal requirements, of course, typically accompany federal funds, and the original 1935 Act specified at least a dozen stipulations.

Through the mid-1960s, AFDC resembled the program enacted by the Congress in 1935: states were in command, setting fundamental rules with minimal federal oversight. But under Lyndon Johnson's Great Society, and for nearly twenty-five years thereafter, AFDC came to incorporate an increasingly large number of federal conditions reflecting an evolving national sense of what constituted proper welfare policy.

This activist welfarism was expressed in detailed federal stipulations on a broad number of subjects. A series of reforms made welfare fairer and simpler, reducing bureaucratic impediments to assistance for those who were eligible, and protecting the due process rights of clients. Other stipulations sought to promote work. To reduce the work disincentives built into AFDC, for example, federal reforms in 1967 created the "$30 and one-third" rule requiring states to allow recipients to keep their initial $30 in monthly earnings, and one-third of remaining earnings, before their AFDC allotments were reduced.[11] Stipulations enacted in the 1980s broadened eligibility, requiring states to provide benefits to needy two-parent families and mandating transitional childcare and Medicaid subsidies for families who had worked their way off welfare.

At the same time, however, there were important devolutionary actions. Federal regulations were somewhat loosened in the 1980s, in keeping with the general tenor of the New Federalism, and a wide range of state welfare experiments were initiated after the 1988 Family Support Act liberalized the Section 1115 waiver program. By the time AFDC was repealed in 1996, forty-three states had been granted waivers from statutory regulations.

Welfare Reformed

In 1996, TANF replaced AFDC with a program far more responsive to state priorities. The federal TANF allocation—around $16 billion a year—is available for the states to use "in any manner reasonably calculated" (i.e., for any purpose that advances the general goals of the legislation). This provides states considerable discretion to organize their welfare programs in their own fashion. TANF funds, for example, can be spent on cash aid, emergency assistance, childcare, job training, or job subsidies. States, if they wish, can limit assistance to particular categories of poor families. They can prohibit cash payments to legal immigrants, or two-parent families, or families failing to meet certain procedural rules. Cash doesn't have to be provided at all—states, if they wish, can structure "assistance" in the form of vouchers, services, or other benefits that meet ongoing basic needs.

Assistance levels, in addition, can vary, just as they did under AFDC. But, different from the old system, states under TANF can impose "family caps," denying mothers additional benefits if they have children while on welfare, and they can also provide uniform benefit levels throughout the state ("statewideness") *or* match levels to the cost of living in a particular city or county, paying more, for example, in areas with high housing costs. They can transfer some TANF funds to other programs, such as Title XX. They can do away with at least some of the broad civil rights protections for reipients that were incorporated into federal welfare law in the 1960s and 1970s. And they can structure service delivery pretty much as they choose. Under AFDC, public assistance was for the most part publicly administered. With TANF, an array of new administrative options are available. Many states have privatized their job-training efforts and several rely on large commercial firms to manage their income-maintenance activities. Under TANF's "charitable choice" provision, moreover, church-affiliated groups are frequently utilized to provide social services.

In extending state control over eligibility, benefit levels, and benefit duration, TANF freed the states of long-standing federal mandates. Symbolizing the changed relationship between Washington and the states, TANF dramatically restricts federal administrative oversight. Although Congress specifies a number of functions for the federal Department of Health and Human Services (DHHS)—reviewing state plans and operations; monitoring state "maintenance of effort" levels; conducting research and analysis; providing technical assistance and information on "best practices"—it cut DHHS oversight staff by 75 percent, substantially reducing the capacity of federal officials to participate in meaningful program oversight.

Welfare reform, nevertheless, is far from the decentralized block grant ideal advanced by devolution purists. While TANF loosened some strings, it fashioned several new ones. As Table 8.3 indicates, TANF incorporates a rather significant array of moralistic "personal responsibility" messages—that it's wrong to have out-of-wedlock babies, that sexual abstinence is the best way to prevent pregnancy, that it's vitally important to work. Accordingly, TANF prohibits federal assistance to teen moms living

TABLE 8.3   *Federal Welfare Conditions, Then and Now*

	AFDC	**TANF**
System of Transfer	Categorical grant-in-aid	Block grants melding AFDC with JOBS and emergency assistance
Federal Funding	Entitlement: open-ended funding guaranteeing aid to poor families meeting state requirements	No entitlement: fixed annual funding
State Funding	State matching required	State maintenance of effort required
Beneficiaries	Mandated Inclusion: all families below state eligibility threshold must be served	Mandated exclusions: states must deny benefits to families not meeting job requirements and time limits; states can deny aid to other categories of poor families
Nature of Social Provision	Chiefly cash assistance	Cash, services, work-support subsidies
Service Delivery	Public agency delivery by state and/or local units	States can select public operations or contracting out
Time Limits?	No	Yes, 5-year lifetime limit, with 20-percent exemption for "hardship cases" (earlier at state option)
Work Requirements?	Yes. WIN and, later, JOBS require states to offer work-training programs	Yes. Work or "work activities" within 2 years or loss of assistance
Statewide Uniformity?	Yes. "Statewideness" required	No. State can vary benefit levels geographically, such as between high- and low-cost areas
Family Cap?	No	Yes
Fund Shifting?	No	Yes. 30 percent can be shifted to childcare and social services
Due Process Protections?	Yes. Client rights to "fair hearings" required	Maybe. Client rights specified in vague terms

CAPSULE 8.4 • *The TANF Contract*

Contracting with nongovernmental entities to provide TANF-funded services occurs in almost every state and exceeds $1.5 billion in federal TANF and state funds for 2001. This level of funding represents 13 percent of total federal and state TANF funds expended for services. About 88 percent of the total funds contracted are with nonprofit providers, which include national organizations, faith-based organizations, and community-based organizations. The most commonly contracted services include education and training, job placement, and support services to promote job entry or retention.

U.S. General Accounting Office, *Welfare Reform*, GAO-02-245, April 2002, 1.

separately from their parents or not attending school, as well as to individuals convicted of significant drug offenses. It also demands that states address out-of-wedlock pregnancies and statutory rape. And, most importantly, it conveys a clear message that welfare is not a right by imposing a sixty-month lifetime limit on federal assistance for most beneficiaries (permitting states to impose even stricter time limits) while compelling states to move a significant portion of their caseload into jobs or work programs.

Rather than eliminating federal controls, then, TANF signifies a marked shift in the *character* of regulation. Under six decades of AFDC, federal law generally served as a liberalizing influence, a vehicle for guaranteed, nonpunitive public aid. To protect the rights of vulnerable parents and children, standards for state conduct were established, and the more egregious and demeaning features of local welfare administration were outlawed. In 1962, for example, Congress prohibited state eligibility conditions that denied assistance to out-of-wedlock children, requiring instead that "illegitimacy" be addressed through services and rehabilitation. Later in the 1960s, Congress, prompted by the U.S. Supreme Court, prohibited unannounced "midnight raids," bed and closet checks to see if the "man-in-the-house rule" was being violated.

Under the new welfare, federal regulations have morphed from the protective to the punitive, from an emphasis on rights to one on responsibilities. Rather than mandating an inclusive rights-based eligibility, TANF is characterized by exclusions and limits. Rather than advancing guarantees, federal funds are denied to several classes of the poor, with the states invited to establish their own restrictions.

Terminating the Guarantee

The most important federal guarantee was the pledge to contribute to the financial support of all eligible parents and children in poverty. For sixty-one years AFDC, and ADC before it, provided a modest income safety net by ensuring open-ended matching grants to the states. No limits were placed on the size of the federal allotment; states determined how much of their own money to spend and the federal government automatically contributed its matching share. The portion paid by Washington varied. In AFDC's last year—fiscal year 1996—it ranged from 50 percent for the highest per capita income states, like Connecticut, to 78 percent for the poorest states, like Mississippi.

This guarantee of open-ended matching made AFDC a federal entitlement—all families meeting state eligibility criteria had a statutory right to assistance. The entitlement, although modest, was important. It never covered all the poor, only those deemed income eligible by the states. And it never carried with it standards for minimum benefits—assistance levels were rarely sufficient to remove recipients from poverty. The guarantee of federal matching, nevertheless, ensured a safety net of material support. Families stranded by the economy, a lack of ability, or just bad luck had a right to aid. Matching also powerfully encouraged state spending because the more the state put in, the more Uncle Sam contributed. Finally, the open-ended character of the grant was responsive to changing conditions. In prosperous times, caseloads could be reduced and AFDC funding (federal and state) dropped. In recessions, caseloads could be increased and, with them, AFDC funding.

In ending the federal entitlement, TANF subordinated assistance to the availability of funds. Rather than matching state spending, the federal government provides a fixed annual sum. Unconnected to state spending—and to changing levels of need—this allotment has generally been adequate, but it could result in benefit rationing in hard times. When more families meet the state need standard than are budgeted for, assistance could be reduced, or denied.

The end of the cash entitlement removed the assurance of a reliable public aid safety net. State policymakers, given unprecedented authority to design their own antipoverty programs, may well sponsor effective and humane welfare interventions. Without federal standards, however, and without a right to assistance, it is equally likely that they may cut benefit levels and narrow eligibility, especially in periods of economic downtown.

Time Limits

While welfare reform imposes a five-year lifetime limit on federal assistance, it permits states to set even lower limits, and nearly half have embraced this authority. Idaho, for example, cuts off aid after just twenty-four months. Some states have also set time limits on *continuous* benefits, placing a maximum (two years is common) limit on any single welfare stay.

To date, the consequences of time restrictions have been limited. In 2003, the first year in which an appreciable number of cases reached their fifth year, less than 1 percent were closed. Some states have simply continued aid using their own funds, either granting exemptions or extending the limit period.[12] New York State, for example, provides a constitutional guarantee that obligates local governments to help all the needy, irrespective of how long they have been on assistance. Other states exempt a portion of welfare families based on hardship. Under federal TANF provisions, states can provide up to 20 percent of their caseloads a "hardship exemption," undefined in the law but illustrated by the so-called "family violence option," designating victims of domestic violence for special consideration.

As one might imagine, selecting the groups eligible for the hardship exemption has engendered considerable controversy. In the years following the enactment of welfare reform, advocates representing needy groups around the country mobilized to protect their constituencies. Perhaps the most active groups were, in fact, advocates for

CAPSULE 8.5 • *Hardship Competition*

The charter buses from New York City rumbled into Albany this week, carrying hundreds of advocates for the poor and disabled. Counselors for battered women and AIDS patients sat side by side, united in their opposition to Gov. George E. Pataki's welfare-overhaul plan. But when the lobbying began, long-time allies became reluctant rivals as they urged legislators to spare their constituents from welfare cuts.

The new Federal law that imposes a five-year limit on public assistance allows states to exempt 20 percent of welfare families from that limit. And as legislators weigh the merits of each group, advocates for battered women, advocates for foster parents and advocates for those infected with H.I.V., among others, find themselves competing for consideration. In their view, they are sparring for space aboard a metaphorical lifeboat, battling over who will survive (and keep welfare benefits) and who will perish (and lose them).

"Welfare reform hurts all of us," said Lisa Cortes, the outreach coordinator for the Boriken Neighborhood Health Center in East Harlem, who helped organize the group trip to Albany on Tuesday. "But you can't help but think, 'Who is going to be saved?'"

With so few seats, the lifeboat is likely to fill up fast. Advocates for battered women, for instance, say that victims of domestic violence are the heads of about 30 percent of all welfare families and could easily consume the coveted exemption slots. Advocates for AIDS patients say that 20 percent of welfare recipients may be H.I.V. positive. Advocates for foster parents, on the other hand, say the number of foster parents caring for toddlers or children with disabilities is so small—fewer than 7,000 families—that no one would be hurt by their inclusion.

domestic violence victims. They argued that public assistance was indispensable for abused mothers, since welfare support provided perhaps the single alternative to victimization by a violent boyfriend or husband. Other groups made their own compelling arguments. Those representing moms with AIDS/HIV, and other chronic disabilities, argued that those conditions often made work impossible, requiring lengthier support. Grandparents caring for grandchildren constituted another group seeking hardship exceptions, since they were often elderly, ill, and unable to work.

Nearly all the states now permit various group exemptions. Thirty-three states have adopted the family violence option exempting abuse victims.[13] Other states exempt adults with disabilities, parents with very young childen, and family heads facing special childcare or transportation needs. Just one state—Wisconsin—prohibits all exemptions, operating on the assumption that *every* welfare recipient should be able to get a job within five years.[14]

Race to the Bottom?

Welfare reform critics originally hypothesized that the structure of the block grant would lead to lowered assistance levels and a denial of help to those families least likely to be able to support themselves. They predicted that the disentitlement of welfare would subject public assistance to competitive cycles of state budget politics, resulting in a significant erosion in welfare spending over time. Public assistance legislation is high-cost, politically unpopular legislation, and the taxes necessary to support it put generous, liberally minded states at a disadvantage. High benefits mean high taxes, which not only produce dissatisfaction among residents but can scare off potential new sources of revenue—industries, new businesses, new residents. What's worse, liberal benefits may serve as a "welfare magnet," attracting poor people from less generous areas.[15]

The old welfare system was explicitly designed to counter the tendency to minimize benefits since states knew that their own AFDC investments would elicit generous federal matching. Mississippi, for example, received more than four dollars in federal AFDC support for every dollar it put up. This provided a significant incentive—some might say "bribe"—for poorer states to maintain at least minimum welfare levels.

Under TANF, however, this incentive has diminished since states are only required to maintain a level of spending equal to their own FY 1994 AFDC budget. And while states are required to maintain their own financial participation, provisions scarcely guard against limiting benefit and service levels or narrowing eligibility.

The "race to the bottom" hypothesis—states competing with one another to avoid welfare costs—remains largely unconfirmed. Up until the crisis beginning in 2008, there was scant evidence of significant cutbacks. Benefit levels increased in the years immediately following TANF's enactment in 1996, leveled off around 2000, and have been relatively stable ever since, although they have not kept up with the cost of living. Payments, however, as under AFDC, still vary significantly from state to state, from a low of $170 a month for a single-parent familty of three in Mississippi to a high of $923 in Alaska.[16]

Cash payment levels, however, provide just one measure of a state's generosity, or lack of it. Under AFDC, welfare, by and large, *was* the monthly cash benefit. But under TANF, states employ their spending for a multitude of antipoverty purposes—many not targeted specifically on welfare recipients at all. Some states, for example, have invested in wage supplements through a state version of the Earned Income Tax Credit in order to increase salaries for low-wage earners. Others, such as New York, have created public jobs. Still others have expanded daycare, transportation, counseling, and job training. As we noted in Chapter 5, welfare spending has shifted markedly from cash to kind (See Figure 8.1).

Welfare to Work

In addition to enforcing time limits, states are required to engage a significant portion of their TANF recipients in work or work-related activities. While the welfare system has long been oriented to jobs, the earlier emphasis was primarily on developing "human capital" (i.e., promoting job training, education, counseling, and financial incentives encouraging employment). Even the JOBS program, the centerpiece of the 1988 reform law, identified its primary goal as reducing "barriers to employment," that is, providing basic education and employment skills.

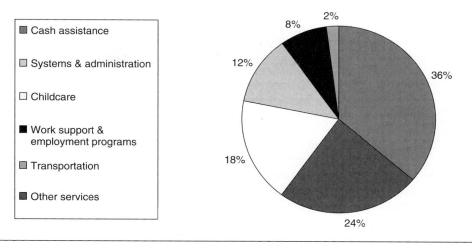

FIGURE 8.1 *TANF Spending, Fiscal Year 2004.*

Welfare reform, on the other hand, incorporates powerful "work first" requirements that emphasize full-time jobs rather than job preparation. Although states have considerable freedom in determining the nature of their work requirements, federal law provides strong incentives for aggressively moving people into jobs. TANF, for example, defines strict employment goals. Each state must ensure that a rising proportion of aid recipients work, with family heads having to work within two years of going on assistance. If states fail to transition clients from welfare to work, federal financial penalties are imposed.

States have initiated a diverse array of employment strategies. A significant set of services and cash incentives, on the one hand, serve as "carrots," pulling clients into job seeking, job taking, and job holding, while coercive penalties, the "sticks," push nonworkers off the rolls.

On the penalty side, welfare reform incorporates some very coercive social policies. Strict time limits, most obviously, send a clear message—"if you don't work, don't count on support." In addition, states have stiffened their welfare rules. While public welfare has never been very "user friendly," new procedures serve both to divert applicants from *seeking* aid and from *remaining* on aid. Welfare "sanctions," such as aid cutoffs or reductions, for example, are frequently applied even for minor infractions of the rules. And many agencies make every effort to place myriad barriers before the applicant seeking aid. Karen Houppert describes one dramatic example at a New York City TANF Job Center:

> Applicants are commonly misinformed. When they first arrive at a job center, receptionists routinely tell them that there is no more welfare, that this office exists solely to see that they get a job, that if they miss any appointments their application will be denied, that emergency food stamps and cash grants don't exist, that there is a time limit on benefits—without explaining that they can apply for Medicaid or food stamps.

Receptionists also tell people who arrive after 9:30 a.m. that they must return another day. If they aren't already deterred, applicants are given a five-page preliminary form to fill out. They must return the next day to get an application. They are fingerprinted, undergo several interviews and are then directed to meet with a financial planner and an employment planner. The financial planner tries to deter people from applying by directing them to churches, charities, and food pantries. At various stages, applicants are orally denied benefits or told they are not eligible to apply, but they receive no written notice of denial or their right to appeal the decision.[17]

While states frequently rely on penalties to induce compliance with their work-first priorities, many also embrace a variety of work incentives. Special financial arrangements, for example, serve to make work as enticing as possible. One of the most common, the earned income "disregard," permits clients to keep a portion of their wages without having their welfare allotment reduced. All the states but one—Wisconsin—protect a portion of client earnings, with around half adopting disregards of 50 percent or more. Over a dozen states permit families to retain up to $1000 in earnings per month before losing TANF payments. These disregards, coupled with the Earned Income Tax Credit, and, often, daycare and transportation assistance, make paid employment far more financially attractive than in the past.

Many states, in addition, have strengthened the role of welfare workers, transforming them from eligibility clerks to job counselors who are able to focus on clients individually, designing strategies to match them with jobs in the community, arranging necessary job supports (Medicaid, food stamps, childcare, transportation), following up to make sure they develop "traction" in their new jobs, and, in some cases, facilitating client, and former client, self-help groups to share job-hunting and job-keeping experiences.

As noted, states are increasinly investing their TANF resources on a multitude of antipoverty purposes beyond simple cash assistance. In 2004, considerably more was spent on social services than on cash aid, as Figure 8.1 indicates. Many states have expanded daycare, transportation, counseling, and job training, typically focusing on families facing the most severe barriers to work—those with low skills and little education, young teen mothers, ex-convicts, the physically or mentally disabled—groups frequently described as the "hard to employ." Substance abusers are a program priority in several states. Michigan, for example, launched a program in the late 1990s requiring welfare applicants to submit to drug tests. Individuals receiving aid were to be tested at random, with users required to get treatment or lose their grant. While this was soon decleared unconstitutional by the courts, other states, more sensitive to civil liberty concerns, administer drug use questionnaires to clients and applicants.

Individuals whose physical, cognitive, and psychological disabilities either prevent or substantially limit employment are also receiving special services in many states, since the disabled constitute a disproportionate segment of the least employable. A major study of welfare reform in Michigan, for example, found that over a quarter of all recipients met the *DSM* criteria for major depression, while 14 percent suffered a traumatic stress disorder, a diagnosis often related to domestic violence. Another 20 percent had health problems resulting in significant functional impairments.[18]

Those with very low levels of education, experience, language, and job skills constitute another target group in many states. A full 30 percent of welfare users have less than a high school education, and nearly a quarter are functionally illiterate. The lack of basic skills, even when the level of personal motivation is great, substantially restricts job opportunities. People with low skills, for example, often can't carry out necessary job-related tasks like understanding written instructions, filling out forms, reading bus schedules, or totaling a bill.[19]

A range of social safety net programs funded through programs other than TANF also assist the hard-to-employ. Daycare programs like Head Start, Title XX counseling services for groups like domestic violence victims, homeless services under the McKinney Act, AIDS-HIV services under the Ryan White Act, and occupational rehabilitation services, for example, are all necessary components of any strategy addressing the needs of families who, even in the best of economic times, have trouble being absorbed into the labor market. And job-training programs sponsored through the Department of Labor, while rather disappointing in their success over the years, are also critical for people with the fewest skills and the least-developed orientation to employment. Subsidized jobs can also be utilized as a step toward regular employment. In many states, TANF has developed a variety of linkages to these efforts and in some has tried to create integrated systems of assistance. Nevertheless, in a comprehensive review of existing programs, the Urban Institute recently concluded that comprehensive support systems rarely exist.[20]

The Responsibility Agenda

In Chapter 4, we discussed teen pregnancy and the assertion of welfare critics that traditional public aid encouraged illegitimacy. Welfare reform, building on this supposition, incorporated a number of features meant to promote personal responsibility among young people, especially in the areas of sexuality, childbearing, and child raising. Responding to the 1996 law, and its 2006 revisions, states have established a great number of programs aimed at reducing illegitimacy, fostering abstinence, increasing the involvement of fathers in the lives of their children, and promoting "healthy marriage."

"Family caps," a key element of the responsibility agenda, are limits on TANF eligibility designed to discourage welfare families from having additional children. Whereas AFDC required states to adjust the welfare grant to family size, increasing monthly payments as the number of children increased, states are now permitted to establish fixed benefit levels, regardless of family composition. While most states continue to vary benefits, twenty-one have instituted caps. Idaho, for example, created an assistance ceiling of $276 a month in 1998, with no allowance for family size. Wisconsin similarly implemented a "one size fits all" policy.

Whether family caps have succeeded in reducing welfare births isn't clear. Findings in one state, New Jersey, appear to show a decline in birthrates, although this seems to have been partially explained by an increase in abortions, a consequence particularly dismaying to social conservatives.[21]

TABLE 8.4 *Welfare Labs*

Michigan Family Independence Program. Michigan started experimenting with welfare reform in 1992. Its program requires recipients to participate in some combination of work, training, general education, and community service. Among the initiatives in the program are "license penalties"—fathers who don't pay their obligated child support can lose their drivers license and other professional licenses.

Illinois TANF. Unmarried mothers under 18 must live with their parents and be enrolled in school or they lose part of their grant. The "family cap" eliminates extra funding when families have additional children. Benefits can be obtained only if paternity is established within six months of birth.

Iowa Family Investment Program. Welfare recipients are encouraged to work and build up savings through "individual development accounts," from which they can make withdrawals only to start a business, buy a home, pursue education or job training, or take care of a family emergency.

Vermont Reach Up. Vermont, one of just a few states refusing to impose a lifetime limit on welfare support, describes its approach as a "kinder, gentler" form of welfare reform. While requiring single parents to work, the state provides a generous cash supplement to poor workers; it has also created its own nearly universal health care program for children. Most recipients must do community service after 2½ years of benefits. If a recipient is unable to secure a private-sector job, the state provides ten months of employment in a public or nonprofit organization.

Mississippi WorkFirst. WorkFirst requires welfare recipients to accept any job offered or else lose all benefits. Employers hiring welfare recipients are provided a TANF subsidy of $3.50 an hour, to which they must add $1.00 an hour. In this fashion, public assistance is turned into a wage subsidy program.

Wisconsin Works (W2). Touted by conservatives as a "welfare miracle," Wisconsin cut its welfare rolls by 80 percent through "diversion," a tough work program requiring nearly all recipients to work for their benefits on penalty (strictly enforced) of reduced (or eliminated) welfare checks. Wisconsin claims that 75 percent of those now off welfare have private jobs; critics argue that a major portion are poorer than ever, many in homeless shelters. Wisconsin has invested heavily in private support services including daycare, health care, wage supplements, and job training.

Wisconsin LearnFare. Wisconsin and several other states penalize TANF families whose minor children are not in school. The penalty is stiff—$50 per month per child. Children who are dropouts, habitual truants, or parents themselves can be exempted from the LearnFare requirement if they participate in case management activities.

New York City Work Experience Program. The nation's largest workfare program requires more than 30,000 residents monthly—10 percent of its welfare population—to don orange workfare vests to clean parks, empty lots, and city offices, to answer phone calls, and to otherwise assist public and non-profit agencies.

TANF Wyoming. One of the nation's most punitive welfare systems, Wyoming requires recipients to meet work requirements *before* their first welfare check either by job hunting, work-related training, or volunteering. As a result, the state has reduced the recipient caseload by 90 percent while substantially increasing employment among single mothers.

Florida Welfare Transition Program. Florida spends less than a third of its welfare allotment on cash grants. The rest goes to services like daycare and mental health treatment for families both on and off the welfare rolls. The maximum TANF grant is 17 percent of the federal poverty line.

Texas Works. The Texas program is largely controlled by twenty-eight local boards composed of local business leaders, educators, and social service workers. It follows a work first philosophy that seeks out quick placements in low-skill jobs rather than emphasizing training and education.

TABLE 8.4 *Continued*

Temporary Assistance for Families in Idaho. Idaho represents a punitive version of welfare reform. On TANF's enactment, the state required all AFDC clients to reapply for aid, immediately reducing its caseload by half. TAFI has a 24-month lifetime limit, with very few hardship exemptions; pays $309 per month, regardless of household size; and requires alcohol- and substance-abuse screening. Only families with incomes below 32 percent of the federal poverty level are eligible.

Other reform initiatives aim at discouraging teen childbearing. TANF, for example, restricts federal benefits to unwed teenage parents under 18 who do not live at home (or another "supervised setting") and attend school. States, at their discretion, can also deny minors all welfare benefits, an option few have exercised to date. TANF requires the U.S. Department of Justice to educate state and local law enforcement officials on the prevention and prosecution of statutory rape. And it provides special financial payments—"illegitimacy bonuses"—to the five states that decrease out-of-wedlock births the most, *without* increasing abortions.

While welfare reform's primary focus has been on single mothers and their children—nearly 90 percent of all adult welfare recipients are unmarried women—the responsibility agenda has also reached out to young men. A number of "fatherhood" programs, especially emphasized in the 2006 welfare reform renewal, have been

CAPSULE 8.6 • *Congress Just Says No*

To qualify for "abstinence-only education" funding under welfare reform's Adolescent Family Life Program, Congress requires that educational or motivational programs for youth have as their "exclusive purpose" the following content:

- Teaches the social, psychological, and health gains to be realized from abstaining from sexual activity.
- Teaches abstinence from sexual activity outside of marriage as the expected standard for all school-age children.
- Teaches that abstinence is the only certain way to avoid out-of-wedlock pregnancy, sexually transmitted diseases and other health problems.

- Teaches that a monogamous relationship in the context of marriage is the expected standard of human sexual activity.
- Teaches that sexual activity outside of marriage is likely to have harmful effects.
- Teaches that bearing children out-of-wedlock is likely to have harmful consequences.
- Teaches young people how to avoid sexual advances and how alcohol and drug use increases vulnerability to sexual advances.
- Teaches the importance of attaining self-sufficiency before engaging in sexual activity.

U.S. Department of Health and Human Services, Adolescent Family Life Program, Abstinence-Only Education Grant Guidelines, 1999.

implemented, some aimed at raising the incomes of noncustodial fathers, others at strengthening ties between dads and their children.

The law, for example, helps states to get absent fathers to pay their obligated child support by requiring welfare applicants to identity the father of all children seeking aid and strengthening efforts to collect court-ordered support. The law requires businesses to identify all new employees to the local child-support authorities so that delinquent parents can be located. Subsequent legislation, chiefly the Welfare-to-Work enactments of 1998, provides job services for noncustodial parents facing major "labor market disincentives," enabling states to establish training and counseling programs for absent fathers. Combined, these father-focused programs have contributed to an appreciable increase in the number of fathers involved with their children. States have had success not only in persuading unwed mothers to identify fathers at the time their children are born, but in confirming paternity from the fathers themselves. Since the mid-1990s, paternity statistics have almost tripled, helping both to ensure that fathers pay child support and to increase the likelihood of their staying in contact with their offspring.[22]

A third responsibility initiative, perhaps the most dramatic one in the law, was tucked away on page 501 of the original 502-page enactment. Promoted chiefly by social conservatives and the right-wing Heritage Foundation, it provided states $50 million annually for "abstinence only" programs emphasizing the "social, psychological, and health" benefits of abstinence along with the negative consequences of premarital sex. (See Capsule 8.6.) Within these rather narrow ideological parameters—comprehensive sex education is *verboten*—states have some latitude in program planning and service delivery. Most have delegated the administration of their abstinence programs to public schools, health departments, and church and other community organizations for activities that teach the importance of chastity, the perils of illegitimacy, and the sanctity of marriage. The program in North Carolina, for example, identifies "mutually faithful monogamous heterosexual relationships in the context of marriage" as the standard for responsible sex. Other states are sponsoring ad campaigns encouraging parents to talk to their children about sex, developing programs that promote self-esteem, and creating mentoring and counseling programs that teach good decision making and "refusal skills."

Given these generally narrow priorities, the denigration of single parenthood, and the refusal to incorporate any elements of the traditional public-health/safe-sex/contraceptive-counseling model of sex education, an increasing number of states have opted out of the progam. In 2007, fourteen states refused to accept abstinence dollars.[23]

Assessing the Evidence

Despite the rather large body of data that has accumulated concerning welfare reform, significant controversy remains concerning its operations, significance, and future. The most dramatic and publicized evidence to date—the startling reduction in caseloads—certainly substantiates one argument for success. Plunging caseloads, down more than half since 1996, reflect a genuine shift from welfare status to work status on the part of hundreds of thousands of household heads, a movement unaccompanied so far, at least, by increased homelessness or broken families, two major disasters originally prophesied by critics.

Given the failure of previous welfare initiatives to appreciably move recipients off the rolls, the remarkable welfare exodus of the last decade seems a decided affirmation of the view that a degree of coercion in enforcing a work obligation does change behavior, and attitudes as well. TANF clearly spurred large numbers of welfare moms to join the workforce. While a good portion of the initial reduction in the welfare rolls reflected the robust economy and soaring demand for labor that charcterized the boom years of the late 1990s, the sustained reduction in caseloads in the years since reflects other factors as well. Certainly, the clear "welfare to work" message has had an impact. But there is no doubt that other policy incentives enacted around the same time as TANF contributed greatly as well. Investigators such as Isabel Sawhill and Douglas Besharov, for example, have estimated that perhaps even more important than the economy in stimulating job seeking were the increases in the minimum wage, liberalized Earned Income Tax Credits, and TANF-supporting state-level enactments that reinforced the spirit of welfare reform.[24]

This combination of factors significantly impacted the job attitudes and the behaviors of family heads. The basic tenet of welfare reform—that poor people who make the effort will get jobs, jobs that put them on the road to escaping poverty—has been realized to an impressive degree. At least half the mothers who left the welfare roles between 1997 and 2007 have secured regular full-time jobs, earning incomes above the welfare level. Indeed, even the economic circumstances of those *remaining* on welfare has improved. According to the Urban Institute, the median income of families on public assistance—many of whom have at least some work income—rose to $11,820 in 2004, some four thousand dollars above the level of 1997.[25]

Looking at the broader picture, welfare reform has contributed significantly to the economic improvement of low-income families in general. Employment and wages among low-income single-mother families, for example, are significantly above what they were in in 1996. Ron Haskins of the Brookings Institution has pointed out

---

CAPSULE 8.7 • *TANF at 10*

- Cash assistance caseloads have been reduced by more than half.
- Employment rates among low-income parents have risen.
- Approximately 80 percent of those leaving welfare enter the workforce; job income averages about $8.50 per hour.
- Child poverty in black single-mother households has dropped significantly.
- Health insurance is rarely available to ex-recipients.

- The proportion of employed low-income single-parent families has increased.
- Those remaining on welfare typically face serious barriers to employment—and targeted, comprehensive, services are rarely available.
- Many who are eligible for welfare don't apply.

Sources: A Decade of Welfare Reform: Facts and Figures, The Urban Institute, June 2006; *Welfare Reform Turns Ten,* The Heritage Foundation, WebMemo No. 1183, August 1, 2006.

that the bottom fifth of all families with children saw their incomes increase by 35 percent in inflation-adjusted terms between 1991 and 2005. In 1991, furthermore, 30 percent of the income of that bottom fifth was composed of welfare payments; in 2005 the figure had dropped to 4 percent. Haskins attributes this remarkable change to the "explosion of work" engendered by welfare reform.[26]

General statistics, of couse, mask significant variations among families. A portion of those transitioning from welfare to work, for example, simply trade public assistance for low-wage, dead-end jobs. Many of the jobs secured by ex-welfare clients, roughly a third, are part time. And many of the available *full*-time jobs—clerks, cooks, fast-food, telephone sales reps, and the like—pay the minimum wage, or just above, and provide few benefits. Fewer than a third of employed ex-recipients, for example, are protected by health insurance—their employers don't provide it and they no longer are eligible for Medicaid.[27] New workers, in addition, are often burdened by significant job-related

---

CAPSULE 8.8 • *Welfare Critiques—Left and Right*

From the Left

One of the fundamental objecties of the twentieth-century welfare state was to make full citizens of everyone. . . . [T]he outcome would be a more cohesive society, with no category of person excluded or less "deserving." But the new, "discretionary" approach makes an individual's claim upon the collectivity once again contingent on good conduct. . . . Modern welfare reform thus returns us to the spirit of England's New Poor Law of 1834, which introduced the principle of least eligibility, whereby relief for the unemployed and indigent was to be inferior in quality and quantity to the lowest prevailing wages and conditions of employment. And above all, welfare reform reopens a distinction between active (or "deserving") citizens and others: those who, for whatever reason, are excluded from the active workforce.

From "The Wrecking Ball of Innovation" by Tony Judt, *The New York Times*, December 6, 2007. © 2007 The New York Times. All rights reserved. Used by permission and protected by the Copyright Laws of the United States. The printing, copying, redistribution, or retransmission of the Material without express written permission is prohibited. www.nytimes.com.

From the Right

Why is welfare reform a failure? While it did reduce caseloads . . . it also caused an explosion of child support. The overall birthrate is at record lows, while the proportion of all births to unmarried women increased to 35.8% in 2004, the highest ever recorded. . . . Poverty is a greater problem than ever for poor men because we placed the burden of the welfare state on them and criminalized their poverty if they cannot pay an arbitrary amount of "child support" that some bureaucrat decided they must pay. . . . We cannot call welfare reformed until marriage is restored as the social norm, in both poor and middle class families.

From "Is Welfare Reform Really a Success?" by David R. Usher, *Human Events Online*, September 5, 2006.

expenses for transportation, daycare, clothing, and meals. While they, and their children, may be happy to be off the dole, many remain close to destitution, churning through an uncertain job market, struggling with the routine hardships of utility and car insurance bills, rent, daycare, and the cost of family meals.

More generally, of course, poverty remains a significant problem in America for one-parent families, as well as for many single men and women. And there is some evidence that levels of *severe* destitution— "deep poverty" below half the poverty line—has increased. While welfare reform has had significant successes, and while companion public assistance programs like Food Stamps and Medicaid have significantly improved their coverage (as we described in Chapter 2), our welfare state remains deficient in confronting poverty and alleviating the challenges faced by our neediest citizens.

Emerging Issues: Immigrants, Social Policy, and the States

The status of immigrants in American society is another issue that has been vitally affected by welfare reform. Historically, the ambivalent attitudes that Americans hold toward immigrants have been reflected in social welfare policy, and in the way policy-making responsibilities around immigration issues have been divided in our federal system. For while *immigration policy*—policy governing the entry of foreigners into the United States—has always been the purview of the federal level of government, what might be called *immigrant policy*—policy that addresses the well-being of newcomers once in America—has come to reflect an inchoate mixture of local, state, and national, and also private agency, activities.

Federal immigration policies, since 1965 at least, have, on the whole, been inclusionary. The Immigration Act of 1965 repudiated a long-standing quota system based on national origins in favor of a relatively open door, and this resulted in a vast increase in the number of foreigners joining the American community. Assimilation, of course, is a complex process—one that is influenced by a myriad of economic, political, social, and cultural factors. Most evidence indicates, however, that assimilation generally proceeds rapidly. Immigrants learn English, get jobs, eat fast food, follow the mainline mass media, and absorb (and influence) the mass culture. Most of this occurs, of course, without specific legislative intervention. And until the last decade or so, immigrant policy—when it wasn't entirely overlooked—was more or less *ad hoc*. Unlike countries like Canada and Israel, countries with systematic national settlement policies for integrating and assimilating newcomers, the United States pretty much assumed that immigrants—who today compose nearly 15 percent of the population—would be able to take care of themselves. For this reason, Congress generally ignored critical social policy questions—including whether new immigrants should be treated the same, or differently, from *citizens* for purposes of service eligibility. Should immigrants, in other words, be excluded from some, or all, social welfare benefits until they are naturalized?

When immigrants *did* receive explicit federal attention, it was generally on a temporary basis. Some modest federal provisions were made, for example, for short-term resettlement assistance for special groups of refugees such as Cubans and Kosovars.

And English language education for children and adults has been promoted through federal aid. For the most part, though, the needs of immigrants have been left to their American sponsors (who have to sign financial responsibility statements), friends, family, voluntary agencies, and state and local governments.

Since the early 1990s, as the number of foreign-born residents has risen to historic highs—with nearly two-thirds not yet citizens—critics have been complaining that immigration has beccome excessive, and damaging to the country. Much of the criticism focuses on the newest arrivals with the fewest skills—immigrants, in particular, from developing countries such as Mexico, the Dominican Republic, the Philippines, Vietnam, and China. Undocumented immigrants have been a particular focus of concern. Some argue that immigrants, legal or not, take jobs away from Americans. Others feel that they impose heavy costs on government—especially on states and localities that have the responsibility for providing services. It has been argued further that many immigrants are taking advantage of the welfare system, even coming to the United States explicitly to get welfare benefits.

It is true, of course, that immigration, as in generations past, has had a major impact on the size and growth of America's poverty population. At present, more than one in five living in poverty reside in immigrant households, compared with less than 10 percent in 1979. Immigration, indeed, is one of the primary explanations for why the overall poverty rate has remained high in recent years, despite significant economic growth and reasonably low unemployment. Some immigrant groups, moreover, are especially likely to be impoverished. Immigrants from Mexico, the Caribbean, and Central America have relatively high poverty rates while those from Europe and Asia have low rates. And, as might be expected, immigrants who are newly arrived tend to be poorer as a group than those who are more established.[29] And while it is hazardous to generalize about welfare use, we do know that some groups of immigrants—refugees and the elderly, for example—have been heavy service users.

But focusing on welfare illustrates only a sliver of the immigrant experience. To the degree that broad statements can be made, most studies find that immigration has been more an economic blessing for the nation than a burden. Enthusiastic, hard-working, and enterprising newcomers bring powerful long-term economic benefits to the United States. They pay taxes, buy homes, serve in the military, and provide valuable resources for U.S. employers. While about 30 percent of all immigrants come to the United States with few skills or education, many more are technically trained and possess a wide array of advanced skills.[30]

Nevertheless, immigration continues to be a volatile public policy issue, with substantial political pressures to restrict immigrant access to welfare. One of the earliest, and most dramatic, manifestations of the public's discontent was the passage of California's Proposition 187 in 1994, which barred undocumented individuals from most public services. Another was the provisions limiting assistance for legal immigrants incorporated into the 1996 welfare reform bill. The devolution theme of welfare reform dramatically changed the way policies affecting immigrants were shaped.

Before welfare reform, immigrants were largely ignored in the welfare debate. No longer. The new law, reflecting the suspicion that immigrants were exploiting the welfare system, significantly reduced immigrant benefits while making state policymakers key players in determining the rules for eligibility and benefits. As Peter Schuck stated, "Congress sought to 'revalue' U.S. citizenship by adopting a firm national policy favoring discrimination against [immigrants] in the distribution of public benefits and by conscripting the states in the implementation of that new policy."[31] Immigrant policy, for the first time, distinguished nonrefugee immigrants into separate eligibility categories, "qualified" and "unqualified," based on when they entered the United States. The "qualifieds," those who entered before welfare reform, were subject to one set of rules; post-enactment immigrants, the "unqualifieds," were subject to another. Only the pre-enactment immigrants, for example, retained their federal eligibility for Supplemental Security Income (SSI), and only pre-enactment immigrant children, elderly, and the disabled (but not working-age adults) were able to maintain their Food Stamps. Eligibility for other programs, chiefly Medicaid and TANF, became a matter for state determination.

For *post*-enactment immigrants, eligibility for most federally supported programs was prohibited for five years. After this period, SSI and Food Stamps, as well as TANF and Medicaid (at state option), could be received. Here, once again, Congress ceded considerable authority to the states. States, if they wish, could bar noncitizens from their programs, or they could create their own programs for immigrants to substitute for the loss of federal support.

Given the new restrictions on welfare in general, and on immigrants in particular, and the decentralization of immigrant policy, how have noncitizen immigrants been affected? One salient consequence of welfare reform has been a substantial reduction in the benefits available to noncitizens—a reduction greater than among the native born. A second outcome has been a dramatic variation in benefits among immigrant groups. Some, Cuban immigrants, for example, have been relatively unscathed while others, typically the most recent immigrants, have suffered considerably. A third result has been divided eligibility within families—children born in the United States (and who therefore are citizens), for example, are often eligible for benefits while their parents or older siblings may not be. A fourth outcome has been a dramatic increase in the number of immigrants seeking citizenship. Since welfare reform put social welfare benefits in jeopardy, the number of immigrants annually securing citizenship has jumped from 400,000 to over 1 million.[32]

The effects of welfare decentralization on the states have been carefully monitored by The Urban Institute, a Washington, D.C., think tank. According to the Institute, the states with the greatest number of immigrants (California, Texas, New York, Florida) have "provided considerable assistance, particularly when the costs are shared with the federal government. Despite fears of a race to the bottom providing as few benefits as possible, nearly every state has opted to maintain TANF and Medicaid eligibility for immigrants who were already in the United States when the federal welfare law was passed."[33]

Even though states must bear the costs, many have elected to provide assistance, and a few have undertaken new initiatives in areas of special importance such as job training, English-language instruction, and other programs designed to foster assimilation. California, despite its anti-immigration rhetoric and the passage of Proposition 187, has devoted more resources than any other state to advancing the well-being of low-income legal immigrants, both the pre- and the post-welfare reform groups, generally replacing lost federal benefits and providing Food Stamps, health insurance, TANF cash support, and SSI payments.

What has been the result of welfare reform? Census bureau data provide a wealth of interesting information on welfare use by both legal and undocumented immigrants. Despite the fact that welfare reform sends the message that discriminating against immigrants *vis-à-vis* citizens in the determination of benefit eligibility is appropriate public policy, many states, incuding California and New York, have strongly defended the rights of immigrants to benefits.

And while the nativist sentiment embodied in welfare legislation has been harmful not only to America's immigrant communities but also to America's traditional image of a welcoming refuge, welfare use among immigrants in need is by no means a thing of the past. It *is* true that very few immigrant households today receive TANF assistance, but when we examine the *range* of public assistance programs—cash aid and food assistance and Medicaid—immigrants remain significantly more likely to receive help than the native born. Considering all these programs, as Table 8.5 indicates, a full third of all immigrant households receive aid, compared with just 19 percent of U.S.-born households.[34]

TABLE 8.5   *Immigrants and Native-Born Americans: A Fact Sheet, 2007*

Foreign Born	37.9 million (14% of the U.S. population)
% Who are Citizens	39%
% Who are Noncitizens	61%
Region of Birth	
Europe	12%
Asia	23%
Latin America	55%
Poverty Rate	
Native Born	11%
Foreign Born	17%
Asian	11%
European	10%
Latin American	21%
Completed High School (Adults)	
Native Born	92%
Foreign Born	71%
Asian	87%
European	84%
Latin American	49%

TABLE 8.5   *Continued*

Receiving Public Assistance (Households)

Native Born	19%
Foreign Born	33%
Asian	20%
European	14%
South American	25%
Mexican	51%

Source: Steven Camarota (November 2007), *Immigrants in the U.S. 2007*, Center for Immigration Studies.

CAPSULE 8.9 • *The Undocumented Dilemma*

As the debate over the residency status of the nation's 12 million illegal immigrants boils, another battle is simmering over what—if any—benefits they deserve while they've here. Some of the most heated arguments on the issue focus on health care. So far, immigrants are losing.

On a national level, an effort to add *legal* immigrant children to the State Children's Health Insurance Program was blocked in the Senate in 2007. Instead, lawmakers added language to ensure that illegal immigrants were excluded. Illegal immigrants can get emergency care through Medicaid, but they can't get non-emergency care unless they pay. They are ineligible for most other public benefits [although they can access] a patchwork of federally funded community health centers, which charge little for basic services and don't seek proof of citizenship.

Some states, including New York, Illinois and Washington, as well as several California counties, cover illegal immigrant children with state dollars.

From "Rising Health Care Costs Put Focus on Illegal Immigrants" by Richard Wolf, *USA Today*, January 21, 2008. © USA TODAY, January 22, 2008. Reprinted with permission.

Notes

1. Richard Ford, *The New Blue Federalists*, MSN Slate, January 6, 2005.
2. Grant McConnell, *Private Power and American Democracy* (New York: Alfred A. Knopf, 1966), 107.
3. "Opening the Third Century of American Federalism: Issues and Prospects," in John Kincaid (ed.), *American Federalism: The Third Century*, The Annals, Volume 509, May 1990, 11–21.
4. Luther H. Gulick, "Reorganization of the State," *Civil Engineering* (August 1933): 420, as quoted in *The Book of the States, 1976–77*, Vol. 21 (Lexington, Ky.: The Council of State Governments, 1976), 21.
5. William E. Leuchtenberg, *Franklin D. Roosevelt and the New Deal* (New York: Harper and Row, 1963), as quoted in *The Book of the States*, ibid., 24.

6. Daniel P. Moynihan, "Comments on 'Re-Structuring the Government of New York City'," in *The Neighborhoods, the City, and the Region: Working Papers in Jurisdiction and Structures* (New York: State Study Commission for New York City, 1973), 15.

7. Ibid., 16.

8. Robert Reischauer, "Fiscal Federalism in the 1980s: Dismantling or Rationalizing the Great Society," in M. Kaplan and P. Cuciti (eds.), *The Great Society and Its Legacy*, 1986, 179.

9. U.S. General Accounting Office, *Homelessness: McKinney Act Reports Could Improve Federal Assistance Efforts*, GAO/RCED-90-121, June 1990.

10. David T. Ellwood, "From Social Science to Social Policy? The Fate of Intellectuals, Ideas, and Ideology in the Welfare Debate in the Mid-1990's," Center for Urban Affairs and Policy Research, Northwestern University, Evanston, Ill., 1996, 23–24.

11. At the time of AFDC's demise, the $30 and one-third disregard was limited to four months; after that, the $30 disregard continued an additional eight months.

12. Judith Havemann, "The Welfare Alarm That Didn't Go Off," *Washington Post*, October 1, 1998.

13. The Family Violence Option, Family Violence Prevention Fund, endabuse.org/display.php3?docID=306.

14. U.S. Department of Health and Human Services, *TANF Seventh Annual Report to the Congress*, 2006, I–25.

15. Paul E. Peterson and Mark C. Rom, *Welfare Magnets* (Washington, D.C.: The Brookings Institution, 1990).

16. U.S. Department of Health and Human Services, *op. cit.*, I-12.

17. Karen Houppert, "You're Not Entitled! Welfare Reform Is Leading to Government Lawlessness," *The Nation* (October 25, 1999).

18. Sandra Danziger et al., "Barriers to Work Among Welfare Recipients," *Focus*, 20(2) (Spring 1999): 31–34.

19. Sheila R. Zedlewski, et al., *Hard-to-Employ Parents*, The Urban Institute, June, 2007.

20. Ibid.

21. Jennifer Preston, "With New Jersey Family Cap, Births Fall and Abortions Rise," *New York Times*, November 3, 1998.

22. Susan Page, "Number of Unmarried Fathers Who Accept Paternity Triples," *USA Today*, June 22, 1999.

23. Rob Stein, "States Spurning Abstinence Funds," *San Francisco Chronicle*, December 16, 2007.

24. Isabel Sawhill, quoted in Michael Kelley, "Assessing Welfare Reform," *Washington Post*, August 4, 1999; and Douglas Besharov and Peter Germanis, "Welfare Reform—4 Years Later," *Public Interest*, 140 (Summer 2000).

25. *A Decade of Welfare Reform: Facts and Figures*, The Urban Institute, June, 2006.

26. Ron Haskins, "The Rise of the Bottom Fifth," *The Washington Post*, May 29, 2007.

27. Pamela Loprest, "Fewer Welfare Leavers Employed in weak Economy," The Urban Institute Snapshots 3 of America's Families, 2003.

28. Christopher Jencks and Joseph Swingle, "Without a Net," *American Prospect*, 11(4) (January 3, 2000): 38.

29. Stephen A. Camarota, *Importing Poverty*, Center for Immigration Studies, September 2, 1999. www.cis.org/povstudy/execsummary.html.

30. For a summary of the fiscal impact of American immigrants, see National Immigration Forum, *A Fiscal Portrait of the Newest Americans*, 1999.

31. Peter H. Schuck, *Citizens, Strangers, and In-Betweens* (Boulder, Colo.: Westview Press, 1998), 199.

32. U.S. General Accounting Office, "Welfare Reform: Public Assistance Benefits Provided to Recently Naturalized Citizens," Washington, D.C., June 23, 1999.

33. Wendy Zimmerman and Karen C. Tumlin, The Urban Institute, "Patchwork Policies: State Assistance for Immigrants under Welfare Reform," Occasional Paper Number 24, 3, April 1, 1999.

34. Steven Camarota, *Immigrants in the United States, 2007*, Center for Immigration Studies, November, 2007.

9

Policy Dimensions: International Trends in the Twenty-First Century

"[T]he beginning of a new century could inspire minds around the world to begin the task of building a new international economic and social order, one that fosters employment creation, that facilitates the exchange of ideas and technological innovations, and that allows men and women to share more equally their home and workplace obligations. Social security on its own cannot achieve these objectives, but it plays a critical role in enabling societies to achieve them. The critical challenge facing the 21st century is thus to find a new balance between economic goals—global and national—and the social protection of the world's citizens. . . . There is, however, a growing consensus that the old ideas and familiar terminology are no longer adequate to guide us into the future. What framework of ideas will therefore dominate in shaping the world's economic and social policies in the years to come?

Dalmer Hoskins
Social Security at the Dawn of the 21st Century, 2001

In preceding chapters, we examined a series of choices affecting the design of social welfare policies. Generally speaking, these choices address questions of what is to be done, what alternative courses of action can fulfill social welfare objectives, and what their implications might be. In this chapter our attention shifts to the international scene to examine some of the ways social and economic forces are transforming the essential character of major social welfare policy choices in many, if not all, welfare states in the advanced industrialized nations. To transform is not to dismantle or obliterate the fundamental institutional arrangements for social welfare—what is being altered, rather, are several of the basic dimensions of social welfare policy choice on which the most progressive welfare states have been modeled.[1] In this final chapter, we examine some of the compelling reasons for this shift, its substantive character, and several important issues it raises.

Pressures for Change

The period from 1960 to the mid-1970s is sometimes referred to as the Golden Age of welfare state expansion. According to Organisation for Economic Co-operation and Development (OECD), social welfare expenditures nearly doubled to an average of over 20 percent of GDP among the 21 member nations in the two decades after 1960. As noted in Chapter 2, this period of growth ended in the wake of the oil crises that hit the world economy during the 1970s. After 1980, as shown in Figure 9.1, social welfare growth rates slowed, almost leveling off since the mid-1990s. The slight rise of social expenditure in the mid-1990s is partly related to unemployment rates in the European Union, which peaked in 1994, then started to fall, although it still remains near 8 percent.

Not only did the rise of social expenditure diminish dramatically by the mid-1990s, but social welfare policies came under renewed criticism. Rather than being advanced as a remedy for the flaws and insecurities of capitalism, social programs were increasingly condemned as part of the very problem they were designed to solve. Critics claimed that the welfare state promised more than could be delivered without creating deleterious effects on the market economy by undermining incentives, hampering competitiveness, inhibiting savings, and increasing national debt.[2] Much of the Reagan–Thatcher welfare state critique of earlier years found a wide audience, even in the countries traditionally associated with progressive, social democratic traditions.

As noted in our discussion of the new social accounting (see Chapter 2), it is now well recognized that direct governmental social expenditures are at best a crude measure of the magnitude of the welfare state since they ignore the impact of taxes, tax expenditures, regulatory transfers, philanthropy, and other forms of voluntary transfers. In analyzing expenditure trends, our point is that social spending has slowed and appears to have hit a ceiling. This is creating a tremendous compression in the welfare

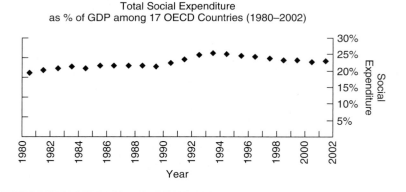

Total Social Expenditure
as % of GDP among 17 OECD Countries (1980–2002)

FIGURE 9.1   *Social Expenditures in Seventeen OECD Countries*

Data source: Public expenditure as percent of GDP from *The OECD Social Expenditure Database (1980–2001)*, http://www.oecd.org/document/2/0,2340,en264920118531612994111,00.html

TABLE 9.1   *Social and Economic Pressures for Change: Four Lines of Influence*

Demographic Transition
Aging, Divorce Rates, Low Fertility, Extramarital Births

Globalization of the Economy
Mobility of Capital to where Production Costs Are Low
Mobility of Labor to where Benefits Are High

Knowledge of Unanticipated Effects
Disincentives to Work
Dependency Traps

Belief in Capitalism
Rising Faith in Market Economy
Privatization

state since the demand for income support and services continue to rise. Simultaneously, *other* forces for change have emerged. Specifically, the welfare state is being challenged by a powerful combination of economic and social pressures. As these economic and social pressures, indicated in Table 9.1, converge, they are significantly reshaping modern social welfare systems.

First, immense fiscal pressures are emerging in response to the interaction of mature social security systems with sociodemographic trends. In most European countries, for example, the proportion of people over age 65 is expected to increase by more than half by 2040, to 22.2 percent of overall populations.[3] In Europe, in addition, the size of the overall population is falling and is likely to continue to fall. In Europe and the United States, life expectancy is increasing and the average age of retirement is declining. In the United States, for example, men and women retired at the median age of 62 in 2002, about seven years earlier than the retirement age in 1940. And workers in the United States retire later than workers in most if not all of Europe.[4] With social security entitlements nearly universal, the rising number of elderly will exact increasing public spending for retirement, health services, and social care, threatening its very solvency. In the United States, estimates by the Social Security Board of Trustees indicate that the cost of Old Age, Survivors, and Disability Insurance (OASDI) will begin to exceed OASDI revenues in 2018—with the cumulated reserves and interest within the OASDI Trust Funds exhausted by 2042.[5] European old-age pension systems face burdens that are even more acute. In France, there are currently three workers contributing for every pensioner, with projections indicating that by 2030 this support ratio will drop to just 1.6 contributors per retiree.[6] And France is by no means the exception. By 2005, the ratio of persons over 65 to the number of people employed will start climbing precipitously among all the advanced industrialized countries.[7]

This demographic shift poses a considerable challenge to the financing of social transfers, particularly old age pensions. Governments could address this challenge by raising taxes, or by lowering benefits, both politically unattractive options. Efforts could also be made to increase the number of the employed by raising the retirement age, a reform already enacted in many countries.[8] Boosting levels of productivity for those currently employed would also be beneficial. Short of a baby boom, however, one of the broadest and most immediate avenues to lowering the "dependency ratio," the ratio of those who are retired compared to those who are working, is by opening national borders to immigrants. Estimates by the United Nations Population Division, for example, reveal that maintaining European population at its maximum level in 1995 would require an average of almost 2 million migrants a year over the next fifty years. These numbers are daunting, as are the cultural implications, particularly for small relatively homogenous countries that may feel culturally threatened.

The rising costs associated with the aging of the population are compounded by other demographic trends. For example, between the early 1980s and the early 1990s, the number of lone-parent families increased an average of 25 percent (and as a percent of all families, they rose proportionately by an average of 17 percent) in twenty-one of the OECD countries for which these data are available.[9] The proliferation of two-income households, as well as lone-parent families, has reduced the modern family's capacity to provide in-person care for children, the elderly, and other infirm relatives, which creates additional demands for the state to supply child and elder care, financial assistance, and other supportive services.[10] Overall, what some are calling the "second demographic transition" forecasts a period of change that will generate new demands while eliminating practically no existing needs.[11]

The second major "line of influence" stems from what is popularly referred to as economic globalization—rapid technological change, particularly in the realm of information and communications, the growth of transnational corporations, and the increased investment of capital in foreign countries. These developments have magnified economic interdependencies and shrunk time and space.

While everyone agrees that globalization is inexorable, there are differences of opinion about what the process represents for the future of state-sponsored social welfare.[12] Although the full impact of globalization is unclear, it does appear that the pressures of a highly integrated worldwide market severely curtail the flexibility of national policymakers. Spending on social benefits, for example, is being squeezed by the mobility of corporations to locate their workforces where production costs are low.[13] As Guy Standing suggests, globalization heightens pressures to scale back labor rights and employee benefits in order to maintain a country's competitive edge in holding and attracting foreign investments.[14]

Globalization not only expedites the mobility of capital, it also provides new highways for the movement of labor. Just as corporations are likely to invest in countries where standards of living, social benefits, and labor costs are low, workers are more and more able to migrate to places, either legally or illegally, where standards of living, wages, and social benefits are high.[15] Thus, while the competitive discipline of the global market exerts pressure to suppress local public spending on social benefits, a counter force of increasing demand is being exerted as new immigrants arrive seeking their fortunes in the lands of opportunity, affluence, and relatively generous social welfare benefits.

The third pressure for change emanates from the realm of ideas and knowledge. Normative views about social welfare are being remolded by the weight of experience gained during the decades of welfare state growth. This experience suggests that social welfare provisions can, indeed, create disincentives to work, a claim, as indicated in Chapter 4, that in the past was advanced mainly by conservatives, most effectively in the United States. Today, the critique has become part of the social policy conventional wisdom in most all welfare states. Thus, for example, a 1991 OECD report on the Netherlands found "clear indications that the generosity of social benefits and the high effective marginal tax rates implicit in income-dependent subsidies create strong disincentives to work and underlie the exceptionally high dependency ratio in the Netherlands, where one employed person supports almost one person on social benefits."[16] To combat what is sometimes known as the "Dutch Disease," corrective measures were initiated—tightening eligibility requirements for disability, reducing benefits, and requiring single mothers to become active in the labor market when their children reached the age of five.[17]

The Dutch experience is not unique. From the *Revenu Minimum d'Insertion* in France to the Newstart program in Australia, recent sociopolitical deliberations in the industrialized welfare states have produced numerous legislative reforms to reduce "poverty traps," social welfare disincentives to work and self-reliance.[18] Even in Sweden, the paragon of progressive social policy, Prime Minister Carl Bildt told the press in 1992 that "if you look at the levels of benefits, they've become so high that they reduce the incentives to work."[19] One might well conclude that Charles Murray's rendition of the disincentive to work bred by public welfare, viewed as heresy by welfare advocates in the mid-1980s, has become a fundamental anxiety of today's welfare state.[20]

Finally, normative views about the proper relationship between the state and the market have undergone a significant conversion as the collapse of central planning in

CAPSULE 9.1 • *Imploding Populations, Exploding Pensions*

Fertility rates across Europe are now so low that the continent's population is likely to drop markedly over the next 50 years and affect its ability to compete and take care of pension obligations, say observers.

The size of Europe's population implosion is staggering:

- By 2050, the number of Italians may have fallen from 57.5 million to 45 million, while Spain's population will drop from 40 million to 37 million.
- Germany's population could fall from 80 million to less than 25 million by the end of the century.

The consequences of a falling economy are severe:

- In Europe there are currently 35 people eligible for pensions for every 100 people of working age.
- By 2050, there will be 75 pensioners for every 100 workers.

This will severely strain government finances in the future. Many countries, like Germany and Italy, are already paying nearly 30 percent of revenues on pensions.

"Europe's Population Implosion," *Economist*, July 17, 2003.

Russia and Eastern Europe raised to record levels the stock of capitalism's public acceptance in the marketplace of ideas. Despite our Enrons, WorldComs, and Tycos, the virtues of the unregulated free market economy have been widely touted—right up until its stock market tumbled in late 2008.[21] While not everyone still believes that *laissez-faire* economic liberalism has triumphed, or that it constitutes a compelling guide to social policy, it has gained powerful converts worldwide. Although the faith in unfettered markets has been shaken by the global financial crisis of 2009, the degree to which government regulation of the market and state intervention are reestablished remain to be seen as this volume goes to press.

In the meantime, complex and multiple forces are lending impetus to the transformation of the welfare state. It is not demographic shifts alone, or globalization, or normative changes, or the faith in the market economy that account for the fundamental change in the character of social welfare policy—it is the confluence of these lines of influence. What lends particular weight to the pressures emanating from these structural and normative forces is that they all press in the same direction, which is away from the traditional model of the welfare state model toward what might be called the Enabling State model.

The emergence of the Enabling State does not signal the end of social welfare programs. No one imagines that social security, health insurance, disability benefits, public assistance, unemployment insurance, daycare, and the rest will be jettisoned. But the social policy environment in which they evolve will be constrained by a set of demographic and market conditions and informed by normative assumptions that are fundamentally different than those underlying the development of social welfare programs through most of the twentieth century. These structural conditions and social norms have given rise to a new institutional framework that increasingly subordinates social welfare policies to economic considerations, such as the need for labor market flexibility, the opening of new markets for the private sector, the pressures of international competition, and the imposition of limits on deficit spending. Within this new framework, social welfare policies are increasingly designed to enable more people to work and to enable the private sector to expand its sphere of activity.

Directions of Change

The Scandinavian welfare state, long and widely regarded as the highest international standard for the provision of social welfare, is characterized by its universal orientation to publicly delivered benefits, benefits firmly held as social rights designed to protect workers against the uncertainties of the market. In terms of the dimensions of policy choice, this model represents an approach under which

- the basis of social allocations emphasize universal eligibility,
- the delivery system operates through the public sector,
- the core social provisions are designed to protect workers, and
- the provision of social welfare benefits are seen as fundamental rights of citizenship.

These characteristics represent a Weberian ideal type, a model of social policy in the progressive social democratic mold, a model that is increasingly on the defensive.

TABLE 9.2   *Shift in Central Tendencies from the Welfare to the Enabling State*

Welfare State	*Enabling State*
Protecting labor	***Promoting work***
Social support ⟶	Social inclusion
Decommodification of labor ⟶	Recommodification of labor
Unconditional benefits ⟶	Use of incentives and sanctions
Universal Entitlement	***Selective Targeting***
Avoiding stigma ⟶	Restoring social equity
Public Provision	***Privatization***
Delivery by public agencies ⟶	Delivery by private agencies
Transfers in the form of service ⟶	Transfers in cash or vouchers
Focus on direct expenditures ⟶	Increasing indirect expenditures
Benefits as Social Rights	***Benefits Linked to Obligations***
Solidarity of shared rights ⟶	Cohesion of shared values and civic duties

Source: Adapted from Neil Gilbert, *Transformation of the Welfare State: The Silent Surrender of Public Responsibility* (New York: Oxford University Press, 2002).

Given the social, political, and intellectual developments we have described, what exactly does the erosion of the traditional progressive welfare state model, and the emergence of the Enabling State, mean for social policy? Table 9.2 summarizes these changes. First, what were previously termed "income maintenance" programs (public assistance, unemployment, and disability benefits) involved benefits that were designed to provide a secure source of income for people who were not employed. This liberated citizens from dependency on wage labor for their survival. Their labor was, in the Marxist expression, "decommodified," made less like a commodity that was bought and sold purely in response to market forces. Recent policy reforms, however, have increasingly tied these benefits to incentives and sanctions that pressure recipients to return to, or to connect to, work as soon as possible. In contrast to an income-support program for social protection, the new work-oriented reforms can be seen as promoting the "recommodification of labor." Indeed, it has become almost universally accepted that unconditioned cash benefits—"passive" income supports based entirely on need—should be replaced by "active" measures designed to stimulate movement into the paid labor force. These reforms have altered the basic requirements to enter and exit programs originally designed to protect people out of work.

Throughout the industrialized nations, therefore, policy reforms have raised the eligibility bar on entrance into social welfare programs and accelerated program exit by reducing the duration of benefits, providing incentives for self-support, and imposing sanctions for continued benefit use. In the realm of old-age pensions, for example, many countries are requiring people (particularly women) to work longer, either directly by raising the formal age of retirement or indirectly by increasing the period of contributions, before being eligible for benefits. Regarding unemployment insurance, many countries are extending the period of paid employment required to qualify for benefits, and a few have introduced or lengthened benefit waiting periods.[22] New Zealand, for example, raised the minimum age to qualify for unemployment benefits.[23] The United States raised the age requirement for social security to 67, to be phased in slowly over a decade, and narrowed the criteria for disability to exclude, for example, people addicted to drugs.

Reforms have not only raised the threshold for access to benefits, they have changed the conditions for continuing eligibility, particularly in unemployment, disability, and social assistance programs. Upon entering these programs, recipients are increasingly being segmented according to characteristics, such as age and length of unemployment, that forecast their service needs and employability. In the United Kingdom, welfare-to-work programs are tailored to the needs of five main groups: the young unemployed, the long-term unemployed, single parents, people with disabilities or long-term illnesses, and partners of the unemployed.[24]

Efforts to differentiate among claimants are also closely linked to what, perhaps, is the most crucial development in the daily administration of social assistance, unemployment, and disability programs—the introduction of quasi-contractual agreements, referred to in Europe as "activation plans," which are formulated by mutual consent between clients and administrative officials. Denmark, Britain, Finland, France, the Netherlands, New Zealand, Australia, and Sweden, among others, have adopted policies requiring individualized action plans, plans spelling out the steps—education, training, job search, subsidized work, and other activities—that will be taken toward employment.[25] The introduction of individually tailored social contracts, which take into consideration different peoples' needs and circumstances, has obvious benefits. At the same time, however, their use converts benefits from entitlements based on impartial and uniform bureaucratic procedures to individualized and discretionary dispensations based on case-by-case assessments. Policy reforms in recent years, finally, have initiated an unprecedented array of work-oriented incentives and services designed to strengthen readiness to work through education and training, to make work pay by subsidizing low-income employment through refundable tax credits, and to heighten the

---

CAPSULE 9.2 • *Paradise Lost*

These days, Europe's northern tier is anything but the high-tax, low-effort "socialist paradise" of popular imagination. Yes, taxes remain high. But Scandinavian welfare systems are built rigorously around the idea of getting people back to work. "The conventional wisdom is that you have to be like the U.S. to be a success. An animal like Sweden shouldn't be able to fly, but in fact we fly faster than others," says Swedish Education Minister Leif Pagotsky, who points out that his country boasts exceptional productivity and an inflation rate of 0.3 percent.

Stryker Mcguire, "The 'Anglo-Social Model'," *Newsweek International*, September 5, 2005.

costs of nonparticipation in work through the impositions of sanctions. The American variants of these reforms have been detailed in this book, especially in Chapter 8.

The reconfiguration of social protection is aptly summarized in the motto of the Dutch "purple coalition" (red Social Democrats allied with blue Liberals), which formed the governing coalition in the Netherlands in the mid-1990s: "Work, work and work again!"[26] Or one might take a leaf from the Norwegian 1992 White Paper on Rehabilitation formulating a "work approach" to social welfare policy premised on the idea "that individual rights are not exclusively tied to cash benefits; each individual has, as far as possible, a right and a duty to work, to participate in rehabilitation programs or enter education. . . ."[27] Or one might refer to the 1998 Green Paper on Welfare Reform issued by the New Labour government in Britain, which identified the Government's aim as rebuilding the Welfare State around work through active work-oriented policies,

CAPSULE 9.3 • *Barriers to Benefits*

For Jobseeker's Allowance claimants the system will look like this:

- Weeks 1–13: self-managed job search. Claimants will have fortnightly jobsearch reviews, and, about half way through, a 'Back to Work session', with a one-week sanction for failure to attend.
- Weeks 14–26: directed job search. Claimants will have to look for and accept lower quality jobs and this stage will begin with 6 weekly jobsearch reviews.
- Weeks 27–52: supported job search. Claimants will have to undertake activities beyond those they have already agreed to in their Jobseeker's Agreements, those with basic skills problems may be directed to take part in a Skills Health Check, with compulsory actions to follow-up.
- Weeks 53–104: flexible New Deal. This will be run by private and voluntary sector contractors, and will replace the existing New Deal programmes. Claimants

will be required to take part in four weeks of either employment or work-related activity. Claimants who fail to take part in activities will face sanctions of up to 26 weeks.
- Weeks 105+: workfare. The Government will test different models of mandatory full-time work or work-related activity for people who have not found paid jobs by the end of the flexible New Deal.

The Government is also considering tightening conditionality in other ways:

- The Government has asked for views on changing the benefit rules to require claimants to declare whether they are addicted to heroin or crack cocaine. They are also considering, for those who are addicted and are not in a treatment programme, to require them to agree and take part in a rehabilitation programme.
- Requiring people aged 60–65 to take part in work-focused interviews.

Opposing Workfare and Privatisation: The TUC response to the welfare reform Green Paper (London: Trade Union Congress, 2008).

supportive services, tax measures that make work pay, and "ensuring that responsibilities and rights are fairly matched."[28]

In 2008, the Labour Government issued another Green Paper on welfare reform, *No One Written Off: Reforming Welfare to Reward Responsibility.* According the Trade Union Congress (TUC), this report proposes a new system that applies harsh conditions to working-age claimants of the Jobseeker's Allowance (previously known as unemployment benefits) and the toughest sanctions the United Kingdom has ever known.

The second major component in the transition from the Welfare State to the Enabling State involves a shift from universal to selective criteria as the basis for social allocation. Since the mid-1980s there has been increasing use of targeting in eligibility designs for social benefits, with eligibility criteria designed not so much to identify new groups of beneficiaries as to reform programs by limiting the number of recipients.[29] Constriction of eligibility, for example, has occurred in the disability programs of many, if not most, industrialized countries.[30] These reforms include narrowing the definition of disabling conditions and more rigorously specifying degrees of disability.[31] Targeting on the basis of impairment allows a program to continue serving its original category of social need while raising the threshold of eligibility. The program appears the same until one looks beneath the surface. Analyzing the "flight from universalism" in Sweden, for example, Sune Sunesson and his colleagues have noted that criteria for elder care have tightened so much that benefits have shifted from services to most elderly people to care for just the weakest and frailest."[32] A similar trend has been documented in the allocation of home help and home care for older people in England.[33]

Like a balloon that expands on one side when squeezed down on the other, however, policy reforms that constrict access and levels of social benefits in one area often create a "bubble effect," shifting recipients from restricted benefits to other program areas. Thus, for example, a high degree of interaction is found among social provisions such as unemployment benefits, disability benefits, and social assistance. When eligibility criteria for unemployment benefits are narrowed, and benefit rates lowered, the reduction in spending may be offset by increased growth in the public assistance and disability rolls.[34]

The third element in the shift toward the Enabling State—increasing privatization—reflects the extent to which public faith in the virtues of the private sector have impelled social welfare transactions to adopt the values and methods of the market economy. This development is conspicuous in the myriad arrangements for the privatization of social welfare functions.[35] (See Chapter 6.) In the United States, corporations large and small have been hired by the states to deliver a wide range of welfare services. The for-profit firm Maximus, for example, contracts with more than a dozen state TANF agencies to provide welfare-to-work and job readiness services, and with other state bodies for child support enforcement, children's health services, and disability programs. Maximus, with its mission to "Help Government Serve the People," has more than 4800 employees in 170 offices nationwide. Another leading corporate player is Affiliated Computer Services, successor to the Lockheed Martin Corporation, which has multiple contracts for TANF services, child support collection, and electronic benefit transfers. In addition, the great majority of the states contract with nonprofit social welfare agencies to provide a broad range of support services in the job training, alcohol and drug treatment, childcare, and pregnancy prevention fields.

And the United States is hardly alone in the movement to privatize welfare. Between 1979 and 1996, for example, the proportion of all public expenditures on personal social services contracted out to the private sector in the United Kingdom more than tripled, from 11 to 34 percent. Most of this increase reflected a change in the provision of residential care, which shifted from facilities operated by local authorities to home care under private auspices.[36] Commercial firms have also moved into services such as in-home meals, cleaning, home nursing, and emergency alarm systems, under contracts with local public authorities who are "expected to be enablers rather than providers."[37]

In Sweden, since the early 1990s, there has been substantial growth in childcare arrangements that are publicly financed and privately operated, mainly by parent cooperatives and other nonprofit organizations.[38] Private for-profit arrangements are also on the rise. For twenty years now, Swedish counties that used to operate local healthcare systems under which physicians were public employees have been contracting for medical services with doctors in private practice. By the mid-1990s, "what [had] started out as a minor revival of private practice [became] a boom."[39] In the area of residential care, the public sector provided almost 90 percent of the beds in residential-care facilities for children and youth in the 1970s. By 1995, close to 60 percent of these beds had shifted over to private institutions, many of them medium-scale operations larger than foster-care homes but smaller than the traditional state-run institutions.[40] A similar trend is evident in contracting out beds in residential treatment homes for alcoholics, where for-profit providers came to dominate the field after the mid-1980s.

In a number of countries, old-age pensions are also marching on a slow but steady course toward privatization. In the United States, between 1976 and 1992, retirement benefits in the form of employee pensions increased from 25 to 33 percent of the total income received by the elderly from employee plans and social security payments.[41] From 1962 to 2001, income from private pensions almost doubled as a share of the total income of the elderly from all sources, including earnings and assets, while Social Security's share of the total rose by less than one third. The U.S. experience tracks that of private pensions in some of the more generous Nordic countries. In Denmark, for example, between 1980 and 1992, private pension expenditure jumped from 20 to 30 percent of the total share of public and private pensions. After 1985, the share of private pensions also increased in Norway, albeit at a slower pace.[42] Sweden, in one fell swoop in 1998, privatized 14 percent of the total public pension contributions.

Implications of Change

In contrast to the emphasis on social rights and citizen entitlements that supported the growth of social provisions during the Golden Age of welfare state expansion, the policy framework of the Enabling State seeks to balance rights with individual responsibilities to work and contribute to the community. The new framework also aims to contain costs by targeting benefits more narrowly on those in need and using the private sector for the delivery of welfare provisions.

Under the new framework, it is increasingly difficult to distinguish substantive differences between political left and the right. The political compass has lost its conventional bearings. Where is the left? In the 2000 United States presidential campaign, Republicans wanted to expand private activity through the use of educational vouchers and a partially privatized in social security. Democrats opposed these measures. At the same time, the privatization of social security contributions and the use of educational vouchers have been approved in Sweden under a Social Democratic regime traditionally to the left of both parties in the United States.

While there are policy experts who argue that privatization, targeting, and "activation" of the unemployed constitute little more than marginal changes from existing policy, it is difficult to deny that serious changes are occurring.[43] Unemployment and disability benefits in the European welfare states that once lasted almost forever are now more time-restricted. Definitions of suitable employment have been broadened well beyond the occupational status of the previous position held. Client–government contracts are now required, which allow for financial sanctions as well as incentives to work. Do these various changes constitute just a fine tuning of existing arrangements—refinements meant to nurture social inclusion through work and responsibility? Or do they signify a pivotal shift toward what has been described as the recommodification of labor? This will be left for the reader to decide.

But, one might ask, does it really matter if these are marginal adjustments or fundamental changes? Is this just some verbal quibbling by academics who have little to do with their time?

While the words used to describe current events in the world of social policy may not be of critical importance, it is clearly vital to understand the nature of today's developments, what they mean, and where they are leading us. Is the movement toward "empowerment," "personal responsibility," and "social inclusion" simply a billowing smoke screen for radical free marketers who are scheming to return us to a nineteenth-century *laissez-faire* capitalism, where "welfare" is but a residual element in society directed at the destitute and disabled? Is the "individualist" perspective on welfare described in Chapter 1—an approach to welfare based on markets and self-help and voluntary agencies and religious charity—to be the model for the decades ahead? Or will the emerging form of social welfare continue to embody our collective "social" consciousness as an effective counterforce to the hazards of social marginalization, poverty, and increasing economic inequality? Can we, should we, maintain principles of fairness and justice in the harsh and fiercely competitive environment of twenty-first-century global capitalism? And how much will the answer to these questions be influenced by the global financial crisis, the depths of which are currently unknown?

The essential challenge for the future is how to sustain, perhaps even improve, our social policies to ensure social justice and the protection of the weak while preserving economic initiative and broad middle-class prosperity? Addressing this challenge will help to clarify the values and principles that ultimately guide social welfare policy choices.

Notes

1. For a more detailed analysis of these changes, see Neil Gilbert, *Transformation of the Welfare State: The Silent Surrender of Public Responsibility* (New York: Oxford University Press, 2002).
2. Some of the most trenchant critical analyses include Douglas Besharov, "Bottom-Up Funding," in Peter Berger and Richard J. Neuhaus (eds.), *To Empower the People: From State to Civil Society* (Washington, D.C.: AEI Press, 1996); Nathan Glazer, *The Limits of Social Policy* (Cambridge, Mass.: Harvard University Press, 1988); Lawrence Mead, *Beyond Entitlement: The Social Obligations of Citizenship* (New York: Free Press, 1986); Charles Murray, *Losing Ground: American Social Policy 1950–1980* (New York: Basic Books, 1984); Dennis Shower, "Challenges to Social Cohesion and Approaches to Policy Reform," in *Societal Cohesion and the Globalization of the Economy: What Does the Future Hold?* (Paris: OECD, 1997); and World Bank, *Averting the Old Age Crisis* (Oxford, UK: Oxford University Press, 1994).
3. OECD, *The Future of Social Protection* (Paris: OECD, 1988).
4. For an analysis of early retirement in Europe, see Susan Devereux, "Pension Systems Reform in Response to the Growth in Retired Populations," in Dalmer Hoskins, Donate Dobbernack, and Christiane Kuptsch (eds.), *Social Security at the Dawn of the 21st Century* (Rutgers, N.J.: Transaction Publishers, 2000).
5. Board of Trustees of the Social Security and Medicare Trust Fund, *2002 Annual Report of the Board of Trustees* (Washington, D.C.: Government Printing Office, 2002).
6. Craig Whitney, "In Europe Too, Social Security Isn't So Secure," *New York Times*, August 31, 1997, E4.
7. One set of projections estimates that between 1995 and 2050, the average percent of GDP spent on old-age pensions in 16 of the wealthiest OECD countries (excluding the United States and Canada) will increase by more than two-thirds, from 8 percent to 13 percent. See Deborah Roseveare, Willi Leibfritz, Douglas Fore, and Eckhard Wurzel, "Population, Pension Systems, and Government Budgets: Simulations for 20 OECD Countries," OECD, Economics Department Working Paper, No. 168, Table 3. (Paris: OECD, 1996).
8. Changes in the standard age of entitlement to pensions are reviewed by Susan Devereux, "Pensions Systems Reform."
9. The mean change over the decade ranged from −10 percent in Sweden to +83 percent in France. OECD, *A Caring World: The New Social Policy Agenda* (Paris: OECD, 1999).
10. Valeria Fargion, "Current Social Service Regimes in Europe: The Rise and Development (1965–1995)." Paper presented at ISA Research Committee Meeting on Welfare State Challenge, Marginalization and Poverty, Copenhagen. August 21–24, 1997.
11. R. Lesthaeghe, "The Second Demographic Transition in Western Countries: An Interpretation," in K. Oppenheim Mason and A. Jensen (eds.), *Gender and Family Change in Industrialized Countries* (Oxford, UK: Clarendon Press, 1995).
12. This advanced period of capitalism is also referred to as postmodern or post-Fordist and includes new information technologies and mass cultural consumption. See, for example, B. Jessop, "From Keynesian Welfare to the Schumpeterian Workfare State," in R. Burrows and B. Loader (eds.), *Towards a Post-Fordist Welfare State?* (London: Routledge, 1994); and Peter Leonard, *Postmodern Welfare: Reconstructing an Emancipatory Project* (London: Sage, 1997). Leibfried and Rieger trace the different phases of globalization back to the turn of the twentieth century; Stephan Leibfried and Elmar Rieger, "Conflict Over Germany's Competitiveness: Exiting from the Global Economy?" Occasional Paper Center for German European Studies, University of California, Berkeley, 1995. For a view of globalization as more of a new form than a modern phase of capitalism, see Robert Reich, *The Work of Nations* (New York: Alfred A. Knopf, 1991).
13. Thus, for example, McKenzie counsels that public spending on redistributive social benefits should be contemplated with the utmost of care. "Otherwise, officials and policy makers can expect to find their fiscal troubles mounting as capital moves elsewhere or is created elsewhere in the world. Those who are concerned about the plight of the poor must realize that there are economic limits to how much society can do for the poor, given the mobility of capital." Richard McKenzie, "Bidding for Business," *Society*, 33:3 (March/April 1996): 60–69.

14. Guy Standing, *Global Labour Flexibility: Seeking Distributive Justice* (London: Macmillan Press Ltd., 1999), 62–63.

15. In 1992, for example, 10.6 million inhabitants of the European Union were nationals of non-EU Member States and an additional 5 million nationals of the EU were living in other than their Member States. Helen Bolderson and Simon Roberts, "Social Security Across Frontiers," *Journal of International and Comparative Social Welfare* XIII (1997).

16. OECD, *Economic Survey: Netherlands* (Paris: OECD, 1991).

17. These reforms were initiated under the Reduction Requirement on Industrial Disability Act of 1993, which introduced a stricter medical evaluation of disability and a reduction of benefits over time and the 1996 reform of the Dutch Social Assistance Act. For discussion of these reforms, see, Hans Ariens, "To Rigorously Combat the Dutch Disease," *World: APB Annual Report 1996* (Heerlen, ND: APB Corporate Communication, 1997) and Romke van der Veen and Willem Trommel, "Managed Liberalization of the Dutch Welfare State." Presented at the SASE Conference on Rethinking the Welfare State, Montreal, July 5–7, 1997.

18. For discussion of concerns about the "poverty trap" in relation to various groups, see Jonathon Bradshaw and Jane Miller, "Lone-Parent Families in the U.K.: Challenges to Social Policy." *International Social Security Review*, 43:4 (1990); Alain Euzeby, "Unemployment Compensation and Unemployment in Industrialized Market Economy Countries," *International Social Security Review*, 41:1 (1988); and OECD, *The Future of Social Protection* (Paris: OECD, 1997).

19. Richard Stevenson, "Swedes Facing Rigors of Welfare Cuts," *New York Times*, March 14, 1993.

20. Charles Murray, *Losing Ground*.

21. Francis Fukuyama, *Trust: The Social Virtues and the Creation of Prosperity* (New York: Free Press, 1995), 17.

22. Mary Daly, "Welfare States Under Pressure: Cash Benefits in European Welfare States over the Last Ten Years," *Journal of European Social Policy*, 7:2 (May 1997): 128–46; Askel Hatland, "The Changing Balance between Incentives and Economic Security in Scandinavian Unemployment Benefit Schemes," Paper presented at the International Social Security Association Conference on Social Security, Jerusalem, January 25–28, 1998, p. 6.

23. Ross Mackay, "Work Oriented Reforms: New Directions in New Zealand," in Neil Gilbert and Rebecca Van Voorhis (eds.), *Activating the Unemployed: A Comparative Appraisal of Work-Oriented Policies* (Rutgers, N.J.: Transaction Publishers, 2001).

24. Ken Judge, "Evaluating Welfare to Work in the United Kingdom," in Neil Gilbert and Rebecca Van Voorhis (eds.), *Activating the Unemployed: A Comparative Appraisal of Work-Oriented Policies* (Rutgers, N.J.: Transaction Publishers, 2001).

25. For an informative discussion of this development, see Tony Eardley, "New Relations of Welfare in the Contracting: The Marketisation of Services for the Unemployed in Australia." Social Policy Research Center Discussion Paper 79, SPRC, University of New South Wales, 1997.

26. Dick Vink, "Will Wisconsin Works Fit into the Dutch Poldermodel?" *Focus*, 19:3 (Summer–Fall 1998): 41–48.

27. Espen Dahl and Jon Anders Dropping, "The Norwegian Work Approach in the 1990s: Rhetoric and Reform," in Neil Gilbert and Rebecca Van Voorhis (eds.), *Activating the Unemployed: A Comparative Appraisal of Work-Oriented Policies* (Rutgers, N.J.: Transaction Publishers, 2001).

28. *Green Paper on Welfare Reform* (London, HMSO, 1999).

29. See, for example, Neil Gilbert (ed.), *Targeting Social Benefits: International Perspectives and Trends* (New Brunswick: Transaction Publishers, 2001).

30. In recent decades, almost every industrialized country has experienced steep growth in their disability rolls, often among young workers. For an analysis of this development and the policy responses, see Christine Kuptsch and Ilene Zeiter, "Public Disability Programs under New Complex Pressures," in Dalmer Hoskins, Donate Dobbernack, and Christiane Kuptsch (eds.), *Social Security at the Dawn of the 21st Century: Topical Issues and New Approaches* (Rutgers, N.J.: Transaction Publishers, 2000).

31. E. Dahl and J. A. Dropping, "The Norwegian Work Approach," op. cit.; and Piet Keizer, "Targeting Strategies in the Netherlands: Demand Management and Cost Constraint," Neil Gilbert (ed.), *Targeting Social Benefits: International Perspectives and Trends* (Rutgers, N.J.: Transaction Publishers 2000).

32. Sune Sunesson, Staffan Blomberg, Per Gunnar Edebalk, Lars Harrysson, Jan Magnusson, Anna Meeuwisse, Jan Peterson, and Tapio Salonen, "The Flight from Universalism," *European Journal of Social Work*, 1:1 (March 1998): 19–29.

33. Linda Bauld, Ken Judge, and Iain Paterson, "Cross-National Study of Continuities and Change in the Welfare State." Paper prepared for the Conference on Continuities and Change in the Welfare State, Bellagio Study Center, Italy, August 7–11, 2000.

34. Knight, for example, provides some evidence that restrictive measures introduced in the United Kingdom and the Netherlands have resulted in a shift of public expenditure from insurance-related unemployment benefits to social assistance. See Mark Knight, "Restrictive Measures in Unemployment Schemes; Impact on Other Social Security Schemes," in Harmonizing Economic Developments and Social Needs: ISSA Technical Conferences (Geneva: International Social Security Association, 1998).

35. The movement toward privatization in the United States and Europe has been widely documented. See Mimi Abramovitz, "The Privatization of the Welfare State," *Social Work*, 34:4 (1986): 257–64; Neil Gilbert, *Capitalism and the Welfare State* (New Haven, Conn.: Yale University Press, 1983); Norman Johnson (ed.), *Private Markets in Health and Welfare* (Oxford, UK: Berg Publishers, 1995); Sheila Kamerman and Alfred Kahn (eds.), *Privatization and the Welfare State* (Princeton, N.J.: Princeton University Press, 1989).

36. Tania Burchardt, *Boundaries between Public and Private Welfare* (London: Center for Analysis of Social Exclusion, London School of Economics, 1997).

37. Norman Johnson, "The United Kingdom," in Norman Johnson (ed.), *Private Markets in Health and Welfare* (Oxford: Berg Publishers, 1995), 29.

38. Anna-Lena Almqvist and Thomas Boje, "Who Cares, Who Pays, and How Is Care for Children Provided? Comparing Family Life and Work in Different European Welfare Systems," in *Comparing Social Welfare Systems in Nordic Europe and France*. Text collected by Denis Bouget and Bruno Palier (Paris: DREES/MiRe, 1999), 265–292.

39. Sven Olsen Hort and Daniel Cohn, "Sweden," in Norman Johnson (ed.), *Private Markets in Health and Welfare* (Oxford, UK: Berg Publishers, 1995), 183.

40. Tommy Lundstrom, "Non-governmental Actors, Local Administration, and Private Enterprise: New Models in Delivery of Child and Youth Welfare" Paper presented at the International Conference on Playing the Market Game, at University of Bielefeld, Germany, March 9–11, 2000.

41. Neung Hoo Park and Neil Gilbert, "Social Security and the Incremental Privatization of Retirement Income," *Journal of Sociology and Social Welfare*, 26:2 (1997).

42. A comparative analysis of these country's experiences suggests that the introduction of a second tier of income-related public pensions in Norway helps to account for the relative containment of private schemes compared to Denmark, where a second public tier did not develop. Axel Pedersen, "Do Generous Public Pensions Crowd Out Private Pensions? Comparative Analysis of Time Series Data for Denmark and Norway." Center for Welfare State Research Working Paper 7 (1997).

43. For the analyses of those who claim that the changes involve only fine tuning or cutting the fat off the welfare state, see Sven Olsen Hort, "From a Generous to a Strong Welfare State? Sweden's Approach to Targeting," in Neil Gilbert (ed.), *Targeting Social Benefits* (Rutgers, N.J.: Transaction Publishers, 2002); Gosta Esping-Anderson (ed.), *Welfare States in Transition* (London: Sage, 1996).

Index